Contents at a Glance

Paint Shop Pro™ 8

Jennifer Fulton

Teach
Yourself

Sams Publishing, 800 East 96th Street, Indianapolis, Indiana 46240 USA

Paint Shop Pro™ 8 in a Snap

International Standard Book Number: 0-672-32389-3

Library of Congress Catalog Card Number: 2001098859

Printed in the United States of America

First Printing: September 2003

06   05   04   03   4   3   2   1

Trademarks

All terms mentioned in this book that are known to be trademarks or service marks have been appropriately capitalized. Sams Publishing cannot attest to the accuracy of this information. Use of a term in this book should not be regarded as affecting the validity of any trademark or service mark.

Warning and Disclaimer

Every effort has been made to make this book as complete and as accurate as possible, but no warranty or fitness is implied. The information provided is on an "as is" basis. The author and the publisher shall have neither liability nor responsibility to any person or entity with respect to any loss or damages arising from the information contained in this book.

Bulk Sales

Sams Publishing offers excellent discounts on this book when ordered in quantity for bulk purchases or special sales. For more information, please contact

U.S. Corporate and Government Sales

1-800-382-3419

corpsales@pearsontechgroup.com

For sales outside of the U.S., please contact

International Sales

1-317-428-3341

international@pearsontechgroup.com

Acquisitions Editor
Betsy Brown

Development Editor
Alice Martina Smith

Managing Editor
Charlotte Clapp

Project Editor
Elizabeth Finney

Production Editor
Seth Kerney

Indexer
Chris Barrick

Proofreader
Katie Robinson

Technical Editor
Dallas Reed

Team Coordinator
Vanessa Evans

Designer
Gary Adair

About the Author

Jennifer Fulton, iVillage's former "Computer Coach," is an experienced computer consultant and trainer with over 20 years of experience. Jennifer is also the best-selling author of more than 100 computer books written for both the education and retail markets, including *Sams Adobe Photoshop Elements 2 in 24 Hours, Sams Teach Yourself Windows ME in 10 Minutes, How to Use Microsoft Publisher 2000, How to Use Microsoft Office XP, Easy Outlook 2000, Sams Teach Yourself Excel 2000 in Ten Minutes, Office 2000 Cheat Sheet,* and *The Complete Idiot's Guide to Upgrading and Repairing Your PC.*

Jennifer lives in the Midwest with her husband, Scott, who is also a computer book author and programmer, and Katerina, an author-to-be. They live together in a small home filled with many books, some of which they have not written themselves.

Dedication

To my husband, Scott, who is my eternal love
and with whom I celebrate ten lovely years in marriage.

Acknowledgments

First, I'd like to acknowledge the invaluable contributions to this book by my husband, Scott. Thanks just aren't quite enough.

I also would like to thank my brother, Michael Flynn, a professional photographer, and thus an incredible source of excellent how-to advice and even more incredible photographs. I challenged him to provide me with photos I could "fix" using Paint Shop Pro, and although he tried hard, it proved difficult for Mike to get it "wrong." So I featured his photographs in areas where the focus was framing and packaging a photograph, rather than fixing it. Thanks for the great photos, Mike! Thanks also to my wonderful father-in-law Scott, my sister Pat, Aunt Betty, and Mom, who trusted me with their precious photographic memories.

I would also like to thank the wonderful PSP community, especially Tyeise Green, whom I met through the newsgroups provided by Jasc during the beta testing period. The beta testers are generous, intelligent, and incredibly gifted. I would also like to thank Jasc's technical support people, who are always understanding and quick to help when you have problems.

We Want to Hear from You!

As the reader of this book, *you* are our most important critic and commentator. We value your opinion and want to know what we're doing right, what we could do better, what areas you'd like to see us publish in, and any other words of wisdom you're willing to pass our way.

You can email or write me directly to let me know what you did or didn't like about this book—as well as what we can do to make our books stronger.

Please note that I cannot help you with technical problems related to the topic of this book, and that due to the high volume of mail I receive, I might not be able to reply to every message.

When you write, please be sure to include this book's title and author as well as your name and phone number or email address. I will carefully review your comments and share them with the author and editors who worked on the book.

Email: **graphics@samspublishing.com**

Mail: Mark Taber
         Associate Publisher
         Sams Publishing
         800 East 96th Street
         Indianapolis, IN 46240 USA

Reader Services

For more information about this book or others from Sams Publishing, visit our Web site at www.samspublishing.com. Type the ISBN (excluding hyphens) or the title of the book in the Search box to find the book you're looking for.

PART I

Fundamentals

IN THIS PART

1

✔ Start Here

TIP

Photo Album is a graphics image organizer and a great companion program to Paint Shop Pro. Use it to organize and backup your images, and to make quick fixes. You can also create slideshows, VCDs, Web galleries, and QuickTime movies with Photo Album. You'll find information on how to use Photo Album in the bonus material for this book located on the Sams Web site.

If you were to make a list of the five most important possessions in your life, there's a very good chance that one of them would be your family photographs. Your photos may be as precious to you as the memories in your own head. But whether or not you've had any formal training in the art of photography, many of the photos you shoot for keepsakes or albums, or for framing in your home or office, may not be as resplendent as the images you keep in your memory.

Why Use a Graphics Program?

Let's not kid ourselves. The reason you own Paint Shop Pro—or one of the key reasons—is because you want to make your own photographs look better. Although Paint Shop Pro's icon is a palette with colors squeezed out on it, most users of Paint Shop Pro today aren't using it to create original paintings *per se*, as much as to retouch photographs. The second most common reason people use Paint Shop Pro is to create buttons, banners, and other graphical gadgets for developing Web sites. Creating original graphics from scratch is an important feature, to be certain. But if that's all Paint Shop Pro could do, chances are it wouldn't be as successful a product as it is today, and you wouldn't be reading this book. For most people, retouching photographs is this product's key strength.

✎ NOTE

PSP 8.0 sports many new or improved features, including the easier-to-use **Tool Options** and **Materials** palettes, enhanced tools such as the **Background Eraser**, **Edge Seeker**, and **Crop** tools, improved multi-image print layout, tool presets, scripts for repeating actions, and an interactive learning center.

What's Possible

The most frequently cited example of digital retouching is the removal of "red-eye" from a portrait—the phenomenon where the backs of the subject's eyes reflect red light from the camera's flash. Naturally, Paint Shop Pro (also known casually as PSP) has features that enable you to make this specific correction to a photo. Red-eye removal is only one of the possible corrections and enhancements you can make to a digital photo with PSP. Here are some examples of actual tasks you can accomplish yourself with Paint Shop Pro—tasks I'll be covering in this book:

- If you've taken a picture of a person standing in front of the sun, you can lighten his face and darken the background.

- You can remove unwanted elements from a photograph—such as an electric cord draped along the floor, a price tag or a logo on a shirt, a blemish on the subject's face or skin, or a hunk of lettuce stuck in his teeth—by selectively copying elements from elsewhere in the photo and using those elements to mask the unwanted ones.

Before ———

After ———

Remove unwanted objects such as your thumb from images.

- You can improve the sense of perspective and dimension in a photograph by selectively blurring and fading elements that are behind your subject.

- You can correct a photograph taken of a painting or other flat artwork so that you restore some or all of its natural, original color balance and contrasts, even if the lighting under which the photo was taken wasn't pure white.

- You can make a picture taken at dusk or twilight appear as though it were taken in the early morning—perhaps all the elements won't be seen crisply, but at least you can see what the picture contains.

Lightening the shadows and improving detail makes a world of difference in this photograph.

- You can let Paint Shop Pro modify your photo, making it look as though it were drawn by Picasso, Titian, Toulouse Lautrec, or Andy Warhol—or, at the very least, by one of their first-year students.

- You can restore the appearance of the oldest and most distressed photographs by scanning them into PSP and then using its spot tools to paint or mask over seams, rips, scratches, and other mutilations. You can add a beautiful sepia tone, in effect re-aging the photo.

Restoring this old photograph involved lightening it, getting rid of the red color cast, and removing several scratches.

- You can remove a friend from an office setting and place her on the beach.

It's just as important to note what you *cannot* do with Paint Shop Pro, or what tasks it simply wasn't designed to do. For example:

You cannot create animated images in PSP, although PSP does include a free program called Animation Studio that is designed to work with PSP in the production of multiframe graphics.

You cannot capture images from a DVD using PSP's screen capture utility, even if you can clearly see both the DVD picture and PSP on your monitor at the same time. There's a sophisticated reason for this, but what it boils down to is that the image produced by a DVD is routed through a separate channel than the image produced by Windows, so that Windows does not actually "see" your DVD picture. If you try a screen capture through PSP, the portion of the screen where your DVD movie appears will show up as all black. This is probably the way the major motion picture studios want things to be.

You cannot restore focus to a blurred photograph. This may be a big letdown to some, especially because it appears that PSP has several commands for doing just this, called *sharpen filters*. What *sharpening* in PSP truly does is restore contrast and distinction between adjacent pixels of slightly differing hues, the result being that their hues differ more than they did before. The result is not necessarily a sharper photograph, but one in which the blurred areas are now more distinct and less translucent. However, digital sharpening can reveal details that weren't obvious before, such as the text faintly written on a tag, or the weaving pattern of a knit sweater. Even so, the sharpen filter actually works better on a photo that is already in focus, or nearly so.

What Are Layers?

Since version 5 of Paint Shop Pro, it's been possible for images to be constructed and composited by way of multiple *layers*. The key purpose of layering in PSP is to give you a way to isolate multiple, individual parts of what will eventually comprise a complete image. A digital photograph, by definition, has one layer; after you import it, PSP treats that layer as the *background*. If you were to add a caption to that photo, placing that element on its own layer enables you to resize, recolor, or reposition it without overwriting and losing those parts of the photo beneath that element. If you were to create an image montage comprised of many photos arranged in an attractive format (such as a Valentine's Day card with multiple pictures of you and your spouse), you could isolate each clipping from that montage on its own layer, enabling you to control not only its position, but its opacity as well.

With layers, you can make changes to one layer without affecting the others. You can also blend two layers together in a multitude of ways, achieving effects you couldn't create otherwise. For example, you might blend two copies of the same image using the **Difference** blend mode, and create instant pop-art. You can also use the contents of a special layer (called an *adjustment layer*) to make subtle or profound changes to the contents of all the layers beneath it. So, layers don't necessarily act as transparencies that simply overlay one another, but as structured elements that can blend and interact with each other.

By isolating each element of this image on its own layer, it's easier to build this illusion.

 TIP

The layer name alone might not tell you enough about a layer for you to know specifically what it refers to. To have PSP remind you what a layer contains, simply *point* to its name on the **Layer** palette—don't click. PSP displays a thumbnail of the contents of that layer.

In PSP, isolating elements of an image is the reason for having layers in the first place, so that you can work on one layer at a time. To tell PSP which layer you want to make changes to, open the **Layer** palette and click the name of that layer in the left column. Knowing which layer is the current one is important because the current layer is the one you affect when you use a tool or select a command. Also, when you select a region of your image (so that you can limit the changes you're about to make to just that selection), the selection will contain pixels *from the current layer only, and they'll be the only ones changed.* Some operations—such as copying the contents of a selection—can address the chosen layer *plus* everything in the same region of all layers beneath the chosen one. But even in that situation, it's important for you to remember which layer you're dealing with.

The list in the **Layer** palette shows you which layers are "on top" of others and which are "beneath." Like a series of animation cels, layers of an image are laid one on top of the other, with each layer obscuring the layers beneath it. "Beneath" in PSP is represented by the hierarchy of the list: Everything listed below the chosen layer is beneath it. You can control the ability of a layer to block the data in the layers below it by changing the layer's opacity. A layer that's 100% opaque is like paint on a wall—it completely blocks the color beneath. Set the opacity to 50% however, and the layer will cover lower layers only partially—like a sheer veil.

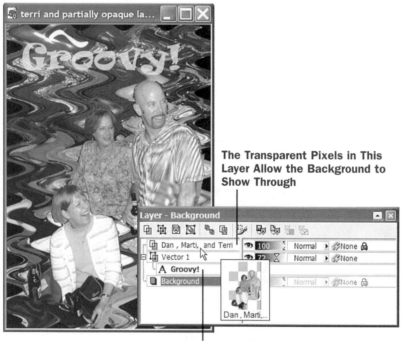

The Transparent Pixels in This Layer Allow the Background to Show Through

The Partially Opaque Text Only Partially Obscures the Wavy Layer Below

Upper layers can obscure lower layers, depending on their opacity.

What It Means to Select a Region

One of the rules of using a coloring book with which I was slowest to comply when I was a child was to color inside the boundaries. The more excited I became with the color of crayon I'd just discovered, the more my work devolved to some splashy, out-of-bounds, freestyle contrivance. Digital images are like that; the individual pixels that make up an area that to you looks like

✎ TIP

If you're not careful with layers, you'll get into a situation where you start painting, and PSP seems to tell you everything's okay, but nothing seems to be happening—for some reason, your paintbrush is dry. The reason is probably that you've accidentally chosen another layer and are painting in an area obscured by pixels in a higher-order layer—the changes you're making on that layer are not visible to you.

a splash of red, more often than not possess characteristics that vary greatly from their neighbors, and yet somehow combine in your mind to form the illusion of a particular shade. So when you want to tell Paint Shop Pro, "Let's make that nose not so red," or, "Let's remove that piece of lint from the subject's hair," there's no way that PSP can *automatically* determine what or where the spot is you want to change. Telling PSP to change red to blue just isn't enough. You must manually select the area of the image you want to change.

PSP gives you a variety of tools and methods you can use to select the area you want to affect. Selecting a region of an image creates a boundary around that region across which PSP will not trespass. It will not, in other words, color across the borders. PSP marks your selection with a flashing *marquee*, like the one you'd see at the entrance to an old-fashioned theatre. The marquee is always in motion (like marching ants), so that your mind can more easily separate it from the image you're working on.

NOTE

A selection doesn't have to be comprised of just one region of adjacent pixels; it can be several nonadjacent regions, or all the pixels in your entire image that have roughly the same color value or brightness.

Selection Marquee

With a selection tool, you define where changes are to take place— here, the pink tulip in the middle of the photograph.

Making a selection that consists of any part or parts of an image protects the rest of the image from any changes you plan to attempt. Even if you were to use a brush tool to paint inside a selection, and even if your pointer were to stray occasionally outside the boundaries of the selection, PSP will not paint outside the selection. Everything outside a selection is safe. In addition, if an area is selected, only that area is affected by whatever command you choose. For example, you could select a person's face and make just that area lighter.

Filters and What They Do

The "horsepower" in Paint Shop Pro is its multitude of *filters*. Professional photographers are familiar with the concept of filters that filter the light coming into a camera lens to create visual effects. PSP filters also create visual effects, but far beyond the capability of a mere lens attachment.

Think of a filter as a little computer program unto itself whose sole job is to make some change, great or small, to your image. For example, you can take any selection and give it a chiseled edge, like the button on a keyboard. You can use a filter to change any part or all of your image as though it were rendered by a watercolor brush, sketched with a charcoal pencil on coarse-bond art paper, or burned into a plate of steel with a blowtorch.

If your image doesn't appear crisp or clear, a sharpen filter can detect the narrowest areas where colors appear to contrast and draw out those contrasts to create a sharper image. By blending some color values with others in their immediate proximity, a blur filter can generate the illusion of motion blur. If you select a specific element of your image first, you can generate the illusion that that element was moving at the time you took the photograph. Other filters can remove scratches, blemishes, and moiré patterns from a photo, especially a photo imported from a scanner where dust specks often abound.

NOTE

PSP gives you three tools for selecting any region or regions of an image: the **Selection** tool (which helps you select a regularly shaped region such as a rectangle or circle), the **Freehand Selection** tool (which allows you to select any region you can draw freehand or by tracing the edge of an object), and the **Magic Wand** (which selects neighboring pixels with similar characteristics such as color or brightness with a single click).

KEY TERM

Filter—A series of computer instructions that modify the pixels in an image.

Before —

After —

*The **Chisel** and **Glowing Edges** filters (with the help of the **Negative Image** command) make a dramatic difference in this image.*

 TIP

Most of the tasks in this book use filters of a more practical nature to clean up photographs and such, but you should take time to experiment with the artistic filters to create special effects and add some fun to an otherwise ordinary picture.

Although some filters exist for the purpose of correcting images, most are, quite frankly, created purely to exploit a new form of artistic expression. You can take all or part of an image and inflate it as though it were the skin of a balloon. You can wrap it around a sphere or a three-dimensional box. You can create circular ripples in an image as though it were rendered on the surface of a pond or a lake of mercury. You can insert a blast of sunlight from any angle, even in a photo where there is no sun—complete with simulated lens flare.

Why You Might Want a Pen Tablet

The prices of digital cameras and digital scanners have plummeted sharply in the last half decade, making true digital photo processing feasible and affordable not only to professionals but to hobbyists as well. Add to this list of more affordable tools the *pen tablet*. You can use a tablet instead of a mouse to make the same kind of drawing or painting motions that you'd make with a real pencil or paintbrush.

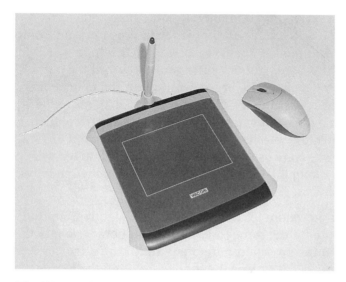

The Wacom Graphire pen tablet (ruby edition).

Today's tablets, such as the Wacom Graphire, are touch sensitive; the tablet can record the difference between a light touch and a firm press. Specifically, it senses 255 different degrees of pressure. If you're using PSP's airbrush tool, for example, the degree of "air pressure" in the brush, and/or the radius of the spray, can be determined by how firmly you press the pen against the tablet. (You can't make this same kind of variation or adjustment using the mouse to paint.) You can even switch back and forth between a pen and a mouse (the Graphire comes with a wireless mouse), so that you can still select menu commands and control Windows with the mouse while you're drawing with the pen.

With a pen tablet, operations within PSP can be a little different than using a mouse. To make an adjustment to a tool setting, for example, lift the pen completely off the tablet—the pointer will stay where it is. Then *hover* your pen over the spot on the table that corresponds with the tool setting location onscreen; the pointer will snap to that spot like a magnet. To move the pointer without actually drawing with it, hover the pen just over the tablet without touching it. To select something with the pen, *tap*, just once. To draw, touch the pen to the tablet and draw normally, remembering that the degree of pressure you use is registered by the tool you're using.

 TIP

If you're unaccustomed to making precise movements with your mouse device—and many people are—you might find a wireless pen much easier to learn and control. And that will make it much easier for you to make minute changes to your photographs or drawn artwork.

NOTE

Most modern tablets, including Wacom models, have a special button on the pen that assumes the function of **double**-clicking the left mouse button. Press this button once, not twice.

◢ NOTE

Believe it or not, many tablets (including the Wacom Graphire) have *erasers* on the back end of the pen. To erase something in a photograph, you can literally turn the pen around and use the blunt eraser end to wipe away unwanted content in an image. PSP associates the eraser end of the pen with its own **Eraser** tool.

The process for picking up and moving something—such as a flower petal you've selected—is different with a pen tablet than it is with a standard mouse. You'll see how to do this in proper detail later in this book; in brief, after you've selected the portion you want to move, plunk the pen down right in the middle of it ("plunk" not exactly being the technical term for it), move the pen in the same direction you want to move the selection, then lift the pen when the selection is in place. From the point of view of your hand, you may as well have used a real pen to scoot a piece of paper along the top of your desk; it feels pretty much the same.

When the pen procedure for a task differs significantly from the mouse procedure for the same task, I'll tell you how to do it both ways. But when the procedures are pretty much the same, I'll defer to explaining the task as though you're using the mouse (drag, click, drag-and-drop, double-click). When there's something you can do with a pen that you cannot do with a mouse (for example, vary the radius of an airbrush stroke *while* you're painting, or using the eraser tip), I'll show you how to do that using pen tablet language.

The Nature of Digital Photography

If you use a digital camera to record an image rather than a film camera, you are more likely to print that photograph at home rather than take the images to a photo shop for printing. Your computer essentially becomes the "film lab," making you responsible for cleaning up any mistakes before printing those photos of your child's fifth birthday party. Don't let this overwhelm you—as you'll learn in this book, PSP provides many simple-to-use tools that help you fix just about any problem caused by a digital camera, scanner, or simple human error. In addition, you'll be able to create illusions and art effects you couldn't get from your neighborhood film lab.

◢ KEY TERM

Photo Album—A graphics image editor and organizer by JASC.

Another fact of life with digital cameras is that your computer will soon be overrun with image files bearing less-than-useful filenames. Do yourself a favor and invest in a graphics file organizer application such as *Photo Album*.

Use PSP to remove digital artifacts (distortions caused by compression or scanning).

Still, there are a few things to remember when making the transition from film to digital photography:

- Film can record more detail than digital media. It's simply the nature of the beast. To compensate, always take photos at your digital camera's highest resolution.

- Digital photos mean digital storage media, so early on you should develop a plan for managing your images. The simplest method is to copy photos from your camera to the hard disk, and then immediately back them up onto a CD-R, Zip disk, or other high-volume, permanent storage medium. Next, print thumbnails of each image, select the best ones to keep on your hard drive (although not as your permanent copies), and delete the rest to reclaim storage space.

- After making changes to your images, save copies of them in a single-layer, universal format that's recognized by other applications—perhaps the same format your digital camera

TIP

Taking digital photos at the camera's highest resolution means that you won't be able to store as many photos on your memory stick/disk, but at least the photos you do save will be worth printing.

NOTE

Although PSP can read photos from Kodak PhotoCDs, it can't store or save photos in the PhotoCD format, mainly because the format can only be used to produce an entire PhotoCD. You can, however, use Kodak's own application to create new PhotoCDs using photos that you retouched in PSP and stored to your hard drive in a universal format such as JPEG or TIFF.

TIP

For occasional photo printing needs, the prices for uploading digital photos and having an online service such as Shutterfly print them are fairly reasonable.

NOTE

Generally speaking, if you are using a standard, low-cost four-color ink jet printer to print photos, you'll get best results by buying that same company's photo paper. With a six-color photo printer however, you'll be fine selecting whatever paper is on sale, as long as it's designed for printing photos.

used to begin with—so that the images are easier to share. Compressed TIFF and JPEG are the two most common universal formats for digital photographs. Back up these images onto a separate CD-ROM, Zip disk, or other device.

- Printing good-quality photos requires a printer designed and tested not only for color, but for photo *paper*. Not all color printers are capable of dealing with thicker, photo-quality paper, which you'll need to make your images proof quality. In addition, today's newer, so-called *photo printers* use six or seven tones of ink, including black, as opposed to the standard four tones you find with common color printers, so they are well worth the extra money if your main goal is to print photos. If you do a mix of photo and standard printing and want to save money, there are some four-tone printer models that *do* print on photo paper, or on photographic paper specifically designed for use with those models. When comparing printer prices, compare not only the photo quality but also the price of inks because that's where the actual expense is.

As an alternative to buying your own color photo printer, consider those do-it-yourself printing machines in the grocery and discount stores that let you bring in your own CD-R or PhotoCD and print your photos on high-quality photo paper. If you decide to go this route, study the instructions on your machine of choice carefully so that you know the format and specifications it requires for your disc and your photos.

- If you intend to use your new PSP skills to repair old photos, invest in a good quality scanner with high resolution. Some higher-end scanner models include special features such as a film reader for scanning film strips and/or slides.

How to Take Better Photographs

Not that using Paint Shop Pro is particularly tedious, or even no fun; but if you learn a few things about what makes a more optically appealing photograph, you can bring that knowledge with you the next time you take pictures—knowledge that could save you time later in PSP. Here are some simple things you can do to correct common problems in photos, things that can save you the time and trouble of having to fix them in Paint Shop Pro:

- **Be prepared.** If you're using a digital camera, you don't have the expense of film and film processing anymore, so you can afford to invest in some extra batteries for your camera and keep them charged and ready to go. That way, you can capture the moments as they happen. Also, if your camera uses flash memory, invest in a few extra-large memory sticks so that you can take lots of pictures when a moment happens. Remember, it's better to waste a few shots than to play it stingy and lose the one that counts.

- **Don't skimp on quality.** Always shoot at the highest resolution your camera allows to give you the most flexibility later on. If you decide after the fact that a photo will make a nice 8" × 10" print, you won't be able to get a quality result if you skimped on the resolution when taking the picture. In addition, if your camera offers the option, select the least amount of compression possible. If needed, buy a bunch of memory sticks to outfit your camera with enough "film," but don't use lower resolutions to save space—you'll definitely regret it later on.

- **Don't be so frugal.** Memory and storage are both cheap and reusable. So to get the best photograph—especially the candid shots or pictures of subjects in motion—go ahead and shoot several photos, one right after the other. This method allows you to easily experiment with exposure and shutter speed settings, and then later choose the best and discard the rest. With a digital camera, you're never wasting anything that can't be written over later.

- **Think first.** Decide what interests you about the scene, and focus on that subject. If needed, move in closer to fill the frame. By framing the subject properly, you can draw more attention to it and create a stronger photograph in the process. For example, when taking a child's picture, kneel down and try to capture the world from her perspective.

- **Think thirds.** Artists know that to create an interesting painting, you simply divide the canvas into thirds vertically

TIP

Low-resolution digital images are always much grainer than their higher-resolution cousins—a problem you can improve but not completely solve using PSP. So don't skimp on resolution—you will always regret it.

and horizontally. The dividing lines intersect at four points on the canvas; these are your focal points—places where the eye is drawn naturally. By placing your subject on one of these four points, as opposed to the absolute center of the frame, you'll create a perfectly pleasing picture.

NOTE

White balancing allows the camera to compensate for color shifts caused by the source of light. For example, under a florescent light, things can look a bit blue because the light source is cool. Outdoors, things tend toward orange because the light source is warmer. If conditions change after you white balance the camera (you move outdoors or it starts to cloud up, for example), be sure to white balance the camera again.

- **Get white right.** Before you take your first picture, white balance your camera. Typically, white balancing involves making a lighting choice from a menu such as indoors, outdoors, snow, cloudy day, nighttime, stage lighting, and so on. When you want to get more precise, most cameras allow you to white balance manually by pressing a button and pointing the camera at something white. (Keeping a small note card in your camera bag for this purpose is a good idea.) When you get the white balance correct, flesh tones will look right (and not too blue or too orange).

Of course, nobody says you have to always follow the rules. Try white balancing your camera for outdoors, then taking a picture inside under candlelight for a warm, romantic photograph.

- **Don't "auto" everything.** Get involved in the picture-taking process. Using the flash, for example, provides fill light even in the daytime, softening shadows on a subject's face. A flash also slows down the camera's shutter speed, letting in more light. Some cameras let you adjust the amount of flash, giving you more control. Get used to thinking of the flash as your filler, and use it at high noon, in sunny shade, and at sunset; let the flash remove dark shadows and provide more detail.

Another way to control the amount of light in a photograph is to change the *f-stop*, or aperture. A large aperture such as F2 helps you capture images under low-light conditions; a smaller aperture such as F16 is more appropriate for daylight conditions. When needed, on some cameras, you can set the shutter speed as well. A fast shutter speed such as 1/1000 second helps you catch the action; a slow shutter speed such as 1 second is perfect for motionless subjects.

Using a large aperture such as F2 may help you capture what light there is in a poorly lit scene, but it also results in a more shallow *depth of field*. A wider depth of field might include not only a subject standing only 3 feet away, but also her surroundings in the background 10 feet behind her. By narrowing the depth of field, you can bring more attention to a single subject, distinguishing it from its surroundings and thus improving the composition of the photograph. However, if you want a larger depth of field so that you capture not only your lovely subject but the crowd of people standing around her, you can combine a smaller aperture such as F12 (which creates a larger depth of field) with a slower shutter speed (for more light-capturing ability).

KEY TERM

Depth of field—The distance between the closest in-focus object to your camera and the furthest in-focus object away from your camera.

Furthest Object in Focus

Out of Focus

Closest Object in Focus

Your own eyes will best help you determine depth of field.

NOTE

Two other factors can jointly affect depth of field: zoom and camera-to-subject distance. As you zoom in on a subject, you lose depth of field. To get a greater depth of field, zoom out. In addition, as you move closer to a subject and then adjust your lens to refocus on that subject, your depth of field becomes more shallow. To increase depth of field, move back from your subject and refocus.

- **Polarize!** A polarizing filter works just as well for your camera as it does for your sunglasses. It instantly removes the glare from lakes, rivers, store windows, car windows, and so on. It also adds depth to a washed-out sky on a sunny day, instantly creating better landscape photos. Even if your camera lens doesn't provide a way for attaching lens filters, you can always hold a polarizing filter in front of the lens when needed, or tape it on. Glare is a very difficult effect to remove from a digital photo during retouching, so a polarizing filter should be your number one accessory.

- **Get rid of the shakes.** Whenever you can, use a tripod to steady your camera and remove unnecessary blur. For some digital cameras, there's an interminable wait between the time you press the button and the time the camera records the image. Holding a camera perfectly still during this waiting period can be almost impossible. And because shutter speeds are slower for digital cameras than they are for film cameras—because electronic light detectors are less sensitive than film—even the brief period while the shutter's open renders the camera extremely susceptible to motion blur. So invest in a small pocket tripod—or use your surroundings for a surrogate tripod.

- **Be careful of zoom.** Most high-end digital cameras currently available "fudge" their maximum zoom factor using a technique where the camera concentrates on a smaller and smaller region of the bigger image its lens is giving it. So if you want a quality photograph, don't zoom in past the natural optical zoom level of your digital camera's lens.

- **Frame it right.** Some cameras come with a viewfinder and a larger LCD screen for displaying pictures. In most cases, you can probably use either one when framing up the scene you want to capture. However, for close shots, use the LCD screen because it provides a realistic view of the actual image to be captured, whereas the viewfinder's optics (by necessity) render its vision a bit to one side of the actual scene.

- **Know the value of exposure.** A lot of cameras allow you to change the exposure value (plus or minus) to compensate for low light/bright light conditions. For example, you might be trying to take a nice picture of your child playing in the snow, but the camera sets the exposure automatically for the brightest object (the snow) and as a result your child's face is underexposed. The same situation happens when the sun is behind your subject and his or her face is in shadow, or the sun is in the picture when you're trying to capture the sunset. To compensate for over-bright elements in a scene, set the exposure value plus 1 or 2 and reshoot. When capturing a scene with deep shadows, dark foliage, or a dark subject against a light background, adjust the exposure value minus 1 or 2.

- **Take better landscapes.** One mistake new photographers often make when taking pictures of a far-off vista is to simply press the shutter button, making the camera focus on that far away mountaintop. The result is a blurring of most of the foreground. To keep more of the foreground in focus, press the shutter button partway and focus on something about 1/3 of the distance between you and that mountaintop (closer to you). Then, while still holding the shutter button partway down, reframe the picture and press the button the rest of the way.

Down to the Nitty-Gritty: The Pixel

The smallest discernable grain of color in a digital photograph is a tiny rectangular block called a *pixel*. Digital TV images and the images on your computer monitor are also comprised of rows of pixels. Within a picture, the smaller all these pixels are, the more pixels you need to fill the same space, and the higher the picture's *resolution*. This is important because your printer also operates at its own resolution. Although most onscreen images are expected to be rendered at between 72 and 106 pixels per inch (ppi), most color inkjet printers are capable of 300 dots per inch (dpi) or, through certain proprietary tricks, as much as 1200 dpi.

So why care about pixels at all? Well, you must be aware of the intended output of your image so that you can tailor its resolution properly. If you want to take photographs for use on the Web, in a PowerPoint presentation, or as a Windows desktop background image, a low-resolution photograph (larger pixels and fewer of them) will do. To print a photograph, you'll need a higher resolution (smaller pixels and more of them) to produce a quality result.

Rasters Versus Vectors

If you view a digital photo at high magnification, it's easy to see that the image is comprised of many pixels arranged in perfect,

KEY TERMS

Raster data—Data comprised of individual pixels, each with their own hue, saturation, and brightness value.

Vector data—Data that's stored as a series of mathematical algorithms that plot the coordinates of points along the edges of a shape, such as a star or a bit of vector text.

Anti-aliasing—The addition of semitransparent pixels along the curved edge of a raster shape or selection. Anti-aliasing helps to make such curves look smooth and not jagged.

TIP

Anti-aliasing also becomes a factor when you are copying or moving a selection from one place to another: You can use an anti-aliasing technique called *feathering* to blur the edge of the selection and blend it into its new surroundings more easily.

NOTE

Although PSP always renders its final graphics using rasters, objects on the vector layer are recalculated before every refresh of the screen as well as before any print job. So, your vector-based lines look as sharp and artifact-free as possible.

horizontal rows. A line of pixels is called a *raster*—a word which dates back to the fourteenth century when it referred to the distance between threads of very finely woven cheese cloth. You don't have to know too much about rasters to use PSP, except when creating a new image or adding layers to an existing image. It's at that point you'll need to choose between *raster data* and its opposite—*vector data*.

To understand the difference between rasters and vectors, consider how drawn objects and text are rendered onscreen. Because each raster in an image is, by definition, one row tall and one row wide, objects such as angular stripes and rounded curves are rendered using a stair-step effect rather than clean, crisp edges. To compensate for this effect, when drawing objects or text on a raster layer, you can turn on **anti-aliasing**, an effect that blurs the edges of objects so that the stair-step effect is less noticeable. Your eye will more readily forgive these watery borders than it will ignore the choppiness of contrasting edges.

Anti-aliasing of this raster (bitmap) text blends otherwise jagged edges with their background by adding shades of the object color along its edges.

Want sharp corners, perfect diagonals, and great looking curves? Then draw your object on a vector layer. Vector objects aren't represented as rows of colored dots as raster objects are, but instead as geometric lines, curves, and angles between points. Because vector objects are rendered geometrically, they'll stay sharp and crisp at literally any resolution—even zoomed in at any magnification.

Another key difference between vector- and raster-oriented graphics—one that isn't obvious on the surface—concerns the printing process. In a vector graphics application such as Corel Draw or Adobe Illustrator, you can give a shape a specific Pantone color and, when you use a printer that recognizes Pantone profiles, get that exact color when the graphic is printed.

By comparison, a raster graphics application—such as Paint Shop Pro—doesn't use named colors (regardless of whether the image contains vector graphics). Instead, each pixel is given a color value that can be addressed using either of two color models: as a blend of red, green, and blue light (RGB), or in terms of hue, saturation, and luminance (HSL). I'll talk more about these two color models later in this chapter; for now, it's important to know that every visible pixel in a PSP image has its own specific color value. That value can be determined by calculating a variety of factors: for instance, the transparency of multiple layers that are all visible at a pixel's location, the opacity of colors for all the points at that same location, whether vector-based shapes with certain coloring instructions reside on some of these layers, and so on. In the end, when the final product of your editing work is "flattened out" (when all the layers are merged together), your image can be described as a point of light, followed by another point of light, followed by another, and so on.

Vector-based elements in a PSP image.

NOTE

Pantone is the developer of the Pantone color-matching system on which numerous profiles for high-grade color photo printers are based. These profiles ensure perfect color matching across systems; for example, from computer screen to computer printer or printing press, or from color chip to wall paint.

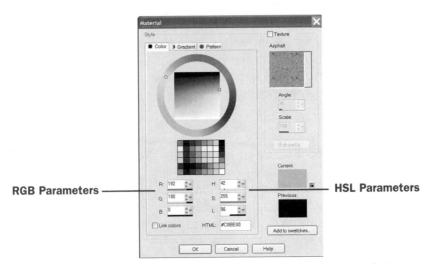

Paint Shop Pro represents pixel colors using two models simultaneously.

RGB Parameters

HSL Parameters

See Also

→ **1** Ensure That What You See Is What You Get

→ **106** Correct Color Manually

Why Printing Isn't a One-Step Task

Many other books on the topic of Paint Shop Pro and other graphics applications forget that printing is the single most important task in all of digital post-production. I could take the easy route and say, "To print your finished image, from the File menu, select Print. Voilà!" But I know better, and instead, I'm going to tell you the full story, because you know as well as I do that the real purpose of using Paint Shop Pro is to help you prepare your images for *permanence*. With the exception of building Web sites, this means *printing*.

In using Paint Shop Pro, you learn right away that no two devices ever worked so differently from one another as your monitor and your printer. You've come to expect your printer to render pretty much whatever you see on your screen in a reliable, representative, "close enough" format. With digital photos, the definition of "close enough" grows very narrow, and with good reason: The ways your monitor and your printer construct colors are almost complete opposites of one another.

Your monitor uses principles of *optics* to blend the color for each pixel in a digital photo. The science of optics is an *additive process,* where colors are added to each other to create other colors. If you think about shining a red and green flashlight on a single spot on the floor, you'll get the idea.

Your color printer mixes colors following the rules of a science you're probably more familiar with: *pigment*, in which yellow is a primary color and not the product of red and green. A color inkjet has as few as four, or as many as seven, different inks to work with. So rather than employing the optical process of *adding* light to attain the desired color, printing employs what's called a *subtractive* process. This theory works in precisely the opposite direction of optics, and even the opposite of how artists are taught to mix paints. The subtractive process presumes that the purest light an object can reflect is white, so an object's color can be simulated by applying colored pigment to mask out, or subtract, just those hues that an object absorbs and does *not* reflect. So during printing, magenta is applied to the color of an object not because the natural hue of that object is magenta or magenta-ish, but instead because the object appears to absorb— or not reflect—magenta light.

Theoretically, if your inkjet printer were to mix equal amounts of cyan, magenta, and yellow ink in a given area, they would cancel out all reflected light, and the product would be black. In practice, however, since cheaper inks tend to introduce certain impurities, the product is actually a muddy brown. So printers add a fourth pass, with black ink, to make darker portions bolder. Thus the name commonly given to the four-pigment process, CMYK (where the *K* stands for black). Recall from our earlier discussion of optics that cyan, magenta, and yellow just happen to be the three secondary hues in optics. This is the critical connection between optics and pigment, and this is why cyan, magenta, and yellow are the three basic inks used in process printing. Still, because the monitor and the printer use two different color models to create color, it's up to your program (in this case, Paint Shop Pro) to do the best job it can in translating between the two. PSP uses certain files called *color profiles* to help it do just that. Color profiles help to translate color information from your monitor's RGB color model to your printer's CMYK color model.

Windows (usually) automatically installs a color profile for translating optical shades to printed shades; when you installed your

NOTES

Optics is the science of light, in which color is created by mixing light of different wavelengths; the three primary colors of light are red, green, and blue. Your monitor adds various amounts of red, green, and blue light together to create other colors.

Because your monitor mixes light to make colors, in its system, red and green make *yellow*, green and blue make *cyan*, and red and blue make *magenta*. This might be a foreign concept for you, especially because it's so different from what you might have done as a child, where mixing yellow and blue make green, red and blue make purple, and so on. A color printer uses a similar color mixing system known as CMYK, where the three primary colors are cyan (the closest thing to blue in a transparent ink), magenta (a kind of red), and yellow.

NOTE

You'll learn more about color profiles and how to install them in **❶ Ensure That What You See Is What You Get**.

printer, the software it uses might have overridden that default color profile with one that's better suited to your printer. But it might not have done so. Color profiling is not a perfect system; in the end, the final judge of which colors truly belong are your own eyes. This is why PSP gives you tools for making subtle color corrections on your own. This book will show you not only how to engage color profiling (in the very next chapter), but also how to make these subtle corrections.

About Color Models and Optics

When you use the Paint program shipped with Microsoft Windows—you've probably played with it once or twice—you choose a brush and a color. Your brush sets the pattern for how the color is applied. You click the image, and the brush stamps that color, with that pattern, onto the image, and there you go. Done.

"Painting" in Paint Shop Pro is a different order of beast. When you're using a painting tool, you might load that tool with a solid color, a color-texture blend, a color gradient, or with a preset wallpaper pattern whose colors are predetermined. The color choice you make directly involves an optical color model. Every color visible on your monitor can be described in either of two ways: as a mixture of the optical primaries red, green, and blue; or as a given hue with a specific brightness (saturation) and lightness (luminance).

NOTE

When you look at the **Colors** tab on the **Materials** palette, you will discover the absence of certain colors you would swear were real—khaki colors, "earth tones," sandy shades.

They're blends that can't be described by an optical color model—one based on light. A digital photograph simulates such impossible blends by placing two or more pixels with wildly varying hues next to each other, letting the mind sort out the resulting illusion.

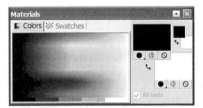

*The **Materials** palette helps you load your brushes with "paint."*

In the first color model—using the optical primaries red, green, and blue, called simply RGB—the three primaries are expressed in terms of their relative intensities, from 0 to 255. As you point to colors in the **Materials** palette, for instance, a ToolTip shows you a sample of the color you're pointing to, and how much red, green, and blue is contained in that color. Every color that it is possible for your monitor to display is shown in the **Colors** tab of the **Materials** palette.

With the RGB model, it's easy to determine how much of the three primary hues to blend with any color to produce white. The purest, brightest red would be defined as RGB value {255,0,0} red with no green or blue. Cyan is created by mixing equal parts of green and blue {0,255,255}. Obviously, if you were to create a pattern of blended red and cyan pixels, the result will appear medium gray at the points where the colors mixed {132,132,132}. White is produced by mixing all three colors evenly {255,255,255}. Black is produced on your monitor by adding no light at all {0,0,0}.

The second color model, named for the three attributes hue, saturation, and luminance (HSL), also describes every color that Windows and your monitor can display. In the HSL model, a set of 256 different colors in the available optical spectrum are each represented by a hue value from 0 to 255. The saturation level (S) refers to how *much* of that hue appears in the blended color—a 0 value is colorless or gray, whereas 255 is "pure" and undiffused (such as a pure yellow). Luminance (L) represents the blended color's degree of light—or, more accurately, *whiteness*. Here, a value of 127 represents "normal" or "balanced," whereas 0 represents total darkness (black), and 255 is total whiteness. Technically, 127 is the *brighter* color because it is not toned down or up. Any visible color for any pixel on your monitor can be represented on both the RGB and HSL scales.

Why Paint Shop Pro Has Its Own File Format

Your digital camera stores its photos in one of the universal image formats: perhaps JPEG (named for the Joint Photographic Experts Group which devised the format) or Tagged Image File Format (TIFF). Your digital scanner probably uses one of these

 NOTE

Okay, there's a third way to specify color in the **Materials** dialog box: by entering a specific HTML color code (actually the RGB value of the color as HTML expects to see it). The code uses six hexadecimal (base-16) digits, where the first pair stands for red value, the second pair for green, and the third for blue. In base-10 everyday numbers, we use digits 0 through 9; hexadecimal proceeds from 0 to 9 and up to A through F (to represent 10 through 15). So A0 represents 160, and FF represents 255.

formats as well. Both JPEG and TIFF images can be mathematically compressed so that they consume less storage space than a format that represents the entire image as a *bitmap*—as colored dots in multiple rows, left to right, top to bottom. (For TIFF files, compression is optional.) But even compressed, a JPEG or TIFF file is made up of one single image component—that is, one picture and not several layers of an image laid on top of each other.

Paint Shop Pro has its own image format, which you use to store works in progress. In Windows, the format's filename extensions are **.psp** and **.pspimage**—the former is the "legacy" extension, while the latter follows the new operating-system-neutral trend of using "-image" as a suffix to identify all image files. The reason PSP has a separate format is because its files may be structured in a much more complex fashion. You can create layers in a PSP file, for example, and use them to build up a complex image. You can also create and save selections for reuse, store *masks* that block part of the layers below, create areas of transparency, and perform other functions unique to Paint Shop Pro. The PSP format represents an image as a work in progress, in a state of transition, with layers kept separate, and hidden image content retained in storage. You'll want to use PSP format for all your work in progress. After a PSP project is complete, you're free to merge all the layers' contents into one, creating a finished product. However, you may opt to leave your image in PSP format as multilayered, and create a single-layer copy of that image in another format (JPEG, for example) for distribution online or to your friends using email.

Become Familiar with the PSP Interface

Every computer application you'll ever work with has its own unique theories of operation, and Paint Shop Pro is no exception. With a new automobile, you can generally be assured that the steering wheel will be located in roughly the same place as every other car you've driven before. The instrumentation should be legible through the steering wheel, and even when there are differences—for example, finding the automatic shift control between the two front seats instead of attached to the steering

> **NOTE**
>
> You won't want to share files using PSP format, even if your friend also uses PSP, because the files are simply too large. Converting finished images to JPEG or TIFF format is smart because the resulting files are much smaller. Back up your original, larger PSP files onto CD for retrieval later on should you need to make changes.

column—they're not so shockingly foreign as to render the car undriveable. In the same way, parts of Paint Shop Pro will be instantly recognizable to you, and some parts will be more difficult to figure out if you are new to paint programs. It's these elements that I want to introduce you to.

Standard Toolbar   **Tool Options Palette**

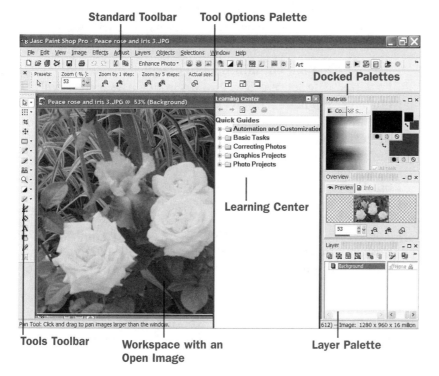

Docked Palettes

Learning Center

Tools Toolbar   **Workspace with an Open Image**   **Layer Palette**

Parts of the PSP workspace.

PSP's functionality is divided among five window regions, whose onscreen arrangement is almost entirely up to you:

- In general, commands that you direct to the program as a whole—for example, "Open a file," "Promote this selection to a new layer," or "Apply this filter from your library"—are accessible from the main menu bar. This is the familiar "File, Edit, View" style of menu you see with most applications.

NOTE

When you start PSP for the first time, it displays a dialog box asking you to select graphic file types you want to associate with the program. Selecting an associated file type will allow you to double-click a file of that type in **My Computer** and display the image in PSP automatically. To change the files you've associated with PSP, choose **File, Preferences, File Format Associations**.

- Common commands are represented with icons on toolbars. To view or hide a toolbar, select it from the **View, Toolbars** menu.

- Tasks that involve manipulating some specific portion of an image are represented by the **Tools** toolbar. The **Tools** toolbar is PSP's equivalent of a caddy on your desk where you keep all your brushes, pens, erasers, and scissors. You'll learn more about the **Tools** toolbar later in this chapter.

TIP

In PSP, you can drag the menu bar from its default location along the top edge of the workspace to any other location on your screen. It fits just fine along the left side, if you don't mind reading the categories sideways. You can rearrange toolbars and palettes as well— toolbars can even be placed next to each other on the same row.

- PSP has two different things, both of which are called "palette." The set of colors that an image uses is, naturally, one type of palette. However, the term also refers to a small floating dialog box. The most commonly used palette is the **Materials** palette, which lets you choose the colors for your tools. Another common palette is the **Tool Options** palette, which lets you change the options for the current tool. To view or hide a palette, select it from the **View, Palettes** menu.

- The rest of the PSP workspace is devoted to showing your images. You can have many images open at one time; the maximum number is theoretically limited by the memory of your computer.

TIP

When you start PSP, it displays the **Materials**, **Overview**, and **Layer** palettes on the right side of the window. Initially, these palettes might not display all the options shown in the preceding figure. To fix this problem, simply drag the docked palette's left edge to the left, making all three palettes wider.

Before I move on to the specifics of working with tools and palettes, I want to mention several unusual viewing modes you might want to use when working on an image.

- **Full Screen Edit.** Choose **View, Full Screen Edit** to display the current image, full screen, with the title bar and status bar hidden from view so as to maximize all available space.

- **Full Screen View.** Choose **View, Full Screen Preview** to display the current image as large as possible, on a screen by itself. Click the image or press **Esc** to return to regular edit mode.

- **Web View.** Choose **View, Preview in Web Browser** to display the current image in your Web browser so that you can see how it might look when viewed over the Internet. After choosing this command, you'll need to select the browser you want to use in the preview, the file type(s) you want to emulate, and the image size you want to use from the dialog box that appears.

You might want to turn on several tools to guide you as you make precise adjustments to an image. For example, when drawing objects of a specific size, you might want to display the ruler (choose **View, Rulers**). Initially, the ruler uses pixels as its unit of measure, but you can change this on the **Units** tab of the Paint Shop Pro 8 **Preferences** dialog box (choose **File, Preferences, General Program Preferences**).

Another useful tool for aligning objects perfectly is the grid, a set of vertical and horizontal lines that cross all over the image forming, well, a *grid*. Turn it on by choosing **View, Grid**. To change the properties of the grid—for example, to make the grid-lines further apart, choose **View, Change Grid and Guide Properties**. On the **Grid** tab of the dialog box, you can choose the unit of measurement used in making the grid and also the distance between the horizontal/vertical gridlines. You can also choose the color used for the gridlines. After turning on the grid, you can automatically align objects to the gridlines by turning on the **View, Snap to Grid** option.

If you like the idea of gridlines but want them at particular points on an image, try using guides instead. To add a guideline to an image, choose **View, Guides**. In addition, make sure that the ruler is turned on. To add a horizontal guideline across the image, click the horizontal ruler at the top of the image and drag down. Place the guideline wherever you want it and then release the mouse button to drop it in place. Drag from the vertical ruler to create a vertical guideline.

Use Toolbars

As in most applications, a toolbar in PSP is a collection of buttons that represent frequently used commands. When you start PSP for the first time, it displays a handful of toolbars, located along the top and left sides of the window. If you move these toolbars and exit the program, PSP remembers their new locations and redisplays them there when you restart the application.

NOTE

To automatically align objects to the guides you create, turn on the **View, Snap to Guides** command. Change the color of the guides and the snap sensitivity by choosing **View, Change Grid and Guide Properties**.

TIP

After you adjust the PSP environment to suit your needs, save your configuration as a workspace: Choose **File, Workspace, Save**. If the program ever crashes, it might hide all toolbars and palettes or lose their last positions. Choose **File, Workspace, Default** to reload the default workspace file, or choose **File, Workspace, Load** to reload your saved workspace and return PSP to normal.

The **Standard** toolbar (located just underneath the menu bar) contains buttons for common commands such as **New**, **Open**, **Print**, and **Save**. To the right of the **Standard** toolbar is the **Photo** toolbar, which contains photograph-fixing commands such as **Automatic Color Balance**, **Fade Correction**, and so on. To the right of that toolbar is the **Script** toolbar, with buttons for recording and playing *scripts*. Along the right side of the window is the **Tools** toolbar.

💡 **TIP**

You can quickly undock a docked toolbar by double-clicking its handle; to dock a floating toolbar to the nearest edge, double-click its title bar.

Handle   **Standard Toolbar**   **Script Toolbar, Repositioned Closer to the Standard Toolbar by Dragging Its Handle**

Tools Toolbar   **Photo Toolbar, Undocked from Its Usual Position and Resized**

Common toolbars.

💡 **TIP**

A floating toolbar always stays "on top," so you never have to worry about accidentally covering it up with an image window.

As I mentioned before, you can hide and display toolbars by selecting them from the **View**, **Toolbars** menu. You can relocate a toolbar by dragging it by its handle to the new location. You can dock any number of toolbars along the sides of the window, or leave them free-floating in the workspace. When a toolbar floats like this, it behaves more like a mini-window, so you can drag its border to adjust its shape from a long rectangle to more of a square box, as shown in the figure.

Use Palettes

Functionally, a palette is very similar to a toolbar. To display or hide a palette, select it from the **View, Palettes** menu. You can also press its shortcut key to display a particular palette:

To Display This Palette	Press This
Brush Variance palette	F11
Histogram palette	F7
Layer palette	F8
Learning Center palette	F10
Materials palette	F6
Overview palette	F9
Script Output palette	F3
Tool Options palette	F4

Arrange palettes onscreen wherever you like by dragging them by their title bars. Dock a palette by dragging it to a window's edge. You can stack several palettes on top of each other by docking them along the same edge. (This is the initial arrangement for the **Materials**, **Overview**, and **Layer** palettes.) After they're stacked, you can take some of the space from one palette and give it to another by dragging the border between the palettes.

Each palette comes with its own window gadgets. For example, to hide a palette (remove it from the workspace), click its close box—the familiar X in the upper-right corner. If the palette is docked and stacked with others along the same edge, you can expand a palette temporarily by clicking its **Maximize palette** button. This action automatically hides the other palettes in the same stack. To restore the arrangement to normal, click the open palette's **Restore palette** button.

NOTE

If a palette is free-floating and you click the up arrow, the palette becomes a self-collapsing window shade. As long as the mouse pointer remains over the palette, the "shade" is open and the palette is fully visible. When your pointer leaves the palette, the palette contracts to just a title bar. To return the palette to its normal state (always open), click the left arrow button.

Docked and Stacked Palettes Have Minimize, Maximize/ Restore, and Close Buttons

Click the Up Arrow on a Free-floating Palette to Roll It Up

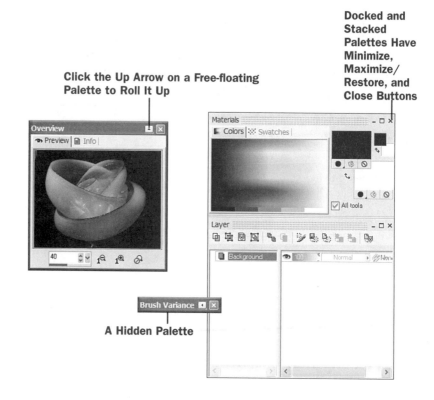

A Hidden Palette

The functional parts of a palette.

Use Dialog Boxes

A dialog box in one application is typically very similar to those you find in any other application. However, the dialog boxes in PSP offer several unique features you should get to know before you use the program. When you select a command that changes an image visually, such as adjusting the brightness, sharpening the edges, or applying a filter, the dialog box that appears provides several ways in which you can display the effects of your selections interactively, so that you can determine what changes you want to make to your image before you make them. These dialog boxes present you with before-and-after previews and close-ups of your image showing what the image will look like if you applied the current settings. This way, you can play with the settings, even making random choices with any of them, just to see what they mean and what they do.

Show/Hide Previews

Zoom Out   Navigate   AutoProof

Zoom In   Proof

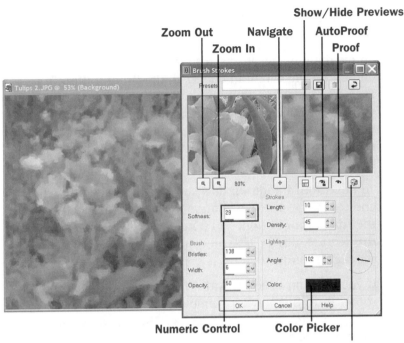

Numeric Control   Color Picker

Randomize Parameters

Dialog boxes in PSP often interact with the image window.

Here's how to use the common features that appear in PSP dialog boxes:

- The two preview boxes at the top of the dialog box show identical segments of the active image. To shift the location currently being shown for *both* of these preview boxes simultaneously, click and hold either box and drag in the direction you want to move the contents. With the pen, touch the tablet and drag the pen.

- Another way to change the area of the image that the preview windows show is with the **Navigate** button. Click and hold this button to bring up a map of your entire image, with a square indicating the region the preview windows currently displayed. Drag this square until it encloses the area you want to see.

- To change the magnification of the preview windows, click the **Zoom Out** button (with the "minus" magnifying glass

 NOTE

By default, the preview boxes generally begin by showing a magnified portion of the very center of the image.

TIP

After you click the **Proof** button, you might have to wait a moment (longer for a slower computer), after which the image will display the results of the settings you've chosen.

icon) to reduce magnification by 20%; click the **Zoom In** button (with the "plus" icon) to increase by 20%.

- To see the possible effects of the settings you've currently chosen on the actual image, click the **Proof** button. You haven't messed up anything; if you don't like your choices, you can make changes to them and try another **Proof**, or you can always click **Cancel**, in which case the image will reset itself to the state it was before you called up the dialog box.

- To have your image window show you the effects of your choices every time you change them in the dialog box, click the **AutoProof** button. You'll need a fast computer to use this feature; otherwise, you could slow down your editing process dramatically.

- If you're using **Proof** or **AutoProof** to inspect your choices rather than the preview windows, and you want more space to see your image, click the **Show/Hide Previews** button to close both preview windows and shrink the dialog box.

- If you're not at all sure what settings to try, click the **Randomize Parameters** button. PSP will make random choices in all the settings in the dialog box. Click again to randomize these choices yet again.

- The numeric control provides several methods for entering a value. You can type the new value into the box, click the spinner button to adjust the value by 1, click and drag the small slider to change the value more quickly, or click the down arrow and drag the larger slider that appears. With a pen, you can easily *draw* either of these sliders to the left or right and stop when the number is what you want it to be.

TIP

At the top of PSP dialog boxes, and on the **Tool Options** palette, you can select a *preset*, which is a set of dialog box or tool options saved in a file so that you can reuse them when needed. You'll learn more about selecting and saving presets in **19** Save Tool Options for Reuse.

Perform Common Tasks with the Help of the Learning Center

I won't mention Paint Shop Pro's Help system very often in this book, except for right here. As part of PSP's improved online help, the **Learning Center** palette guides you step by step through some of the more common PSP tasks. To display the

Learning Center palette, choose **View, Palettes, Learning Center** or press **F10**. Inside, the Learning Center works like a small Web page, complete with hyperlinks to different sections and browser-like buttons that enable you to go back to the page you just read or to the home page (the Quick Guides listing). After you choose a task, the Learning Center lists the steps you must follow to complete that task. Sometimes, the hyperlink, **Perform this step for me** is included underneath a step to help you complete it properly. At the bottom of most tasks you'll find links to related tasks.

The **Learning Center** *guides you through common tasks.*

> **TIP**
>
> The **Learning Center** is just like any other palette; you can dock it, float it, or roll it up. You can also resize the window, as shown in the figure.

What Undo Undoes

Finally, a few words about the **Undo** feature: Like a lot of programs, Paint Shop Pro remembers the changes you make to your image and allows you to undo them as needed. When you click the **Undo** button or select **Edit, Undo** from the menu, PSP resets the image to the state it was before you made the most

TIP

The **Edit, Undo** menu command will tell you the name of the operation you're about to undo, before you undo it. The limit to the number of changes PSP can undo is set on the **Undo** tab of the **General Preferences** dialog box (choose **File, Preferences, General Preferences**). Unless you change this setting, the number of changes you can undo is unlimited except by the total amount of disk space an image can take up (usually set to 500MB).

NOTE

If PSP can only undo and redo "changes," what's a change? Any operation you make with a tool from the **Tools** toolbar, from when you click on the image to when you release the mouse button, is *one change*. With a pen, that's any job you do with a tool from when your pen touches the tablet to when you lift the pen (a one-mark operation). Selecting **Edit, Undo** "erases" that mark. If you paint a picture without releasing the mouse or lifting the pen, you can undo the whole thing with one **Undo** command.

recent change. Because PSP remembers the changes you made, in the order in which you made them, whenever the image is reset by an Undo command, the change you made before that point is the one PSP can undo next if you click the **Undo** button or choose **Edit, Undo** again.

If you have several images open, PSP remembers separate sequences of changes—or "diaries," if you will—for each image. Switching between images is not one of the commands that PSP remembers. If you draw something onto a layer of Image 1, then move to Image 2, cut out a portion of that image, move back to Image 1, and paste that part in as a new selection, then with Image 1 as your active image, the Undo command would reset these changes in this sequence: the paste, followed by the drawing. The cut from Image 2 would remain. If you switch back to Image 2 and select Undo, the cut operation would be reset. The portion you cut from Image 2 would return. However, the portion you pasted into Image 1 would not disappear—you cannot undo the change made to Image 1, while Image 2 is the active window.

Whatever can be undone can also be redone. Every time you undo an operation—thereby going back one step—the operation PSP resets is remembered in a separate "redo" sequence for the image. If, after you click **Undo**, you click the **Redo** button or select **Edit, Redo** (the menu command will tell you the name of the operation that's being redone), the active image is reset to the stage it was in before the Undo command.

Any change made to an image through the use of a filter is also something that PSP can undo. The image is reset to its state at the time you called up the filter's dialog box. The act of selecting a region of an image can be undone. Any operation that involves changing the order or position of layers, or the creation of new layers, or the removal of layers, can be undone.

What can't you undo? When you make some change to the Paint Shop Pro *application*—for instance, the location of the toolbars and palettes in the workspace—those changes aren't remembered and cannot be reversed with an Undo. Undo only remembers changes you make to images, not to the program. Of course, you can move a toolbar wherever you want it at any time without negatively affecting any of your open images, so this is the sort of change you can manually undo.

If you have multiple changes to undo, rather than clicking the **Undo** button repeatedly, use the Command History. Select **Edit, Command History** from the menu to open a dialog box listing all the changes you can undo. Select any change you want to undo, click **Undo**, and all the changes made up to that point will be undone in one step.

That's all the general information you need to know about PSP before getting to work. From this point on, I'll be concentrating on real-world tasks you can do with digital photos and original artwork in Paint Shop Pro. Don't read the rest of this book like a book—instead, just jump to whatever task you want to do right now. And don't worry; if you need some background information or if there's a related task you might also want to do, I'll point you in the right direction.

 TIP

Even if you save an image in progress, you can still undo a change. When you save and close a file, however, the undo history is erased. When you open that file again, you will no longer be able to undo the changes you saved before you closed the file.

2

Getting an Image into Paint Shop Pro

IN THIS CHAPTER:

Paint Shop Pro comes with many tools for creating and manipulating graphics. With its help, you can create cool Web buttons, remove red eye before you can blink, or take Johnny out of a snowy scene and place him on the beach.

Before you can perform any of this graphics wizardry, however, you must first import the graphic you want to work on or tell Paint Shop Pro you want to start from scratch. In the tasks presented in this chapter, you will learn not only how to start something new, but also how to locate and open image files already stored on the hard disk. In addition, you'll learn how to scan in a photo or other graphics, import photos from your digital camera, and take pictures of data shown on your screen.

1 Ensure That What You See Is What You Get

See Also

→ **5** Scan an Image
→ **33** Print an Image

 TIP

You can improve the quality of your scans by installing an ICM profile for your scanner (if one is available). Just follow the general steps listed here.

 **NOTE**

To match what you see onscreen with what prints, you start by adjusting your monitor and then installing profiles specifically designed for your monitor and printer. With these profiles installed, each device can tell exactly what colors the other device can produce, and how best to map colors from one device to the other to create as close a match as possible between onscreen appearance and print result.

What you see onscreen is often very different from what you get when you print an image on paper. Your monitor, printer, and even your scanner not only use different methods to render color images, but each device works with a different range of possible colors (also called a *gamut*). The best way you can deal with this messy situation is to create an environment that simulates on your screen what an image will look like when it's finally printed. To do that, you use *color management*.

What color management does is match up the gamut of colors your monitor uses with the gamut of colors your printer is capable of reproducing so that, in the best of all worlds, what you see onscreen as a pale shade of greenish blue approximates that shade when printed out. Translating colors from one device to another requires specific ICM (Image Color Management) profiles of the devices involved, and needless to say, the process is not perfect.

A new technology called Exchangeable Image File Format (EXIF) and Print Image Managing (PIM, an Epson-based derivative) for color management is taking hold, and if your digital camera and printer support EXIF or PIM, you can achieve near-perfect photographic prints. EXIF/PIM digital cameras store data specific to the image being taken in the EXIF header of the JPEG file, which is later read and interpreted by your PIM printer. Newer

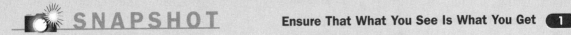
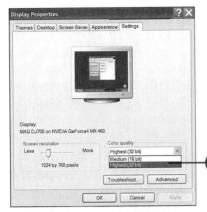

1 Change to 32-Bit Color

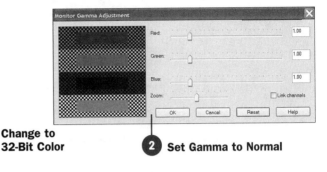

2 Set Gamma to Normal

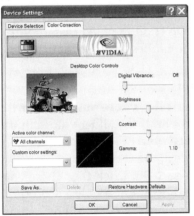

3 Calibrate Your Monitor

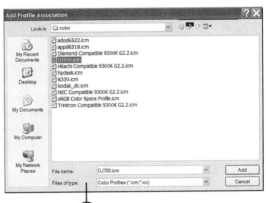

4 Install the Monitor ICM Profile

5 Install the Printer ICM Profile

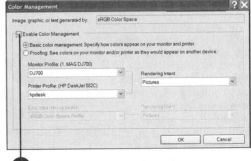

6 Turn on Color Management

photo printers, digital cameras, and most graphics editing programs (Paint Shop Pro included) support EXIF. And even though PSP does not currently support PIM (the Epson EXIF add-on), you can still achieve excellent results using an Epson printer. To take advantage of EXIF technology in Paint Shop Pro, you must retain the EXIF data of an original image when you edit it by saving the image in JPEG or PSP format.

NOTE

If you're low on video memory, reduce the screen resolution by dragging the **Screen resolution** slider to the left. For graphics processing, it's always better to go with a higher color than a higher resolution (if you have to choose).

① Change to 32-Bit Color

Right-click the Windows Desktop and choose **Properties** to display the **Display Properties** dialog box. Click the **Settings** tab. Open the **Color quality** list and choose **Highest (32 bit)**. If this option isn't available, it's because your system does not have enough video memory to support it; in that case choose the highest setting you can. Click **OK**.

② Set Gamma to Normal

In Paint Shop Pro, choose **File, Preferences, Monitor Gamma** from the menu bar. If the slider values in the **Monitor Gamma Adjustment** dialog box that opens are not already set to 1.00, drag the **Red, Green,** and **Blue** sliders to set their values to **1.00**. Click **OK**. These values set the amount of gamma adjustment; a value of 1.00 means no adjustment at all. By setting the gamma adjustment to none in PSP, you can more properly correct the monitor adjustment in step 3.

NOTE

If you can adjust the white point on your monitor, set it at 6,500K. You might make this adjustment using the monitor's physical controls, or by changing video settings in the **Display Properties** dialog box: Right-click the Desktop, choose **Properties**, click the **Settings** tab, click **Advanced**, and then click the tab for your video card.

③ Calibrate Your Monitor

Using the appropriate control for your monitor, set the **contrast** at 100%. (Consult the owner's manual for help in locating this control.) Open your Web browser and display **www.jasc.com/monitor1.asp**. Using the chart you'll find on that Web page, adjust the **brightness** control on your monitor as needed. Scroll down to the bottom of the page and estimate the monitor gamma. A typical Windows computer registers around 2.5; however, as long as the gamma is between 2.35 and 2.55, you're okay.

If you can set the gamma manually on your monitor, set the gamma value anywhere between 2.0 and 2.2. This will give you a nice average of the typical gamma used by a Mac (1.8) and that used by a PC (2.5). Some video cards don't let you set a gamma value, but rather, the amount of gamma adjustment. I've set my video card at 1.10 (1.00 normal value plus 1.10 adjustment gives me a total of 2.1).

WEB RESOURCE

www.photoscientia.co.uk/Gamma.htm

A series of charts you might find helpful when adjusting monitor gamma.

4 Install the Monitor ICM Profile

Right-click the Windows Desktop and choose **Properties**. Click the **Settings** tab and then click **Advanced**. Click the **Color Management** tab and click **Add**. Select a profile that matches your monitor's brand and model number and click **Add**. Click **OK** twice to return to the Desktop.

Determine whether a particular profile was designed for use with your monitor by right-clicking the profile name and choosing **Properties**. If you don't see a compatible profile, you might be able to locate the file on the disk that came with the monitor, or download a profile from the manufacturer's Web site. Save the file to the **Windows\System\Color** folder for Windows 98, 98SE, or Me; save it to the **Windows\System32\Color** folder for Windows NT, 2000, or XP.

If you happen to choose a profile that's not designed for your monitor, you won't get good color matching results (as you would with a profile specifically designed for the equipment you're using). If you can't find a profile for your specific monitor's make and model, install a profile that's close and see what happens. If the result is worse than no profile at all, uninstall the profile (go back to the dialog box and select the Windows default profile).

5 Install the Printer ICM Profile

Click the **Start** button and choose **Printers and Faxes** or open the **Control Panel** and double-click the **Printers and Faxes** icon. Right-click the printer icon and choose **Properties**. Click the **Color Management** tab and click

Add. Select a profile that matches your printer's make and model number and click **Add**.

If needed, set this printer to be the default printer by right-clicking its icon and choosing **Default**.

6 Turn on Color Management

Start Paint Shop Pro. Choose **File, Preferences, Color Management** from the menu. The **Color Management** dialog box appears. Choose **Enable Color Management**. Choose the **Basic color management** option because this option suits most graphics editing purposes without slowing down your system too much. Open the **Monitor Profile** list and select the monitor profile you installed in step 4. Open the **Printer Profile** and select the printer profile installed in step 5. Open the **Rendering Intent** list and choose **Pictures**, which is the best choice if your intent is to match what you see onscreen as closely as you can with what you get when you print an image. If you need to match several colors exactly (such as a company logo), you might want to choose **Match** instead. Click **OK**.

2 Create a New Image

Before You Begin

✔ **1** Ensure That What You See Is What You Get

✔ **13** Select a Color to Work With

✔ **28** About Size and Resolution

✔ **36** About Image Types

See Also

→ **29** Change Image Size or Resolution

→ **31** Change Color Depth

→ **39** Save an Image As Another File Type

As with other programs, if you want to use Paint Shop Pro to create new art such as a Web page button, you must start with a new, empty image file. You might also create a new image file when you want to combine portions of several photographs into a collage or panorama. After creating a new image file, you should save it in Paint Shop Pro format.

When you create a new image file, you set several initial parameters, such as the image's width and height. You are not stuck with your initial choices; in most cases, you can change your selections later on as you work. In addition to width and height, you must set the image's *resolution*. Finally, you'll select the background type and color, and the image *color depth*. As you make your selections, memory requirements and final dimensions are displayed at the bottom of the dialog box. You'll actually need about three times the amount of memory shown to work on an image; if necessary, reduce the image size, resolution, or color depth to make the memory requirement more manageable for your system.

❶ Click New

Click the **New** button on the **Standard** toolbar. The **New Image** dialog box appears; the dialog box contains many presets to fit common image types, such as a 5-by-7-inch photo or a 125-by-125-pixel Web button. To use any of these presets, open the **Presets** list and click the one you want. You can modify the settings that appear by following these additional steps.

❷ Set Desired Width and Height

Open the **Units** list and choose the unit of measurement you want to use. Then set the **Width** and **Height** values for the desired finished image size.

❸ Select Desired Resolution

Set the **Resolution** value to the number of pixels you want per inch/centimeter. If the image will only be viewed onscreen, the default of 72 pixels per inch is sufficient; for images you intend to print, consider a higher resolution of about one-fourth to one-half your printer's resolution.

❹ Select a Background Type

If the new image will contain mostly *vector data* (drawn objects and text), choose **Vector Background**; if it will contain mostly *raster data* (photographs, gradients, and color fills), choose **Raster Background**.

❺ Choose a Color Depth

Open the **Color depth** list and select the size of the color gamut you want to work with. Some tools and commands are available only in 24-bit or grayscale images, so keep that in mind when making a selection. Typically the best way to go is to choose **16 Million Colors (24 Bit)**, and to reduce the color depth if necessary before saving the final image (so as to reduce the file size as well).

🔍 KEY TERMS

Resolution—The number of pixels (dots of color) per inch/centimeter. Higher-resolution images can hold greater amounts of detail but are also larger in file size.

Color depth—The color depth of an image determines the amount of colors you can work with; it also affects the image's file size—the larger the color depth, the larger the file size.

💡 TIP

A typical ink jet printer uses a resolution of 600 dpi (dots per inch); if you're printing on a home ink jet, select 300 ppi (pixels per inch). Newer photo printers average 1200 dpi, so you're still fine with 300 ppi resolution, although you could try 600 ppi and compare the results.

🔍 KEY TERMS

Raster data—Data comprised of individual pixels, each with its own hue, saturation, and brightness values.

Vector data—Data that's stored as a series of mathematical algorithms that plot the coordinates of points along the edges of a shape, such as a star or a bit of vector text.

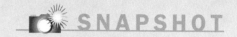
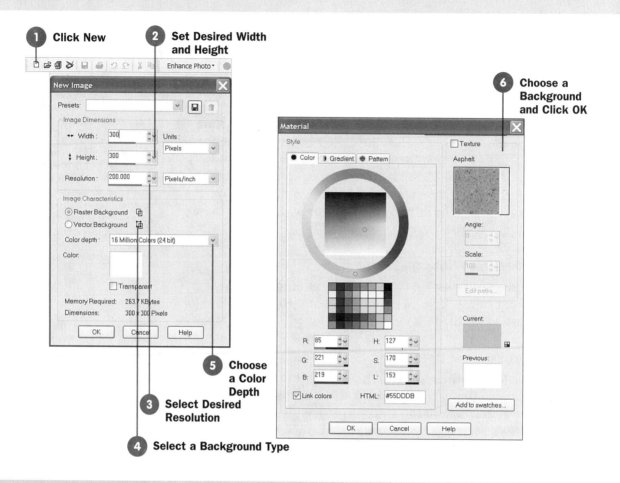

1 Click New

2 Set Desired Width and Height

6 Choose a Background and Click OK

5 Choose a Color Depth

3 Select Desired Resolution

4 Select a Background Type

TIP

If you don't want to use any material, click **Transparent** in the **New Image** dialog box. (This option is available only in 24-bit and grayscale images.) To select from materials you've chosen recently, right-click the **Color** box and select a color.

6 **Choose a Background and Click OK**

Click the **Color** box; the **Material** dialog box opens. Choose a color, gradient, or texture and then click **OK**. The color/gradient/texture you choose will fill the bottom layer of your image—the background layer. After selecting a background, click **OK** to create the new image file.

③ Open an Existing Image

Before you can make changes to a graphic within Paint Shop Pro, you must open its file. You can open files saved in Paint Shop Pro format and other common graphic types such as TIFF, JPEG, GIF, and so on. After opening an image in another format, you might want to use the **Save As** command to resave it in Paint Shop Pro format.

Before opening an image, you can view its *thumbnail*. Image thumbnails help you select the correct image for editing. You can also open multiple images at one time if you like.

① Click Open

Click the **Open** button on the **Standard** toolbar. The **Open** dialog box appears.

② Change to the Image Folder

Files stored in the currently selected folder are displayed in the **Browse** window at the top of the dialog box. To change to another folder, open the **Look in** list and select a different folder.

③ Select the Images to Open

Normally, all graphic files in the selected folder are listed in the **Open** dialog box, but you can narrow the display by opening the **Files of type** list and choosing a particular graphic type such as TIFF. Click a file in the **Browse** window at the top of the dialog box to select it; press and hold the **Ctrl** key and click additional files if you want to work on several images at once.

④ Click Open

Click the **Open** button to open the selected images.

Before You Begin

✔ ③⑥ About Image Types

See Also

→ ④ Browse for an Image

🔍 KEY TERM

Thumbnail—A small version of an image generally appearing in a group of other small images, but just large enough so that you can easily distinguish one from another.

💡 TIP

When you started Paint Shop Pro for the first time, it asked you to select the file types you wanted to associate with the program. If you double-click a file of an associated type in **My Computer**, Paint Shop Pro will start and open the file for you automatically.

✏ NOTE

Windows typically displays files as small thumbnails, although you can change the way in which files are listed by opening the **View** menu. If you use an earlier version of Windows that does not display thumbnails, Paint Shop Pro can provide previews for you if you enable the **Show preview** check box at the bottom of the **Open** dialog box. To display details for a single selected file, click the **Details** button.

1 Click Open

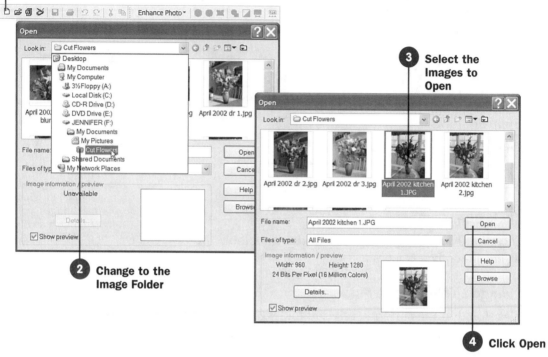

3 Select the Images to Open

2 Change to the Image Folder

4 Click Open

---

4 Browse for an Image

See Also

→ **3** Open an Existing Image

→ **6** Browse Images on a Digital Camera

→ **8** Rename Digital Images in One Step

→ **34** Print Contact Sheets

You can locate and open a file quickly with the Paint Shop Pro **Browser**. In the **Browser**, a list of folders appears on the left side of the window, and thumbnails for the images in the current folder appear on the right in a manner similar to the way **My Computer** displays files. The advantage is that you don't have to switch from Paint Shop Pro to perform tasks you might typically do in **My Computer**—such as quickly checking several folders for a file; copying, moving, renaming, or deleting a file; or viewing file information. You can also print a *contact sheet*—a sheet of thumbnail images—from within the **Browser**—see **34** **Print Contact Sheets**.

1 Click Browse

Click the **Browse** button on the **Standard** toolbar to display the **Browser** window. Alternatively, you can click the **Browse** button in the **Open** dialog box to display the **Browser**.

2 Change to the Image Folder

From the list of folders on the left side of the window, click the folder that contains the image or images you want to open, copy, move, rename, or delete.

3 Select Images

From the display of thumbnails on the right, click the image you want to work with. To select multiple images, press and hold the **Ctrl** key and click additional images.

To quickly select similar files in the same folder, choose **File, Select** from the menu, choose the attributes that make the files similar (such as filename, type, date of creation, image size, and so on), and click **OK**.

4 Perform a File Management Task

To open the selected images, choose **ImageFile, Open** from the menu bar. If you selected a single image, you can simply double-click it to open it, or you can drag the file from the Browser window into the PSP workspace.

To copy or move the selected images, choose **ImageFile, Copy To** or **ImageFile, Move To** from the menu bar. Select a folder to which you want to copy/move the files from the **Browse for Folder** dialog box and click **OK**.

To delete the selected images, choose **ImageFile, Delete** from the menu bar and click **Yes** to confirm.

To rename the selected image, choose **ImageFile, Rename** from the menu bar. Type a new name for the file and click **OK**. You can rename only one file at a time using this command.

TIP

You can leave the **Browser** open while you work in Paint Shop Pro if you like.

TIP

To help locate the image(s) you want, sort the thumbnails by choosing **File, Sort** from the menu. You can set a primary and a secondary sort (such as filename within file date). Make your choices on the appropriate tabs in the **Sort** dialog box and click **OK**.

TIP

To display details about the selected image, choose **ImageFile, Information** from the menu bar. (You can select only one file at a time with this command.) Click **OK** to close the **Information** window. To send images using email, choose **File, Send**. Select the **Selected thumbnails** or **All** option as desired and click **OK** to open an email message. Address the message and send it as normal.

SNAPSHOT

1 Click Browse

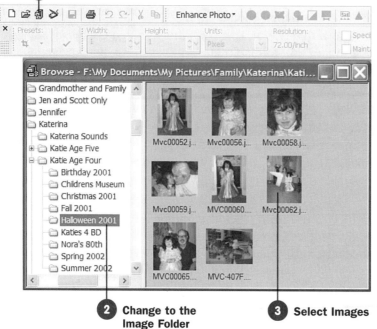

2 Change to the Image Folder

3 Select Images

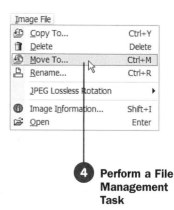

Image File	
Copy To...	Ctrl+Y
Delete	Delete
Move To...	Ctrl+M
Rename...	Ctrl+R
JPEG Lossless Rotation	▶
Image Information...	Shift+I
Open	Enter

4 Perform a File Management Task

---

5 Scan an Image

Before You Begin

✔ **1** Ensure That What You See Is What You Get

✔ **28** About Size and Resolution

See Also

→ **29** Change Image Size or Resolution

→ **94** Clean Up Scans of Printed Material

→ **97** Improve a Dull, Flat Photo

→ **112** About Sharpness

Most computer systems sold today include a scanner, but if yours did not, you'll find scanners readily available at a low price. With a scanner, almost any printed photograph from a photo album or even a magazine becomes eligible for graphic manipulation directly by you. (Of course, be sure not to use copyrighted material without permission.) After connecting and installing a scanner, you can scan a printed image directly into Paint Shop Pro.

Before scanning an image, decide how you intend to use it. If you want to use it onscreen (on a Web page, for example), you can scan the image at relatively low resolution such as 100 *dpi* or lower. Scanning at a lower resolution reduces the file's size, making it much easier to work with, and faster to download from the Web. If you intend to print the image, however, you should scan it at 300 dpi if you have a photo-quality ink jet printer, at 150 dpi if you have an ink jet printer and plain paper, or at 200 dpi for black-and-white laser printers. If you're scanning text, 300 dpi will work in most cases.

However, if you're scanning images from a magazine, book, or newspaper—any source where halftone process printing was used—scan at 600 dpi or higher. Then use PSP to remove any *moiré patterns* and improve the detail. Scanning printed images at twice the needed dpi (at 600 dpi instead of 300 dpi, for example) allows you to resample the image down (essentially *blending* the pixels together) to the print size you actually want, eliminating any moiré patterns.

① Start the Scanner Program

If your scanner is *WIA*-compliant, choose **File, Import, From Camera or Scanner** to start it. If you have several WIA devices, select the scanner from the list that appears and click **OK**.

If the preceding instructions do not start your scanner program, your scanner might be *TWAIN*-compliant. Click the **TWAIN Acquire** button on the **Standard** toolbar. If a list of several TWAIN devices appears, select your scanner from the list and click **OK**.

② Set Scanner Options

Use the options in the scanner program window to select the scanner resolution (dpi) that suits your intended purpose. For my scanner (an HP ScanJet 4100C), I must click the **Adjust the quality of the scanned picture** link to access the scanner settings.

KEY TERMS

dpi (dots per inch)—The higher the dpi, the larger the file and the higher the resolution. Because a printer uses dots of ink to produce an image, dpi is used to describe printer output; a monitor uses pixels to display an image, so ppi (pixels per inch) is used to describe the quality of onscreen images. Generally, the two terms are interchangeable.

Moiré pattern—The optical illusion that occurs when one regular geometric pattern—such as a grid made up of dots—overlays another similar pattern slightly askew. For example, two window screens placed on top of each other at an angle form a moiré effect.

 TIP

If you're scanning a newspaper or magazine page, and the text on the back side is bleeding through, place a black piece of paper over the item and rescan it.

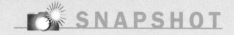

Start the Scanner Program

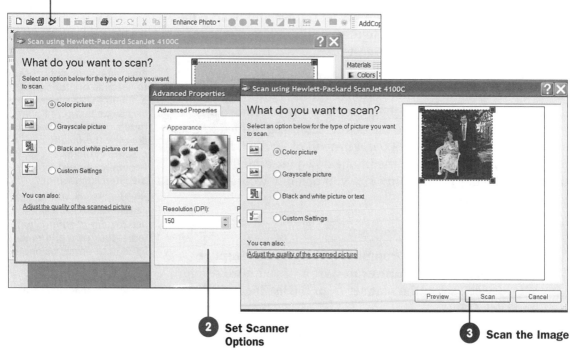

2 Set Scanner Options

3 Scan the Image

3 Scan the Image

Some scanner programs allow you to **Preview** the scan first, and then scan again using other settings as needed. After previewing an image, you might be able to select a portion of the image for scanning by resizing the bounding box. Click **Scan**. The image opens in its own window in Paint Shop Pro.

If your scanner program comes with a descreen option, turn it on as needed to reduce the moiré effect associated with images from newspapers, magazines, and books. Do not use the descreen option with photographs because it will blur them. If your scanner program does not have a descreen option, increase the scanning resolution (dpi) and see **94** **Clean Up Scans of Printed Material** for help.

6 Browse Images on a Digital Camera

Digital cameras provide a vast array of options for copying their images onto your computer. With some cameras, you simply remove the floppy disk and insert it into your computer. With others, you remove a smaller memory stick and insert that into a special card reader. Some cameras provide a method of direct communication—through a docking port, a FireWire hub, or a USB hub. Typically, each of these options creates a "virtual drive" visible in **My Computer**. It's then a simple matter to use **My Computer** to copy the files to the hard disk and then open them in Paint Shop Pro, or to use the PSP **Browser** to view the images on the virtual disk and open them as needed. This task shows you how to connect a camera to a computer using USB or FireWire, browse its images with the **Browser**, and open one for editing in PSP. If your camera is WIA-compatible, you can import its images directly into Paint Shop Pro. See **7** **Import Images from a Digital Camera** for help.

1 Connect the Cable to the Camera

Connect the USB/FireWire cable that came with the camera to the appropriate port on the camera.

If your camera connects to the computer through a special docking port, place the camera in its port and skip to step 3.

2 Connect the Cable to the Computer

Connect the USB/FireWire cable to the appropriate port on the computer.

3 Turn the Camera On

Flip the camera switch to the upload setting. This setting sends a signal to the computer, letting it know that the camera is ready to upload images.

4 Start the Browser

In Paint Shop Pro, click the **Browse** button on the **Standard** toolbar to start the **Browser**.

See Also

→ **4** Browse for an Image

→ **7** Import Images from a Digital Camera

→ **8** Rename Digital Images in One Step

→ **40** Convert a Group of Images to Another File Type

🔆 TIP

You can browse digital camera images using Photo Album. Just click the arrow on the **Camera** button and click **View Images**. Select an image and click **Get** to copy the image to your computer. If Photo Album does not detect your camera, select **Connection** from the **Camera** menu and choose the connection type your camera uses.

✎ NOTE

Although most digital cameras come with their own program for importing and managing images, why mess with it when you can bring the images directly into PSP and start working on them right away?

SNAPSHOT

2 Connect the Cable
to the Computer

1 Connect the
Cable to the
Camera

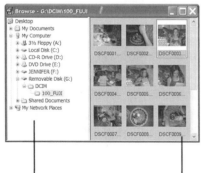

3 Turn the
Camera On

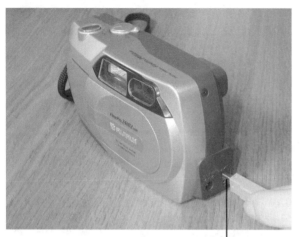

4 Start the Browser   **5** Browse Images

6 Open an Image

⑤ Browse Images

Windows creates a virtual drive containing the images stored on the camera. Change to this drive using the file list on the left side of the **Browser** window. Select the appropriate folder (if any) to display the camera images.

⑥ Open an Image

Double-click an image in the **Browser**. That image is displayed in the Paint Shop Pro window. You might want to save the file to your hard disk in PSP format before making any changes.

> **TIP**
>
> If you look carefully at the **Browser** window shown here, you'll notice that the images being displayed are stored on a *virtual drive*. Before closing the **Browser**, you might want to copy the images to a permanent place such as your hard disk; if you don't, the images are still safe and sound on the camera's storage medium (until you erase it).

---

⑦ Import Images from a Digital Camera

Although you might be able to connect to your camera and browse its images using the **Browser** in Paint Shop Pro (as described in ⑥ **Browse the Images on a Digital Camera**), that approach is not always the most convenient. In a perfect world, you should be able to talk to your camera more directly and display its images in Paint Shop Pro without having to navigate endless drives and folders to find them. Luckily, with digital cameras that are WIA-compliant, you can do just that.

① Initiate the Camera

After connecting your camera to the computer with its cable or docking port and turning the camera on, start Paint Shop Pro. Choose **File, Import, From Camera or Scanner**. If you have several WIA devices, select the camera from the list and click **OK**.

See Also

→ ④ Browse for an Image

→ ⑥ Browse Images on a Digital Camera

→ ⑧ Rename Digital Images in One Step

→ ④⓪ Convert a Group of Images to Another File Type

> **TIP**
>
> You can import images using Photo Album. If your camera is connected to your computer with a memory card reader, select **Camera, Get All Images**. If your camera uses a TWAIN connection, select **File, Acquire**, select the camera from the devices listed, and click **OK**.

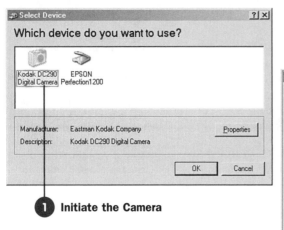

1 Initiate the Camera

2 Import
Desired
Image

NOTE

Windows XP might detect your camera the moment you switch it on, and display a dialog box asking you what you want to do. If the dialog box contains an option for displaying the images in Paint Shop Pro, choose it. Otherwise, ignore the dialog box and follow these steps.

2 **Import Desired Image**

Click an image to select it. To select multiple images, press and hold the **Ctrl** key and click each additional image. Click **Get Pictures** to open the selected images in Paint Shop Pro, each in its own image window.

Always save your imported digital images *without any changes, in their native format.* These digital image files act as your original "negatives." Resave the files in PSP format before making any changes.

8 Rename Digital Images in One Step

Images captured by a digital camera are, by necessity, given generic filenames such as **MVC-57IF**. Retaining these generic filenames will not help you identify each image later on, so Paint Shop Pro offers a solution: batch renaming. With the batch renaming feature, you can rename a collection of images using more descriptive filenames such as **Hawaii Vacation 10-2003 01**, **Hawaii Vacation 10-2003 02**, and so on.

When renaming files, you can include custom text such as "Tamika's 30th Birthday," the file date or time, the current filename, and the file's location within the file selection, such as 01, 02, and so on.

1 Select Images to Rename

Choose **File, Batch Processing, Rename** from the menu bar. The **Batch Rename** dialog box appears. Open the **Look in** list and choose the folder that contains the files you want to rename. Then press **Ctrl** and click the files you want to rename to select them.

You can type a generic filename using wildcards in the **File name** box and click **Start** to display a list of matching files. To select all the files, click **Select All**.

2 Specify New Filenames

Click the **Modify** button to display the **Modify Filename Format** dialog box. Select a variable from the **Rename Options** list on the left side of the dialog box and click **Add >**. The variable appears in the **Included** list on the right. Continue to select and add more variables as you like. As you make your selections, a sample filename appears in the **Example output** area. When you're satisfied with your choices, click **OK**.

Some of the file-naming variables have options. For example, if you choose the **Custom Text** variable, you must type the text you want to use in the **Custom Text** box that appears. If you choose the **Date** or **Time** variable, you can select the date/time format you prefer.

Before You Begin

✔ **6** Browse Images on a Digital Camera

✔ **7** Import Images from a Digital Camera

See Also

→ **40** Convert a Group of Images to Another File Type

💡 TIP

You can batch rename files in Photo Album: Select the images to rename from the **Album View** window. Then select **Edit, Rename Image**. Type the new filename in the **New title** box. This filename will be appended with a number, starting with **000**. To start with a different number, type the number in the **Append title with count from** box. Click **OK**.

📝 NOTE

If you've used this dialog box before, the old filename variables are displayed in the **Included** list. Simply select any variables you want to delete and click **< Remove**, or click the variable and type replacement text or change its options as desired.

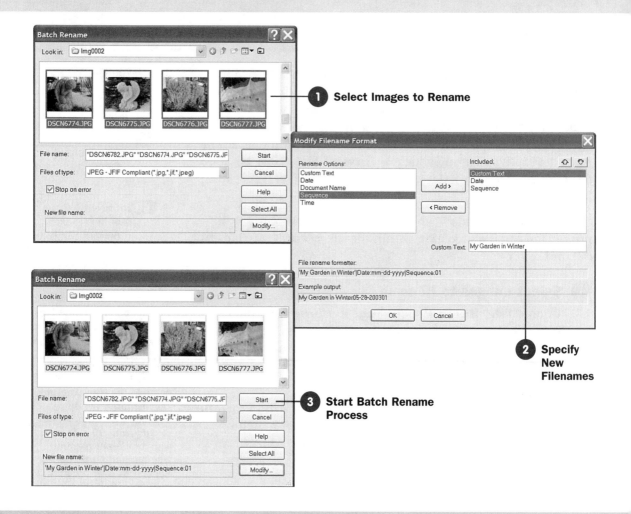

1 Select Images to Rename

2 Specify New Filenames

3 Start Batch Rename Process

3 Start Batch Rename Process

Click **Start** to rename the selected images using the variables you've chosen.

After you click **Start**, the files are renamed almost instantly, and then the **Batch Rename** dialog box disappears. This might leave you with the impression that nothing has happened. However, when you display the images again in the **Browser**, the **Open** dialog box, or **My Computer**, you'll notice that the images are using the new filenames.

9 Capture Images Displayed on Your Screen

Using Paint Shop Pro's screen capture utility, you can capture the image displayed on your screen and save it in a file. For example, if you want to show Uncle Bob your recent Galaxy Pinball score, you could display the scoreboard onscreen and take a picture of it. Screen captures were used to illustrate the steps in this book, and you could capture similar images to show Aunt Agnes how to attach a file to an email message. Screen captures are also useful in taking pictures of error messages so that you can relay detailed information to technical support personnel. After capturing a screen image, you can edit it using the tools in Paint Shop Pro, and then save it in any format you want.

The screen capture utility allows you to capture all of the screen or just portions of it. Your choices include **Area** (any rectangular portion of the screen), **Full Screen**, **Client Area** (the workspace of the current window), **Window** (the active window including its title bar, toolbars, and status bar), and **Object** (a toolbar, palette, or some other special window feature).

1 Set Screen Capture Options

Choose **File, Import, Screen Capture, Setup** from the menu bar. The **Capture Setup** dialog box appears. From the five options in the **Capture** area, select the portion of the screen you want to capture. Then choose how you want to activate the screen capture utility—by clicking the right mouse button, by pressing a hotkey (you can then select the specific hotkey you want to use), or after a few seconds' delay (you can specify the length of the delay).

2 Turn on the Screen Capture Utility

After selecting setup options, click **Capture Now** to immediately turn on the screen capture utility. If you want to capture a screen a little later, click **OK**; when you're ready to capture a screen, turn on the utility by choosing **File Import, Screen Capture, Start** from the menu or by pressing **Shift+C**.

Before You Begin

✔ **36** About Image Types

See Also

→ **38** Save an Image in Paint Shop Pro Format

TIP

To quickly capture a screen image anytime, press **Print Scrn** on your keyboard. The entire screen is captured and placed on the Clipboard. To create an image from this data, return to PSP and select **Edit, Paste as New Image**.

NOTE

Select other capture options as applicable. You can include the mouse pointer in the screen capture by choosing **Include cursor**. If the screen is changing fast, you can capture several images one right after the other by choosing **Multiple captures**.

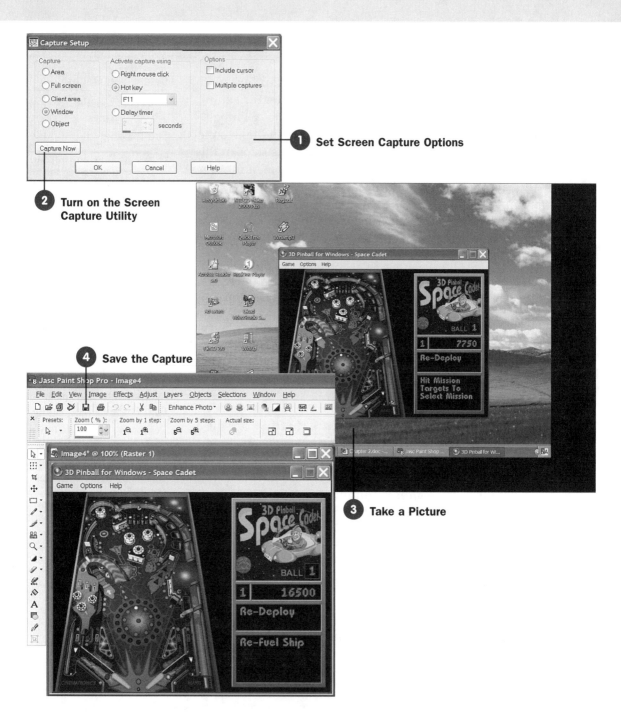

1 Set Screen Capture Options

2 Turn on the Screen Capture Utility

4 Save the Capture

3 Take a Picture

When you start the screen capture utility, PSP automatically minimizes itself to get out of the way. If you want to take a picture of PSP, you must start it twice—initiate the capture in one PSP window and take a picture of the second one.

③ Take a Picture

After turning on the screen capture utility, arrange the screen as you like. Then take a picture by right-clicking the mouse, pressing the hotkey you choose, or waiting the number of seconds you designated in the **Delay timer** box.

If you chose **Area** in the **Capture Setup** dialog box, you'll have to select the area to capture. Wait until the mouse pointer changes to a crosshair, and then click in the upper-left corner of the area you want to capture and drag down and to the right. If you chose **Object**, move the mouse pointer over the object you want to capture (its border automatically darkens so that you know which object PSP will capture) and click.

④ Save the Capture

After you capture a screen image, it appears in the Paint Shop Pro window. (If you captured multiple images, each appears in its own image window.) Make any changes you like, then save the image(s) to a file by clicking the **Save** button, typing a filename, selecting a file type, and clicking **Save**.

NOTE

If you chose **Multiple captures** in the **Capture Setup** dialog box, the screen is captured repeatedly each time you right-click, press the appropriate hotkey, or after a few seconds delay. When you're through capturing screens, simply activate PSP and it will stop.

3

Working with Tools

IN THIS CHAPTER:

Every tool in PSP can be customized with options you can set and adjust at any time. In this chapter, you'll learn how to choose the tool you want and set its options. For each of the painting, filling, and text tools, you'll also learn how to select a material to use with it, such as a color or pattern. You'll also learn how to save these selections permanently, so that you can reuse them without having to re-enter all the options each time you use the tool.

10 About Tools and Tool Options

Before You Begin

✔ **58** About Making Selections

✔ **120** About Layers and the Layer Palette

See Also

→ **11** Select a Tool to Use

→ **19** Save Tool Options for Reuse

→ **149** About the Painting Tools

→ **150** About Drawing Objects

→ **152** Add Text

 TIP

If you've hidden the **Tools** toolbar, redisplay it by choosing **View, Toolbars, Tools.** For more information on how to use toolbars in general, see Chapter 1, "Start Here."

 TIP

Sometimes it's hard to find the tool you're looking for because its icon is not currently displayed on the group tool button. But if you remember what group the tool is in, you can find it easily enough.

The **Tools** toolbar is perhaps the central functional component of Paint Shop Pro. Almost everything you do in this application begins there. If you want to crop an image, for example, you select the **Crop** tool first. Clicking a tool on the **Tools** toolbar determines what your mouse pointer will do when it enters the area of your image's window. For example, if you click the **Crop** tool, the mouse pointer changes to a crop pointer as you move it over an image. This tells you that PSP is ready for you to crop out a portion of the image and throw away the rest.

Notice that some of the buttons on the **Tools** toolbar have arrows. The arrow hides a menu of tools in the same category as the one shown on the tool button. For example, click the arrow on the first tool button to reveal a menu that contains both of the image viewing tools, **Pan** and **Zoom**. If you choose **Zoom** from this menu, the **Zoom** icon is shown on the first toolbar button, rather than the **Pan** icon, which appears there by default.

After you've chosen a tool, but before you use it on an image, you set its options. The **Tool Options** palette shows the options for the currently chosen tool. Each tool has its own specific options; in the tasks that follow, I'll tell you exactly how to adjust the tool's settings so that you can accomplish that specific task. But first, it's useful to learn what all the options are for, so that you can make your own adjustments to the instructions whenever you want.

Deform, Straighten, Perspective Correction, and Mesh Warp Tools

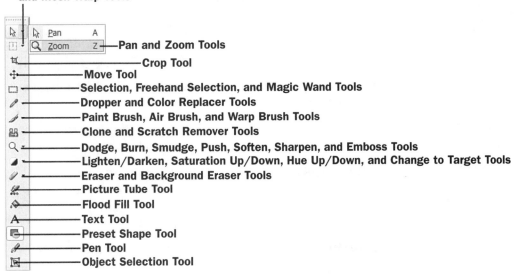

—Pan and Zoom Tools
—Crop Tool
—Move Tool
—Selection, Freehand Selection, and Magic Wand Tools
—Dropper and Color Replacer Tools
—Paint Brush, Air Brush, and Warp Brush Tools
—Clone and Scratch Remover Tools
—Dodge, Burn, Smudge, Push, Soften, Sharpen, and Emboss Tools
—Lighten/Darken, Saturation Up/Down, Hue Up/Down, and Change to Target Tools
—Eraser and Background Eraser Tools
—Picture Tube Tool
—Flood Fill Tool
—Text Tool
—Preset Shape Tool
—Pen Tool
—Object Selection Tool

*The **Tools** toolbar.*

To help me demonstrate what these options mean, I'm going to pretend that I want to use the **Flood Fill** tool, and explain the **Tool Options** palette in relation to it. In brief, when you click a pixel with the **Flood Fill** tool, you coat an entire area with a chosen color, pattern, gradient, or texture. You can fill an entire layer or selection with this material, or you can have PSP change *only those pixels* within the image, layer, or selection that is similar in some regard to the pixel you clicked. With that in mind, the following sections offer brief descriptions of the more common tool options.

Match Mode

The purpose of the match mode options is to inform PSP how to evaluate the pixels that surround the one you clicked. This way, during a flood fill operation, PSP can determine how far the flooding is supposed to extend, and where the boundaries are that stop the flood. Here are the settings you can select and what they mean:

 TIP

At first, PSP places the **Tool Options** palette in the horizontal area just above your image, but you can move it elsewhere. If you've hidden it, select **View, Palettes, Tool Options** to redisplay it.

 NOTE

Not all the tool options described here apply to every tool you select. When you choose a particular tool, only the options applicable to that tool appear on the **Tool Options** palette. The painting tools, for example, provide additional options, displayed on the **Brush Variance** palette.

NOTE

If you set the match mode to **None** when using the **Flood Fill** tool, all pixels in the current selection or layer are changed. For example, if you click a tree with the **Flood Fill** tool, the entire layer or selection is filled with that material, not necessarily just the tree. Select a specific area before flood-filling it to limit the fill to just the selected area.

- **RGB Value.** Only pixels with the same RGB value (the same amount of red, green, and blue) as the pixel you click are changed.

- **Color.** Only pixels with the same hue and saturation values as the pixel you click are changed.

- **Hue.** Only pixels with the same hue value as the pixel you click are changed.

- **Brightness.** Only pixels with the same luminance (brightness) value as the pixel you click are changed.

- **All Opaque.** Only pixels that are *not transparent* are changed. A transparent pixel on one layer reveals part of the contents of other layers beneath it; so any pixels where transparency applies remain unaltered.

- **Opacity.** Only pixels with the same opacity are changed.

- **None.** All pixels are changed.

KEY TERM

Neighboring pixels—Pixels that physically touch each other. When trying to judge which pixels will be affected by a change, only pixels that match the criteria *and that touch the original pixel you click or another matching pixel* are included.

Tolerance

After you've selected a match mode, the **Tolerance** setting comes into play. Here, 100 means "total forgiveness" of any differences between the pixel you click and *neighboring pixels*, 0 means no differences are tolerated (neighboring pixels must be exactly the same to be affected), and 50 is in between—for instance, if the fill starts on a red point, PSP might change an orange neighbor but not a green one.

Opacity

The **Opacity** setting is a percentage representing the extent to which new paint covers up the old paint. Think of opacity as transparency in reverse; when you set **Opacity** to less than 100, you're "watering down" your paint. With the **Flood Fill** tool, you can use **Opacity** to change the amount that the fill color replaces the qualified pixels (those your match mode and **Tolerance** settings indicate are to be flooded over). For example, if you set **Opacity** to 40, 60% of the pixel's original color is blended with 40% of your tool's color. More precisely, imagine the original pixel reduced to 60% intensity, and then blended with your tool's color at 40% intensity.

With the **Airbrush** tool, the **Opacity** setting controls the speed at which paint flows through the nozzle, as it were. Set to 100%, the airbrush completely covers the area you're pointing to with your chosen color, although along the edges of the airbrush path, you'll notice some fuzziness. But when you set **Opacity** to a much lesser number, such as 25%, paint "flows" more slowly from the nozzle, and the *speed* at which you paint becomes a factor. The longer you hold the airbrush over a spot, the more that spot becomes covered over by your paint; if you hold it at one spot for a few moments, eventually the area is entirely covered.

Blend Mode

Blend mode is one of the more complex options in Paint Shop Pro. The blend mode you set determines how the color on your tool blends with a color in your image. The result of this blending of tool color and target color is determined on a pixel-by-pixel basis, depending on the blend mode you select. You can also select a blend mode for a layer, and that blend mode determines how the colors on that layer blend with the colors on the layers below.

There are several blend modes, all of which are available both for the various painting tools as well as for multiple layers in an image. You start with a *blend color*—the color on your painting tool/upper layer. This blend color mixes with the *base color*—a color already on the current layer/lower layer. The *result color* you get depends on the blend mode you select.

Each of the images shown here contains two layers: The bottom layer contains a gradient that changes gradually from a very dark red to white. On the upper layer, where I'll change the blend modes, there are three stripes. The upper-left stripe is a fully saturated yet very pale yellow {HSL: 44/255/220}. The middle stripe is a medium light, medium saturated blue {HSL: 168/120/128}. The lower-right stripe is a dark, lightly saturated green {HSL: 71/85/57}. Both layers are set at 100% opacity. So you have a better idea of the result of using a particular blend mode, be sure to look for these same figures in the Color Gallery in this book.

NOTE

A separate setting for the **Airbrush** tool called **Rate** also affects the flow of paint.

NOTE

If you're using blend modes with the layers of an image, select a blend mode on an *upper layer* to affect how its colors blend with the color of the layer just below it.

NOTE

The color of a pixel may be described using the HSL (hue/saturation/lightness) color model. The first value is the hue (such as yellow); the middle value is the saturation (from middle gray to full color); the last value is the amount of white (from black to full color to white).

Normal blend mode.

Darken blend mode.

Lighten blend mode.

Hue blend mode.

With a **Normal** blend mode, the blend color replaces the base color. It's then up to the **Opacity** setting to determine to what extent that replacement is made: totally (**Opacity = 100**) or partially (**Opacity < 100**). With **Opacity** set to less than 100, a percentage of the base color, equal to 100 minus the **Opacity** setting, is mixed with the blend color.

With the **Darken** blend mode, the blend color is blended with the base color to produce a result, and this result replaces the base color only if it is darker than the base. If you're using a tool to apply the blend color, the color will appear only when the result is *darker* than the existing color. If you're using **Darken** mode with layers, the colors on the top layer replace those on lower layers only if the result is darker. If the base color is replaced, the **Opacity** setting determines by how much. Notice that the result of blending a very light yellow with the background gradient doesn't produce a darker result, so that stripe disappears. The medium stripe gets darker as a result of the **Darken** blend mode, while the already dark green stripe remains unchanged.

Lighten blend mode, predictably, works the opposite way of **Darken**: The result color replaces the base color only when the result color is *lighter* than the base color. If you use the **Lighten** blend mode with layers, the colors on the top layer replace those on lower layers only if they are lighter. Again, use the **Opacity** setting to control the amount of replacement. With **Lighten** mode, the dark green stripe disappears; the medium blue stripe disappears when it's blended with the light colors of the base color gradient in the upper-right corner but shows through slightly in the darkest portion of the gradient in the lower-left corner. The light yellow stripe appears unchanged.

With the **Hue** blend mode, only the blend color's hue value (the *H* in the HSL color model) is applied to the base color. As a result, the base color retains its original saturation and luminosity values, but it changes hue. Remember, in the HSL color model, there are only 256 possible hues, and all possible color values are variations of those 256. When **Opacity** is set to less than 100, (100 – **Opacity**)% of the base color's original hue remains after the blend. With this mode, you can clearly see the colors used in each of the three stripes on the upper layer, but they are shaded from dark to light because of the underlying gradient's change in luminosity.

PSP 8 also includes several legacy blend modes such as **Hue (Legacy)** and **Color (Legacy)**. These modes do not work as described here; instead, they re-create the way in which that particular blend mode worked in PSP 7 (which was not how the Help system described them).

Saturation is a most unusual blend mode, with often unanticipated results. Its purpose is to adjust the saturation (the *S* in the HSL color model) of the base color to match that of the blend color. This blend mode doesn't take the hue or luminosity of the blend color into account at all. By turning **Opacity** down below 100, you can reverse the saturation effect somewhat and tone down the amount by which the base color's saturation level is changed. In our example, the light yellow stripe that is fully saturated doesn't change the underlying colors at all because they are fully saturated as well. As a result, the yellow stripe seems to disappear. The medium-saturated blue stripe in the middle retains only a bit of the red color from the gradient layer. The lightly saturated green stripe on the bottom-right becomes gray throughout, managing to erase all the red value of the fully saturated bottom layer.

Saturation blend mode.

With the **Saturation** blend mode, you can load your painting tool with a very pure green, apply it to a beige or tan area, and have the result be bright orange. Beige, optically speaking, is an unsaturated orange; if you resaturate a beige area to a level equivalent to that of a pure green, you get an orange result.

Color blend mode has perhaps the most confusing name of the lot. This mode uses both hue (H) and saturation (S) but not luminance (L). The base color is changed to the same hue and saturation levels as the blend color, while retaining its original luminance. Thus, our three stripes retain their color and saturation levels, while changing from dark to light as a result of the underlying gradient's change in luminance values.

Color blend mode.

Luminance blend mode.

Multiply blend mode.

Luminance blend mode achieves exactly the opposite results of **Color** blend mode in that it doesn't apply the blend color (its hue or saturation) to the base color, but just its luminance component. **Luminance** blend mode applies as much whiteness to the base color as appears in the blend color, without affecting the existing "color value" from the artistic perspective. In the sample, the three stripes become various shades of red, from light to dark, based on their original luminance values.

Multiply blend mode appears to work very similarly to **Darken** blend mode, although there are important differences: With **Darken** blend mode, the base color is left as-is when it's already darker than the blend color. With **Multiply** blend mode, the darkness of the base color is compounded with the darkness of the blend color, so the result color is always darker. When used with layers, the **Multiply** blend mode most closely simulates the effect of laying one color transparency over another and projecting one light through both. The result in our sample is a light-orange-to-yellow stripe on the left (yellow blended with red), a dark-purple-to-blue stripe in the middle (blue blended with red), and a brownish-green-to-green stripe on the right (green blended with red).

In the HSL model, luminance is defined by how much *whiteness* a pixel contains. Luminance allows there to be a definite distinction between a light blue (a soft pastel) and a bright blue (a vibrant shade).

Multiply blend mode takes the luminance value of the blend color, multiplies it by the luminance value of the base color, and divides the result by 256. The resulting color blends both hues, but its brightness is as much darker than the base color's brightness as the blend color was darker than pure white.

With **Screen** blend mode, the lightness of the base color is compounded with the lightness of the blend color, so the result is always lighter. **Screen** blend mode uses the inverse formula of the one **Multiply** uses: Luminance values from both the base and blend colors are subtracted from 255 to obtain two "darkness values"; those values are multiplied together and divided by 256. The result is then subtracted from 255 to convert it back into a luminance value. The **Screen** blend mode for two layers most closely simulates the effect of projecting images of both layers onto the same screen with separate projectors. Our sample shows a light-yellow-to-almost-white stripe on the left, a dark-to-light-magenta stripe in the middle, and a medium-brown-to-light-tan stripe on the right.

Screen blend mode.

The **Dissolve** blend mode gives you the opportunity to apply some visual effects and relies entirely on the **Opacity** setting. When you set **Opacity** to less than 100, rather than making the blend color partially transparent, **Dissolve** removes pixels from the blend color at random locations to let the base color show through. If you're using a painting tool, your tool color may or may not overwrite the target pixel—the lower the **Opacity** value, the less likely your tool will do so. When you're overlaying one layer atop another, **Dissolve** covers up some pixels in the lower layer entirely while letting others show through; the higher the **Opacity** setting, the fewer of the lower-layer pixels show through. In the sample, I've set the **Opacity** to 50%, so about half of the base color shows through the stripes on the upper layer at random intervals.

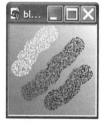

Dissolve blend mode.

The **Overlay** blend mode is one way for PSP to combine the virtues of **Multiply** and **Screen** modes. Essentially, the formula is adjusted so that light compounds with light, and dark compounds with dark. If the base color has a luminance value less than 128, PSP applies the **Multiply** formula; otherwise, it applies the **Screen** formula. The result of an **Overlay** blend for two layers is that the base layer appears to have been adjusted somewhat—though not strongly—by the blend layer. The **Overlay** blend mode is one way to create a ghostly image of the contents of the blend layer on top of a base layer. The stripes in our sample have a lightness value of 220, 128, and 57 reading left to right.

Overlay blend mode.

Hard Light blend mode.

The **Hard Light** blend mode applies almost exactly the same formula as **Overlay** blend mode, except that it's the *blend* color that's tested for brightness or darkness. As a result, **Hard Light** blend mode for two layers appears to show a ghostly image of the contents of the *base* layer, applied to the blend layer. With **Hard Light**, what you're adding (the blend color) becomes more prominent; with **Overlay**, what you're adding to (the base color) remains prominent. Here, the colors of our three stripes are very apparent, but they have been changed somewhat by the lightness values of the underlying gradient.

Soft Light blend mode.

Despite its title, **Soft Light** blend mode is not the opposite of **Hard Light**. It's actually another attempt to achieve the effect of **Overlay**, only by executing both a **Multiply** and a **Screen** blend *together*—a result that favors the base color slightly more than does **Screen**. To compound both brightness and darkness, the blend and base colors are blended using **Multiply**, then the product is multiplied back into the inverse of the base color. Separately, the two colors are blended using **Screen**, with the result multiplied back into the base color. The two results are then added together. The practical purpose of **Soft Light** blend mode for two layers is to create a more hazy, ghostly image of the blend layer on top of the base layer. And that's just what's happened in our sample: The three stripes appear as ghosts on top of the gradient red layer.

Overlay blend mode compounds the darkness of generally dark colors and the lightness of generally light colors. It uses roughly the same formulas as **Multiply** and **Screen**, but the result is divided by 128, not by 255. This way, darks fall within the range {0, 127}, while lights fall within the range {128, 255}.

Difference blend mode.

Difference is a blend mode you use to create special effects rather than to create a photorealistic look. Using a different math formula altogether, **Difference** subtracts the color value of the blend color from that of the base color. But the result isn't necessarily what common sense tells you it might be. The purpose of **Difference** is not only to subtract color values from one another, but to create a new and altogether *different* color wherever the two blended colors differ the *most*. To accomplish this, the blend color values—R, G, and B—are subtracted from the base color values. When the result dips below zero (because negative values can't be represented on the RGB scale), the sign of the number is removed. As a result, if you subtract more red from the base color than it actually has, at some point below zero, the result color will start *gaining* red. In the sample, you'll see some interesting results using **Difference** mode. The light-yellow stripe is now light-to-dark green; the blue stripe blends from purple to yellow-brown; the green stripe becomes red to light-purple.

Consider these rules when working with **Difference** blend mode: First, black is considered "zero," and subtracting zero from anything leaves you with what you had to begin with. Second, subtracting a color from itself results in black. Third, subtracting double a color's value results in that same value, so medium gray minus white equals medium gray.

If you place an all white layer below a layer using **Difference** mode, you will get a negative image—roughly the same effect you will get if you choose **Adjust, Negative Image** (to invert the colors in current layer) or **Layers, New Adjustment Layer, Invert** (to add an adjustment layer which only inverts the colors of the layers below it).

Dodge blend mode.

Dodge blend mode is named for a term used in photographic developing, where selected portions of a print are masked to block the light during exposure, causing the developed image to be lighter in those areas. In PSP, **Dodge** blend mode can simulate the effects of underexposure by lightening the base color. **Dodge** lightens the base colors using the lightness values of the blend colors. In the sample, you can see that the light-yellow stripe has been totally burned out of color by **Dodge** mode. The medium-blue stripe manages to retain a bit of its blended purple color, while the dark-green stripe (which, when blended with red, becomes brownish) manages to hang onto most of its color.

In practice, **Dodge** works best when the blend color is darker than the base color. When the blend color is lighter, **Dodge** can actually burn out most colors, turning them white. This blend mode's best use is for bleaching areas of a photograph.

Burn blend mode.

Exclusion blend mode.

Burn blend mode was so named because burning is the opposite technique of dodging in photo developing: It increases exposure in certain areas to darken the print. **Burn** mode darkens the base colors using the reverse-lightness values of the blend color. A dark or medium-dark blend color has the effect of darkening, or even blackening, the base color; while a lighter blend color lightens the base color and might even replace it a bit. In our sample, the very light stripe darkens the gradient layer just a bit; the dark-green stripe darkens the gradient layer by quite a lot.

Exclusion blend mode is the closest mode to a "negative" that PSP offers. It works like **Difference** mode, blending the base color with the blend color to create a color that's exactly halfway between the two on the color scale. **Exclusion** then uses the exact opposite of the lightness value of the blend color to darken the base color. If you use a light blend color, you'll darken the base color by quite a bit more than if you use a medium blend color. To create a negative for a photograph, add a blend layer filled with a light color (for interesting color effects), or pure white (for a more normal negative look). On the sample, each stripe becomes the color of its opposite, and much darker or lighter than the gradient below.

Size

The **Size** tool option, when available, controls the size of the tool and, of course, the size of the tool's effect on an image. For example, after choosing the **Paint Brush** tool, you can select a small brush to do fine work on an image or a large brush to make sweeping changes.

Hardness

The **Hardness** value determines the softness of the tool you select. If you choose the **Paint Brush** tool for example, and set the **Hardness** value to 100, you'll create a very sharp-edged stroke of color. If you reduce the **Hardness** value to 20, you'll produce a very fuzzy, soft-edged stroke.

Step

If you imagine your painting tool as though it were a guy walking along a sidewalk, casting seeds for the birds with each step, you can imagine the **Step** option as a way to increase the distance between casts. As you move a painting tool along your image, the **Step** value determines the amount of *space* (not time) between points at which the tool dispenses paint.

Density

The **Density** tool option controls the concentration of material on a tool's brush tip. For example, when you're using the **Paint Brush** tool, the **Density** setting controls the concentration of paint pixels; the higher the density, the more paint pixels, and thus, the more paint that's delivered each time the brush tip hits the image. Change the **Density** to a low number to paint with speckles of paint.

Thickness

The **Thickness** value controls the width of a tool's brush tip. If you select a round brush, for example, and then change the **Thickness** value to a high number, you'll get an oval brush tip that's wider than it is tall. Change the **Thickness** value to a low number, and you'll get an oval tip that's taller than it is wide.

Rotation

The **Rotation** tool option controls the angle of a tool's brush tip. Naturally, you should use this option only when you've chosen a brush tip that's not perfectly round or square. You can rotate a tip 360 degrees; the tip rotates clockwise. Thus, a value from 1 to 180 rotates the tip to the right; a value from 181 to 359 rotates the tip to the left.

Sample Merged

When a tool has to evaluate the characteristics of a pixel to determine whether the pixel can be affected by the tool, the

 TIP

If you increase the **Step** value and make the steps far apart, when you drag with the tool, you'll get breaks where the tool has no effect. Make the steps smaller, and you'll get more of a continuous line of effect wherever you drag.

 TIP

To simulate a calligraphy pen with the **Paint Brush** tool, choose a square brush tip with **Thickness** set to 25 and **Rotation** set to 30.

Sample Merged option instructs it to evaluate the pixels from all layers of an image, rather than just the current layer. This option applies only to images that contain more than one layer. For example, if you use the **Sample Merged** option with the **Magic Wand** selection tool, you can select pixels based on how they look when blended together in the final image, and not by the actual characteristics of the pixels on the current layer.

Anti-alias

NOTE

When used with the **Magic Wand** selection tool, the **Anti-alias** option can be added along the inside, outside, or both sides of a selection curve.

The **Anti-alias** option is used with the vector drawing tools, the selection tools, and the **Text** tool to smooth the appearance of curves and diagonal lines. With the **Text** tool, for example, the **Anti-alias** option adds partially opaque pixels along curves to soften the stair-step effect seen in raster text. With a selection tool, the **Anti-alias** option softens the edge of a selection, creating a gentler curve to the selection.

Continuous

TIP

Using the **Continuous** option helps you avoid the stripes you might ordinarily see when overlapping your strokes with a painting tool.

The **Continuous** option is applicable only to the painting tools, such as the **Paint Brush**, **Clone Brush**, **Dodge Brush**, and **Lighten/Darken Brush**. When the **Continuous** option is on, you can click and drag over pixels as many times as you want, but the effect caused by the tool is applied to those pixels only once. For example, if you drag the **Paint Brush** over an area and then drag it again over a neighboring area while slightly overlapping the two areas, the overlapped pixels are only the same color as the nonoverlapped pixels—not twice as dark.

Although these are by no means all the options you might find associated with a particular tool, they are the more common ones. Other options will be explained along the way as you learn to use a particular tool to accomplish some task.

11 Select a Tool to Use

As you saw in **10** **About Tools and Tool Options,** all the tools you need to select, alter, or paint any particular spot on an image are located on the **Tools** toolbar. Some tools with similar purposes share the same slot on the **Tools** toolbar, so to access one of these related tools, you click the arrow on the tool to bring up a submenu of all the tools in that group. After you select a tool, the **Tool Options** palette reveals only the options that pertain to that tool, and you can change those options as desired. Any changes you make to these options remain set until you change them again, even if you do something else in the program—or even shut down the program—and then return to that tool later.

Before You Begin

✔ **10** About Tools and Tool Options

See Also

→ **13** Select a Color to Work With

→ **14** Select a Gradient to Work With

→ **15** Select a Pattern to Work With

→ **16** Select a Texture to Work With

→ **19** Save Tool Options for Reuse

1 Select a Tool

Click the tool you want to use on the **Tools** toolbar. If the tool you want is not displayed, find the tool in the same group as the one you want, click the arrow to the right of that tool, and select the tool from the submenu. For example, when you want the **Airbrush** but only the **Paint Brush** is showing, click the arrow on the **Paint Brush** tool to display a menu of other painting tools and then select **Airbrush**.

2 Choose a Preset if Desired

Some tools have a number of preselected options settings, called *presets*, which enable you to configure your tools in a useful way with just one click. To choose a preset, click the **Presets** button on the **Tool Options** palette. A dialog box appears; select a preset from those listed and click **OK**.

3 Adjust Options as Needed

Whether you chose to start with a preset or not, you can still adjust the settings for the tool as desired. Simply make your selections from those shown on the **Tool Options** palette.

 TIP

A tool remembers its previous options settings when you return to it. You might start using a tool only to discover that it doesn't behave normally but instead uses the characteristics of some previous job. Reset a tool to its default settings by clicking the **Presets** button and clicking **Reset to default**. You can save your own settings for a tool as a preset and then restore those same settings later. See **19** Save Tool Options for Reuse.

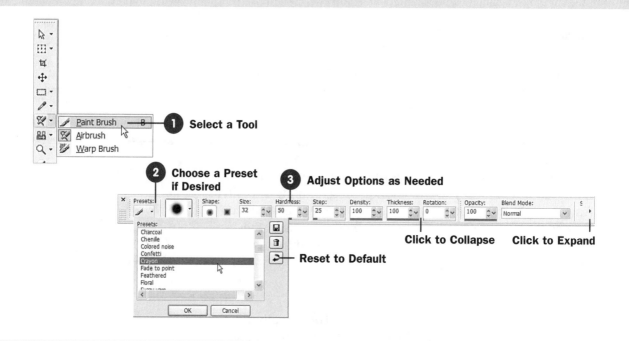

1 Select a Tool

2 Choose a Preset if Desired

3 Adjust Options as Needed

Click to Collapse   Click to Expand

Reset to Default

TIP

The dividing lines in the **Tool Options** palette are toolbar handles; most palettes, including **Tool Options**, are really collections of smaller toolbars. If a palette contains so many options that you can't see them all, you can drag one of these small toolbars by its handle below the main toolbar.

Depending on the resolution of your monitor, not all of the options for a tool can be displayed on the **Tool Options** palette at the same time. To display hidden options, click the **right pointing arrow** in front of that option section. To collapse a section, click the **dividing line** to the left of that section.

12 About Materials

Paint Shop Pro gives you lots of choices of materials for painting, drawing, filling areas of an image, and adding text. You can choose from many *styles*—a color, **gradient**, or **pattern**. Add a *texture* to any style to create a unique *material* for use with your tool.

You select the material for a tool from the **Materials** palette, shown here. As you can see, the **Materials** palette has two tabs: the **Color** tab and the **Swatches** tab. Like those sample cards you get from a paint store, a *swatch* is any material that you've saved for reuse: a single color, a combination of colors, gradients, or patterns, perhaps in addition to a texture. To reuse a swatch you've saved, click the **Swatches** tab and then click the swatch. You'll learn how to select a material and save your own swatches in upcoming tasks.

Colors Tab

Swatches Tab

Foreground Materials Box

Foreground Color Box

Background Color Box

Background Materials Box

Swap Colors Icon

Swap Materials Icon

Available Colors Panel

The Materials palette.

To the right of the **Available Colors** panel are samples of the *two* materials that are currently chosen for use by your active tool. Notice there are two pairs of samples; the smaller pair is reserved just for colors, while the larger pair shows the currently

Before You Begin

✔ **10** About Tools and Tool Options

See Also

→ **13** Select a Color to Work With

→ **14** Select a Gradient to Work With

→ **15** Select a Pattern to Work With

→ **16** Select a Texture to Work With

→ **18** Save Materials for Reuse

🔍 KEY TERM

Gradient, pattern, or texture—A gradient is a gradual transition between two colors, sometimes by way of a third (or more) color. A pattern is a design that repeats at regular intervals, like wallpaper. A texture is an irregular pattern that simulates a textured surface such as wood, fur, or marble.

💡 TIP

The **Materials** palette is normally docked along the right side of the window. If it is not in view, redisplay it by selecting **View, Palettes, Materials**. Some swatches have already been saved for you on the **Swatches** tab; these were created by PSP, and you can remove them if you like.

chosen *material*—a combination of the current color, pattern, gradient, and texture. Having two sample pairs allows you the flexibility of changing just the color without having to adjust the material as well. For example, you can use the **Foreground Color** box to change from red to yellow without affecting the pattern, gradient, or texture shown on the **Foreground Materials** box. You'll learn how to select colors and materials in the next few tasks.

The **Materials** palette contains many shortcuts you can use to save yourself some time when choosing the material you want to work with:

- To swap the currently selected foreground and background colors, click the **Swap Colors** icon.

- To swap the currently selected foreground and background materials, click the **Swap Materials** icon.

- To bring back a color or material you've used recently, right-click the appropriate samples box and then click a material or color from the **Recent Materials** list that appears.

- To apply your material selections to all painting, drawing, fill, and text tools, enable the **All tools** check box at the bottom of the **Materials** palette. When this box is disabled, any materials choices you make apply only to the active tool; when you select a new tool, the previously chosen materials for that tool are recalled.

To toggle between the most recently selected color, gradient, or pattern, click the **Style** button and select the style you want. To turn on/off the currently selected texture, click the **Texture** button. To turn off both style and texture and use transparency, click the **Transparency** button.

 TIP

A smaller version of the **Recent Materials** list is also available from within the **Material** or **Color** dialog box discussed in upcoming tasks. Just click the **Recent Materials** button displayed to the right of the **Current** color box to display the list.

13 Select a Color to Work With

In Paint Shop Pro, there are two colors you can select: a *foreground color* and a *background color*. You can combine the color with a pattern, gradient, or texture to create a material, as you'll learn in upcoming tasks. In this task, you'll learn how to choose just the color you want to work with.

With a painting tool, the foreground material is applied when you press the left mouse button; if you press the right mouse button, the background material is applied instead. When you create a shape using the **Preset Shapes** tool, the foreground material is the stroke color (outline), and the background material is the fill (the interior color). If you insert text with the **Text** tool, the text is filled with the background material and is outlined or stroked with the foreground material.

1 Click a Color Box

To change the foreground color, click the **Foreground Color** box in the **Materials** palette. To change the background color, click the **Background Color** box. The **Color** dialog box appears.

2 Choose a Color from the Color Wheel

There are several ways in which you can choose the color you want. The most common method is to click the **Color Wheel** to select the hue you want, and then drag the **Saturation** and **Lightness** slider boxes to adjust those characteristics for the hue.

3 OR Choose a Color from the Basic Colors Panel

A list of commonly used colors is displayed below the Color Wheel, in the **Basic Colors** panel. To select one of these common colors, click its box.

4 OR Choose a Color by Entering Its Value

Another way to choose a color is to enter its **RGB** or **HSL** values in the appropriate boxes. You can also enter the HTML value for a color in the **HTML** box.

Before You Begin

✔ **12** About Materials

See Also

→ **16** Select a Texture to Work With

→ **17** Select a Color Already in Your Image

→ **18** Save Materials for Reuse

NOTE

If your image has a color depth of less than 24-bit (16 million colors), the **Color** dialog box (or the **Color** tab of the **Materials** dialog box) displays a table containing only the colors belonging to the image's own color palette. You can only choose a color from this palette.

TIP

Choose a color without displaying the **Color** dialog box by clicking the color in the **Available Colors** panel in the **Materials** palette. Left-click to choose a foreground color; right-click to choose a background color. Notice that white, black, and three shades of gray are displayed at the bottom of the panel.

2 Choose a Color from the Color Wheel

3 OR Choose a Color from the Basic Colors Panel

1 Click a Color Box

5 OR Choose a Color from the Image

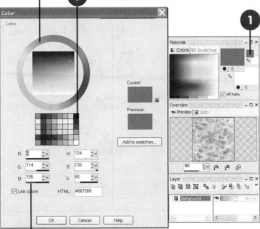

4 OR Choose a Color by Entering Its Value

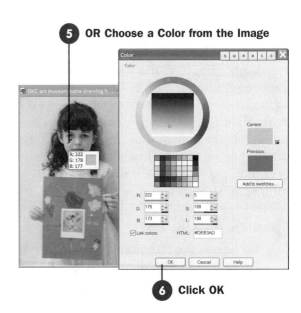

6 Click OK

TIP

You can select a color from anywhere on the screen—even the Windows desktop. To do that, move the mouse pointer over a **Color** or **Materials** box on the **Materials** palette, then press and hold the **Ctrl** key. Move the mouse pointer anywhere on the screen and click to select a screen color.

5 OR Choose a Color from the Image

Move the mouse pointer over the image; it turns into a dropper. Click anywhere on the image to select that color.

6 Click OK

As you change color settings in the **Color** dialog box, the corresponding color is displayed in the **Current** box. Click **OK** to change the foreground/background color.

14 Select a Gradient to Work With

In images whose color palettes are 24 bits (16 million colors) or grayscale, you can create gradients. A *gradient* is a gradual transition between one color and another, and can be used to fill the interior of objects, selections, or layers. You can even paint with gradients if you like, or use them in text. Another reason for using gradients is to create a *mask*, which is used with a layer to block or filter the effect of that layer on the layers below it. Where a mask is black, the effect is totally blocked; where it is gray, the effect is partially blocked; where it is white, the effect is not blocked at all. For example, you might use a mask to block the effect of the **Blur** filter. Imagine this: If you copied an image to a layer, completely blurred the copy, and then added a mask with a black center gradually fading to white at the edges, the resulting image would show a clear picture in the center with blurred edges. That's because the black part of the mask would block the blurred image layer, allowing the blurred image to show through only at the edges where the mask is white. To create a mask with a black center gradually fading to white, you use a gradient fill.

You can choose from several different predefined gradient types. Three use either or both of the foreground and background colors, and all the others use preselected colors. The easiest way to use your own specific colors for a gradient is to change the foreground and background colors as desired and then follow the steps given here to select the gradient.

1 **Click a Material Box**

Click the **Foreground Material** or the **Background Material** box in the **Materials** palette. The **Material** dialog box appears.

2 **Click the Gradient Tab**

The **Gradient** tab might already be displayed in the **Material** dialog box; if not, click it.

Before You Begin

✔ **12** About Materials

See Also

→ **16** Select a Texture to Work With

→ **18** Save Materials for Reuse

 TIP

Use gradients to give your shapes a three-dimensional look. For example, you might design a button for your Web page and use a gradient to make the button appear raised toward you. To make it appear pushed down, simply reverse the gradient colors.

TIP

To change back to the previously used gradient, click the **Style** button in the **Materials** palette and click the **Gradient** icon. To select from recently used materials, right-click the **Foreground Material** or **Background Material** box.

2 Click the Gradient Tab

1 Click a Material Box

5 Set Angle

4 Select a Style

6 Set Repeat

7 Invert Gradient if Desired

3 Select a Gradient Type

9 Adjust Focal Point and Click OK

8 Adjust Center

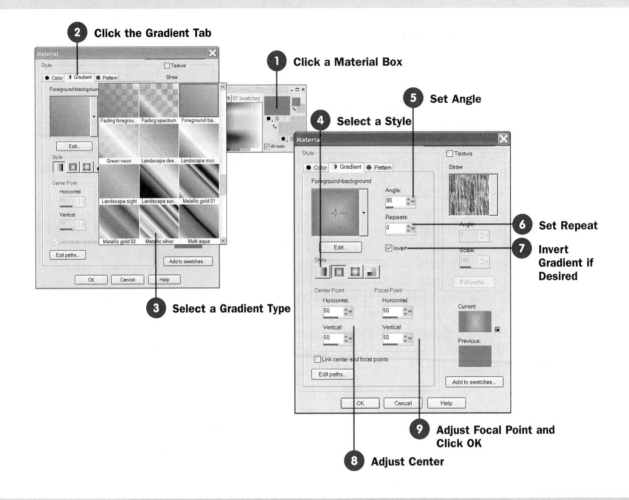

TIP

You can customize the selected gradient type, adding or changing colors, changing the points of transition, and adding transparency. Just select a gradient and click **Edit**. Make changes in the **Gradient Editor** and click **OK**.

3 Select a Gradient Type

Click the **down arrow** next to the sample box and choose a gradient from the **Gradient Type** list that opens.

4 Select a Style

Click one of the **Style** buttons to choose the gradient style you want: **Linear**, **Rectangular**, **Sunburst**, or **Radial**.

5 Set Angle

If you selected a linear, rectangular, or radial gradient, you can change the angle at which the gradation occurs. Enter the angle you want to use in the **Angle** box.

6 Set Repeat

If desired, in the **Repeats** box, enter the number of times you want the gradient to repeat. A repeated gradient transitions back and forth between its start and end colors; if your gradient progresses between red and orange, with **Repeats** set to 1, the gradient will transition from red to orange and then from orange back to red.

7 Invert Gradient if Desired

To reverse the colors in the gradient, enable the **Invert** check box.

8 Adjust Center

On a rectangular, sunburst, or radial gradient, you can adjust the location of the central point from which the gradient begins. Simply drag the center point in the large sample box and drop it where you like, or enter coordinates in the **Center Point Horizontal** and **Center Point Vertical** boxes.

9 Adjust Focal Point and Click OK

On a rectangular or sunburst gradient, you can change the point toward which the gradient gravitates, thus making one side more weighted than another, or giving the gradient a certain slant. Disable the **Link center and focal points** check box, drag the focal point in the large sample box, and drop it where you like. Alternatively, enter coordinates in the **Focal Point Horizontal** and **Focal Point Vertical** boxes. Click **OK** to create the gradient.

NOTE

Instead of typing an angle value, drag the control needle in the large gradient sample box to change the angle of the gradient.

15 Select a Pattern to Work With

Before You Begin

✔ **12** About Materials

See Also

→ **16** Select a Texture to Work With

→ **18** Save Materials for Reuse

 TIP

If you want to use all or part of an image as a pattern, open it and select the area before beginning the following steps. To create your own pattern, save any image in any format and copy it to the **Patterns** folder in the **Paint Shop Pro 8** folder. The pattern can contain transparent pixels if you like.

 **NOTE**

If you have other images open, they will appear as choices at the top of the pattern list. Any patterns you have created and saved to the **Patterns** folder appear in the **Pattern Type** list as well.

 TIP

If you set the **Scale** to a low value, the pattern repeats more frequently; use a large value to repeat the pattern less frequently.

Like Windows wallpaper, a *pattern* is a small design or picture that repeats at regular intervals both vertically and horizontally. Patterns make great backgrounds for Web pages, greeting cards, business cards, brochures, and CD labels. Paint Shop Pro provides you with many patterns you can use as fills for shapes, selections, or layers, as paint for a painting tool, or as text. You can also supply your own patterns, even creating a pattern from an image if you want. Like gradients, patterns can only be used in 24-bit or grayscale images.

1 Click a Material Box

Click the **Foreground Material** or the **Background Material** box in the **Materials** palette. The **Material** dialog box appears.

2 Click Pattern Tab

The **Pattern** tab might already be displayed in the **Material** dialog box; if not, click this tab.

3 Select a Pattern

Click the arrow next to the **Pattern Type** sample box and click a pattern to select it.

4 Set Angle

You can adjust the direction of the pattern repeat by entering an angle in the **Angle** box. You can also drag the control needle in the sample box to change the angle.

5 Adjust Scale and Click OK

Adjust the size of the pattern graphic by entering a percent in the **Scale** box. (A value of 100 displays the pattern at 100% or actual size.) After making selections, click **OK** to save the pattern.

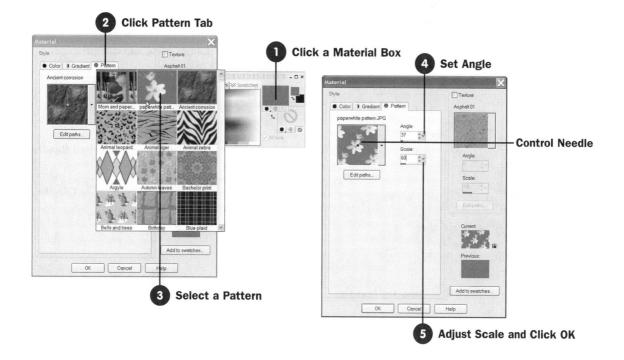

2 **Click Pattern Tab**

1 **Click a Material Box**

4 **Set Angle**

Control Needle

3 **Select a Pattern**

5 **Adjust Scale and Click OK**

16 **Select a Texture to Work With**

A *texture* is an irregular pattern that simulates a textured surface such as grass, silk, burlap, bricks, or wool. Paint Shop Pro provides many textures for you, but you can also add your own. Because it's semitransparent, a texture must be laid over a color, pattern, or gradient. After creating a textured material, you can use it with the paint or fill tools to apply the texture to any object, selection, or layer. When needed, you can apply the textured fill or paint multiple times to darken the texture and make it more apparent.

As I mentioned earlier, you can create your own textures from any image. Simply save the image in any format and copy it to the **Textures** folder in the **Paint Shop Pro 8** folder. If you have **.TEX** files from an older version of Paint Shop Pro, they will work too, if you copy them to this folder.

Before You Begin

✔ 12 About Materials

See Also

→ 13 Select a Color to Work With

→ 14 Select a Gradient to Work With

→ 15 Select a Pattern to Work With

→ 18 Save Materials for Reuse

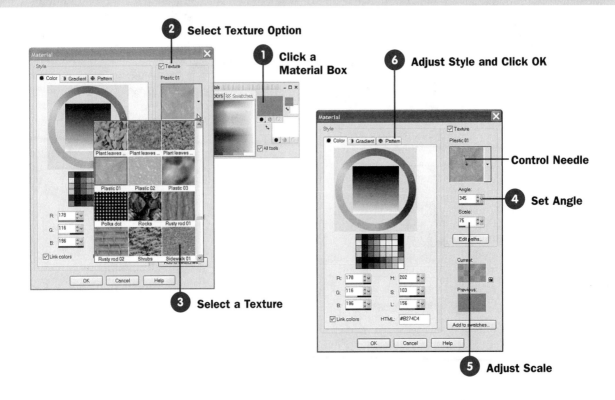

2 Select Texture Option

1 Click a Material Box

6 Adjust Style and Click OK

Control Needle

4 Set Angle

3 Select a Texture

5 Adjust Scale

TIP

To remove a texture from the current material, click the **Texture** button below the **Foreground** or **Background Material** box in the **Materials** palette.

TIP

For best results when using a texture, apply it so that it shows through opaque pixels, rather than transparent ones. For example, fill the layer below the texture with white.

1 Click a Material Box

Click the **Foreground Material** or the **Background Material** box in the **Materials** palette. The **Material** dialog box appears.

2 Select Texture Option

To add a texture to the current color, pattern, or gradient, enable the **Texture** check box.

3 Select a Texture

Click the arrow next to the **Texture Type** sample box and click a texture to select it.

4 **Set Angle**

You can adjust the direction of the texture's pattern repeat by entering an angle in the **Angle** text box. You can also drag the control needle in the sample box to change the angle.

5 **Adjust Scale**

Adjust the size of the texture pattern by entering a percent in the **Scale** box. (A value of 100 displays the pattern at 100% or actual size.)

6 **Adjust Style and Click OK**

You can click the appropriate tab and make adjustments to the *style* of the material as needed—the color, gradient, or pattern you're using with the texture. After you're done, click **OK** to finalize your material choices.

NOTE

If you set the scale to a low value, the pattern will repeat more frequently; use a large value to repeat the pattern less frequently. To make the plastic pattern more noticeable, I decreased the scale to 75%. If I had chosen a woven pattern, I might have increased the scale instead.

17 Select a Color Already in Your Image

In **13** **Select a Color to Work With**, you learned how to pick up a color in an image and use it for the foreground or background color. This process involved first opening the **Color** dialog box, selecting a color, and clicking **OK**. When you're hard at work on an image, it's difficult to set aside what you're concentrating on just to scrounge through a bunch of dialog boxes. Luckily, Paint Shop Pro provides an easier way for you to pick up a color from an image while bypassing those dreaded dialog boxes: the **Dropper** tool.

The **Dropper** tool doesn't have a lot of options, but it does allow you to select a *sample size*. You can select a sample size as small as one pixel, which means that the pixel you click is the color you get. On the upper end, you can set the sample area as large as 11 by 11 pixels. When you choose a wider sample area, PSP blends all the colors in that area to create the color that is absorbed by the dropper.

Before You Begin

✔ **12** About Materials

See Also

→ **13** Select a Color to Work With

KEY TERM

Sample size—The area from which a color is derived by computing the average color of the pixels in that area.

1 Select Dropper Tool

2 Select Sample Size

3 Set Layers to Sample

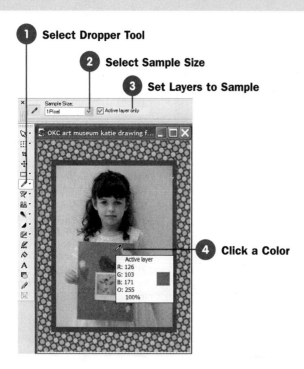

4 Click a Color

Active layer
R: 126
G: 103
B: 171
O: 255
100%

1 Select Dropper Tool

Click the **Dropper** tool on the **Tools** toolbar. If you don't see the **Dropper** tool, click the arrow on the **Color Replacer** tool and select the **Dropper** tool from the list that appears.

2 Select Sample Size

Click the arrow on the **Sample Size** list and select a sample size.

3 Set Layers to Sample

NOTE

To select a layer and make it the current one, click its name in the **Layer** palette.

Normally, the **Dropper** tool selects the color based on what you're seeing, which is a compilation of the data on all *visible* image layers. But if you want to select a color from the current layer only, enable the **Active layer only** check box.

4 **Click a Color**

As you move the **Dropper** tool around the image, you'll notice that the RGB values of the sampled color appear in a small pane. In addition, you'll see a value and a percentage; these represent the opacity of the layer(s) being sampled. Values of 255 and 100% indicate that the color is fully opaque.

Click the image with the **Dropper** tool to select a color for the foreground color. Right-click the image to select a color for the background color. With a pen tablet, tap the color you want to select for the foreground color. For the background color, hover the pen over the sample area and touch the pen's menu button (whatever corresponds to the right mouse button).

18 Save Materials for Reuse

After carefully selecting a color, gradient, or pattern, and possibly adding a texture, the last thing you want is to lose all that work. Granted, you can easily reselect a material if you've used it recently by right-clicking the **Foreground Color**, **Background Color**, **Foreground Material**, or **Background Material** box on the **Materials** palette and choosing the material from those listed in the **Recent Materials** list. The **Recent Materials** list, however, can hold only 20 of the most recently used materials. So if you think you might reuse a material after selecting 20 other materials, or if you think you might need the material for use in another image, save it as a swatch.

Swatches are displayed on the **Swatches** tab of the **Materials** palette. You can control the type of swatches displayed by clicking the **View** button at the bottom of the tab and clicking a swatch type, such as **Gradient**. To select a swatch for the foreground color, click it; to make it the background color, right-click the swatch instead. To delete a swatch, click it and then click the **Delete Swatch** button at the bottom of the tab.

Before You Begin

✔ **12** About Materials

See Also

→ **13** Select a Color to Work With

→ **14** Select a Gradient to Work With

→ **15** Select a Pattern to Work With

→ **16** Select a Texture to Work With

 TIP

You can also create a swatch while creating a material in the **Material** dialog box; just click **Add to swatches** to add the current material to the **Swatches** tab of the **Materials** palette.

1 Click the Swatches Tab

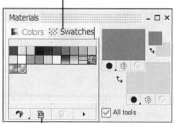

2 Click Create New Swatch Button

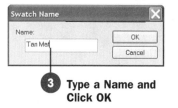

3 Type a Name and Click OK

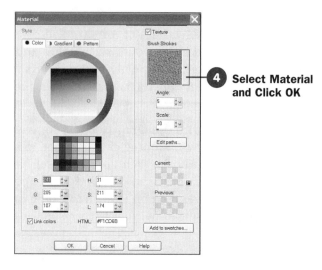

4 Select Material and Click OK

---

1 Click the Swatches Tab

On the **Materials** palette, click the **Swatches** tab to display it.

2 Click Create New Swatch Button

Click the **Create New Swatch** button at the bottom of the tab. A **Swatch Name** dialog box opens.

3 Type a Name

Type a name for the swatch and click **OK**. Later, when you hold the mouse pointer over the swatch on the **Swatches** tab, that name will appear in the tooltip.

TIP

You can change the materials associated with a swatch; just double-click the swatch on the **Swatches** tab to reopen the **Material** dialog box.

4 Select Material and Click OK

The **Material** dialog box automatically appears after you name the swatch. Make your selections from this dialog box and click **OK**.

19 Save Tool Options for Reuse

After choosing a tool and refining the options you want to use with it from the **Tool Options** palette, it's difficult to think about having to do it all over again if you need those exact settings again at some later time. Granted, you can switch to a different tool and come back to this one later, and the settings you used before will still be there. But if you change the settings of a tool to use it for some new task, you don't want to go through that long refinement process all over again just to recall its former purpose. Well, don't resort to ginkgo biloba to aid your memory recall; instead, save those settings in a tool *preset*.

1 Display Presets List

Select the **Tool Options** settings you want to save with a tool. If the tool is a painting tool, you can select settings on the **Brush Variance** palette to save as well. Click the **Presets** button to display the **Presets** list.

2 Click Save Preset

Click the **Save Preset** button. The **Save Preset** dialog box appears.

3 Enter a Name

Type a descriptive name for the preset into the **Preset name** box.

4 Turn Off Settings As Desired

Click the **Options** button to expand the **Save Preset** dialog box. A list of all possible options associated with the tool appears in the **Preset includes** list, along with their current values. For example, the **Opacity** was currently set to 100% for my **Paint Brush**. You can turn off any option you don't want to save as part of the preset by clicking its **Save** icon. When you do, a red **X** appears over the **Save** icon to indicate that the option will not be included in the preset. For example, I turned off the **Opacity** setting because I don't want the preset to change the current **Opacity** setting when I reload it at a later time.

Before You Begin

✔ **10** About Tools and Tool Options

See Also

→ **20** Save Dialog Box Options

🔍 KEY TERM

Preset—A collection of saved settings for use with a specific tool or a dialog box.

🖌 NOTE

A tool preset is a series of saved settings for use with a specific tool, such as **Airbrush**. If you want to make the settings available to all the painting tools, save them as a *brush tip*. See **149** About the Painting Tools.

💡 TIP

When using a tool you haven't used in a while, it's usually a good idea to reset the tool to its default settings. Click the **Presets** button and choose **Reset to default**.

💡 TIP

When saving a preset for the **Paint Brush** tool, you might not want to save the current foreground and background material with the preset. That way, when you select the preset later on, your current materials won't be replaced by the one in the preset.

① **Display Presets List**

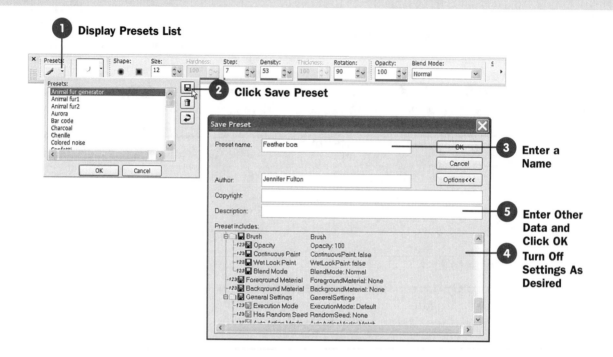

② **Click Save Preset**

③ **Enter a Name**

⑤ **Enter Other Data and Click OK**

④ **Turn Off Settings As Desired**

NOTE

To use a preset after creating it, change back to the tool for which you saved the preset, click the **Presets** button, select the preset and click **OK**. Current tool settings are replaced by those saved with the preset. Any current tool settings you did not save with the preset are not overridden.

⑤ Enter Other Data and Click OK

In the expanded dialog box, you can also enter an **Author** name, **Copyright** data, and a **Description** for the preset if desired. Click **OK** to save the preset.

20 Save Dialog Box Options

As I discussed in **19** **Save Tool Options for Reuse**, a *preset* is a collection of tool or command settings saved in a set so that you can reuse the settings without having to manually make all the same choices again. If you spend awhile making selections in a dialog box that you think you might need again in a similar situation, save them as your own preset.

Whether you create your own presets or not, it's always best to start out in a new dialog box by opening the **Presets** list to see whether there is already a preset that fits your current situation. To reset a dialog box to the default settings, select **Default** from the **Presets** list or click the **Reset to Default** button located to the right of the **Presets** list. To reset the dialog box to the same settings you used the last time, select **Last Used** from the **Presets** list. To choose any other preset, select it from the **Presets** list instead.

1 **Click Save Preset**

After making your selections in a dialog box, click the **Save Preset** button to save the settings in a preset. The **Save Preset** dialog box opens.

2 **Enter a Name**

Type a descriptive name for the preset into the **Preset name** box.

3 **Turn Off Settings As Desired**

Click the **Options** button to expand the **Save Preset** dialog box. A list of all the possible options associated with the dialog box appears in the **Preset includes** list, along with their current values. For example, the color of the light shining on the bevel was set to white {255,255,255}. Turn off the options you don't want to save as part of the preset by clicking the appropriate **Save** icon. When you do, a red **X** appears on the **Save** icon to indicate that the option will not be included in the preset. For example, I wanted to

See Also

→ **19** Save Tool Options for Reuse

TIP

In many dialog boxes, PSP offers the **Factory Defaults** preset, in which you can save your own custom default settings. To recall your personal default settings, select **Factory Defaults** from the **Presets** list.

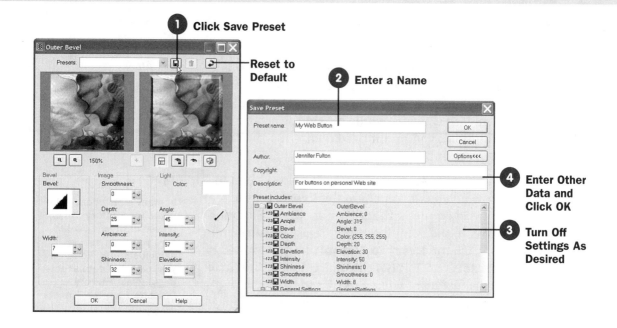

1 Click Save Preset

Reset to Default

2 Enter a Name

4 Enter Other Data and Click OK

3 Turn Off Settings As Desired

select a light color based on the images I'm currently using to make my Web buttons, so I didn't want that value saved with the preset.

NOTE

To use a preset after creating it, redisplay the dialog box for which you saved the preset, open the **Presets** list, and select the preset you want to load. Dialog box settings saved with the preset replace any current dialog box settings you might be using.

4 **Enter Other Data and Click OK**

In the expanded dialog box, you can also enter an **Author** name, **Copyright** data, and a **Description** for the preset if desired. Click **OK** to save the preset.

4

Performing Basic Image Tasks

IN THIS CHAPTER:

This book is designed around you, the busy user, enabling you to quickly jump to whatever topic you're interested in at the moment. However, it seems that no matter what kind of image you're working on—a Web button, an old black-and-white photo, or pictures from your child's recent birthday party, you'll find yourself performing some of the same tasks. In this chapter, you'll learn how to accomplish the most common PSP tasks, such as displaying image information, zooming in and out, scrolling, magnifying an area so that you can perform detail work, protecting your photos with a copyright stamp, resizing an image, and changing the number of colors you can work with.

21 About Image Information

When needed, Paint Shop Pro can display information about the basic characteristics of an image—its file type, resolution, size, and data specific to the conditions under which it was taken. To display this information for any currently open image, change to that image first, then select **Image**, **Image Information** from the menu bar. The **Current Image Information** dialog box opens, containing three tabs, all loaded with information about the current image.

The *Current Image Information* dialog box.

On the **Image Information** tab, you'll find this data:

- **Source file.** Here you'll see the filename and file type (such as JPEG or TIFF).

- **Image.** The dimensions of the image are displayed in pixels and inches. The example shown here uses a resolution of 300 pixels per inch, resulting in a print size of 6.827" × 5.120". These two values are interconnected; you'll learn more about changing resolution and resizing images in **28** About Size and Resolution.

- **Status.** Here you can tell whether any changes have been made to the image, and whether it contains any current selections, layers, or *alpha channel* information.

- **Memory used.** If your computer resources are running low, you can look here to see how much memory your image editing is consuming.

KEY TERM

Alpha channel—Data saved with an image for reuse when needed, such as selections, masks, and creator information.

The data on the **Creator Information** tab of the **Current Image Information** dialog box is entered by you and stored in the alpha channel of the image file. If you intend to publish your PSP image to public places, such as a personal Web page, you can claim your copyright by typing copyright information and your name into this tab.

Many newer digital cameras are capable of saving additional data, such as the camera type, date the photo was taken, and shot conditions such as f-stop, shutter speed, and focal length. This data is stored in the image's Exchangeable Image File (EXIF) header. You'll find this data on the **EXIF Information** tab of the **Current Image Information** dialog box. Some of this data can be used by an EXIF-compatible printer to print your photo more accurately, with better color and brightness matching.

To make sure that you don't lose this valuable EXIF data, save your image file using an EXIF-compatible program (PSP happens to be one), in an EXIF-compatible format (PSPImage or JPEG). See **1** Ensure That What You See Is What You Get for more information.

EXIF data may be stored with an image.

The **Overview** palette also displays some image information, because you might need to refer to it while considering changes to an image. Click the **Info** tab on the **Overview** palette to see the size of your image in pixels (useful to know, especially if you're working with the image zoomed in). You'll also see the **Pixel Format** listed—this is essentially the *color depth*. Some of Paint Shop Pro's features are not available unless an image is currently using 16 million colors, so looking here first can save you the trouble of looking for an option that you won't be able to select. On the **Info** tab, you'll also see the amount of memory being used—again, this is useful information to have if you're using an older computer with limited resources.

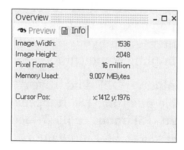

*The **Info** tab of the **Overview** palette.*

At the bottom of the **Info** tab, you can see the relative location of your mouse pointer as a pair of x (horizontal) and y (vertical) coordinates. In this coordinate system, {0, 0} is considered the upper-left corner of the image. The x value increases as you move the pointer to the right, and the y value increases as you move it down. When you're selecting a rectangular area of an image to be cut out or copied, the **Info** tab will also show you the selection's size in pixels and the relative locations of both the upper-left and lower-right corners of the selection.

The data on the **Info** tab of the **Overview** palette also appears at the right end of the status bar. At the left end of the status bar, you'll find a brief description of any tool, toolbar button, or menu command you point to.

TIP

Before placing text or other data in a precise location within an image, display the **Info** tab of the **Overview** palette so that you can see the x and y coordinates as you work.

*The **Status** toolbar displays vital information.*

22 Zoom In and Out with the Zoom Tool

Whether you're making changes to a photograph or some artwork you've created yourself, you must be able to view the image clearly to make precise changes. Typically, this means zooming in on some area that doesn't look right so that you can discern the problem, and later zooming back out again to see whether the change you made looks right when the image is viewed at its regular size. To zoom in on an image and back out again, use the **Zoom** tool and its **Tool Options** buttons.

❶ Select the Pan/Zoom Tool

Click the **Pan** or **Zoom** button on the **Tools** toolbar.

See Also

→ **23** Zoom In and Out with the Overview Palette

→ **25** Magnify Your Work

 TIP

To zoom quickly, click the image with the **Zoom** tool. Right-click to zoom back out.

To zoom in on a particular area of an image, simply drag with the **Zoom** tool to select the area. The selected area is enlarged to fit the size of the image window.

① **Select the Pan/Zoom Tool**

② **Choose a Zoom Amount**

Fit Window to Image

Fit to Window

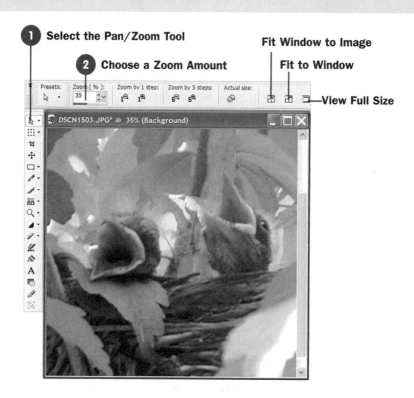

—**View Full Size**

You don't actually have to choose the **Zoom** tool if you simply want to use the controls on the **Tool Options** palette to zoom—so just click whichever button is currently displayed.

To zoom to 50%, 200%, 500%, or 1,000% *and increase the size of the image window to fit the available workspace*, click the **Presets** button, select a zoom amount, and click **OK**.

② **Choose a Zoom Amount**

The **Tool Options** palette for the **Zoom** tool provides many ways in which you can zoom. To view an image at a particular zoom level (such as 50%), type that percentage in the **Zoom (%)** box.

To zoom gradually, click either of the **Zoom by 1 step** buttons—if you click the **1 minus** button, you'll zoom out gradually; if you click the **zoom plus** button, you'll zoom in gradually.

To zoom in or out more quickly, click either of the **Zoom by 5 steps** buttons. To view the image at 100% (actual size), click the **Actual size** button.

The image window can be larger or smaller than the image; to shrink the window so that it fits the image exactly, click the **Fit Window to Image** button. To enlarge the image to fit the size of the window, click the **Fit to Window** button instead. To enlarge the image to fit the available workspace, click **View Full Size**.

TIP

If your mouse has a scroll wheel, you can use it to zoom in and out: Roll the wheel up to zoom in or down to zoom out.

23 Zoom In and Out with the Overview Palette

In the last task, you learned how to zoom in or out using the **Zoom** tool and its buttons on the **Tool Options** palette. However, if the **Overview** palette is displayed, you can use it to zoom in and out without changing to the **Zoom** tool first.

See Also

→ **22** Zoom In and Out with the Zoom Tool

→ **25** Magnify Your Work

1 **Display the Overview Palette**

Choose **View, Palettes, Overview** from the menu bar or press **F9**.

2 **Choose a Zoom Amount**

To view an image at a particular zoom level (such as 50%), type a percentage in the **Zoom (percent)** box.

To zoom gradually, click either of the **Zoom by 1 step** buttons.

To view the image at 100% (actual size), click the **Actual size** button.

TIP

Another way you can zoom without changing to the **Zoom** tool first is to use the scroll wheel on your mouse (if it has one). Scroll the wheel forward to zoom in; scroll it backward to zoom out.

NOTE

You might have noticed the "do not" red slash/circle on the **Actual Size** icon and wondered, "Will this blow something up if I click it?" The answer is no—the symbol simply means, "no magnification," or 100% zoom.

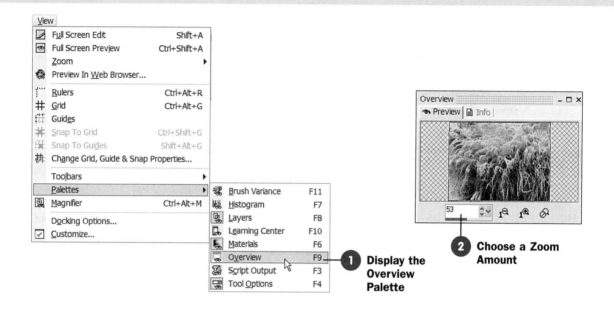

1 Display the Overview Palette

2 Choose a Zoom Amount

---

24 Scroll a Large Image

See Also

→ **22** Zoom In and Out with the Zoom Tool

→ **23** Zoom In and Out with the Overview Palette

If an image is being shown with a magnification larger than the image window can display, parts of that image will be obscured from view. If you need to make changes on a part of the image you can't currently see, you'll have to scroll to view it. To do that, use the **Pan** tool, the scrollbars, or the **Overview** palette.

1 Select the Pan Tool

Click the **Pan** button on the **Tools** toolbar.

2 Drag with the Tool

Click the mouse in the image window and drag with the hand pointer to display the portion of the image you want to view. For example, drag down to view a part of an image that's hidden just above the currently displayed portion.

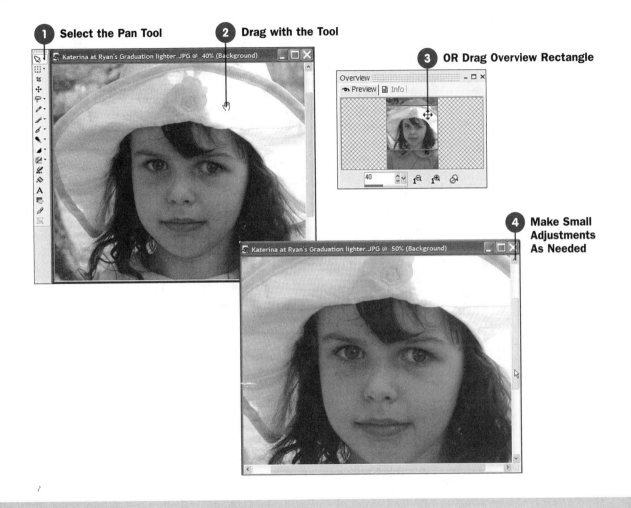

① **Select the Pan Tool**

② **Drag with the Tool**

③ **OR Drag Overview Rectangle**

④ Make Small
Adjustments
As Needed

③ **OR Drag Overview Rectangle**

You can also reposition the viewable portion of the image
by dragging its rectangle within the **Overview** palette.

④ **Make Small Adjustments As Needed**

Click the scroll arrows on the horizontal/vertical scrollbars
or press the arrow keys to move the viewable portion of the
image by a small amount.

25 Magnify Your Work

Some changes you'll want to make to an image will involve working in a small confined area. For example, perhaps you want to remove a small mole or other distraction from a person's face. To do that, you can use the **Clone** tool, but what if you can't see the area you want to fix all that clearly? You could zoom in, of course, but it might be nice to be able to view the changes as you make them, using a more zoomed-out view. Of course, there's always the **Overview** palette and its small image thumbnail, but your tiny changes might not be noticeable in that window. What you need is the ability to quickly zoom in on your work while still maintaining the big-picture view of your changes. To accomplish this task, you use the **Magnifier** palette.

1 **Display the Magnifier Palette**

Choose **View, Magnifier** from the menu bar or press **Ctrl+Alt+M**.

2 **Magnify the Work Area**

Move the mouse pointer anywhere over the image to magnify the area directly beneath the pointer.

3 **Change the Zoom**

Change the zoom level of the **Magnifier** palette by pressing **Ctrl++** to zoom in or **Ctrl+−** to zoom out.

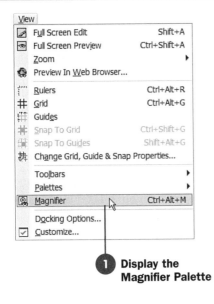

View
- Full Screen Edit — Shift+A
- Full Screen Preview — Ctrl+Shift+A
- Zoom ▸
- Preview In Web Browser...
- Rulers — Ctrl+Alt+R
- Grid — Ctrl+Alt+G
- Guides
- Snap To Grid — Ctrl+Shift+G
- Snap To Guides — Shift+Alt+G
- Change Grid, Guide & Snap Properties...
- Toolbars ▸
- Palettes ▸
- Magnifier — Ctrl+Alt+M
- Docking Options...
- Customize...

1 Display the Magnifier Palette

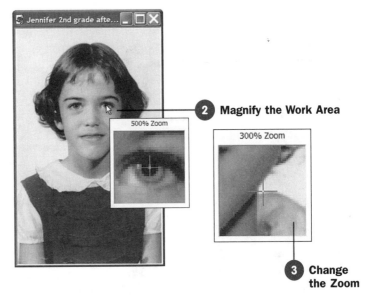

2 **Magnify the Work Area**

500% Zoom

300% Zoom

3 Change the Zoom

---

26 **Add Copyright Information**

Digimarc Corporation, a world leader in digital watermarking, in coordination with Paint Shop Pro's **Image, Watermarking, Embed Watermark** command, can provide you with a secure method of protecting your copyrighted images and tracking their use on the Web. The cost, however, is practical only for a professional photographer. In this task, I'll show you a simple way to watermark your own images—for free! This method creates a copyright notice that you can embed softly within your own images.

The photographs you take are already your property and protected by law. All you have to do to claim copyright over your photo is to place your © mark in some visible location. With a PSP image, you can place your © mark in the **Image Information** dialog box, but that notice can easily be stripped away, even though it's actually illegal for someone other than you (the

Before You Begin

✔ **2** Create a New Image

✔ **13** Select a Color to Work With

✔ **29** Change Image Size or Resolution

✔ **120** About Layers and the Layer Palette

See Also

→ **57** Repeat Adjustments on Multiple Images Automatically

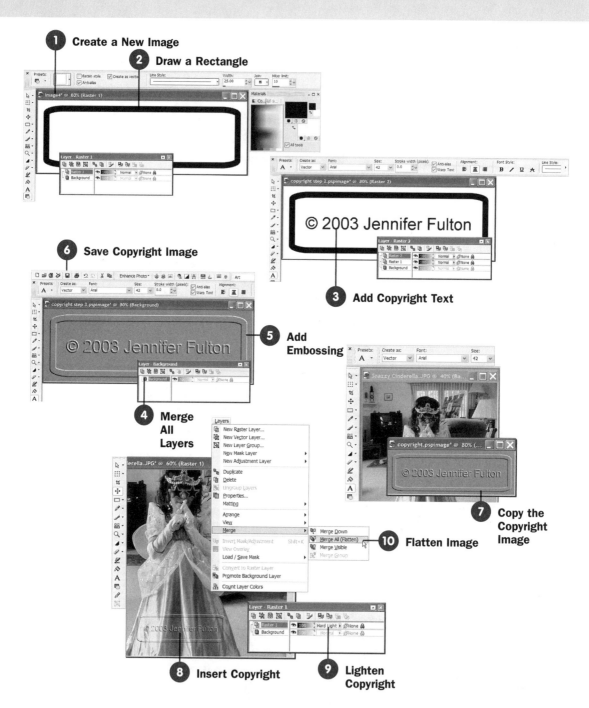

1 Create a New Image

2 Draw a Rectangle

6 Save Copyright Image

3 Add Copyright Text

5 Add Embossing

4 Merge All Layers

7 Copy the Copyright Image

10 Flatten Image

8 Insert Copyright

9 Lighten Copyright

claimant) to do so. This is where direct embedding of the copyright notice within the image itself comes in handy. Of course, you can't copyright just anything. For example, you can't copy an image off a Web page, make changes to it, and then copyright the result.

1 Create a New Image

Start a new image by clicking the **New** button on the **Standard** toolbar. Set **Width** to **900**, **Height** to **300**, and **Units** to **Pixels**. Set the **Resolution** to **72 Pixels/inch**. Select **Raster Background**, with **Color depth** at **16 Million Colors**. Click the **Color** box, choose white, and click **OK**. Click **OK** again.

2 Draw a Rectangle

On the **Materials** palette, change the foreground color to **black** and the background color to **white**. On the **Tools** toolbar, click the **Preset Shape** tool. On the **Tool Options** palette, from the **Shape** list, select **Rounded Rectangle**. Enable the **Anti-alias** and **Create as vector** check boxes and disable **Retain style**. Select the **#1 Solid Line Style** and set the **Width** to **25**. In the image window, draw a rectangle that nearly fills the window. From the menu bar, choose **Layers, Convert to Raster Layer**.

3 Add Copyright Text

On the **Tools** toolbar, click the **Text** tool. On the **Tool Options** palette, choose the **Arial** font, **42** point **Size**, and center **Alignment**. Set the background color to black. In the image window, click in the center of the rectangle. The **Text Entry** dialog box appears. Press and hold the **Alt** key and type **0169** on the numeric keypad to enter the copyright symbol (the © symbol). Type the year followed by your name. Click **Apply**.

If necessary, you can adjust the position of the text by dragging it. You'll want to center the text within the rectangle. When you're done, choose **Layers, Convert to Raster Layer** from the menu bar.

TIP

To make it easier to add a copyright to other images, record steps 7 to 10 as a script. You can then invoke the script during batch processing of new images, or within any open image. See **57** **Repeat Adjustments on Multiple Images Automatically**.

NOTE

The U.S. Copyright Office states that official notice of copyright must contain the word *copyright* or the circle-C symbol, the year the work was first published, and the claimant's name. The use of the copyright notice does not require advance permission from, or registration with, the Copyright Office.

4 Merge All Layers

Choose **Layers, Merge, Merge All (Flatten)** from the menu bar to flatten the image so that you can add embossing.

5 Add Embossing

Choose **Effects, Texture Effects, Emboss** from the menu bar. The **Emboss** effect changes the copyright notice to a mostly gray image with raised text. The edge of the rounded-rectangle appears raised as well.

6 Save Copyright Image

Click the **Save** button. Type **copyright** in the **File name** box. Select **Paint Shop Pro Image** from the **Save as type** list. Click **Save**.

7 Copy the Copyright Image

When it comes time for you to attach a copyright notice to an original image, open the `copyright.pspimage` file. Resize the copyright notice to fit the image you want to watermark by choosing **Image, Resize**, entering new dimensions, and clicking **OK**. When the copyright notice is the correct size, click the **Copy** button on the **Standard** toolbar.

8 Insert Copyright

Open any image you want to copyright. Choose **Edit, Paste, As New Layer** from the menu. The copyright notice is placed on its own layer, on top of the image. Use the **Move** tool if needed to reposition the notice.

9 Lighten Copyright

On the **Layer** palette, select the copyright layer. (It will be on the top of the list because it was the layer most recently created.) Click the **Blend Mode** list and choose **Soft Light**.

TIPS

Place the copyright over an important part of the image—something that cannot be cropped out without ruining the photo.

If the copyright fades away too much, select **Hard Light** instead. Lighten the effect even more by adjusting the copyright layer's opacity by dragging the **Opacity** slider in the **Layer** palette to the left.

10 **Flatten Image**

Choose **Layers, Merge, Merge All (Flatten)**. The copy-right notice is now permanently "embedded" in the image file. Save the image. Look for this in the Color Gallery.

27 Share Images Using Email

One reason you take the time to clean up digital photographs or to create your own art in Paint Shop Pro is so that you can share your work with friends and family. If you have a connection to the Internet, sharing your images by attaching them to email messages is a simple process.

If you have Photo Album, you can also use it to send images using email. Photo Album has the advantage here because it can compress images on the fly, making them smaller and thus easier to send electronically. To send images using Photo Album, select the images to send by clicking them in the **Album View** window, and then click the **Email** button on the toolbar. An email message with the images compressed and attached is automatically created for you to address and send.

1 **Click Browse**

Click the **Browse** button on the **Standard** toolbar. The **Browser** appears.

2 **Select Images to Send**

Select the folder that contains the images you want to send. If you don't want to send all the images in the folder, click the first image and then press and hold **Ctrl** as you click each additional image you want to send.

3 **Choose File, Send**

Choose **File, Send** from the main menu. The **Send** dialog box opens.

Before You Begin

✔ **4** Browse for an Image

NOTE

To send images by email using PSP or Photo Album, your computer must have a MAPI-compatible email program installed such as Outlook, Outlook Express, Eudora, or Pegasus Mail. AOL, Yahoo!, and Hotmail mail programs will not work.

TIP

If you want to send all the images in the current folder, skip step 2.

1 Click Browse

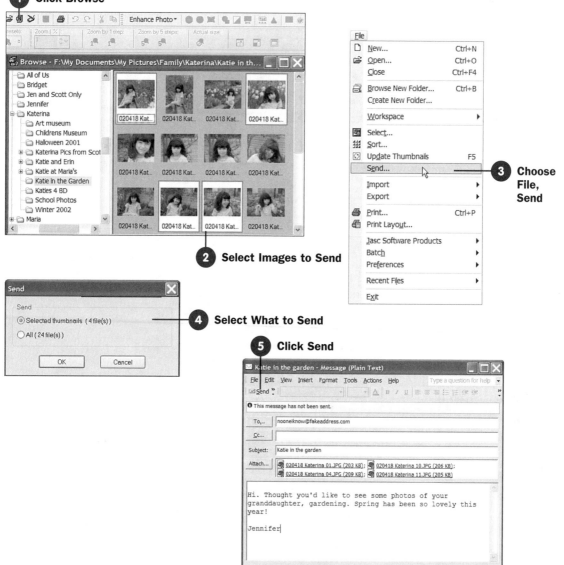

2 Select Images to Send

3 Choose File, Send

4 Select What to Send

5 Click Send

4 Select What to Send

Choose either **Selected thumbnails** (to send only the images you've selected) or **All** (to send all the images in the current folder). Then click **OK**.

5 Click Send

An email message with the images attached is automatically created. Notice the list of image files that have been attached to this message. Address the email message in the usual manner and click **Send** to send it on its way.

28 About Size and Resolution

Two of the most common changes you'll make to an image are to adjust its size and to change its resolution. By *size*, I'm referring to an image's dimensions when printed, not its size onscreen. An image's *resolution* is determined by the number of pixels (dots) per inch.

To compute an image's print size, Paint Shop Pro looks at the number of pixels in an image and their relative size (the number of pixels per inch). Take a look at the first figure here, which depicts an image that's 10 pixels wide by 5 pixels high, using an imaginary scale of 16 pixels per inch. Based on the size of these pixels, the printed image will be about 1.6" wide by .81" high.

See Also

→  **29** Change Image
Size or Resolution

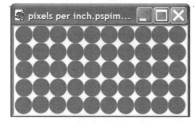

An image that's 10 pixels wide by 5 pixels high.

To compute the resolution of an image, you simply count the number of pixels per inch. Luckily, PSP does that for you, and you can view the print size and resolution of an image in the **Image Information** dialog box (choose **Image, Image Information** from the menu bar). The print size is listed as

NOTE

High resolution (over 200 pixels per inch) is unnecessary for an image destined to be displayed on a computer monitor or a television screen because NTSC standard TV resolution is 72 dots per inch and computer screen resolutions average 102 pixels per inch.

NOTE

To increase the size of an image without changing its resolution, use the **Image, Resize** command to resample it. See **29** Change Image Size or Resolution.

Dimensions and the resolution as **Pixels per Inch**. If you never plan to print a certain image, the image won't need a high resolution (a great number of pixels). But for you to print an image, you need the highest number of pixels you can get—the more the better. As I explain in **32** About Printing Images, you must have an image resolution of 300 ppi (pixels per inch) to create a high-quality print using an outside lab; for home printing, 200 ppi usually does just fine.

An image's print size and its resolution are interdependent; changing one without changing the other will affect the image's print quality. Reducing resolution while maintaining the same print size for example, decreases the number of pixels per inch and, as you can imagine, inflates the size of each pixel. If the pixels become too large, a mosaic effect called *pixelation* might distract you from seeing the image as a whole. Look at the first figure showing the 10 × 5 rectangle. If you change the size of the pixels and make them twice as big (as shown in the second figure), you'll get a much larger rectangle, but the pixels will be much more apparent. When printed, the rectangle might look more like a mesh of dots than a solid rectangle, which is probably not the effect you're going for. The same is true of any graphic image: Make the image larger without increasing the number of pixels (resolution), and the pixels will become bigger and more evident in the final print.

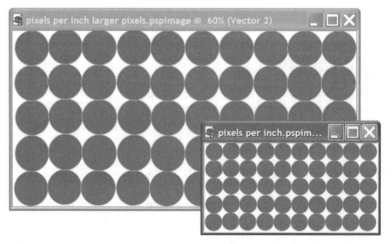

Enlarging the pixels increases the image size while decreasing its quality.

Suppose that, instead of changing the size of the pixels, you maintain their relative size, but double their number. Once again, you'll also double the print size, although the print quality will remain the same, as shown in the third figure.

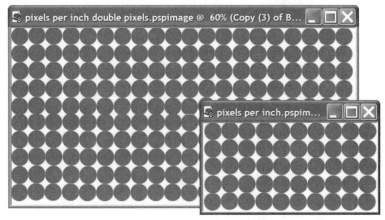

You can also enlarge an image without sacrificing quality by adding to the number of pixels.

29 Change Image Size or Resolution

As you learned in **28** **About Size and Resolution**, an image's size is tied directly to the number of pixels in the image as well as the relative size of the pixels. When you create images with a digital camera, or scan printed images with a scanner, you choose the resolution you want to use—for instance, 300 pixels per inch. The resolution you choose also determines the resulting print size. For example, an image that's 2,048 pixels wide by 1,536 pixels tall (the typical dimensions of an image taken with a 3 MP camera), whose resolution is 300 pixels per inch, will print at 6.827" by 5.120".

So what do you do if you want your image to print at a larger size, but remain at 300 dpi? In other words, what do you do if you want to increase its size without inflating the size of pixels? The answer is, you ask PSP to *resample* the image. When resampling is employed either to increase an image's print size or its resolution, new pixels are inserted between existing ones. The colors for these new pixels are determined by a process that

Before You Begin

✔ **28** About Size and Resolution

See Also

→ **8** Scan an Image

→ **30** Change the Working Area Without Affecting Image Size

→ **94** Clean Up Scans of Printed Material

🔍 KEY TERM

Resample—The process of creating new pixels based on the value of surrounding pixels.

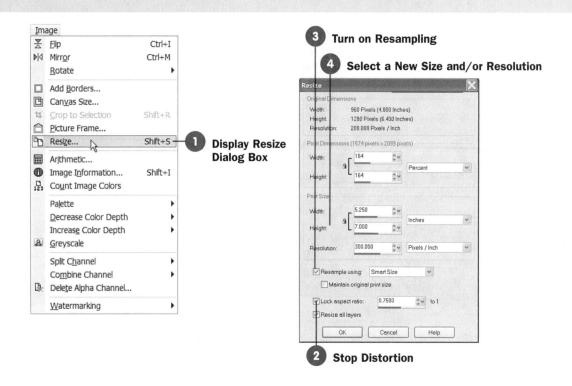

3 Turn on Resampling

4 Select a New Size and/or Resolution

1 Display Resize Dialog Box

2 Stop Distortion

samples the values of surrounding pixels and uses estimated values in between. Resampling can also be used when reducing an image's print size or resolution. In such a circumstance, pixels are removed from an image, and the colors of the remaining pixels are determined through sampling of all the original colors and approximating their blended values.

Because resampling is based on best-guess estimation, using it to change an image's size or resolution by more than 20% often produces poor results. You can resize or change an image's resolution without resampling by telling Paint Shop Pro that you want to maintain the relationship between the size and the resolution. In this manner, you can double an image's print resolution by cutting its print size in half. The image will contain as many pixels as it did before, but the pixels will be smaller, and there will be more of them per inch. Onscreen, you won't see any change at all.

TIP

One fast way to remove moiré patterns, fuzziness, and spots from an image is to scan the image at 600 dpi and then reduce its resolution to 300 dpi *while maintaining its print size*. See **94** Clean Up Scans of Printed Material.

① Display Resize Dialog Box

Choose **Image, Resize** from the menu bar or press **Shift+S**. The **Resize** dialog box appears.

② Stop Distortion

If you do not want the image distorted during the resizing process, select the **Lock aspect ratio** option to turn it on.

If the image contains multiple layers, and you want all the layers resized to the same size, enable the **Resize all layers** option as well.

③ Turn on Resampling

To have PSP estimate colors for pixels when you change the print size or resolution, enable the **Resample using** option and select a sampling formula from the list. Typically, the **Smart Size** option works best because it determines the appropriate formula based on the image's unique requirements. Here's a brief description of the other formulas:

- **Bicubic**—Estimates each new pixel's color value based on the values of the 16 nearest pixels to the new pixel's location relative to the original image, in a 4 × 4 array. This method is best used when enlarging an image.

- **Bilinear**—Estimates each new pixel's color value based on the values of the four nearest pixels to the new pixel's location relative to the original image. This method is best used when reducing an image.

- **Pixel Resize**—Copies the color value of each new pixel from the exact value of its nearest neighbor. Fast and dirty, with often poor results including jagged edges and stair-step effects.

- **Weighted Average**—Estimates each new pixel's color value based on the values of all the pixels that fall within a fixed proximity of the new pixel's location relative to the original image. Here, the pixel residing in the same proportionate location in the original image as that of the new pixel in the resized image is given the extra "weight" when estimating the new color value. This method is best used when reducing the size of an image.

NOTE

If you don't choose the **Resize all layers** option, only the current layer or active selection is resized. Leaving this option disabled is a handy way to resize a selection or an image copied to a new layer.

NOTE

To avoid resampling an image, turn off the **Resample using** option and change either the **Height/Width** or **Resolution** values in the **Print Size** area of the **Resize** dialog box. If you increase the **Resolution** without resampling, for example, the image will be resized smaller.

④ Select a New Size and/or Resolution

If you know what size you want the final image to be, type a value in the **Print Size Width** box; the **Height** value changes proportionately (or vice versa).

You can also change an image's size by adjusting its pixel dimensions. For example, if you want the image to be twice as big, select **Percent** from the **Pixel Dimensions** list and type **200** in the **Width** and **Height** boxes. This changes the number of pixels without affecting their size (assuming **Resample** is on).

To change the resolution, type a value in the **Resolution** box. Altering resolution in this manner does not change the image's print size, unless you entered new print dimensions earlier. Because the **Resample using** option is selected, new pixels are created as needed to meet your print size and resolution requirements.

TIP

Because resampling often leaves an image a bit fuzzy, it's best to follow up by treating your resampled image to an **Unsharp** mask. See **114** Sharpen an Image.

---

30 **Change the Working Area Without Affecting Image Size**

See Also

→ **29** Change Image Size or Resolution

KEY TERM

Canvas—In PSP, the canvas is the geometric platform that provides the coordinate system for every image, and to which the background layer is attached.

TIP

There are other methods you can use to create a frame around an image. See **135** Frame a Photograph.

Each image begins with a *canvas*—essentially the image background. The benefit of thinking of an image's background layer as a canvas is that it helps you conceive how that layer can be stretched to change the size of the area on which you can paint. For a newly imported digital photo, the image is "painted," if you will, to fill the canvas. You can expand the background layer (the canvas) of an image such as a photograph, for example, to make room for a frame, and then fill the new area with color or texture. Or you might simply want to expand the canvas to create more room in which to add a clip from another image, an object, or some text.

When you expand the canvas for an image, you expand the background layer. If you've already created other layers in the image, all those layers are expanded by the same amount. If the background layer is transparent, then any extra space you create is filled with transparent pixels. You can choose to fill the extra space in the background layer with a color you select.

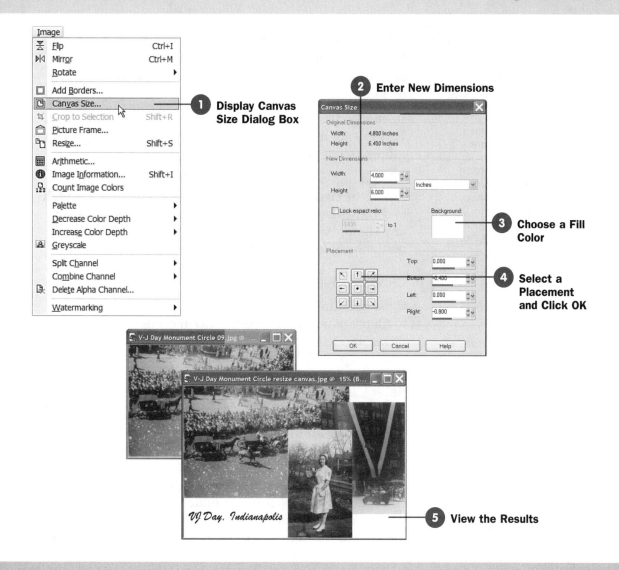

1 Display Canvas Size Dialog Box

2 Enter New Dimensions

3 Choose a Fill Color

4 Select a Placement and Click OK

5 View the Results

1 Display Canvas Size Dialog Box

Choose **Image, Canvas Size** from the menu bar. The **Canvas Size** dialog box is displayed.

2 Enter New Dimensions

If you want the image to retain its ratio of height to width after stretching the canvas, enable the **Lock aspect ratio** option.

To change the aspect ratio to fit a specific format—such as 1.33 to 1 for a standard television screen—enter the aspect ratio you want in the box.

Select a unit of measure such as inches or pixels from the **New Dimensions** list box. Then type values in the **Width** and **Height** boxes. If you've selected **Lock aspect ratio**, any change you make to the **Width** value is reflected proportionately in the **Height** value, and vice versa.

3 Choose a Fill Color

If the background is not transparent, you can choose a color to fill the extra canvas space. Click the **Background** color picker and select a color. You can also click anywhere in the image to pick up that color with the dropper.

4 Select a Placement and Click OK

To choose how you want the new canvas space distributed, click a **Placement** button. The button you click indicates where the image should appear in relation to the new canvas areas. If you click the center button for example, the new canvas space is distributed around the image evenly; if you click the upper-left corner button, the image is placed there and the new canvas areas are inserted along the bottom and to the right. Click **OK**, and the canvas is expanded as directed by your selections.

5 View the Results

In the sample figure, the canvas was expanded to the right and along the bottom, text was added, and several new images were pasted into the image to fill the new space.

31 Change Color Depth

One of the key factors affecting the size of an image file is the maximum number of colors it can include. If you're working on an image to be shared over the Internet, small file size is often a high priority. One way you can reduce a file's size is to reduce its color depth. Of course, reducing the number of colors in an image's palette can also reduce its quality because a limited number of colors are used instead of a full spectrum.

Because some commands are available only for grayscale images or for those that use 16 million colors, you might sometimes find yourself temporarily *increasing* an image's color depth. This won't, however, improve the resolution of a low-resolution image—increasing an image's color palette simply makes more colors available for use; it does not tell PSP where to use them in an image to boost detail and clarity.

If file size is your main priority, you can *compress* an image into GIF, JPEG, or PNG format (for example), a process that also reduces its color palette a bit more scientifically than the method discussed here. You can also convert an image to grayscale to reduce its color depth.

① **Display Increase/Decrease Color Depth Menu**

Choose **Image, Increase Color Depth** from the menu bar to increase the number of colors in an image; choose **Image, Decrease Color Depth** to reduce the number of colors instead.

② **Select Color Depth**

Select the color depth you want from the submenu that appears. If you're increasing color depth, the image is not changed, but more colors become available for you to use.

If you're reducing the color depth, a dialog box appears, allowing you to choose how Paint Shop Pro will narrow the color palette and adjust image colors. Continue to step 3.

See Also

→ **41** Compress an Image Using GIF Format

→ **42** Compress an Image Using JPEG Format

→ **43** Compress an Image Using PNG Format

→ **143** Change a Colored Photograph to Black and White

✎ NOTE

A 16-million-color image might not actually contain 16 million colors, even though it is capable of doing so. Reducing the color depth for images that are generally monochromatic to start with might not appreciably reduce the quality but will shrink the file sizes considerably.

TIP

If you're curious about how many colors your image is currently using, choose **Image, Count Image Colors**. To check the current color depth, look at the right end of the status bar.

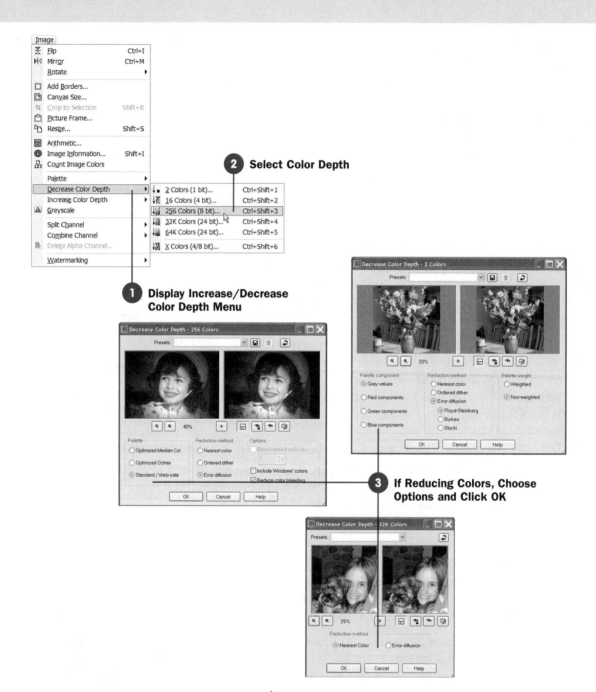

2 Select Color Depth

1 Display Increase/Decrease Color Depth Menu

3 If Reducing Colors, Choose Options and Click OK

3 If Reducing Colors, Choose Options and Click OK

If you're reducing colors in an image, select how you want PSP to choose the colors for the palette by selecting options in the dialog box that appears. (The dialog box you see depends on which color depth option you selected in step 2.) Here are some choices you might encounter—select one of the following and click **OK**:

- **Palette Component**—When reducing an image to two colors (black and white), you must tell Paint Shop Pro how to choose which pixels to change to white: based on their gray values, or their red, green, or blue components.

- **Palette**—When reducing an image to 16 or 256 colors, use the **Palette** options to tell PSP how you want it to select the optimal range of colors for the image's palette. To select the most common colors used in the image, choose **Optimized Median Cut**. To choose the most common color in each of several small quadrants throughout an image, choose **Optimized Octree**. To make the image appear the same on a wide variety of computers, choose **Standard/Web-safe**.

- **Reduction method**—Select the method you want PSP to use to reduce the color palette: **Nearest color**, **Ordered dither**, or *Error diffusion*. Choose **Nearest color** to have PSP choose the nearest color in the color wheel when substituting an original color for a new color in the palette. Choose **Ordered dither** to tell PSP to use a checkerboard pattern when working with two colors to create a blended color. Choose **Error diffusion** if you want PSP to use a more random pattern when color blending with two colors. Because it uses a mathematical formula, **Error diffusion** (when used in images with a very limited color palette) can sometimes generate artifacts in a color blended area, more so than using the **Ordered dither** method.

- **Palette weight**—This option appears only when you're reducing an image to two colors. Choose

🔍 KEY TERM

Error diffusion—Any of several mathematical techniques that attempt to compensate for large error values (differences between the intensities of an original pixel and its replacement in a reprocessed image) by dividing this difference into parts and distributing it to neighboring pixels, thus masking the obvious inaccuracy.

Weighted to balance out the color palette with an even number of light, dark, and medium tones. Choose **Non-weighted** to let the balance of tones in the image decide which colors belong in the palette.

- **Boost marked colors by**—To use this option in 16 or 256 color images, select an area whose colors you want to favor, enable the **Optimized Median Cut** reduction method, and set a relative boost factor between 1 and 10.

- **Include Windows' colors**—If you intend to use the image exclusively within a Windows program such as PowerPoint, enable this option to include the Windows standard palette of 32 colors in the image palette.

- **Reduce color bleeding**—As the **Error diffusion** reduction method moves from left to right across an image substituting colors, a loss of color integrity might occur, with colors becoming too blended and more muted. Enable this option to prevent this from happening to your image.

5

Printing and Saving Images

IN THIS CHAPTER:

Retouching an image and then printing it are probably the two most common Paint Shop Pro tasks. If printing was as easy as clicking a button, I wouldn't have devoted so much of this chapter to it. But don't worry; by following the steps in the appropriate task in this chapter, you'll be printing great-looking images in no time.

Saving an image is also one of those tasks that is sometimes not as simple as it looks. When it comes to saving an image, a lot of questions come up, such as where do you intend to use the image—on the Web, on your screen, or in print? Do you want to reduce the image's file size as you're saving it? Are you making a copy of an image so that your changes won't affect the original? With the answers to these questions in hand, you can easily select the right task to help you save the image correctly.

32 About Printing Images

Before You Begin

✔ **1** Ensure That What You See Is What You Get

See Also

→ **33** Print an Image

→ **34** Print Contact Sheets

→ **35** Print Portrait Sheets

NOTE

Match the print size of an image as shown in PSP with the size of the paper you're printing on. For example, if you're using 4" × 6" photo paper, you must adjust the print size of your image so that it's exactly 4" × 6" or *smaller* so that it doesn't print off the edge of the paper.

After working on an image and perfecting its beauty, there are several things you should consider before printing it.

- **What size do you want the image to be when printed? Is this size the same as the image is now?** As you'll learn in **33** Print an Image, you can make quick adjustments to the size of the image when printing, *without changing the image file's actual size*. Still, it's nice to have an idea of the image's final size when making modifications—you don't have to be as picky with image quality for a wallet-size photo as you do with an 8" × 10", for example.

- **What kind of quality do you expect?** In other words, is this just a quick print to see roughly how something looks, or is this a "keeper"? As you can when printing documents from other programs, you can change the print quality of a PSP image just before printing. For test prints, choose your ordinary ink jet or laser paper and draft quality; for final prints, choose a high-quality (20 to 24 lb.) paper and best-quality print speed. For photos, choose a glossy or matte photo paper.

If you want to save a few bucks and buy your paper online, consider only those sources that provide ICC profiles that match your printer *and* their paper type. ICC profiles are customized to match the capabilities of your printer to the brand and paper type you buy, creating prints of high quality.

TIP

For best results, use photo paper made by the same manufacturer as your print-er, because the printer's ink and paper are designed to work together.

WEB RESOURCE

www.Pictorico.com

Online photo paper store that also offers free ICM pro-files that match their paper types with Canon and Epson Stylus Photo printers (they pledge to add profiles for HP Photosmart printers soon).

- **Do you need more than one copy of the image?** As you can with other programs, you can select the number of copies you want when you print the image. However, Paint Shop Pro has one feature many other programs don't have: the capability to arrange multiple images (or copies of the same image) on a single sheet of paper, like the photo sheets you get from a professional photographer. So if you decide you want to share your photos, you won't need to waste a lot of paper printing each copy on its own sheet. **see 35 Print Portrait Sheets** for more information.

- **Will you be printing the image on a home printer or taking it to a lab for professional printing?** If you're printing at home, enhance the final quality of your prints by buying photo paper for photos you intend to frame or place in an album, and high-quality paper for greeting cards, calendars, business cards, and reports. If they are available for your printer, buy high-quality inks that resist fading.

TIP

You can directly upload images to Shutterfly, a digi-tal image sharing and pro-cessing Web site, from both Photo Album and Paint Shop Pro.

If you plan on taking the image to a professional service bureau or photo kiosk for printing, make sure that you know exactly what that service expects from you: specifical-ly, media type (CD, floppy, memory stick) and image type (JPEG, TIFF, Kodak Picture CD, and so on). For example, the Kodak Picture Maker machines in many retail stores accept most digital camera memory sticks, Kodak Picture CD, or JPEG format only. If your local choices are too limited, try the Internet. There are any number of high-quality photo labs on the Internet that will accept images sent by email or FTP.

Whether you plan on printing a photograph locally or with a service, here are some tips for preparing the image properly:

NOTE

Makers of scanners, digital cameras, and the imaging community at large typically refer to an image's resolution in terms of "dots per inch," or dpi. Printer manufacturers refer to print resolution in terms of ppi, or "pixels per inch." They mean essentially the same thing, but Paint Shop Pro uses mostly the term ppi when referring to an image's resolution.

KEY TERM

Resampling—A process that creates new pixels for an image by sampling the colors of surrounding pixels, or that drops pixels that are no longer needed. Resampling occurs when the ratio between the image file's original dpi (dots per inch) and the printout's ppi (pixels per inch) is no longer 1:1.

TIP

Online film labs typically require images of only 150 dpi to achieve good quality prints on Kodak paper, so if you don't like the results you get on your home printer, try a film lab instead.

- **Start with enough pixels.** Typically, you'll want your final print resolution to be 200 to 300 ppi, so make sure that you scan at that resolution. If you plan on resizing and *resampling* to remove moiré patterns, scan at double that resolution—400 to 600 dpi. If you're shooting an image with a digital camera, *always use the camera's highest resolution.* You can always reduce the print size of an image later by reducing the ppi or by compressing it, but you can never increase an image's resolution after it has already been shot.

- **Check the print size and resolution.** The dimensions of the original image, when viewed using the **Image**, **Image Information** command, must correspond to the final print size you want to achieve, or you'll have to resample the image to add pixels, resulting in a loss of print quality. For example, if you want to print an image in 6" × 4" format at best quality (300 ppi), the image file's dimensions shown in the **Image** pane of the **Image Information** dialog box must be least 1800 × 1200 pixels (300 ppi times 6 inches by 300 ppi times 4 inches). You can usually achieve acceptable quality results at 150 ppi, and for that, the dimensions of your original image must be at least 900 × 600 pixels. To get a really good quality image printed at home, you typically need only 200 ppi, or image dimensions of at least 1200 × 800 for a print size of 6" × 4".

The highest quality images produced by a 1.2-megapixel (Mp) camera are stored at 1280 × 960 (1,280 times 960 = 1,228,800 pixels, or 1.2 Mp). This means that you can print 4" × 6" images at home with good quality (200 dpi), but if you want to print larger images, you must resample. If you own a 2.1 Mp camera, its highest quality images are stored at 1600 × 1200 resolution, which means that you can print good quality images up to 5" × 7" without resampling. If you own a 3.34 Mp camera, its images are stored at 2048 × 1536, and you can achieve good quality images up to 8" × 10" without resampling. With the newer 4.1 and 5 Mp cameras, you can print even larger images without sacrificing quality.

- **Save the image using a lossless format such as PSP or TIFF.** JPEG format allows for invisible, or semi-visible, selective reductions in image quality to achieve smaller file sizes. If you plan on using an outside photo service that requires JPEG format, edit your image first, making sure that you save changes in PSP or TIFF format. When you're completely done with the image, save a *copy* as JPEG, using as low an amount of compression as your photo lab allows. If the lab accepts TIFF format, use it instead because TIFF files are certain to provide higher quality prints.

- **Size the image to fit the photo size you want.** If you are printing the image yourself, you can adjust its print size in the **Print** dialog box to approximate the proper photo size. If you plan on turning the image over to a photo lab, limit the amount of cropping the photo lab might have to do on your uploaded image by making sure that the image's aspect ratio (its height to width ratio) *exactly* matches the photo size you want. For example, the aspect ratio of a 4" × 6" print is 1:1.5, a 5" × 7" print is 1:1.4, and an 8" × 10" print is 1:1.25. An unedited digital image typically has an aspect ratio of 1:1.33, which is the same as a computer screen. You can change the aspect ratio of a photo by cropping or resizing/resampling.

TIP

To crop an image at exactly 4" × 6", for example, simply select that preset from the **Presets** list for the **Crop** tool. Then move the crop rectangle around the image to select the best portion to crop. You can also resize the crop rectangle by dragging from a corner without losing the aspect ratio.

33 Print an Image

Before printing an image in Paint Shop Pro, you can use the **Print** dialog box to make quick adjustments to get the final result you're looking for. For example, if your image size is not the same as the paper you want to print on, you can scale the image proportionately so that it fits better. You can also place the image on the paper wherever you like—centering it, for example, or offsetting it from the left edge by a certain amount. The **Print** dialog box also allows you to change from **Portrait** to **Landscape** orientation, specify the number of copies you want, print in grayscale, select the highest print quality, set the paper

Before You Begin

✔ **32** About Printing Images

See Also

→ **34** Print Contact Sheets

→ **35** Print Portrait Sheets

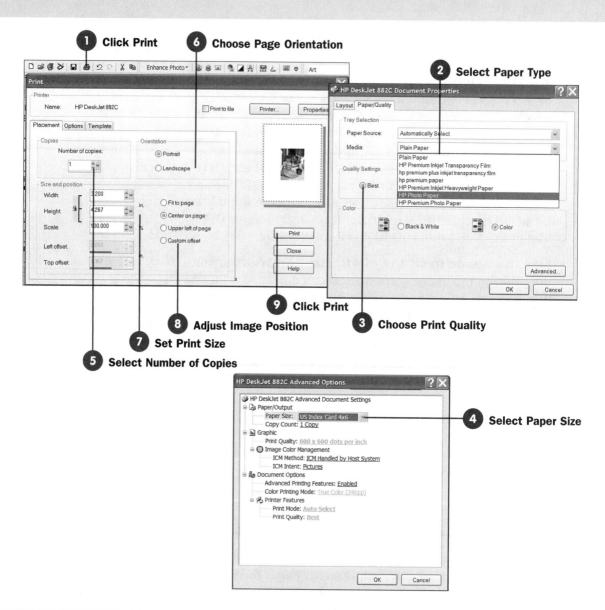

1 Click Print

6 Choose Page Orientation

2 Select Paper Type

9 Click Print

8 Adjust Image Position

3 Choose Print Quality

7 Set Print Size

5 Select Number of Copies

4 Select Paper Size

type to photo paper, change the paper size to 4" × 6", and print other useful information such as crop marks and the filename.

When printing a photograph on photo paper, allow a few minutes for the ink to dry before touching the print. Also, be sure to keep copies of your image files in a safe place so that you can reprint them when needed.

1 Click Print

Click the **Print** button on the **Standard** toolbar. The **Print** dialog box appears.

2 Select Paper Type

Click the **Properties** button. Windows displays a **Properties** dialog box specifically for your printer. Select the paper type you want to use.

Your dialog box might look a bit different than the one shown here for an HP DeskJet 882C. In this dialog box, I open the **Media** list and choose the paper type I want, such as Plain Paper or HP Premium Photo Paper. You'll find your paper type selections in a similar list.

3 Choose Print Quality

In the **Properties** dialog box for my HP printer, I simply click the **Quality** option I want—typically **Best** for fine quality, **Normal** for okay quality, or **Draft** for I-just-want-to-get-a-quick-look-at-this quality.

4 Select Paper Size

On my HP printer, I must click the **Advanced** button in the **Properties** dialog box to display options for changing paper size. Your printer will probably provide a similar button for accessing the paper size. From here, I open the **Paper Size** list and choose the paper size I need—typically **Letter** for 8.5" × 11", although I have used **US Index Card 4 x 6** for 4" × 6" photos. Click **OK** as many times as needed to return to the **Print** dialog box.

5 Select Number of Copies

Set the **Number of copies** value to the number of printed copies you want. Each copy prints on a separate page. If you want to fit multiple copies of an image on a single page, see **35** **Print Portrait Sheets**.

NOTE

Unless you are using archival inks and special papers, most home-printed photos will fade within a few years (more quickly if exposed to direct sunlight, extreme heat, or high humidity). After your prints are thoroughly dry (about a day), place them under anti-UV-coated glass or in archival albums.

TIP

Before printing an image on photo paper, do a test print on high-quality white paper first so that you can make further adjustments if needed.

6 **Choose Page Orientation**

Normally, the page orientation is set to **Portrait**. However, if your image is wider than it is tall, you might want to choose **Landscape**, which prints the image across the greatest width of the paper (on an 8.5" × 11" paper, **Landscape** orientation prints across the 11" width).

7 **Set Print Size**

To adjust the size of the printed image (which will not affect its actual image size in the file), type a desired **Width** or **Height**. If you type a new width, for example, the height is adjusted proportionately.

You can also adjust the **Scale** if you like—for example, you can change this value to 200% to print the image at twice its normal size. If you click the **Fit to Page** option, the image is scaled to fill the page completely.

8 **Adjust Image Position**

Click the **Center on page** option to place the image in the middle of the paper. Select the **Upper left of page** option to place the image against the upper-left margin.

To place the image on the paper in any other position, click **Custom offset** and enter **Left offset** and **Top offset** values. A positive value places the image that far away from the left or top margin; a negative value places the image into the margin, essentially cropping it off.

9 **Click Print**

Click the **Print** button to print your image.

NOTE

If you enlarge an image for printing using the **Scale** or **Fit to Page** options, the print quality will be poor. A better alternative is to resize and resample the image first. See **29** Change Image Size or Resolution.

TIP

On the **Template** tab, you can select a template to print the image multiple times on a single sheet of paper. See **35** Print Portrait Sheets.

34 Print Contact Sheets

Before the days of the digital darkroom, the first task a photographer would perform after developing a roll of film was to create a *contact sheet*. Using Paint Shop Pro's **Browser**, you can quickly print contact sheets of your images as well.

① **Open Browser**

Click the **Browse** button on the **Standard** toolbar.

② **Select Images**

On the left side of the **Browser**, click the folder that contains the images you want to print as thumbnails.

③ **Click Print**

Click the **Print** button on the **Standard** toolbar. The **Browser Print** dialog box appears.

④ **Set How to Print**

By default, all images will be printed in thumbnail size, with a filename appearing beneath each image. If you'd like to use some other print layout template, deselect the **Auto-create a template** check box, then click **Select template** to select a print layout from the **Templates** dialog box.

To print each thumbnail in a slightly larger size, choose **Mini Wallets** from the templates listed in the **Templates** dialog box. To learn more about print layouts, **see 35 Print Portrait Sheets**.

Change the orientation from **Portrait** to **Landscape** if desired.

⑤ **Choose Images and Click Print**

In the **Print range** area, select what to print: **All** images in the current folder, a specific range of **Pages**, or just the current **Selection** of images. Choose the **Number of copies** you want printed. Click **Print** to print the images.

Before You Begin

✔ **32** About Printing Images

See Also

→ **35** Print Portrait Sheets

KEY TERM

Contact sheet—A printout of a group of images, where each image is displayed in a small, thumbnail size. Contact sheets are useful in cataloging groups of images for easy reference.

NOTE

If you want to print all the images in the folder, you do not have to select the images individually. However, if you want to print selected images only, press **Ctrl** and click the ones you want to include.

NOTE

To enter a range of pages to print, first estimate the number of print pages by dividing the total number of images by the number of images per page.

 SNAPSHOT

1 Open Browser

3 Click Print

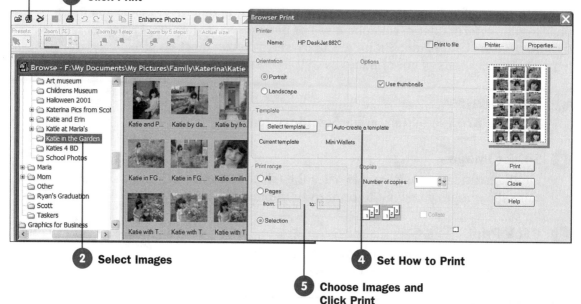

2 Select Images

4 Set How to Print

5 Choose Images and Click Print

---

35 Print Portrait Sheets

Before You Begin

✔ **32** About Printing Images

See Also

→ **33** Print an Image

→ **34** Print Contact Sheets

If you've ever had your picture taken by a professional photographer, you are probably familiar with *portrait sheets*. In Paint Shop Pro, you can re-create this same type of printout using one or more images of your choice.

The **Print Layout** window gives you total control over your printout. Here you can select from standard portrait sheet formats such as two 5" × 7"s or one 4" × 6" and several wallet-sized photos. You can also create a custom portrait sheet with your own unique size combinations.

1 **Open Image(s)**

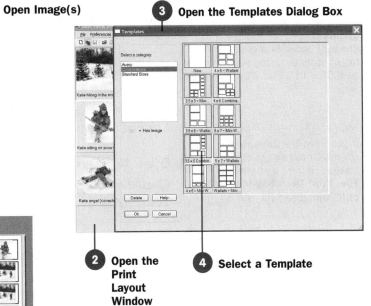

3 **Open the Templates Dialog Box**

2 **Open the Print Layout Window**

4 **Select a Template**

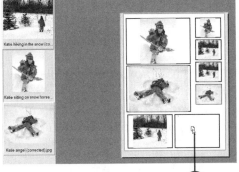

5 **Arrange the Photos**

Fill Template with Image Button

7 **Print the Sheet**

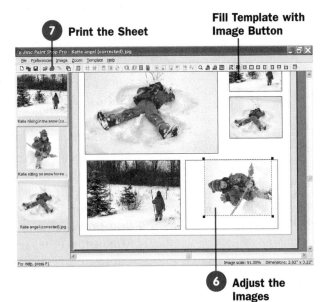

6 **Adjust the Images**

KEY TERM

Portrait sheets—Multiple copies of the same photograph or multiple photographs printed on a single sheet of paper, in a grouping of standard sizes such as 8.5" × 11", 5" × 7", and wallet.

TIP

If you have the **Browser** open, you can select the images to print and choose **File, Print Layout** instead of following steps 1 and 2.

1 **Open Image(s)**

Open the images you want to print by clicking the **Open** button on the **Standard** toolbar, selecting the images, and clicking **Open**.

2 **Open the Print Layout Window**

Choose **File, Print Layout** from the menu bar. The images you opened in step 1 appear on the left side of the **Print Layout** window.

3 **Open the Templates Dialog Box**

Click the **Open Template** button on the toolbar. The **Templates** dialog box opens.

4 **Select a Template**

Choose a category of templates from the **Select a category** list. **Avery** is a grouping of templates that use layouts standard to Avery brand photo papers. **Combinations** is a grouping of templates that combine common photo sizes such as 5" × 7" and wallet. **Standard Sizes** is a grouping of templates in which a common photo size is used to fill a sheet.

After choosing a category, click the template you want to use from those displayed on the right. Click **OK.** You're returned to the **Print Layout** window.

TIP

To fill the entire sheet with the same image, drag the image to any cell in the template and then click the **Fill template with image** button on the toolbar.

5 **Arrange the Photos**

Cells appear in the template on the right. Fill each cell with the photo you want to print there. Select a photo from the list of open photos on the left side of the window and drag-and-drop it onto the appropriate cell. For example, to print an image at 3" × 5", drop the image onto a 3" × 5" cell (assuming the template you selected has one). Continue to drag-and-drop images onto the template until all the cells are full.

6 **Adjust the Images**

Click an image on the template. A red border appears around the cell, telling you that it's active. Adjust the image to fit the cell as desired. Here are some choices from the toolbar in the **Print Layout** window:

- **Rotate 90+**—Rotates image 90 degrees to the right.

- **Rotate 90–** —Rotates image 90 degrees to the left.

- **Remove from Layout**—Removes the image from the template. The image is still displayed on the left so that you can place it somewhere else on the template if you want. The image is not deleted from the hard disk.

- **Free format**—Allows you to resize the image and place it wherever you want within the cell.

- **Size and Center**—Allows you to resize the image while automatically centering it within the cell.

- **Fit, fill, and center to cell**—Fills the cell with the image while retaining its proportions. If the image doesn't fit exactly, portions of it might be cropped.

- **Fit and center**—Adjusts the size of the image proportionately so that it touches the top and bottom of the cell and then centers it between the left and right boundaries of the cell.

- **Fit and adjust left**—Adjusts the size of the image proportionately so that it touches the top and bottom of the cell and then places it against the left boundary of the cell.

- **Fit and adjust right**—Adjusts the size of the image proportionately so that it touches the top and bottom of the cell and then places it against the right boundary of the cell.

NOTE

The **Rotate 90+/90–** and **Remove from Layout** buttons are located in the middle of the toolbar; you'll find the rest of these buttons in the last group, located on the far right.

- **Fit and adjust to top**—Adjusts the size of the image proportionately so that it touches the top and bottom of the cell and then places it against the top boundary of the cell.

- **Fit and adjust to bottom**—Adjusts the size of the image proportionately so that it touches the top and bottom of the cell and then places it against the bottom boundary of the cell.

 TIP

If you want to save the portrait sheet to print it again, click the **Save template** button on the toolbar. In the dialog box that opens, click **Save with images**. Select the existing template name in the **Name** box, type a new template name, and then click **OK**.

7 **Print the Sheet**

Click the **Print** button on the toolbar. One copy of the portrait sheet as it is shown in the window is printed. Click the **Close Print Layout** button on the toolbar to return to PSP. Click **No** if you do not want to save the template with your changes.

---

36 **About Image Types**

See Also

→ **37** About Saving

 NOTE

Officially, to publish a GIF or TIFF (with **LZW** compression) image to the Web, you're required to obtain a written license from Unisys (patent holders of the LZW compression technology). Unisys has prosecuted selected people who failed to seek this permission. See www.unisys.com/about__unisys/lzw for more info, or email LZW_INFO@UNISYS.COM to see whether further licensing on your part is required.

Digital images can be saved in any number of different formats. The format you choose for your images will depend on the purposes you have in mind for them. For example, if you want to use an image on a Web page, you'll need to save it in a Web-compatible format: GIF, JPEG, or PNG. Each of these formats uses compression—JPEG and PNG in variable amounts—to make image files smaller. Compressed images are a benefit to Web users who have lower bandwidth and, thus, longer download times. Here's a brief description of each format:

- **GIF.** One of the oldest compressed formats in wide use. PSP supports GIF under license from Unisys, its current patent holder. On its own merits, GIF is great for use with line art such as cartoons and illustrations, and artwork with large areas of similar color. GIF format supports animation—basically multiple copies of almost-the-same image stored in one file. GIFs can also include transparent pixels, where background pixels of a selected RGB value that surround the main image are ignored, and the graphics beneath them are allowed to show through. When a transparent GIF is placed on a Web page, its rectangular edges disappear, and the image appears to sit right on top of the page as shown here.

Katerina's Web Page

Hi! My name's Katerina, and welcome to my Web page! Although I'm only five, I have lots of favorite things I like to do, such as working on my computer, playing with my puppets, swimming, and ballet. To see my complete list of favorite things, click here.

We just got back from a wonderful vacation in Oklahoma, where I got to visit with my Grandma Ria, Granddad, Nana, and Great-Grandmother. You can see some pictures from my trip if you click here.

Here's a home movie my mommy made—of course, it features me! To view this movie, you'll need an MPEG player. Ready? Well, here I am!

A transparent GIF blends into the Web page background.

- **JPEG.** JPG/JPEG images are perfect for use with photographs or other images with lots of color. JPEG uses a lossy compression technique, where certain color values in similarly shaded regions are blended with one another in a barely noticeable way, resulting in a smaller color palette and a smaller image. But if you save a JPEG file over and over again, it will develop *artifacts*. So you should only save an image in JPEG format when you are finished with it. When you start to retouch a previously saved JPEG image in PSP, start by saving it immediately in PSP format, and save a copy of it as JPEG only when you're done. Artifacts also appear in a JPEG file whenever it is compressed too much. Artifacts can appear in a JPEG file if the image contains sharp edges, such as a border, a line, or the edges of large text.

  If you own a digital camera, it probably uses JPEG format. As long as you choose relatively high quality, however, the JPEG compression will be minimal and you'll still get a good quality image (at highest quality, no compression whatsoever is used). However, if your camera gives you a choice between JPEG and TIFF format (which I'll talk about in a minute), choose TIFF.

- **JPEG 2000.** JPEG 2000 or JP2 format is similar to JPEG, but because it uses a different compression scheme, JPEG 2000 can produce smaller files, retain image quality, and produce minimal artifacts even at high compression. JPEG 2000 handles anti-aliased text better than JPEG, so if you have an image such as a photograph with text, JPEG 2000 might be the format to use. Be sure to see this figure in the Color Gallery section of this book.

A JPEG 2000 file contains image information in its header about the color space used, which helps to ensure that the file is displayed and printed properly. JPEG 2000 supports lossless and lossy compression, *alpha transparency*, and 16-bit color.

JPEG 2000's major drawback right now is that litigation concerning the originality of its compression scheme has compelled many manufacturers to suspend their support for it. For example, no Web browsers currently support JPEG 2000 (at least, not without third-party plug-ins); you might not want to use them on your Web pages.

This JP2 image is smaller than its JPEG counterpart, yet it retains a higher quality.

KEY TERM

Alpha transparency—Supported by JPEG 2000 and PNG image formats, alpha transparency is simply variable transparency, or the ability to vary the amount of transparency in an image. This allows you to gradually fade an image against a Web page background, for example.

- **PNG.** PNG is a format that's fairly new on the Web scene, so using it might mean that some users with older Web browsers won't be able to view your Web graphics correctly—and sometimes not at all, especially if the images use transparent backgrounds. PNG has the advantage, though, of using a lossless compression method as does GIF. PNG files, when compared to GIF files, are typically smaller. They also offer other advantages, such as alpha transparency, gamma correction for cross-platform control, and faster *interlacing*.

- **TIFF.** A great format to use when saving photographs or other color-intensive images because there is no loss of image data. Unlike JPEG, which uses a lossy compression scheme, TIFF uses a lossless compression scheme—100% of the data that goes into a compressed image survives the decompression process when the image is loaded into PSP or another program.

- **PSPImage.** In most cases, while you're retouching a digital photo or creating original graphics, you'll want to work in Paint Shop Pro's native format, PSPImage. Doing so allows you to save critical image data such as layers, alpha channels, and vector object information. When you're done making changes to an image, you can always save it in an alternative format, such as JPEG or TIFF.

If you're not going to use your image on a Web page, but simply send it over the Web using email, the image can be saved in just about any format (as long as the recipient has a program capable of reading that format). The same is true if your purpose is to simply print the image; you can use any format compatible with the program you're using to print—in this case, any format supported by Paint Shop Pro.

KEY TERM

Interlacing—Also known as *interleaving*. A method of downloading a Web graphic for viewing in which the image is displayed progressively—typically, the image appears on the Web page quickly but without much detail, and as the download progresses, the image gains detail and sharpness.

NOTE

If you want to be able to make changes to vector text, vector objects, elements on layers, or use data stored in alpha channels, you must save the image in PSP format. When you save an image in any other format, vector data is converted to raster (bitmapped) data.

Before You Begin

See Also

Saving changes in PSP is roughly the same as saving a document with any other program. There are, however, some notable differences I thought I would mention here, before we get into any of the tasks in which you actually save anything.

Like lots of other programs, Paint Shop Pro can save your work for you automatically, as you continue to make changes. To use this feature, you must turn it on: Choose **File, Preferences, Autosave Settings** from the menu. Click **Enable Autosave**, adjust the number of **Minutes** between saves as desired, and click **OK.**

If you don't have PSP save changes for you automatically, you should get into the habit of saving them on your own. You'll know when there are unsaved changes to a file because PSP displays the image's filename in its title bar with an asterisk. To save new changes to the image file, click the **Save** button on the **Standard** toolbar. One important difference between PSP and other programs: *Saving changes does not prevent you from undoing them as needed.* So you don't lose the ability to undo an experimental change simply because you were thoughtful enough to save your own work.

If changes have not yet been saved, the filename appears with an asterisk in the title bar.

Another interesting thing you'll notice about PSP's Save commands is that there are three of them:

- **Save.** This command works as you might expect; it saves changes to the current file, overriding the existing version of the file.

- **Save As.** Use this command to save changes to another, separate file. After using this command, the original file is closed (without saving changes) and the new file (with the changes) is displayed.

- **Save Copy As.** This command is useful for saving versions of a work in progress. After processing this command, the original file remains displayed, without recent changes having been saved to the original image file. Changes are instead saved to a separate image file with a different filename, and that file is not opened in PSP after the save.

In the following tasks, you'll learn how to use each of these commands to their fullest.

38 Save an Image in Paint Shop Pro Format

Before beginning work on any image, you will most likely want to open it in Paint Shop Pro and then save it in Paint Shop Pro's native format, PSPImage. Doing so gives you access to all of Paint Shop Pro's features, such as alpha channels, layers, transparency, vector objects, and masking, while preserving the integrity of your original image's data.

After copying files from a digital camera onto your computer, or scanning images using a scanner, your first step should be to perform some type of backup. Typically, this involves burning copies of the image files onto a CD-R. After backing up your images, feel free to open them in PSP, save them in PSPImage format so you can access all of PSP's features, and then make adjustments before printing, emailing, or posting them on a Web site.

Before You Begin

✔ **37** About Saving

See Also

→ **39** Save an Image as Another File Type

→ **40** Convert a Group of Images to Another File Type

→ **41** Compress an Image Using GIF Format

→ **42** Compress an Image Using JPEG Format

→ **43** Compress an Image Using PNG Format

→ **44** Save a Copy of an Image

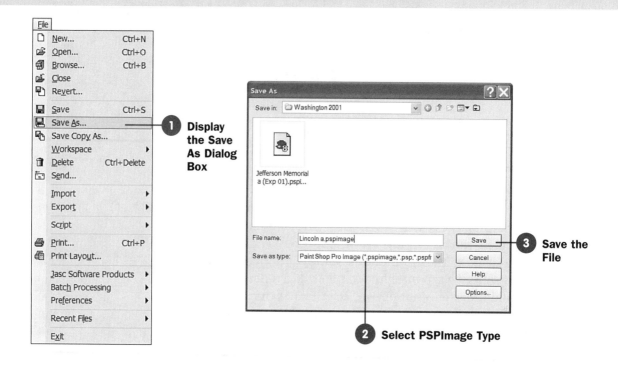

1 Display the Save As Dialog Box

2 Select PSPImage Type

3 Save the File

---

1 Display the Save As Dialog Box

Choose **File, Save As** from the menu bar. The **Save As** dialog box opens.

TIP

Paint Shop Pro fully supports EXIF, which means that you will not lose important digital camera data when you save your original file in PSP format (PSPImage).

2 Select PSPImage Type

If necessary, change to a new location in which to save the file by opening the **Save in** list and selecting a different folder. Type a new name for the file in the **File name** box. When saving an image in PSPImage format, you can use the same filename if you like; the PSP file will not override it because the two images will have different file extensions.

Finally, open the **Save as type** list and choose **Paint Shop Pro Image**. Rather than scrolling, you can press **P** to jump to the **Paint Shop Pro Image** file type.

3 **Save the File**

Click **Save.** The original image is closed and no changes are saved to it; instead, all changes are saved in a new file that uses PSPImage format.

39 Save an Image as Another File Type

You can save any image in a different format. You might do this, for example, to resave a file back to its original format after working on it for a while in PSPImage format. Typically, you'll save an image in a non-PSP format only after making all your changes to it.

1 **Display the Save As Dialog Box**

Choose **File, Save As** from the menu bar. The **Save As** dialog box opens.

2 **Select a File Type**

If necessary, change to a new location in which to save the file by opening the **Save in** list and selecting a different folder. Type a new name for the file if you like in the **File name** box. You can keep the image's original filename if you want; the new file will not override it because it will have a different file extension. Finally, open the **Save as type** list and choose the file type you want to use.

3 **Choose Options**

Click the **Options** button to display a list of options associated with the selected file type. The dialog box shown displays options associated with the TIFF file format.

After choosing any options, click **OK** to return to the **Save As** dialog box.

4 **Save the File**

Click **Save.** The original image is closed and no changes are saved to it; all changes are instead saved in a new file that uses the format options you selected.

Before You Begin

✔ **36** About Image Types

✔ **37** About Saving

See Also

→ **38** Save an Image in Paint Shop Pro Format

→ **44** Save a Copy of an Image

💡 TIP

If you want to save an image in GIF, JPEG, or PNG format, see **41** Compress an Image Using GIF Format, **42** Compress an Image Using JPEG Format, or **43** Compress an Image Using PNG Format.

💡 TIP

Rather than scrolling through the **Save as type** list, you can press the first letter of the file type name to jump to that file type. If more than one file type begins with that letter, the first file type will be selected, so make sure that you click the exact file type you want.

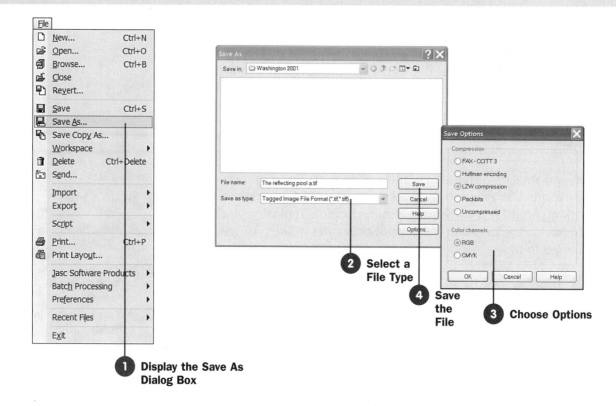

1 Display the Save As Dialog Box

2 Select a File Type

3 Choose Options

4 Save the File

---

40 Convert a Group of Images to Another File Type

Before You Begin

✔ **37** About Saving

✔ **57** Repeat Adjustments on Multiple Images Automatically

See Also

→ **39** Save an Image as Another File Type

→ **44** Save a Copy of an Image

It's easier than you might think to collect hundreds, if not thousands, of digital photos before you even realize it. Managing these photos can quickly become a full-time job if you don't establish a method for dealing with common tasks that are part of the process. Establish a routine for processing new images that includes copying the files to your computer, backing them up onto CD-R or similar media, and converting those you want to work with to PSP format or some other lossless format, such as TIFF. You should follow a similar process for images you copy to the computer using your scanner.

Luckily, Paint Shop Pro provides a method called Batch Conversion for easily converting a group of files from one format to another *all at once*. Actually, what happens is that PSP copies the original files and converts the copies—so this process is perfectly safe. If you're converting several images from your digital camera format to PSPImage, you might also want to run a *script* to process changes to them after conversion. For example, you could select the **One Step Photo Fix** script, which applies a series of common corrections such as **Auto Contrast** and **Auto Saturation** to the images.

1 Display the Batch Process Dialog Box

Choose **File, Batch, Process** from the menu bar. The **Batch Process** dialog box opens.

2 Select Files to Convert

If necessary, change to a different folder by opening the **Look in** list and selecting a folder. Limit the display of files by selecting the type you're looking for from the **Files of type** list. Then select the files you want to convert.

Select non-adjacent files by pressing **Ctrl** and clicking each one. Select files adjacent to each other by clicking the first file in the group, pressing **Shift**, and then clicking the last file. To quickly select all the files in the current folder, click **Select All**.

3 Select a Script to Run

If you want, you can run a script on the selected files to apply the same kind of changes to each one. PSP's own scripts are typically located in the **\Scripts**, **\Scripts-Restricted**, and **\Scripts-Trusted** subfolders of the **Paint Shop Pro 8** folder. To select a script, click the **Browse** button next to the **Script** box. Select the script file and click **Open.**

4 Select New Type Save Mode

Select the **New Type** option in the **Save Mode** pane. This option causes PSP to read the file, run the selected script (if any), and resave the file with its new name and type.

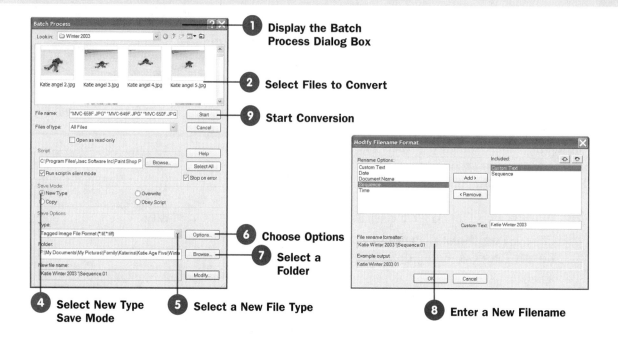

1 Display the Batch Process Dialog Box

2 Select Files to Convert

9 Start Conversion

6 Choose Options

7 Select a Folder

4 Select New Type Save Mode

5 Select a New File Type

8 Enter a New Filename

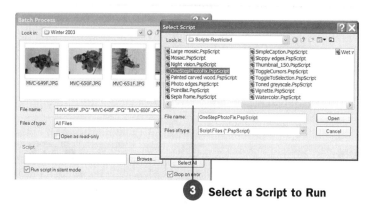

3 Select a Script to Run

The other **Save Mode** options require that you select a script: the **Copy** option creates a new file with a new name like the **New Type** option does; the **Overwrite** option overwrites the original file; the **Obey Script** option doesn't save the file but just runs the script.

5 **Select a New File Type**

Near the bottom of the **Batch Conversion** dialog box, open the **Type** list and select the file type to which you want to convert the selected files.

6 **Choose Options**

Click the **Options** button and set the options you want use with the file type you selected. Click **OK.**

7 **Select a Folder**

Click the **Browse** button next to the **Folder** text box and select the folder in which you want to save the converted files. Click **OK.**

8 **Enter a New Filename**

Digital photos straight from the camera have non-descriptive filenames such as **MVC-413G.JPG**. If you have a group of photo files with a common theme, you can rename them **Paris at Night 01**, followed by **02**, **03**, and so on in sequence. Click the **Modify** button to display the **Modify Filename Format** dialog box. Select a property from the **Rename Options** list and click **Add >**. The property name appears in the **Included** list on the right. Continue to select and add more properties as you like.

As you make your selections, a sample filename appears in the **Example output** area. When you're satisfied with all your choices, click **OK.**

9 **Start Conversion**

Click **Start**. A **Batch Progress** box is displayed. When the conversion process is complete, click **OK.**

NOTE

Some properties require further input from you. For example, if you choose the **Custom Text** property, you must type the text you want to use in the filename in the **Custom Text** box that appears. If you choose the **Date** or **Time** property, you can select the date/time format to use.

41 Compress an Image Using GIF Format

🔍KEY TERM

Dithering—A technique for
simulating a color whose
value does not appear in
an image's palette by mixing pixels of the two closest available shades, in
either a predefined or
mathematical pattern.

💡 TIP

Click the **Use Wizard** button in the **GIF Optimizer**
dialog box to let PSP make
more choices for you. If you
don't like the result, you
can always try the more
manual method described
in the steps.

As you learned in **36** **About Image Types**, GIF format is used
with images that contain a palette of 256 or fewer colors—
typically with large patches of one color, with line art images
such as cartoons and illustrations, and with images that contain
transparent backgrounds. You'll also find GIF format used to create
small, animated images such as a flag waving in the breeze.

Saving a file in GIF format gives you a number of options, such
as how you want color variations to be simulated and whether
you want transparency. The latter is a sticky issue, not only
because there are so many ways you might have varied transparency in your original image (reducing the opacity of a layer,
feathering a selection, or using a brush with a lower opacity
level), but also because GIF supports transparency only in an "all
or nothing" manner. So if you have semi-transparent pixels in
an image, you must tell GIF what to do with them: change them
to a fully opaque pixel or simulate partial transparency by
dithering, or "sprinkling" totally opaque pixels throughout the
transparent region, either by means of a regular pattern or a
mathematical formula. To make it easier for you to make the
right selections when saving GIF files, I present them here as a
separate task.

❶ Display the GIF Optimizer

Choose **File, Export, GIF Optimizer** from the menu bar.
The **GIF Optimizer** opens.

If you have the **Save As** dialog box already open, select
CompuServe Graphics Interchange from the **Save as
type** list, click **Options**, and then click **Run Optimizer**.

❷ Select Transparency Level

The left preview is the uncompressed image in its native format; the right preview shows how the image will appear if
you compress it using the choices you make in the optimizer. The sizes of the uncompressed and compressed image
files are shown beneath the corresponding previews.

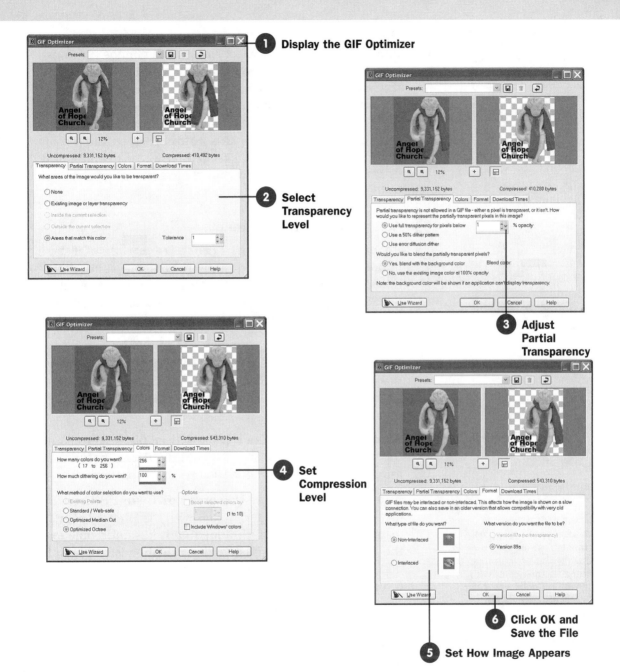

1 Display the GIF Optimizer

2 Select Transparency Level

3 Adjust Partial Transparency

4 Set Compression Level

6 Click OK and Save the File

5 Set How Image Appears

TIP

You can choose a color from the image that you want to make transparent by simply clicking on it with the color picker.

On the **Transparency** tab, if you don't want to use transparency in this image, select **None.** If the image contains transparent pixels and you want them retained, select **Existing image or layer transparency**. If necessary, choose **Inside** or **Outside the current selection.** To replace pixels of a particular color with transparent ones, select **Areas that match this color**. Then choose a color from the picker and set the **Tolerance** value to enable PSP to register colors similar to your choice as transparent as well.

③ Adjust Partial Transparency

If you selected **None** on the **Transparency** tab, or if the image does not contain partially transparent pixels, skip this step. Otherwise, on the **Partial Transparency** tab, tell PSP how to change the partially transparent pixels into opaque ones:

Choose **Use full transparency for pixels below XX% opacity** to change the partially transparent pixels to fully transparent, using the tolerance value you set. Partially transparent pixels above this opacity are changed to fully opaque.

Alternatively, choose **Use a 50% dither pattern** to blend the partially transparent pixels with the **Blend color** you select by means of a "checkerboard" dither pattern.

NOTE

In the 50% dither and error diffusion methods, partially transparent pixels are changed to opaque ones by blending their color with the **Blend color** you select. These pixels are then placed near fully transparent pixels using the 50% dither or error diffusion pattern.

As a third option, choose **Use error diffusion dither** to blend partially transparent pixels with the **Blend color**, using a mathematical technique that is less noticeable to the viewer. The error diffusion dither method is best used for a PSP image whose native palette contains more than 256 colors; otherwise, use the 50% dither pattern.

To blend partly transparent pixels with a color of your choice (creating opaque pixels), choose **Yes** and select a blend color by clicking the **Blend color** sample and making a selection from the **Color** dialog box or from the image window. To retain the color of all partially transparent pixels and to simply make them entirely opaque, choose **No**.

4 Set Compression Level

On the **Colors** tab, you can adjust the amount of compression used by changing various options. To reduce the number of colors in the image, change the **How many colors do you want** value.

To reduce the side effects caused by using a smaller number of colors, increase the amount of dithering by changing the **How much dithering do you want** value. You might not want to use dithering on an image that has large solid blocks of color—for instance, comics art—because the dithering might produce unwanted dots of color in those areas.

Next, choose which range of colors to use in the reduced color palette. To make sure that the image appears the same on most computers, choose **Standard/Web-safe**. To create a palette that better fits the colors in your GIF image, PSP offers two alternative palette creation methods: **Optimized Median Cut** uses ordinary averaging to determine the most common color values throughout the entire image; **Optimized Octree** subdivides the image into quadrants and subquadrants, and determines the most often-used colors based on their distribution throughout these regions.

If you select **Optimized Median Cut**, you can select a region of colors in your image before you launch the **GIF Optimizer** so the Optimizer can give those colors priority when creating the palette. Choose **Boost selected colors by** and set a relative "boost factor" between 1 and 10. Preferential treatment for certain colors created by the **Boost selected colors by** option comes at the expense of others; for example, if you select a generally blue region of your image for boosting, a greater priority will be set for creating blue slots in the palette, but orange slots will suffer most.

If the image will be used mostly onscreen by Windows users (in PowerPoint, for example), choose **Include Windows' colors** to include its array of 32 standard colors among the other colors being generated.

 TIP

Each time you reduce the total number of colors by a factor of two (from 256 to 128, from 128 to 64, from 64 to 32, from 32 to 16) you reduce the file size. When reducing colors, be sure to zoom in on any anti-aliased (round) edges to verify that they don't suddenly appear jagged.

 TIP

Determine which optimization method is best for your image by experimenting. **Median Cut** is generally best for images with widely varied colors, and **Octree** is best for images with many subtle variations for one basic hue.

TIP

Before saving the file, click the **Download Times** tab and view how your selections affect the size of the file and its approximate download time. Feel free to return to any of the tabs and make changes as needed to adjust the download time.

5 Set How Image Appears

Click the **Format** tab and select how you want the image to appear on a user's system when it's downloaded from the Web. The GIF file can be made to appear one line at a time from the top down (**Non-Interlaced**), or in several cycles, with details filled in gradually (**Interlaced**).

6 Click OK and Save the File

When you are done making choices, click **OK**. The standard Windows **Save As** dialog box opens. In the **File name** box, type a name for the compressed file. Click **Save** to save the image.

42 Compress an Image Using JPEG Format

Before You Begin

✔ **36** About Image Types

✔ **37** About Saving

See Also

→ **40** Convert a Group of Images to Another File Type

→ **41** Compress an Image Using GIF Format

→ **43** Compress an Image Using PNG Format

NOTE

If your photograph contains added text, you'll get better results if you compress the image using JPEG 2000 format. With JPEG format (especially at mid to high compression levels), a lot of artifacts are created around the edges of the text. Yet at these same compression levels, the photograph looks fine.

In **36** **About Image Types**, you learned that JPEG images are typically photographs or other complex images with lots of colors or variations in tone. Among the chief purposes for the creation of the JPEG format was to achieve very small file sizes; however, the degree of compression you apply to a JPEG image is variable—from none at all to a level so high you can no longer tell what the image is. The most important point to remember about JPEG format is that you should use it to save a PSP image project only when you are done manipulating the image. Constantly changing and resaving a JPEG file can generate artifacts and other degradations to the image.

One of the key options you'll find in PSP's **JPEG Optimizer** concerns a methodology called *chroma subsampling*, a compression technique that takes advantage of the fact that the human eye will recognize fluctuations in brightness or luminance before it notices variations in color. The idea is to compress a file by saving the difference in brightness between pixels, while sacrificing some color differences because they aren't noticed anyway. Thus, in a compressed JPEG file, the individual brightness of each pixel is saved, while the color of each pixel is determined by the dominant *chroma* in a block of pixels (typically two pixels wide by two pixels high). PSP's **JPEG Optimizer** lets you change the size of the subsampling block, including turning it off altogether. Disengaging subsampling eliminates one factor in the generation of artifacts and graininess, especially in portions of images that depict thin, multicolored stripes, like those on a shirt or flag. You can also increase subsampling to make files even smaller— although the result might be that your colors seem washed out.

1 ## Display the JPEG Optimizer

Choose **File, Export, JPEG Optimizer.** The **JPEG Optimizer** appears. To display the optimizer from within the **Save As** dialog box, select **JPEG** from the **Save as type** list, click **Options**, and then click **Run Optimizer**.

2 ## Set Compression Level

The left preview pane displays the uncompressed image; the right preview pane shows how the image will look when compressed using the selections you've made so far. The file's compressed and uncompressed size is also shown just below the corresponding image.

On the **Quality** tab, adjust the compression level by changing the **Set compression value to** value. The higher the number, the more the file is compressed (made smaller). However, at high compression levels, a loss of quality will occur.

3 ## Set Chroma Subsampling

The mode you choose from the **Chroma subsampling** list determines the type of information removed from the JPEG file to reduce its size. The default mode, **2×2 1×1 1×1**, is typically a good choice. The first number, **2×2**, describes the sample size (2 pixels vertically by 2 pixels horizontally); **1×1** describes the number of pixels sampled from that area to create the coordinate for the blue to yellow axis; while the third number, **1×1**, indicates that a similar number of pixels is sampled to create the coordinate for the red to green chroma axis.

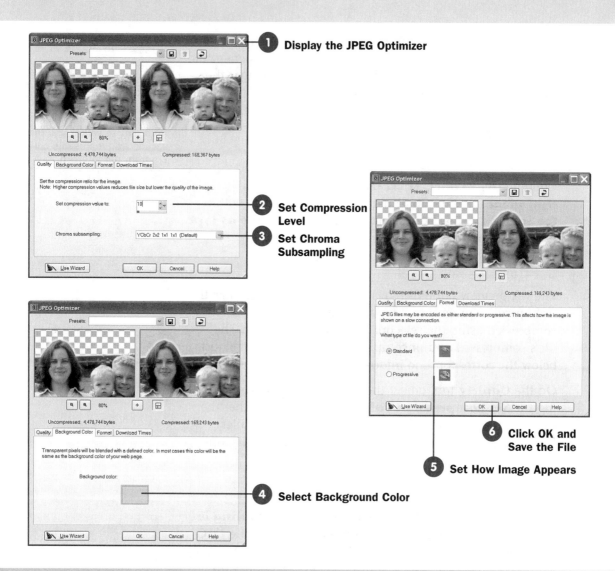

1 Display the JPEG Optimizer

2 Set Compression Level

3 Set Chroma Subsampling

6 Click OK and Save the File

5 Set How Image Appears

4 Select Background Color

Alternately, 1×1 1×1 1×1 (essentially no subsampling) might provide a higher quality image (that's also larger in size) but makes little sense when compressing an image from a digital camera because digital cameras do not store chroma information at that frequency. So you end up with a larger file size with no improvement in quality over the 2×2 1×1 1×1 choice.

4 Select Background Color

If the image contains transparent pixels, a **Background Color** tab appears. Click the **Background color** picker and select the color you want to blend with these pixels. Typically, you'll want to set the **Background color** to the same color as your Web page so that the non-transparent part of your image can "float" on top of the background seamlessly.

5 Set How Image Appears

Click the **Format** tab and select how you want the image to appear on a user's system when it's downloaded from the Web. The JPEG file can be made to appear one line at a time from the top down (**Standard**), or in several cycles, with details filled in gradually (**Progressive**).

6 Click OK and Save the File

When you are through making changes click **OK**. The standard Windows **Save As** dialog box opens. In the **File name** box, type a name for the compressed file. Click **Save** to save the image.

> **TIP**
>
> Because digital still camera technology is derived directly from video camera technology, most digital cameras subsample along the horizontal axis. So you could conceivably choose 2×1 1×1 1×1 (for vertical images) or 1×2 1×1 1×1 (for horizontal images) for maximum resolution from a digital camera photo—or even 4×1 for an image captured from digital video—without loss of data.

> **TIP**
>
> Before saving the file, click the **Download Times** tab and view how your selections affect the size of the file and its approximate download time. You can return to any of the tabs and make changes as desired.

---

43 Compress an Image Using PNG Format

As you learned in **36** **About Image Types**, PNG is a file format that's compatible with certain Web browsers, but not all. Because it isn't uniformly accepted as a Web format, you might not want to use PNG images on your Web site. PNG format, like GIF and JPEG formats, offers a variable amount of compression, depending on the choices you make in the **PNG Optimizer**. Unlike JPEG, PNG offers a lossless compression method.

1 Display the PNG Optimizer

Choose **File, Export, PNG Optimizer.** To start the **PNG Optimizer** from within the **Save As** dialog box, select **Portable Network Graphics** from the **Save as type** list, click the **Options** button, and then click **Run Optimizer**.

Before You Begin

✔ **36** About Image Types

✔ **37** About Saving

See Also

→ **40** Convert a Group of Images to Another File Type

→ **41** Compress an Image Using GIF Format

→ **42** Compress an Image Using JPEG Format

2 Set Compression Level

The left preview pane displays the uncompressed image; the right preview pane shows how the image will look when compressed using the selections you make in the dialog box. The file's compressed and uncompressed size is shown just below the corresponding image.

On the **Colors** tab, you can adjust the amount of compression through the choices you make. To reduce the number of colors in the image, choose either **Grayscale** or **Palette-Based.**

If you choose **Palette-Based**, additional options appear. Select the number of colors to place in the palette by adjusting the **How many colors** value. Reduce the effect of using a smaller number of colors by adjusting the amount of dithering with the **How much dithering** box.

You can improve quality in an image with a small color palette by selecting the optimal range of colors. To make sure that the image appears the same on most computers, choose **Standard/Web-safe**. Otherwise, experiment by choosing either **Optimized Median Cut** or **Optimized Octree**.

If the image will be used mostly onscreen by Windows users (in PowerPoint, for example), choose **Include Windows' colors** to have the image's palette include Windows' standard array of 32 colors.

3 Select Transparency Level

On the **Transparency** tab, if you don't want to use transparency, select the **No transparency** option. If you want to use transparency in the image, you can choose between **Single color transparency** and **Alpha channel transparency.** Because transparency is one of the features not universally supported by Web browsers, you might not want to use transparency in your PNG image. In particular, the alpha channel in a PNG file allows you to store pixels of varying degrees of transparency regardless of color; however, this feature is not supported by Internet Explorer.

 TIP

You might not want to use dithering on an image that has only large solid blocks of color because the dithering might produce unwanted dots of color in those areas.

 TIP

If you've selected an area in advance whose colors you want preserved, and you selected **Optimized Median Cut** to determine the color palette, choose **Boost selected colors by** and set a boost factor from 1 to 10.

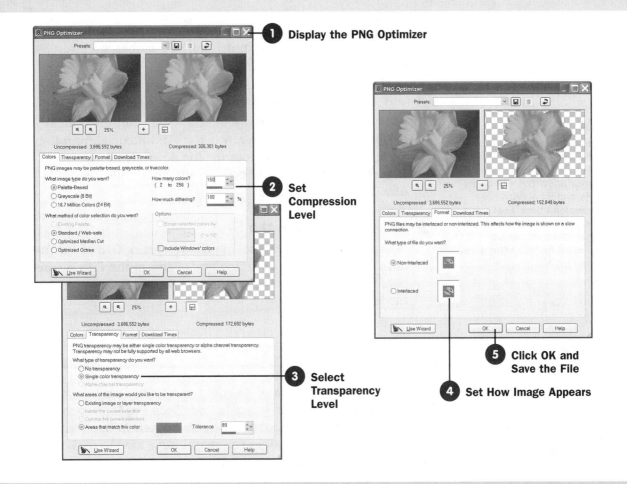

1 Display the PNG Optimizer

2 Set Compression Level

3 Select Transparency Level

4 Set How Image Appears

5 Click OK and Save the File

If the image contains transparent pixels and you want to retain them, select **Existing image or layer transparency**. If you've selected an area of the image in advance that represents the portion you want to make transparent, choose **Inside the current selection**. If the area you've selected represents the portion you want to leave opaque, choose **Outside the current selection**.

To replace pixels of a particular color with transparent ones, select **Areas that match this color**. Then choose a color from the color picker or use the dropper to sample a color from the image itself. Set the **Tolerance** factor to either a low level (for exact color matching) or a higher level (to allow for variation).

4 Set How Image Appears

Click the **Format** tab and select how you want the image to appear on a user's system when it's downloaded from the Web: one line at a time from the top down (**Non-Interlaced**) or in several cycles, with details filled in gradually (**Interlaced**).

5 Click OK and Save the File

When you are through making changes, click **OK**. The standard Windows **Save As** dialog box opens. In the **File name** box, type a name for the compressed file. Click **Save** to save the image.

💡 TIP

Before clicking **OK**, click the **Download Times** tab and view how your selections affect the size of the file and its approximate download time. Feel free to return to any of the tabs and make changes as needed to adjust the download time.

---

44 Save a Copy of an Image

Before You Begin

✔ **37** About Saving

See Also

→ **40** Convert a Group of Images to Another File Type

When you use the **File, Save As** command to save an image as described in **38** **Save an Image in Paint Shop Pro Format**, the open image is closed without changes, and a new image is created using any unsaved changes you might have tried to make to the original image. Sometimes, you want to continue to work on your open image, and yet save a copy of what you've done so far in a different file. This way, you can track your progress in stages and give yourself "fallback positions" you can return to if you decide to abandon new changes.

1 Display the Save Copy As Dialog Box

Choose **File, Save Copy As** from the menu bar. The **Save Copy As** dialog box opens.

1 Display the Save Copy As Dialog Box

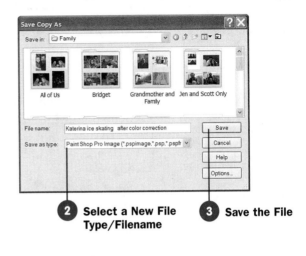

2 Select a New File Type/Filename

3 Save the File

2 Select a New File Type/Filename

If necessary, change to a new location in which to save the file by opening the **Save in** list and selecting a different folder. If desired, type a new name in the **File name** box. If you don't change the filename, you should select a different file type by opening the **Save as type** list and choosing a type from those listed.

3 Save the File

Click **Save.** The original image remains open and no changes are saved to it; all changes are instead saved to the new file.

TIP

You must change either the filename or file type to prevent overriding your original file.

 Prepare an Image for the Web

Before You Begin

✔ **29** Change Image Size or Resolution

✔ **36** About Image Types

✔ **57** Repeat Adjustments on Multiple Images Automatically

NOTE

PNG format is only partly compatible with most Web browsers; a PNG image might not appear correctly, if at all, especially if it uses partial transparency. With some third-party plug-ins, JPEG 2000 images can be viewed with most Web browsers.

If you want to use an image on a Web page, your most important consideration when preparing it for publication is its file type. Of all the types you can choose, only three are compatible with the majority of Web browsers: GIF, JPEG, and PNG. Use GIF format for drawn art or images that use a limited color palette to reduce bandwidth and download time (speeding up the loading of the Web page). GIF is also useful for including transparency in the image, especially along the borders, as you might want to do when you want the image to appear as an integral part of a Web page instead of something just glued to it. PNG can be used in place of GIF format because it offers the possibility of smaller files with faster load times. Use JPEG for digital photos or images with a large color palette.

After choosing a file type that suits the image, you'll want to use the optimizers that come with PSP to help you compress it. Compression reduces the time a user has to wait to download the image from the Web. In a situation where your image is a photograph that appears as part of a gallery—for instance, recent snapshots of your family—you can reduce download time for the Web page by creating a thumbnail for each image. Thumbnails are miniatures of the images that load more quickly, providing your user with small previews of the actual images. You can set up your Web page so that clicking the thumbnail triggers downloading of the original, larger image. This gives a user with a slow Internet connection the option to not display larger images that might take a long time to appear. In this task, you'll learn how to create image thumbnails. Even if you don't plan on creating your own Web pages for images, you might want to create thumbnails for attaching to email messages or uploading to Shutterfly, an image-sharing Web site you can use to share images with designated recipients.

① Open an Image

Open the image for which you want to create a thumbnail by clicking the **Open** button on the **Standard** toolbar, selecting the image's filename, and clicking **Open**.

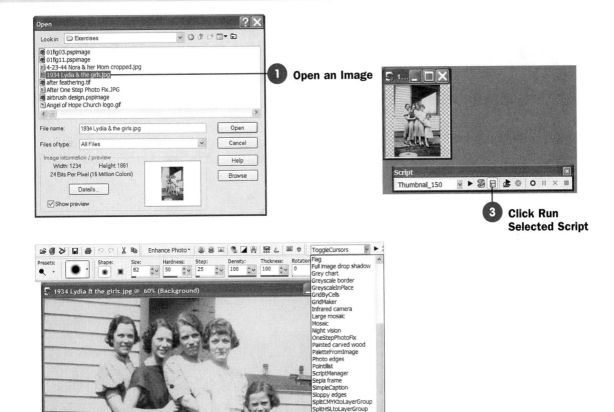

1 Open an Image

3 Click Run
Selected Script

2 Select Thumbnail Script

2 Select Thumbnail Script

On the **Script** toolbar, from the **Select Script** list, choose
Thumbnail_150.

NOTE

The **Thumbnail 150** script resizes the image so that one of its dimensions is 150 pixels. If you want larger thumbnails, create your own script. See **29** Change Image Size or Resolution and **57** Repeat Adjustments on Multiple Images Automatically.

3 **Click Run Selected Script**

Click the **Run Selected Script** button on the **Script** toolbar. The script processes its commands automatically, resizing the image proportionately to a standard thumbnail size, where the width or height—whichever is larger—is scaled back to 150 pixels.

Be sure to save the image with a new name, so that you don't override the regularly sized image with the new thumbnail.

6

Making Quick Corrections to a Photograph

IN THIS CHAPTER:

TIP

Even if PSP's automatic adjustment tools leave you with less than satisfactory results, it's always worth the time to try them out as a first course of action. You can always undo changes you don't like, or leave them and make further adjustments manually.

Sometimes, no matter how careful you are when taking a picture, something goes wrong to make it less than perfect. Perhaps it turned out too dark or overexposed. Perhaps the focus isn't as sharp as it could be. Or—as is often the case when you shoot portraits—your image is sideways and should be tipped 90 degrees. After you have the photo, it doesn't matter why it isn't what it should be—your focus is on making it better. Paint Shop Pro provides you with a sophisticated array of tools you can use to improve your digital images. Some of these tools work automatically, without further input from you. It's these tools I'll discuss in this chapter.

46 About Common Corrections

See Also

→ **5** Scan an Image

→ **7** Import Images from a Digital Camera

→ **38** Save an Image in Paint Shop Pro Format

→ **57** Repeat Adjustments on Multiple Images Automatically

There are certain changes you will find yourself making to almost every image, even if the changes are just experimental. But before you start, you need to give yourself a safety net. Follow these steps:

1. Copy the image from your camera's medium (memory device or diskette), or from your scanner, to your hard disk.

2. Immediately back up the original image to some type of permanent media, such as CD-R. When you work with one image at a time, be sure to copy it to a folder that contains only original, nonretouched images. Back up the entire folder at your earliest convenience.

3. Open the image in Paint Shop Pro and save a working copy of it in PSPImage format. This format allows you to work on the image using all of PSP's digital correcting tools, save changes as often as you like, revert to saved copies when an experiment you attempt turns out wrong, and not worry about accidentally introducing artifacts.

4. After you're done making changes to a photo, save it in a portable format that's compatible with its use. For example, if you want to share the image through email, choose some type of format that compresses it (makes it smaller) without noticeably affecting its quality, such as JPEG, JP2, PNG, or TIFF. To include the image on a Web page, you should only use JPEG, GIF, or PNG format. To send the image out for printing, you'll most likely need to use JPEG or TIFF.

After converting an image to PSPImage format, you can make any number of quick corrections to it. These adjustments, which require very little (if any) input on your part, include the following:

- Rotating, flipping, and straightening an image.

- Cropping an image to remove distracting detail and to improve composition.

- Applying a "quick fix"—a series of automatic adjustments that fix the color balance, contrast, saturation, and sharpness of an image.

- Applying automatic adjustments that fix one specific problem, such as brightness/contrast, color saturation, color balance, or sharpness.

- Changing the print size of an image while maintaining its quality (resolution).

- Adding a blank work area around an image to create a greeting card, picture frame, and so on.

In this chapter, you'll learn how to apply each of these quick changes to an image. If the quick changes discussed in this chapter do not fix the image enough, you can apply manual changes as described in later chapters.

You can undo any change you make, *even after you save an image (as long as you don't close it)*, by simply clicking the **Undo** button. You can back through a series of recent changes by repeatedly clicking **Undo**. You can click **Undo** multiple times in any image, even if it uses some format other than PSPImage.

You can make the changes listed here without converting an image to PSPImage format first, but you really should use PSPImage as your working format whenever possible because it provides access to all of PSP's features.

You can convert a group of images to another file type such as PSPImage and, at the same time, apply a quick fix correction to them. See **40** **Convert a Group of Images to Another File Type** and **57** **Repeat Adjustments on Multiple Images Automatically**.

47 Rotate an Image

Before You Begin

✔ **46** About Common Corrections

See Also

→ **48** Flip an Image Horizontally

→ **49** Flip an Image Vertically

→ **50** Straighten an Image

NOTE

You can rotate an image by any amount—not just 90 degrees—to straighten its contents. For example, you might want the horizon in your beach shot to appear perfectly horizontal, or the side of a building not to appear to be leaning. See **50** Straighten an Image. After you've straightened the image, however, the borders of your image won't be square. Crop the image to correct this problem. See **51** Crop a Portion of an Image.

You can also rotate images in 90-degree increments using Photo Album. Open the image for editing, click the arrow on the **Rotate** button, and select **Rotate Right** or **Rotate Left**. You can also just click the **Rotate** button to rotate the image in the direction shown on the button.

When a digital camera stores an image, it orients the image with the longest side displayed horizontally, regardless of how you took the picture. So, if you rotate the camera vertically, perhaps to shoot a picture of a standing figure, tree, building, or other tall subject, the image will be saved sideways, and it will appear that way when you open it in PSP. Often, one of the first "corrections" you'll ever do on an image is to orient it so that the subject is "heads up." Images can be quickly rotated clockwise or counter-clockwise 90 degrees as desired.

1 **Choose Image, Rotate**

Choose **Image, Rotate** from the menu bar. The **Rotate** submenu opens.

2 **Choose Direction**

Click **Rotate Clockwise 90** (to rotate the image 90 degrees to the right) or **Rotate Counter-clockwise 90** (to rotate the image 90 degrees to the left). All layers in the image are rotated in the direction chosen.

If you want to rotate a single layer, or rotate by something other than 90 degrees, select **Free Rotate** from the **Rotate** menu, enter the number of degrees to rotate in the **Free** box, select a direction (**Right** or **Left**), turn off the **All layers** option if desired, and click **OK**.

3 **View the Result**

Here's what the scarecrow and Dorothy image looks like after rotating it counter-clockwise 90 degrees.

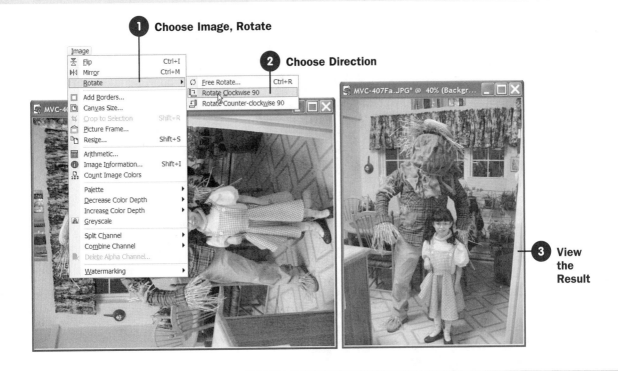

1 Choose Image, Rotate

2 Choose Direction

3 View the Result

---

48 Flip an Image Horizontally

Flipping and rotating an image are two different things. *Rotating an image* pivots it on its center point. Imagine looking down on a spinning top, and you'll get the idea. To understand what *flipping an image* does, imagine a horizontal bar across the middle of the image over which the image "falls," like a gymnast flipping over one of the uneven bars during a routine. Typically, you'll find yourself rotating an image to restore the ground to the bottom instead of the side. You might find yourself flipping an image you scanned in if your original photo was inserted upside down.

1 Choose Image, Flip

Choose **Image, Flip** from the menu bar, or press **Ctrl+I**. The image is flipped horizontally.

Before You Begin

✔ **46** About Common Corrections

See Also

→ **47** Rotate an Image

→ **49** Flip an Image Vertically

NOTE

You can flip an image while editing it in Photo Album if you like; just choose **Image, Flip, Horizontal** while editing the image.

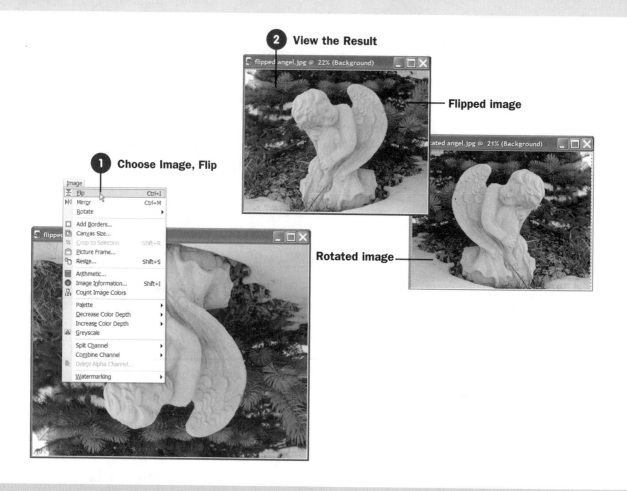

2 View the Result

Flipped image

Choose Image, Flip **1**

Rotated image

---

2 **View the Result**

After flipping the angel image horizontally, the angel is upright, its head still on the left, and its wings remain on the right. If you rotate the image 180 degrees after you flip it, the angel's head is on the right, and its wings are on the left—the opposite of their positions in the original image.

49 Flip an Image Vertically

Flipping an image vertically allows you to change how objects face in a photograph. Suppose that you are creating an invitation to your daughter's birthday party, with text on the right and a space for a photo on the left. While browsing through recent photographs of your daughter, you spot a great shot of little Benita looking to her left. If you flip the image vertically, it will appear as if Benita is looking at the invitation text, rather than away from it—and you'll look as if you'd planned the card layout months ago when the photo was taken.

Flipping vertically is called "mirroring" in Paint Shop Pro. Mirroring flips an image over a vertical bar running down the middle of the image. If you imagine the image etched on a piece of glass and then skewered on the center pole of a carousel, you'll get the idea.

1 **Choose Image, Mirror**

Choose **Image, Mirror** from the menu bar, or press **Ctrl+M**. The image is flipped vertically.

2 **View the Result**

After mirroring the image, the man is facing left, and his daughter is facing right—exactly the opposite of what they were doing in the original photograph.

Before You Begin

✔ **46** About Common Corrections

See Also

→ **47** Rotate an Image

→ **48** Flip an Image Horizontally

 NOTE

To flip an image vertically while editing it in Photo Album, choose **Image, Flip, Vertical**.

NOTE

If you're selling your images for use in a publication of any type, make your editors aware of any changes you make that alter the "truth" of an image. For example increasing an image's contrast simply improves its quality, whereas flipping a cup upside down that wasn't in the original photo alters its "reality."

① Choose Image, Mirror

Flip an Image Vertically

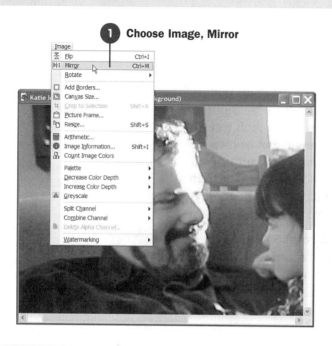

② View the Result

50 Straighten an Image

Before You Begin

✔ **46** About Common Corrections

See Also

→ **47** Rotate an Image

→ **51** Crop a Portion of an Image

→ **87** Repair Holes and Tears

→ **137** Change Perspective

 TIP

To straighten part of an image, move that portion to its own layer.

In Paint Shop Pro, straightening an image is simply the process of rotating it by just a few degrees. The main reason for straightening an image is to draw the viewer's attention away from distractions such as a sidewalk running downhill, a slanting horizon, a pole that's leaning to one side, and so on. You might also use this technique to deliberately place an image on a slant to make it more interesting for use on a greeting card, Web page, scrapbook page, and so on.

PSP's **Straighten** tool is a line that you arrange on an image to help tell PSP what part of your image isn't straight. In the image window, the line starts out horizontal, with nodes on both sides called "rotation points." You arrange the line by placing these two rotation points along the edge of the object you want to straighten, such as the side of a building or the horizon. PSP determines just how non-straight this line is and straightens it, straightening the image by exactly the same amount.

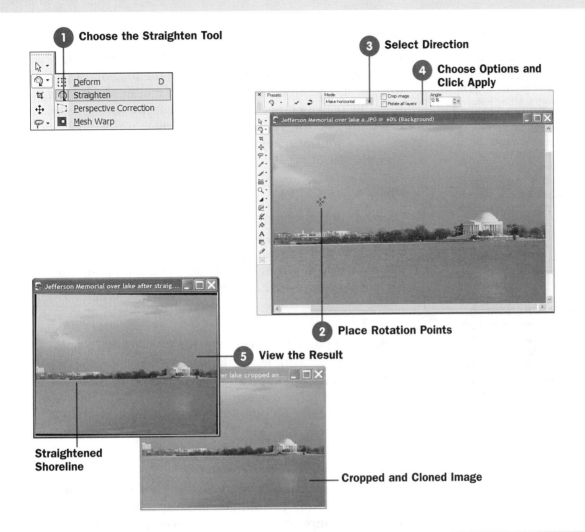

① **Choose the Straighten Tool**

③ **Select Direction**

④ **Choose Options and Click Apply**

② **Place Rotation Points**

⑤ **View the Result**

Straightened Shoreline

Cropped and Cloned Image

After straightening an image, empty spots will appear along the sides of the image; you might want to crop to remove these areas. As an alternative, you can use the **Clone Brush** tool as explained in **87** Repair Holes and Tears to "paint in" the empty areas with colors and details from other parts of the photograph.

You might also want to do more than straighten an image—you might want to adjust its perspective. See **137** Change Perspective.

NOTE

It's not easy to perfectly straighten an image in Photo Album, but you can easily rotate it in any direction to create a special effect. Choose **Image, Rotate, Free**. Then drag the image right or left with the mouse pointer to rotate it in that direction.

NOTE

Suppose that you have a photo in which the subject appears crooked but the background seems straight, or vice versa. Using selection tools, you can separate the elements into different layers, and then use the **Straighten** tool to straighten just one and leave the other as it is. You will then have to use various tools to paint in the gaps. For more on layer separations, see **79** Copy a Selection to a New Layer.

 TIP

The rotation points must lie perfectly on the edge you want to straighten, or PSP will not be able to make the proper correction. To move the entire line closer to the non-straight edge, click and drag the line anywhere between the rotation points.

 NOTE

Regardless of whether the image is straightened vertically or horizontally, the straighten bar still appears in a horizontal position after straightening. That makes it easy for you to use it again to straighten the image some more. If you like the results, simply click another tool to remove the bar.

1 Choose the Straighten Tool

In the **Layer** palette, choose the layer to straighten, and then choose the **Straighten** tool from the toolbar. (If you want to straighten all layers, it doesn't matter which layer is currently active.) If necessary, click the arrow on the second tool button on the **Tools** toolbar to display the complete list of image transformation tools and then select **Straighten** from the list.

2 Place Rotation Points

Drag one of the rotation points at either end of the bar that appears on the image, placing it on the edge of the object to be straightened. For example, drag a rotation point and place it on the horizon. Drag the other rotation point and place it elsewhere on that same edge.

3 Select Direction

In the **Mode** list on the **Tool Options** palette, choose the orientation you want for the line once it has become straight: **Make horizontal** or **Make vertical**. If the line is *almost* horizontal or *almost* vertical, you can leave this option set to **Auto** because PSP can easily guess what you want.

4 Choose Options and Click Apply

Enable the **Crop image** check box in the **Tool Options** palette if you want PSP to automatically crop the image to remove the empty areas that will appear after it straightens the image. Note that some image content alongside those empty areas will be cropped as well.

Enable the **Rotate all layers** check box to have PSP rotate all layers of the image at the same time, by the same amount.

Click the **Apply** button (the check mark) on the **Tool Options** palette to straighten the image. Click any other tool to cancel changes.

⑤ View the Result

Because I didn't enable the **Crop image** check box, the straightened image has some gaps on either side, as shown in the image on the left. On the right is the image after I cropped it to fit a common print size (4" × 6") and painted with the **Clone Brush** tool to fill in the gaps I didn't crop out.

51 Crop a Portion of an Image

Cropping an image might allow you to improve it in several different ways. For example, you might crop to remove a distraction such as a truck from the left side of an image. Or you might crop to improve an image's composition—placing your subject on a crucial "focal point" (one of four points that are one-third of the way in from two connecting sides, such as the top and left sides). Finally, you might crop an image before printing to make it proportional to a standard print size such as 3.5" × 5" or 8" × 10", or to size it for use with an object of specific size, such as a business card or CD insert.

Paint Shop Pro gives you many methods to crop your image. You can crop it manually to any size using the **Crop** tool, or you can load a preset such as **4 × 6 in horizontal** or **Postcard horizontal** to crop an image to that exact size. As you crop, a rectangle appears on the image. The area inside this rectangle is kept, while the area outside the rectangle is discarded.

① Choose the Crop Tool

Click the **Crop** tool on the **Tools** toolbar.

② Select Preset if Desired

If you're cropping an image to fit a particular print size, click the arrow on the **Presets** button, select a preset from those listed (such as **CD insert**), and click **OK**. To manually select the size of the area you want to keep, skip this step.

Before You Begin

✔ **46** About Common Corrections

See Also

→ **50** Straighten an Image

Cropping—The process of selecting a portion of an image to keep. Unselected portions are permanently removed.

TIP

You can select a nonrectangular portion of an image using any of the selection tools, and crop to that selection. The area outside the selection is filled with the current background color. Use this technique to create photo vignettes, as explained in **142** Age a Photograph.

TIP

If there isn't a preset that matches your exact size requirements, you can enter a **Width** and **Height** measurement on the **Tool Options** palette.

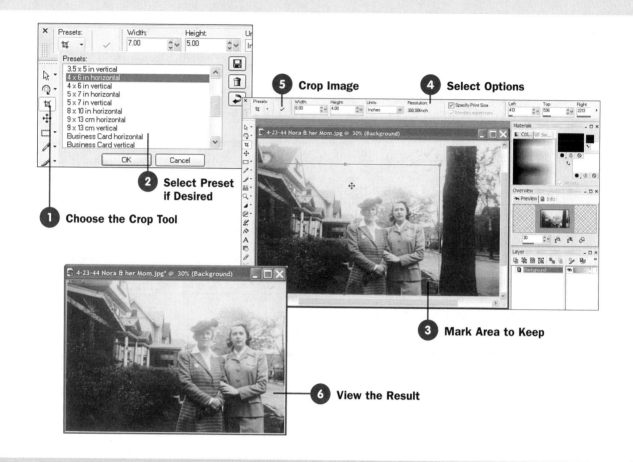

5 Crop Image

4 Select Options

2 Select Preset if Desired

1 Choose the Crop Tool

3 Mark Area to Keep

6 View the Result

3 Mark Area to Keep

If you skipped step 2, drag the **Crop** tool to select the portion of the image you want to crop: Start at the upper-left corner of the area to keep and drag down to the lower-right corner. A rectangle appears, marking the cropped area. You can adjust the size of the cropping rectangle by dragging one of its sides or a corner. You can adjust the position of the cropped area by clicking in the middle of the rectangle and dragging it around the image.

If you selected a preset in step 2, a cropping rectangle appears on the image. Move the rectangle around the image to adjust the area to crop. Resize the area proportionately by dragging a corner.

4 Select Options

Select other options from the **Tool Options** palette as desired. Enable the **Specify Print Size** check box if you want to crop to a desired print size rather than to an image size. See **35** **About Size and Resolution** for more information. Enable the **Maintain aspect ratio** check box to maintain the image's original height/width ratio in the cropped region.

5 Crop Image

Click **Apply** (the check mark) on the **Tool Options** palette to crop the image; right-click the image to cancel the cropping attempt. After cropping, the area outside the cropping rectangle is discarded. To undo the crop, click the **Undo** button.

6 View the Result

After cropping this image of Grandma and my mom, the annoying tree is eliminated, and the composition becomes more interesting. Notice how the ladies are now positioned on one of the four possible focal points. This arrangement makes your eyes automatically look first at their faces. I still have to adjust their contrast, but the image is already much improved.

NOTE

If you expand the **Tool Options** palette, you'll see some additional options on the far right. The **Left**, **Top**, **Right**, and **Bottom** values are coordinates that mark the corners of the cropped region. You can use them to crop the same area on several images. The **Snap crop rectangle to** options allow you to crop precisely around a currently selected region or an opaque (non-transparent) area of the current layer or layers.

52 **About the Photo Toolbar**

Before You Begin

✔ **46** About Common
 Corrections

See Also

➡ **53** Apply a Quick Fix

➡ **54** Achieve Color
 Balance
 Automatically

➡ **55** Adjust Brightness
 and Contrast
 Automatically

➡ **56** Adjust Saturation
 Automatically

TIP

If the **Photo** toolbar is not displayed, make it reappear by selecting **View, Toolbars, Photo**.

KEY TERM

Black and white points— Items in a photo that should be pure white or pure black. By identifying these key items, you can correct the color balance throughout an image.

The **Photo** toolbar is like a "one-stop photo fix shop," with tools for quickly correcting many common photo problems. Unless you've moved it, you'll find the Photo toolbar just to the right of the **Standard** toolbar, near the top of the PSP window.

Here's a brief description of each button on the **Photo** toolbar:

- **Enhance Photo Menu.** This menu contains commands for making easy, one-step corrections to a photograph such as adjusting the brightness and contrast. You'll learn how to apply all of these quick fixes in this chapter.

- **Barrel Distortion Correction.** Displays a dialog box that allows you to manually correct a problem sometimes caused by the use of a wide-angle lens. See **92** **Remove Barrel, Pincushion, and Fisheye Distortion**.

- **Fisheye Distortion Correction.** Displays a dialog box you can use to manually correct distortion in an image captured by a fisheye lens. See **92** **Remove Barrel, Pincushion, and Fisheye Distortion** for more help.

- **Pincushion Distortion Correction.** Displays a dialog box you can use to correct a problem sometimes caused by the use of a zoom lens set at maximum zoom. See **92** **Remove Barrel, Pincushion, and Fisheye Distortion** for more information.

- **Fade Correction.** Displays a dialog box you can use to adjust the brightness and saturation levels in an old, faded photograph. See **108** **Restore an Old Photograph** for help.

- **Black and White.** Displays a dialog box you can use to establish the *black and white points* in an image. See **111** **Remove a Color Cast**.

- **Manual Color Correction.** Displays a dialog box that allows you to correct color in an image, such as pale skin tones caused by a close flash. See **106** **Correct Color Manually**.

Fade Correction

Black and White
Pincushion Distortion Correction
Fisheye Distortion Correction
Barrel Distortion Correction
Enhance Photo Menu

Manual Color Correction
Histogram Adjustment
Adjust HSL
JPEG Artifact Removal
Unsharp Mask

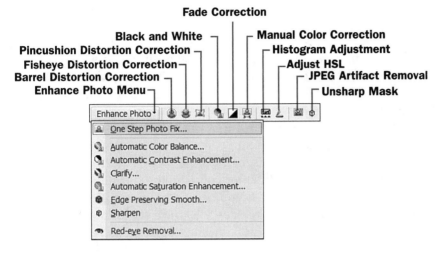

*The **Photo** toolbar helps you correct photos quickly.*

- **Histogram Adjustment.** Displays a graph you can change to manually adjust the distribution of lights, darks, and midtones in an image. See **96** **Improve Brightness and Contrast**.

- **Adjust HSL.** Displays a dialog box that allows you to manually adjust the hue, saturation, and lightness of an image. See **107** **Adjust Hue, Saturation, and Lightness Manually** for more information.

- **JPEG Artifact Removal.** Displays a dialog box you can use to remove artifacts from an overly compressed JPEG image. See **93** **Remove Imperfections Caused by File Compression**.

- **Unsharp Mask.** Displays a dialog box that allows you to sharpen an image by varying degrees. See **114** **Sharpen an Image**.

Before You Begin

✔ **46** About Common Corrections

EY TERM

Color cast—The predominance of a particular color throughout an image, such as an overall reddish tone. This condition might occur for an image originally shot with a digital camera that was not properly white-balanced.

TIP

Photo Album offers something similar to Paint Shop Pro's **One Step Photo Fix** command, although Photo Album's version adjusts only the brightness, contrast, and color balance. In the **Image View** window, click the **Quick Fix** button. To quickly fix multiple images, select them in **Album View**, click the arrow on the **Batch** button, and choose **Quick Fix**.

EY TERM

Script—A series of recorded commands that can be played back in sequence, applying the same alterations to other images.

The best place to start when correcting an image is with the **One Step Photo Fix** command, located on the **Enhance Photo** menu of the **Photo** toolbar. With this single command, you can automatically improve an image by balancing the color in non-grayscale images and removing a *color cast* (if present), improving an image's brightness and contrast, adjusting the saturation levels if necessary, and sharpening the focus. All these tasks are performed automatically; after you give the command, you don't have to do anything else. If you don't like the results, you can undo them with a single click of the **Undo** button, or keep them and make additional manual changes as desired.

1 **Open Enhance Photo Menu**

Click the **Enhance Photo** button on the **Photo** toolbar to display its menu.

2 **Click One Step Photo Fix**

Click the **One Step Photo Fix** command. The *script* starts, applying each recorded command in turn. You can watch the script apply each adjustment by looking at the status bar.

3 **View the Result**

The before photo is on the left; the result of using **One Step Photo Fix** is on the right. As you can see, the command made a dramatic difference in the photo, but there might still be room for improvement. For example, I might decide to make manual adjustments to the brightness.

PSP provides many prerecorded scripts (including One Step Photo Fix) you can use to quickly perform common adjustments. You can record your own scripts as well; see **57** **Repeat Adjustments on Multiple Images Automatically**.

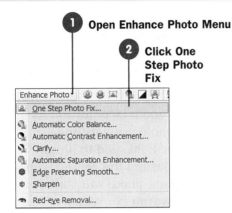

1 Open Enhance Photo Menu

2 Click One
Step Photo
Fix

Enhance Photo	
One Step Photo Fix...	
Automatic Color Balance...	
Automatic Contrast Enhancement...	
Clarify...	
Automatic Saturation Enhancement...	
Edge Preserving Smooth...	
Sharpen	
Red-eye Removal...	

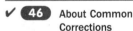

3 View the Result

54 Achieve Color Balance Automatically

When the colors in an image are out of balance, a single color seems to dominate the picture, appearing in places where it should not. For example, a reddish tone might appear in the sky, in everyone's hair, and might make white shirts seem almost pink. When a single color dominates an image, that image is said to have a "color cast." You'll find color casts often in older photographs that have not been stored properly; a color cast might also occur in a digital photograph taken with improper settings. For example, if you *white-balance* your camera for a bright sunny day outside and then take a shot indoors, the

Before You Begin

✔ **46** About Common
Corrections

See Also

→ **106** Correct Color
Manually

KEY TERM

White-balance—A process that adjusts a digital camera so that it can automatically compensate for the natural bluish tone of photographs taken outdoors and the natural orange-ish tone of indoor ones.

TIP

If you're not satisfied with the way **Automatic Color Balance** attempts to balance the colors in an image taken outdoors, you might want to try **Adjust, Color Balance, Grey World Color Balance**. It balances color making sure that the average of all the colors in an image is a middle gray.

TIP

To vary the degree to which PSP will change colors in your image to achieve color balance, adjust the **Strength** value (the default setting of 30 is typically best for most images). If flesh tones seem a bit too red or orange, try simulating "cooler" light by sliding the **Temperature** setting *to the right*. If a landscape seems too cold—as though everything were covered by a layer of frost—try sliding the **Temperature** setting *to the left* to "warm up" the light.

image assumes an orange cast. If your goal is to warm up a romantic fireside photograph, the orange color cast might be welcome; but if you were trying to achieve a more natural look for your image, use the steps in this task to remove the color cast and achieve color balance.

To remove the color cast from an image, you'll be adjusting its "illuminant temperature." Professional photographers understand this to mean the temperature of the light used to illuminate the subjects of a photograph. By adjusting this setting, you can make it appear as though your original photo was shot using light that was stronger or weaker, warmer or cooler.

1 Open Enhance Photo Menu

Click the **Enhance Photo** button on the **Photo** toolbar to display its menu.

2 Click Automatic Color Balance

Select the **Automatic Color Balance** command. The **Automatic Color Balance** dialog box appears.

3 Make Adjustments and Click OK

If necessary, click the **Reset to Default** button, and let PSP guess what temperature setting will fix your image the best. If there is a strong color cast to the image, enable the **Remove color cast** check box.

If you want to make minor adjustments to the results, watch the preview as you adjust the **Strength** and **Temperature** settings as desired. When you're satisfied with the adjustments, click **OK.**

4 View the Result

In this old school photograph with a reddish color cast, selecting the **Remove color cast** option worked best. However, it made the girl's skin tone appear a bit cold, so to warm it up, I adjusted the **Temperature** setting by dragging it to the **Warmer** end. See these before and after photos in the Color Gallery in this book.

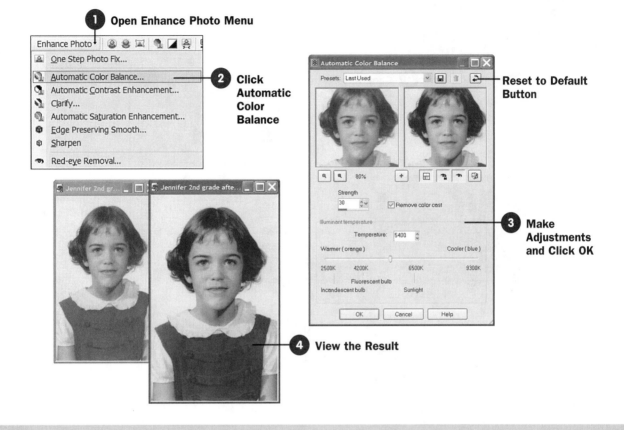

1 Open Enhance Photo Menu

2 Click Automatic Color Balance

Reset to Default Button

3 Make Adjustments and Click OK

4 View the Result

---

55 **Adjust Brightness and Contrast Automatically**

One of the more common problems with digital images is that they are often simply too dark. This problem might be caused by improperly setting the camera's controls so that not enough light is taken in during the recording process, but more often it's simply the nature of digital imaging and scanning to produce an image that's darker than the original. In any case, if brightness and contrast are the only problems with an image, try the steps in this task to improve it.

Before You Begin

✔ **46** About Common Corrections

See Also

→ **96** Improve Brightness and Contrast

① **Open Enhance Photo Menu**

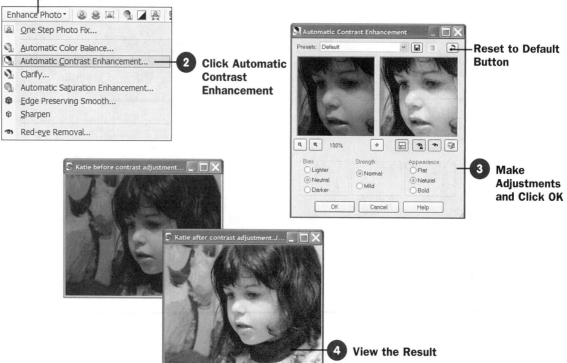

② **Click Automatic Contrast Enhancement**

Reset to Default Button

③ **Make Adjustments and Click OK**

④ **View the Result**

TIP

You might want to lighten the image even further than the default settings do by changing the **Bias** option to **Lighter**. You might want to tone down the effect by changing the **Strength** option to **Mild**. However, unless you're going for a special effect, it's unlikely that you'll want to change the **Appearance** setting to something other than **Natural**.

① **Open Enhance Photo Menu**

Click the **Enhance Photo** button on the **Photo** toolbar to display its menu.

② **Click Automatic Contrast Enhancement**

Select the **Automatic Contrast Enhancement** command. The **Automatic Contrast Enhancement** dialog box appears.

③ **Make Adjustments and Click OK**

If necessary, click the **Reset to Default** button and use the default settings to adjust the image (these default settings typically work best).

Adjust the **Bias**, **Strength**, and **Appearance** settings as desired. When you're through making changes, click **OK.**

4 View the Result

Brightening this photo improved it immensely.

56 Adjust Saturation Automatically

An old, faded image can often be fixed simply by increasing its *saturation*. Doing so makes the colors in the image appear more vibrant, similar to how they might have looked when the now-faded photograph was first taken. You might also want to improve the saturation in an image where the flash was too close to the subject (making it almost white and devoid of color), or too far away (making the subject too gray and colorless).

1 Open Enhance Photo Menu

Click the **Enhance Photo** button on the **Photo** toolbar to display its menu.

2 Click Automatic Saturation Enhancement

Select the **Automatic Saturation Enhancement** command. The **Automatic Saturation Enhancement** dialog box appears.

3 Select Skintones Present if Applicable

If necessary, click the **Reset to Default** button, and use the default settings because they typically look best.

Next, enable the **Skintones present** check box if there are people in the image.

4 Make Adjustments and Click OK

If you're not satisfied with the result, adjust the **Bias** and **Strength** settings as desired. When you're through making changes, click **OK.**

Before You Begin

✔ **46** About Common Corrections

See Also

→ **107** Adjust Hue, Saturation, and Lightness Manually

KEY TERM

Saturation—The amount of a particular hue present in a pixel. A fully saturated red pixel is bright red; a less saturated red pixel has more gray, and its reddish tone is more subtle.

NOTE

The **Skintones present** option enables PSP to account for the special variations of hues—including even cyan—necessary for a digital photo to create a realistic approximation of flesh tones. Disabling this selection can create unrealistic variegations in skin tones, so your subjects might appear to have more freckles and pockmarks than normal.

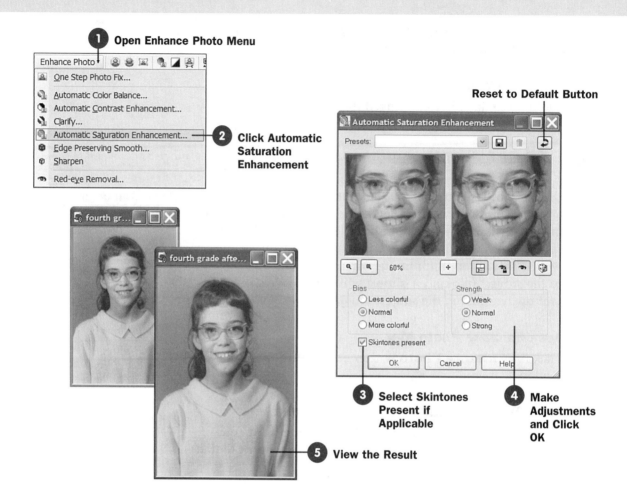

1 Open Enhance Photo Menu

2 Click Automatic Saturation Enhancement

Reset to Default Button

3 Select Skintones Present if Applicable

4 Make Adjustments and Click OK

5 View the Result

5 View the Result

Increasing the saturation just a bit brought out the pinkish undertone in the little girl's skin, the reddish highlights in her hair, and the lovely yellow in her sweater. To appreciate the difference, see these two photos in the Color Gallery.

57 Repeat Adjustments on Multiple Images Automatically

If you've ever used a spreadsheet program such as Excel, you're familiar with the concept of a *macro*, where a sequence of operations is executed with a single keystroke or menu command. Paint Shop Pro includes a similar feature in which sequences of commands are recorded as a *script*. The purpose of a script is to simplify common operations by automating them. As you record a script, PSP "watches" you as you perform a set of steps on an existing image.

You don't have to keep every script you record forever, but you can take advantage of scripts to repeat certain actions on an entire set of images. Suppose that you use your digital camera to shoot a dozen or more portraits in the same outdoor setting. All these portraits require the same fixes—perhaps all the faces are similarly washed out, or the lighting ended up being too low and the subject and the background on all shots were too blue and color-imbalanced. Using the script feature, you can make the necessary changes to one image in the set as you would normally, and then replay the script to apply those same changes to the remaining images in the set.

1 Begin Recording

Click the **Start Script Recording** button on the **Script** toolbar.

2 Perform Your Task and Click Save Script Recording

Execute the steps you want PSP to record, in the order in which you want them to be recorded. When your task is complete, click the **Save Script Recording** button on the **Script** toolbar. The **Save As** dialog box opens.

See Also

→ **40** Convert a Group of Images to Another File Type

→ **46** About Common Corrections

KEY TERM

Script—A series of recorded commands that can be played back in sequence, applying the same alterations to other images.

NOTE

You can play a script while converting a group of images from one file format to another, as described in **40** Convert a Group of Images to Another File Type. You might do this to fix a group of new images while converting them to PSP format, for example. You can also assign the finished script to a toolbar button and run it with a single click. To do that, you must name the script **BoundScript***n*, where *n* is a number from 1 to 9.

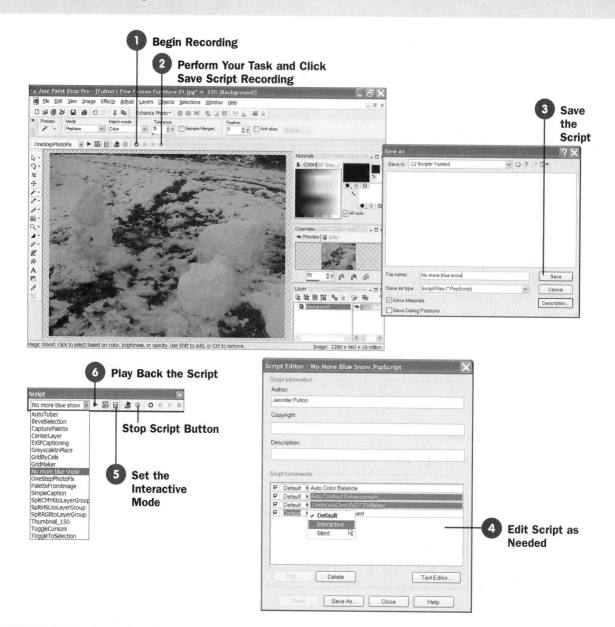

1 Begin Recording

2 Perform Your Task and Click Save Script Recording

3 Save the Script

6 Play Back the Script

Stop Script Button

5 Set the Interactive Mode

4 Edit Script as Needed

3 Save the Script

In the **File name** box, type a phrase that briefly but adequately describes the function of the script. To have the script include the specific options of all the tools you used in the recording, enable the **Save Materials** check box. To have the script remember the locations of dialog boxes you used during the recording process, enable the **Save Dialog Positions** check box. Click **Save** to enroll the script in PSP's menu of active scripts.

④ Edit Script as Needed

If you perform a step and immediately undo it, PSP records both the step and the **Undo** command. With script editing, you can safely remove both unwanted elements. On the **Script** toolbar, choose the script title from the list and then click **Edit Selected Script**. Select the command you never meant to do and click **Delete**.

In addition to removing actions from a recorded script, you can control whether or not dialog boxes appear when the script is played. For each command, open the **Execution Mode** list and select the mode you prefer: **Silent** performs the action without displaying the dialog box; **Interactive** performs the action and displays the dialog box so that the user can adjust the settings if she wants; **Default** displays dialog boxes only if the **Interactive** mode is turned on (as described in step 5). Click **Save** and then click **Close**.

You can turn off an action just before running a script if you decide you don't want to perform that action just now, and you don't want to remove the action permanently. To turn off an action without removing it, disable its check box in the **Script Editor**.

⑤ Set the Interactive Mode

Normally, dialog boxes that opened during the recording of a script are displayed when that script is run so that you can make adjustments to the settings. If you'd prefer not to display the dialog boxes, click to turn *off* the **Interactive Script Playback Toggle** button.

TIP

Take your time as you go through the actions you want to record, using a "guinea pig" image. PSP records only what you do, not how long you take to do it.

NOTES

To execute commands without including them in the script, click **Pause Script Recording** on the **Script** toolbar, and do what you need to do. To resume recording, click **Pause Script Recording** again.

To include a description of your script to refresh your memory later, or to help you distribute it to colleagues, click the **Description** button in the **Save As** dialog box and enter descriptive data under **Author**, **Copyright**, and **Description**; click **OK**.

TIP

Remove both the command you want to pretend never happened and the **Undo** command, which is listed as **UndoLastCmd**.

NOTE

If the script has been edited so that particular actions use **Silent** or **Interactive** mode, toggling the **Interactive Script Playback Toggle** has no effect.

 TIP

If the results of the script for the second image are not what you want, you can undo them. To undo *all the changes* made to your active image by the entire script, select **Edit, Undo Script**. (No, you can't undo just some of them.) You can, however, make additional changes to an image even after running a script.

 **Play Back the Script**

Open another image. Open the list on the **Script** toolbar and choose the script you want to run on the new image. Click the **Run Selected Script** button in the **Script** toolbar. PSP runs the selected script immediately and does not respond to regular menu, toolbar, or palette commands until the script is completed, or until you click **Stop Script** to abort.

PART II

Making Selected Changes to an Image

IN THIS PART

7

Selecting Portions of Images for Manipulation

IN THIS CHAPTER:

58 About Making Selections

See Also

→ **59** Select a Rectangular, Circular, or Other Standard-Shaped Area

→ **60** Select by Drawing Freehand

→ **64** Select Areas of Similar Color, Brightness, or Opacity

TIPS

Not only can you use a selection to limit what you paint or fill, or where you adjust the brightness, for example, you can also use a selection to delete a portion of an image.

To remove the marquee and return to editing an entire image or layer, right-click the image with a selection tool. To cancel a selection while drawing it, press **Esc**.

Several tasks in this book include—generally as an option—the job of selecting a part or parts of an open image. Selecting a portion of an image allows you to use a command or tool to change *just that portion*, in a sense creating a boundary across which PSP will not trespass. Making a selection protects the rest of the image from any changes you attempt. For example, if you use a brush tool to paint inside a selection, even if your pointer were to stray occasionally outside the boundaries of the selection, PSP will not paint outside the selection. Everything outside a selection is safe from changes.

As you've probably guessed, a selection doesn't have to be comprised of just one region of adjacent pixels; it can be several non-adjacent regions, or all the pixels in your entire image that have roughly the same color value or brightness. A selection is typically made only on the current layer, although you can opt to select through all layers if you like. PSP marks your selection with a flashing *marquee*, like the one you'd see at the entrance to an old-fashioned theatre.

The three selection tools in PSP.

Paint Shop Pro gives you three tools for selecting any region or regions of an image, and multiple options for using each of these tools. Using one or more of these selection tools, you can isolate an object in the foreground from material in the background, or specifically designate the lint ball in the hair and not the hair, or specify the nose despite the face. It may take a series of motions to do it—often, you'll find yourself adding to a selection by selecting an area to add, or subtracting from a selection by selecting an area to remove. When it's perfected, a selection can be saved and reused in the same image or in a completely different one.

The selection tools are located on the fifth **Tools** toolbar button (which always displays the currently chosen selection tool):

- The classic **Selection** tool lets you mark a regularly shaped area, such as a rectangle, ellipse, star, or hexagon. Most often, you'll find yourself using this tool when filling areas in an image with a color, pattern, or gradient, when cutting or copying a portion of one image for pasting into another, or when creating unique borders around an image.

- With the **Freehand Selection** tool, you carefully draw an outline all the way, or most of the way, around the area you want to select. With the mouse, this can be a slow and often imprecise process; on the other hand, with a pen tablet it can be quite simple.

- The **Magic Wand** tool lets you point to a spot, a patch, an area where the colors are similar or equal in some way, and have PSP select that spot with one touch.

As you create an initial selection using any of these tools, you can add or remove pixels from the selection using the same tool or any other tool you choose. Although you can base your selection on data contained on other layers in an image, the pixels contained in a selection are located within the current layer only.

You can have PSP include a buffer zone inside and/or outside the border you've drawn making pixels more transparent as they move towards the selection border (inside *feather*) or farther away from it (outside feather). The effect of feathering the selection results in a removal of the hard edge that generally accompanies a cropped region. You might use feathering when you're

TIP

You can select areas of an image or layer and then invert them to select everything except the area(s) you originally selected.

TIP

If the area you're selecting borders the edge of the image, you can draw "out-of-bounds" (to be sure that you include that outside edge) by dragging the pointer off the side of the image.

KEY TERM

Feather—To produce a fuzzy border around the inside, outside, or both edges of a selection. PSP feathers a selection by changing pixels along the edge of the selection to make them gradually more transparent. The result is a soft, transitive effect that can be preferable to a hard edge.

TIP

You can select the marquee itself, rather than the pixels inside it, by choosing **Selections, Modify, Select Selection Borders**. This is especially handy after you've feathered a selection to widen its border—after selecting the border itself, you could fill that border with a color to create a frame, for example.

KEY TERM

Interpolating—The process of mathematically mixing the component values of one pixel with those of a pixel on a layer that overlays it or that replaces it partially, so that the result appears to be an in-between color value.

cropping a portion of an image for pasting somewhere else. The feathering softens the edge of the cropped region, keeping it from becoming too distracting in its new location.

You might use feathering to create a new image in which a feathered selection from an original image has been clipped and magnified, and then pasted onto the old image as a "blow-up." The fuzzy border of the clipped, relocated selection will blend better into the background of the old image. PSP produces this fuzziness by *interpolating* the values of the copied pixels along the edges, in varying degrees, against the values of the original pixels on top of which the new pixels are being pasted. You can't see this blending taking place until after you've pasted, even though the **Tool Options** palette tells you quite clearly that you're using feathering during the selection process. You can also add feathering after making a selection. See **66** **Soften the Edge of a Selection**.

Feathering a selection adds a fuzzy border to the region you've indicated to ease the selection into its new surroundings.

Another non-obvious aspect of the selection process concerns cases in which the intensity of all of the pixels in the selected region may vary. You've already seen this with feathering, in

which some of the pixels along the edge are only partially selected, creating a fuzzy border around the selection. As discussed in
73 **Edit a Selection**, you can use the **Paint Brush** to vary the
amount that a pixel is selected. Imagine taking a rubber eraser
to a colored pencil drawing and erasing a portion of it just partway, and you'll get an idea of the effect I'm talking about. The
marquee around a selection in a PSP image only tells you which
pixels are being selected, but not by how much. But there's a way
you can find out: by displaying the selection overlay.

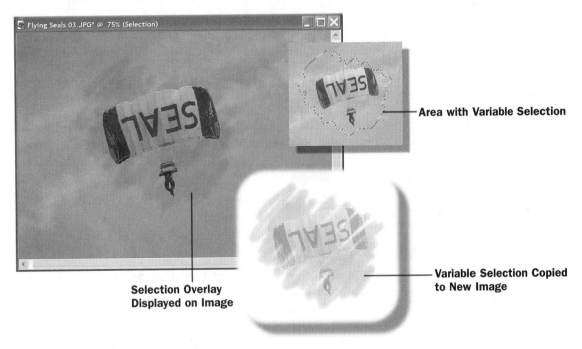

Area with Variable Selection

Variable Selection Copied
to New Image

Selection Overlay
Displayed on Image

A selection with variable intensity.

As you'll learn in **73** **Edit a Selection**, when the selection overlay is displayed, it takes the form of what Jasc poetically chris-
tened the "ruby lithe." Actually, it looks like you've just spray-
painted your image with a can of red. Don't worry. This overlay
is not treated as a real region of color, but instead as a graph of
the area you've selected, with fully selected areas indicated by a
more opaque red, and those of lesser selection indicated by a
more transparent red (refer to this image in the Color Gallery).
This mode of viewing a selection, as you'll see, was devised to

help you make careful alterations to a selection, although you can also use it to preview the amount of feathering or variations in your selection before you copy it to the Clipboard.

59 Select a Rectangular, Circular, or Other Standard-Shaped Area

Before You Begin

✔ **58** About Making Selections

See Also

→ **65** Add Areas to or Subtract Areas from a Selection

→ **70** Select Everything But the Current Selection

→ **73** Edit a Selection

→ **120** About Layers and the Layer Palette

🔅 TIP

If you're using the **Selection** tool with a unique shape such as a star or ellipse to create a frame around a subject, it's often difficult to get the selection marquee exactly where you want it. To move the marquee, switch to **Edit Selection** mode, as described in **73** Edit a Selection.

NOTE

PSP remembers the shape you choose (as well as any other options); the next time you use the **Selection** tool, it will retain the shape and options you last used.

With the **Selection** tool, you can select any regularly shaped area in an image, such as a rectangle, square, circle, ellipse (oval), a rectangle or square with rounded corners, a three-, five-, six-, or eight-sided object, an arrow, or a star. These shapes can help you create a decorative frame for a clipping you make from an original image.

① Choose the Selection Tool

Change to the layer that contains the pixels you want to select, then choose the **Selection** tool on the **Tools** toolbar.

② Choose a Shape

Open the **Selection Type** list on the **Tool Options** palette and choose a new shape from the list.

③ Set Options

Set options as desired on the **Tool Options** palette. To give your selection a fuzzy or semi-transparent edge, set the value for **Feather** to a number above **0**. The **Feather** value represents the thickness of the fuzzy border, measured in pixels. You can also feather a selection after the fact; see **66** Soften the Edge of a Selection for help.

For a selection with a curved border (**Circle**) or a partly diagonal border (**Hexagon** or similar shape), enable the **Anti-alias** check box to have PSP eliminate jagged or stair-stepped edges.

Under **Create selection from**, click the appropriate button to indicate how you want to make your selection: **Current selection** (to select pixels from the current layer that lie within the marquee), **Layer opaque** (to instantly select all the nontransparent pixels on the current layer), or **Merged**

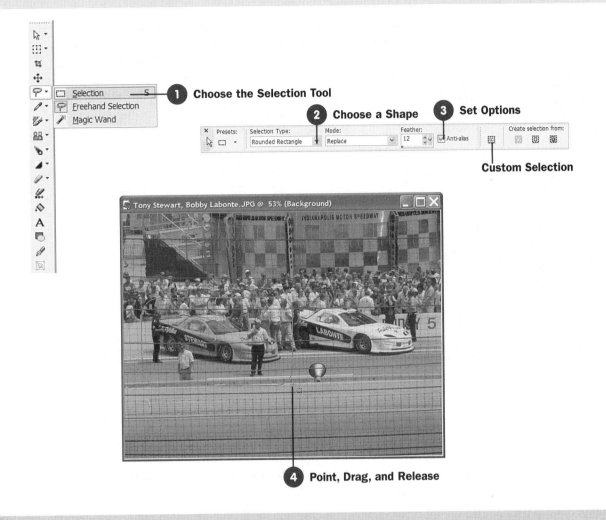

1 **Choose the Selection Tool**

2 **Choose a Shape**

3 **Set Options**

Custom Selection

4 **Point, Drag, and Release**

opaque (to instantly select all nontransparent pixels in the merged image).

4 **Point, Drag, and Release**

If your **Selection Type** is **Circle** or **Ellipse**, point to the *center* of the area you want to select, click and hold the left mouse button, then drag the mouse pointer to expand the selection to the size you want. With the pen, touch the tablet at the center of the area and draw toward the outer rim.

 NOTE

By default, the **Mode** option is set to **Replace**, which means that any new selection you make cancels the existing one. You'll learn to add or subtract from a selection by changing the mode in **65** **Add Areas to or Subtract Areas from a Selection.**

NOTE

If you click the **Layer opaque** or **Merged opaque** option, a rectangular selection border is drawn around the indicated pixels *regardless of the shape you selected in step 2.*

TIP

If you want to select a rectangular or square area, you can designate the area to select by clicking the **Custom selection** button and entering the coordinates of the four corners of the selection marquee into the dialog box that appears.

For other selection types, point to the upper-left corner of the area you want to select, click and hold the left mouse button, and drag the pointer downward and to the right. With the pen, touch the tablet at one corner of the area and draw toward the opposite corner. When you release the mouse button or lift the pen, a selection marquee appears. Here, I've drawn a rounded rectangle around Tony Stewart's race car.

60 Select by Drawing Freehand

Before You Begin

✔ **58** About Making Selections

See Also

→ **65** Add Areas to or Subtract Areas from a Selection

→ **70** Select Everything But the Current Selection

The **Freehand Selection** tool lets you indicate an area by drawing its border. You can draw a selection border around a person's head and hair, one flower in a bouquet, one car parked on a street, one snowball being tossed in the air, one bandage on a runner's leg, one ketchup stain on a white shirt. The **Freehand Selection** tool takes many forms: freehand drawing (which you'll learn to do in this task), edge drawing (it has two edge modes to help you draw a border along the edge of an object), and point-to-point (which fences in the selection area with short straight "fence sections").

1 **Select Freehand Selection Tool**

Change to the layer that contains the pixels you want to select, then choose the **Freehand Selection** tool on the **Tools** toolbar.

2 **Select Freehand Type**

Open the **Selection type** list on the **Tool Options** palette and select **Freehand**.

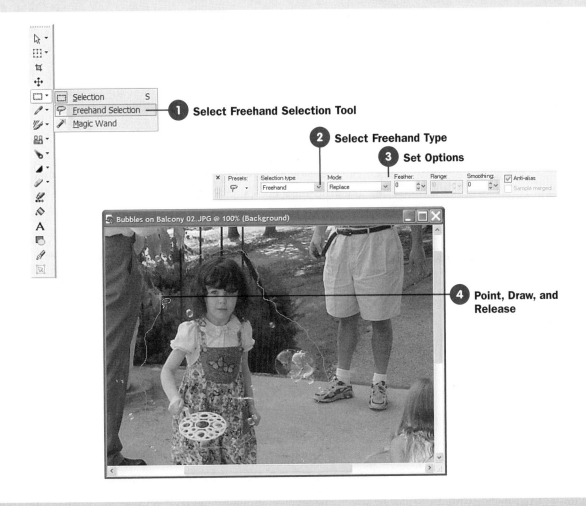

1 Select Freehand Selection Tool

2 Select Freehand Type

3 Set Options

4 Point, Draw, and Release

3 **Set Options**

Set options as needed on the **Tool Options** palette. To give your selection a fuzzy or semi-transparent edge, set the value for **Feather** to a number above **0**.

To smooth the edge of the selection, set the value for **Smoothing** to a number above **0**. Enable the **Anti-alias** check box to have PSP eliminate jagged or stair-stepped curves by adding semi-selected pixels along the edge of the selection.

NOTE

To feather a selection after it is made, see 66 **Soften the Edge of a Selection.**

TIP

To make the border you're drawing smoother—to blunt sharp points and get rid of small zig-zags caused by a shaky hand—you can set PSP's **Smoothing** factor to a number above zero, **40** being the maximum setting. To the degree you've chosen, PSP will smooth the line you've drawn.

4 Point, Draw, and Release

Draw the freehand selection by dragging. With the pen, touch the tablet and draw along the edge you want to select. A shadow line trails your pointer, showing the edge you're drawing. Release the mouse button to complete the selection. If you trace most of the way, and then stop and release before you've reached your start point, PSP automatically connects the end points of your border, enclosing your selection. Here, I've quickly selected the general area of my daughter and the bubbles so that I can paste it into a greeting card.

61 Fence in a Selection

Before You Begin

✔ **58** About Making Selections

✔ **60** Select by Drawing Freehand

See Also

→ **65** Add Areas to or Subtract Areas from a Selection

→ **70** Select Everything But the Current Selection

NOTE

Point-to-point selection works best when you're marking an area whose precise shape is unimportant. If you're trying to eliminate a bothersome reflection, the shape isn't important; you just need to mark the general area in which the reflection appears. With the area marked, you can apply a softening filter or reduce brightness to eliminate the problem.

Drawing a freehand loop around a selection is just one way to use the **Freehand Selection** tool. An alternative method is for you to mark points along the perimeter of a selection, and extend lines between those points until they form a closed border or fence that encloses the area you want to select. The result is an irregular polygon or, if **Smoothing** is set above **0**, a wobbly ring.

1 Select Freehand Selection Tool

Change to the layer that contains the pixels you want to select, then on the **Tools** toolbar, select the **Freehand Selection** tool.

2 Choose Point to Point Type

In the **Tool Options** palette, choose **Point to point** from the **Selection type** menu.

3 Set Options

Set options as desired from the **Tools Options** palette. To give your selection a fuzzy or semi-transparent edge, set the value for **Feather** to a number above **0**.

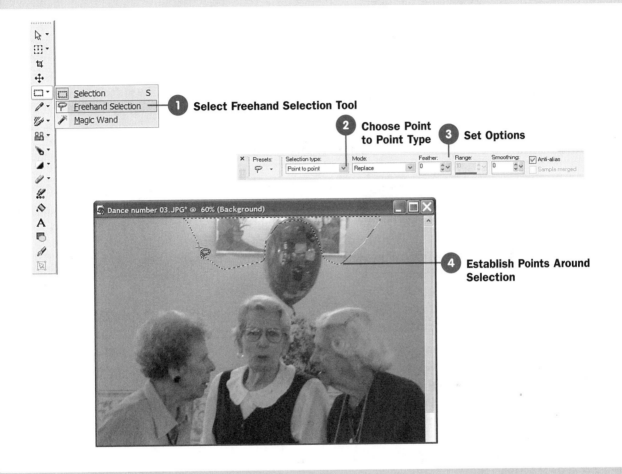

1 **Select Freehand Selection Tool**

2 **Choose Point to Point Type**

3 **Set Options**

4 **Establish Points Around Selection**

To smooth the edge of the selection, set the value for **Smoothing** to a number above **0**. Enable the **Anti-alias** check box to have PSP eliminate jagged curves.

4 Establish Points Around Selection

Click the mouse to establish the first "fence post." Continue clicking on the image to add more posts at points where the edge is likely to change direction substantially. For each successive click, PSP plots a shadow line, showing you the "fence" under construction. With the pen, tap a series of spots along the edge of the area to be selected.

NOTE

To feather a selection after it is made, see 66 Soften the Edge of a Selection.

To close the fence around the selection, point to the last "fence post" and double-click. PSP joins the last fence post to the first one, fencing in the selection. To finish the selection with the pen, touch the tablet and (for most newer models) rock the thumb switch back. Here, I've selected a bright reflection behind the singers so that I can darken it a bit.

62 Trace an Object's Edge with Edge Seeker

Before You Begin

✔ **58** About Making Selections

✔ **60** Select by Drawing Freehand

See Also

→ **63** Trace an Object's Edge with Smart Edge

→ **65** Add Areas to or Subtract Areas from a Selection

→ **70** Select Everything But the Current Selection

 TIP

An "edge" is determined by the level of contrast between pixels. High-contrast edges are easiest for Edge Seeker to follow, although it can follow a low-contrast edge without problems if you place your "fence posts" more precisely.

When an object you want to select is *very* irregularly shaped—for instance, the edge of a cupcake shell, a flying duck, or a branch of a tree—and you absolutely need the border of your selection to tightly surround that object, one option available to you is the **Edge Seeker**, a variation of the **Freehand Selection** tool. Using your click points as a guide, Edge Seeker determines the border of an object by looking for the difference in nearby pixels. The result is a border that appears to tightly describe the edge of an object.

Edge Seeker works—and even feels to some extent—the same as point-to-point selection, where you plant "fence posts" around the edge of your selection, and PSP adds straight lines between the posts. Edge Seeker differs from point-to-point selection by moving the "posts" as needed to follow the closest edge.

1 Select Freehand Selection Tool

Change to the layer that contains the pixels you want to select, then on the **Tools** toolbar, select the **Freehand Selection** tool.

2 Choose Edge Seeker Type

In the **Tool Options** palette, choose **Edge Seeker** from the **Selection type** menu.

3 Set Options

On the **Tool Options** palette, set the tool's characteristics. To set the radius of the area in which Edge Seeker searches for the edge of an object, set **Range** to a value above **0**. The higher the **Range** setting, the more likely PSP is to find a

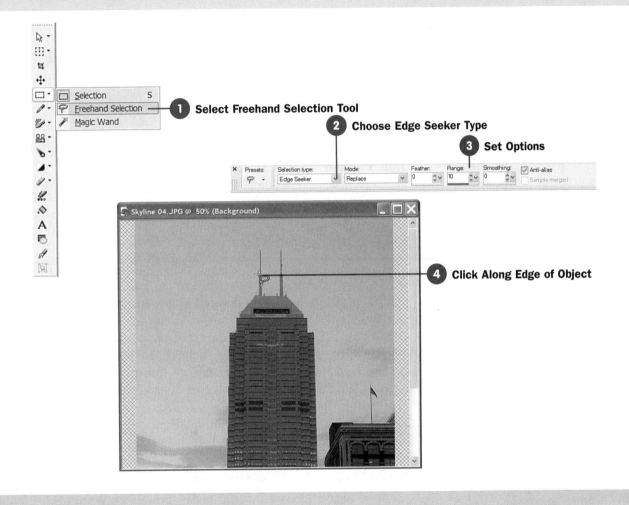

1 Select Freehand Selection Tool

2 Choose Edge Seeker Type

3 Set Options

4 Click Along Edge of Object

clear edge, but also the more likely the border it draws will stray from a straight line between your points.

For best results, set **Smoothing** to **0** so that Edge Seeker will not move the marquee away from the object's edge by smoothing its jaggedness. For this same reason, you should turn off the **Anti-alias** option as well.

NOTE

Although you can feather the selection as you make it, you'll get better results by selecting the edge first, then feathering, as described in **66** Soften the Edge of a Selection.

TIP

Change the Edge Seeker tool into the **Point to Point** tool on the fly by holding down the **Alt** key and clicking. Straight lines are joined between points, ignoring the edge. By dragging with the **Alt** key down, you activate the **Freehand Selection** tool so that you can draw that part of the selection manually.

4 Click Along Edge of Object

Click along the edge of the object. It's important to click as closely as you can along the edge of the object you're trying to select. To help you, turn on the **Magnifier** by pressing **Ctrl+Alt+M**.

With the pen, tap a series of points in the vicinity of the edge that borders your intended selection. To close the selection and join the first and last points, double-click.

---

63 Trace an Object's Edge with Smart Edge

Before You Begin

✔ **58** About Making Selections

✔ **60** Select by Drawing Freehand

See Also

→ **62** Trace an Object's Edge with Edge Seeker

→ **65** Add Areas to or Subtract Areas from a Selection

→ **70** Select Everything But the Current Selection

NOTE

You might find Edge Seeker easier to use in a photographic image, because Edge Seeker is superior to Smart Edge at following the exact edge you want, even if it's a low-contrast one. Edge Seeker is not as good as Smart Edge at turning sharp corners, however, so you might prefer to use Smart Edge in certain situations.

The Smart Edge option works very similarly to Edge Seeker. When you mark two points along the perimeter of your selection, Smart Edge finds the most logical border between contrasting elements along that path. The result is a border that appears to tightly describe the edge of an object. The key difference between Edge Seeker and Smart Edge is that Edge Seeker's marquee runs exactly through your click points, while Smart Edge adjusts their position to fit what it perceives as the closest edge. In addition, the width of Smart Edge's search area is fixed at approximately 15 pixels, while Edge Seeker's is adjustable.

1 Select Freehand Selection Tool

Change to the layer that contains the pixels you want to select, then in the **Tools** toolbar, select the **Freehand Selection** tool.

2 Choose Smart Edge Type

In the **Tool Options** palette, choose **Smart Edge** from the **Selection type** menu.

3 Set Options

On the **Tool Options** palette, select desired options.

Trace an Object's Edge with Smart Edge **63**

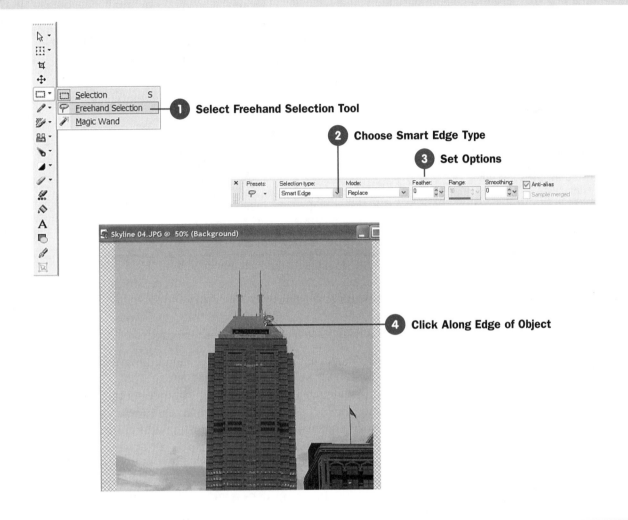

1 **Select Freehand Selection Tool**

2 **Choose Smart Edge Type**

3 **Set Options**

4 **Click Along Edge of Object**

---

4 **Click Along Edge of Object**

Click along the edge of the object. It's important to click as closely as you can along the edge of the object you're trying to select. To help you, turn on the **Magnifier** by pressing **Ctrl+Alt+M**.

NOTE

You'll help Smart Edge find the edge of your object more easily if you set **Feathering** to **0**, **Smoothing** to **0**, and turn off the **Anti-alias** option. You can always modify the selection after the fact, adding feathering, smoothing, and anti-aliasing as needed.

CHAPTER 7:   Selecting Portions of Images for Manipulation   **209**

TIP

Change the **Smart Edge** tool into the **Point to Point** tool on the fly by holding down the **Alt** key and clicking. Straight lines are joined between points, ignoring the edge. By dragging with the **Alt** key down, you activate the **Freehand Selection** tool so that you can draw the selection manually.

With the pen, tap a series of points in the vicinity of the edge that borders your intended selection. To close the selection and join the first and last points, double-click.

Select Areas of Similar Color, Brightness, or Opacity

Before You Begin

✔ **58** About Making Selections

See Also

→ **10** About Tools and Tool Options

→ **68** Remove Specks and Holes from a Selection

→ **71** Select a Portion of an Image with Channels

→ **72** Select a Portion of an Image with Threshold

NOTE

To be included in the selection, a pixel must match the qualities you select, and must either touch the target pixel or some other qualified pixel.

Most digital photographs you see can be described in terms of patches of similar shades or colors. Although you might see a landscape as leaves, branches, sky, clouds, and water, another way to perceive these is as sewn-together patches of similar colors and shades.

When you click a pixel with the **Magic Wand** tool, Paint Shop Pro begins by selecting that pixel. It then proceeds to evaluate neighboring pixels for similarity. The **Match mode** you select from the **Tool Options** palette determines what characteristic PSP should look for in the neighboring pixels to create a match, and the **Tolerance** level determines how much variance to allow. Pixels that match closely enough to the target pixel are added to the selection—all with a single click. This makes the **Magic Wand** the perfect tool for selecting all sorts of odd shapes, provided that the pixels share something in common—color, brightness, or opacity.

① Select Magic Wand Tool

Change to the layer that contains the pixels you want to select, then in the **Tools** toolbar, select the **Magic Wand** tool.

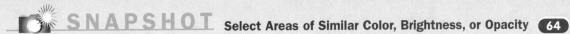
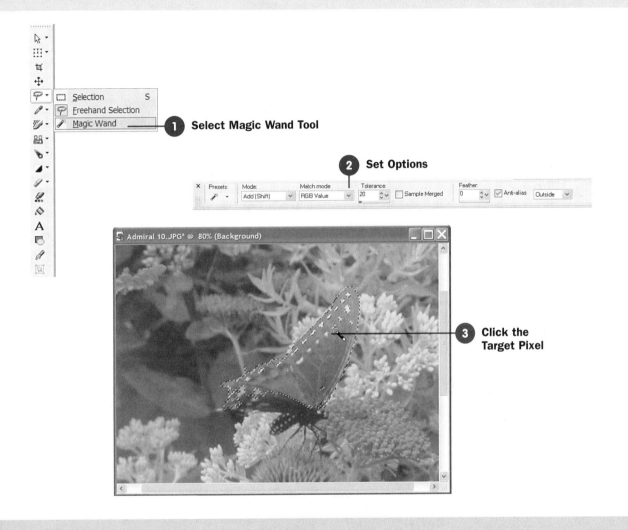

Select Magic Wand Tool ①

Set Options ②

Click the Target Pixel ③

② **Set Options**

In the **Tool Options** palette, open the **Match mode** list and choose the characteristic you want PSP to evaluate in neighboring pixels. The selection spreads out from the point you touch with the Magic Wand, to include all pixels that pass the **Match mode** test you choose here.

NOTE

Forget what the **Match mode** values mean? Check out **10** About Tools and Tool Options for a description.

Set **Tolerance** to a value that represents how much variance from the chosen pixel PSP should allow when creating a match. **Feather** the selection and turn on **Anti-alias** as desired to soften the edge of the selection.

3 Click the Target Pixel

Although pixels are selected from the current layer only, PSP can evaluate pixels for inclusion in the selection based on their merged value—the value that would result if all layers were merged together. To turn this feature on, click **Sample Merged** on the **Tools Option** palette.

In the image window, locate the point that best exemplifies the entire area you want to select, and click that point. With the pen, simply touch that point. PSP selects similar pixels based on your option settings.

 TIP

Inevitably, you won't get all the pixels you want to select with just a single click; either adjust the **Tolerance** value and click again, or add to your selection as described in **65** Add Areas to or Subtract Areas from a Selection.

---

65 Add Areas to or Subtract Areas from a Selection

Before You Begin

✔ **58** About Making Selections

See Also

→ **70** Select Everything But the Current Selection

→ **73** Edit a Selection

TIP

You can change any tool options you want before adding or subtracting from a selection. You can also change to another selection tool, if you think that a different tool might work better.

When you're selecting an area to be retouched or adjusted, there's a good chance that the selection process won't be quick. You will want the marquee to wrap itself tightly around the precise area you want to alter, to effectively exclude everything else. Normally, the selection tools work in **Replace** mode, which means that each time you click, you create a different selection. To add to a selection or subtract from it, you need only change the selection tool's **Mode** option. However, it's often much easier to use the keyboard shortcuts for Add and Remove: **Shift** and **Ctrl**, as described in this task.

1 Make Your Initial Selection

Use any selection tool to mark the first part of the selected region.

2 Add or Subtract Areas

Continue to use the same selection tool, or switch to another one. To add to the current selection, hold down the keyboard **Shift** key. To subtract from a selection, hold down the

1 Make Your Initial Selection

2 Add or Subtract Areas

Ctrl key. Should part of the new selection overlap the existing one, the two will merge. Noncontiguous selections will generate their own selection marquees, without affecting the original selection.

NOTE

As you hold down the **Shift** key, the **Mode** box in the **Tool Options** palette reads **Add (Shift)**, and the pointer appears with a + (plus) mark. If you hold down the **Ctrl** key, the **Mode** box reads **Remove (Ctrl)**, and the pointer appears with a – (minus) mark. After you release the **Shift** or **Ctrl** key, the **Mode** box reverts to read **Replace**. However, if you changed the mode before pressing the **Shift** or **Ctrl** key, the **Mode** option returns to that same mode (**Remove** or **Add**).

66 **Soften the Edge of a Selection**

Before You Begin

✔ **58** About Making Selections

See Also

→ **67** Smooth the Edge of a Selection

→ **69** Remove Jaggies from a Selection

→ **142** Age a Photograph

NOTE

Although feathering is an option you can choose while making a selection, this task shows you how to add feathering to an existing selection. You can then preview the selection *before* you apply feathering to the selection; with the other method it's hard to know whether the feather amount will be enough until after you've made the selection.

NOTE

You can remove the feathering from a selection later on with the **Selections, Modify, Unfeather** command.

Normally, when you cut or copy a selected region to a new location, the edge of the pasted region is hard or sharp, and perhaps even jagged with the lack of anti-aliasing. You can easily set up PSP to apply feathering to the selection boundary. Feathering gives the selection a soft, semi-transparent transition from the region you selected—which is left totally opaque—to the pixels that surround it after the selection is filled, pasted, or otherwise modified. Imagine a group photo of 30 or so people, where one face is selected with an oval-shaped marquee, copied, pasted in an unobtrusive location, and expanded in size. If left with a hard edge, the pasted face would draw too much attention away from the group of people, and it would look stark against its new background. With a feathered edge, the face becomes more subdued and pleasing in the photo.

1 Open Inside/Outside Feather Dialog Box

After selecting the area you want to feather, choose **Selections, Modify, Inside/Outside Feather** from the menu. The **Inside/Outside feather** dialog box opens.

2 Select Feather Type

Choose **Inside** (to feather pixels inside the selected area), **Outside** (to feather pixels outside the selected area), or **Both.**

3 Set Degree of Feathering and Click OK

Set the **Feather amount** to a value between 1 and 200. This value represents the radius in pixels that the region you selected will be extended, using semi-selected pixels. Click **OK**.

4 View the Result

Here I've cut and pasted the feathered selection into a new image with a cream background, creating an old-time vignette.

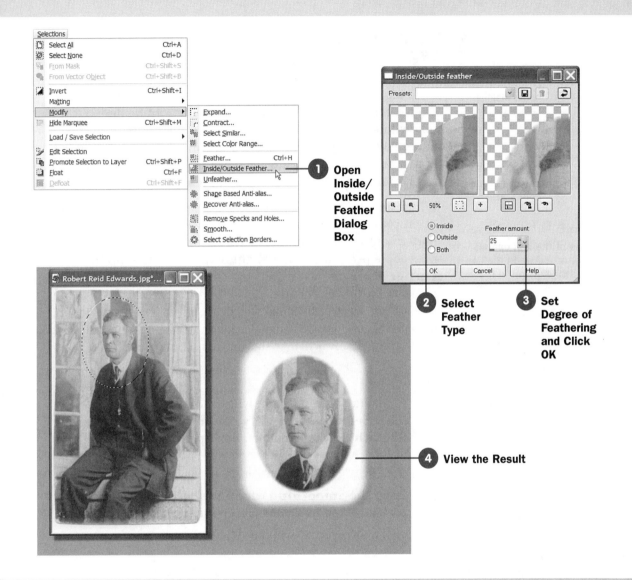

1 Open Inside/ Outside Feather Dialog Box

2 Select Feather Type

3 Set Degree of Feathering and Click OK

4 View the Result

67 Smooth the Edge of a Selection

Before You Begin

✔ **58** About Making Selections

See Also

→ **66** Soften the Edge of a Selection

→ **69** Remove Jaggies from a Selection

NOTE

None of the tool options you applied when making the selection in the first place—for instance, the Magic Wand's **Match** mode—apply to the smoothing effect. So some portion of the image you might have meant to exclude could end up included, and other portions you meant to include could end up smoothed out.

TIP

If you paste a feathered selection to its own layer, semi-transparent pixels appear along its borders, making it look jagged. Clean up the edge by selecting **Layers, Matting** and then choosing a command based on the color of the background the selection was copied from: **Remove Black Matte, Remove White Matte,** or **Defringe** (if the selection was copied from a colored background).

After you've used the **Magic Wand** tool to select a region from an image, there's a good chance that the selection will have a jagged edge. In some circumstances, this might be fine; but usually whatever you do to a selection, you don't want it to show. Using PSP's **Smooth** command, you can iron out the boundary of any selection so that the perimeter appears to flow fluidly and easily from point to point, as though it were drawn by hand.

When smoothing, PSP uses ordinary geometry to create a series of simple curves whose paths most closely fit the more irregular pattern of the selection border. These curves might include noticeable peaks and valleys, although by turning up the **Corner scale** option setting, you can have PSP round off the peaks to create very gentle convex and concave curves. The purpose of this kind of smoothing is not to create precise selection areas but more general ones—areas that appear more naturally cut out, especially when pasted into another image.

1 Make an Initial Selection

After making a selection whose border you want to smooth, select **Selections, Modify, Smooth** from the menu. The **Smooth Selection** dialog box opens.

2 Set Degree of Smoothing

Select the **Smoothing amount** you want. Watch the right preview pane for the result, and adjust as needed.

3 Set Corner Scale

To adjust how many pixels are added at the corners to smooth them, change the **Corner scale** value as desired. To preserve the crispness of a corner and not smooth it, enable the **Preserve corners** check box.

4 Set Anti-Aliasing and Click OK

Ironic though this might seem, the smoothing of your selection can lead to the same stair-step phenomenon as drawing a vector-based curved shape on a low-resolution canvas.

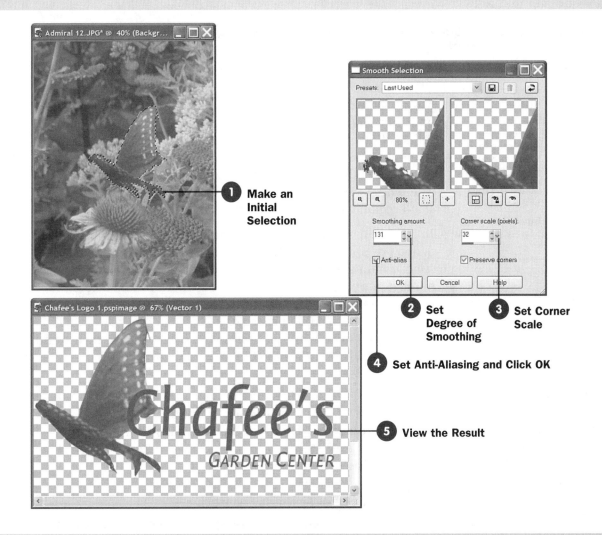

1 Make an Initial Selection

2 Set Degree of Smoothing

3 Set Corner Scale

4 Set Anti-Aliasing and Click OK

5 View the Result

To enable PSP to soften these jaggies, enable the **Anti-alias** check box. Variable opacity is used to soften the edges of the selected region. To finalize your choices, click **OK**.

5 View the Result

Here I've cut and pasted the smoothed selection into a new image with two other vector-based text elements. The graininess of the original selection boundary is gone, and the real butterfly integrates more cleanly with the other elements.

TIP

Turning off the **Preserve corners** option often has the effect of smoothing the selection much more than it might normally be smoothed, at the risk of losing the actual corners you might want to keep.

68 Remove Specks and Holes from a Selection

Before You Begin

✔ **58** About Making Selections

See Also

→ **65** Add Areas to or Subtract Areas from a Selection

→ **66** Soften the Edge of a Selection

→ **67** Smooth the Edge of a Selection

NOTE

When you're making a selection with anti-aliasing turned on, some pixels might be partly selected (using variable opacity) to compensate for the stair-step effect. Sometimes, choosing **Remove Specks** counteracts anti-aliasing, restoring the stair-step effect to places where you don't want it. When removing specks, be sure to preview the effect before applying it.

TIP

If the selection contains holes you don't want filled, and yet the current settings leave holes or specks that you want added to the selection, add them manually. See **65** Add Areas to or Subtract Areas from a Selection.

Although the **Smoothing** dialog box efficiently rounds off the edges of selections, covering up the jagged edges created by the **Magic Wand** tool, the method does precisely nothing to clean up the *interior* of a selection—namely, the occasional holes and specks of pixels that didn't satisfy the **Match mode** conditions at the time you made the selection. When referring to patchy selections in the interior of an image, a *hole* is a small region where no pixels are selected at all, whereas a *speck* is an equally small region with partially selected pixels.

To remove specks and holes, you must define their size. In the dialog box shown in the following steps, you'll enter a value and select a multiple, such as 4×1000. This defines the maximum number of pixels in area that a hole or speck can be before it is removed. In other words, with a setting of 4×1000, a hole can be no larger than 4,000 pixels (20×200, 10×400, or 40×100, for example) to be removed from the selection. A hole measuring 50×100 pixels would be too big to be removed.

1 **Make an Initial Selection**

After you've made a selection full of tiny holes that you want to remove, choose **Selections, Modify, Remove Specks and Holes** from the menu. The **Remove Specks and Holes** dialog box opens.

2 **Select Specks, Holes, or Both**

Choose whether to **Remove Specks**, **Remove Holes**, or both (**Remove Specks and Holes**).

3 **Adjust Size of Areas to Fix and Click OK**

PSP identifies a hole or a speck as an area that fits into a test square of a given size, where nothing (hole) or little (speck) has been selected. To specify the size of this test area, enter a value in the first box and select a multiple from the list. Increase the size of the test area until all holes and specks are removed from the selection. Click **OK**.

CHAPTER 3

10 **About Tools and Tool Options**

Many tools offer the option of blend modes.
Here's what you need to know about blend modes:

In **Normal** blend mode, the blend color completely replaces the base color.

In **Lighten** blend mode, the blend color is blended with the base, but replaces the base color only if the result is lighter.

In **Saturation** blend mode, only the blend color's saturation value is applied to the base, which retains its original hue and luminance values.

In **Luminance** blend mode, only the blend color's luminance value is applied to the base, which retains its original hue and saturation values.

In **Screen** blend mode, the lightness of the base color is compounded by the lightness of the blend color.

In **Overlay** blend mode, the lightness/darkness of the base color is compounded with the lightness/darkness of the blend color.

In **Soft Light** blend mode, the base and blend colors are blended and multiplied back into the base color, creating a ghostly image of the blend layer on top of the base layer.

In **Dodge** blend mode, the base color is lightened using the luminance value of the blend color.

In **Darken** blend mode, the blend color is blended with the base, but replaces the base color only if the result is darker.

In **Hue** blend mode, only the blend color's hue value is applied to the base, which retains its original saturation and luminance values.

In **Color** blend mode, the blend color's hue and saturation values are applied to the base, which retains its original luminance value.

In **Multiply** blend mode, the darkness of the base color is compounded by the darkness of the blend color.

Dissolve blend mode removes pixels from the blend color at random locations to let the base color show through.

In **Hard Light** blend mode, the lightness/darkness of the blend color is compounded with the lightness/darkness of the base color.

In **Exclusion** blend mode, the blend color is subtracted from the base color, and the inverse luminance value of the blend color is applied.

In **Difference** blend mode, the blend color is subtracted from the base color.

In **Burn** blend mode, the base colors are darkened by the inverse luminance values of the blend colors.

CHAPTER 4

26 Add Copyright Information

Protect your precious photographs when you place them online by embedding your copyright.

CHAPTER 5

36 About Image Types

This JP2 image file is smaller than its JPEG counterpart, yet it retains a higher quality.

JPEG 2000 Format

My Washington Trip

JPEG Format

My Washington Trip

CHAPTER 6

54 Achieve Color Balance Automatically

*The **Automatic Color Balance** feature instantly removed the reddish cast in this old school photo.*

COLOR GALLERY

CHAPTER 6

56 Adjust Saturation Automatically

*The **Automatic Saturation Enhancement** feature was just enough to bring out the pinkish undertone in the little girl's skin, the reddish highlights in her hair, and the lovely yellow in her sweater.*

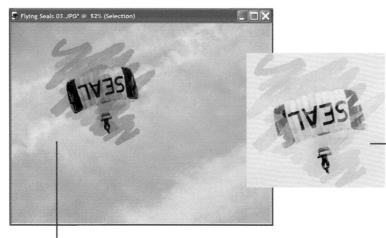

Flying Seals 03.JPG* @ 52% (Selection)

CHAPTER 7

58 About Making Selections

The ruby lithe enables you to see the various levels of selection.

Variable Selection Copied to New Image

Selection Overlay Displayed on Image

CHAPTER 8

79 Copy a Selection to a New Layer

I pasted a four-year-old version of my daughter next to a three-year-old version. Now they can play together.

CHAPTER 8

81 **Copy Data into a Selected Area**

To create this image, I did three "paste into selection" tasks: one to paste my daughter into the star shape, a second to paste a portion of Dorothy's dress into text created as a selection, and a third to paste the dress fabric again, this time into a freehand frame.

CHAPTER 9

89 **Remove Freckles and Minor Blemishes**

Remove freckles, wrinkles, and minor blemishes with a slight blur.

CHAPTER 10

95 **About Making Histogram Adjustments to Brightness and Contrast**

Because the Red channel has shifted to the right, dominating the light tones in this faded Kodak print, the image looks very pink.

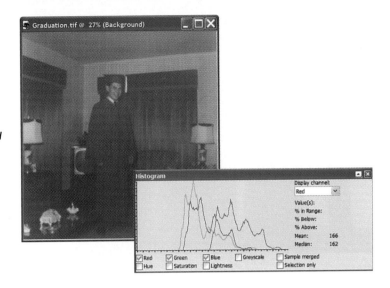

Original Image

Gamma Lowered to .70

Gamma Raised to 1.5

CHAPTER 10

95 **About Making Histogram Adjustments to Brightness and Contrast**

Adjusting the gamma can lighten or darken the midtones in an image, as it did with this rose.

CHAPTER 10

96 Improve Brightness and Contrast

A histogram adjustment allowed me to improve the contrast in this low-light image while maintaining its quiet solitude.

CHAPTER 10

98 About Making Curves Adjustments to Brightness and Contrast

*A small **Curves** adjustment in the Blue channel to remove blue in selected pixels changed the pale yellow accents of these daffodils to a bright yellow.*

CHAPTER 10

99 Restore Color and Improve Detail

*Using **Highlight/Midtone/Shadow** and **Curves** adjustments, I was able to restore color balance and contrast to this faded image of Grandmother Era.*

COLOR GALLERY

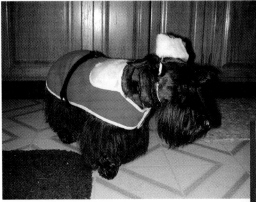

CHAPTER 11
106 **Correct Color Manually**

Manual color correction removed the yellowish cast from this image and returned Santa's coat to a bright red.

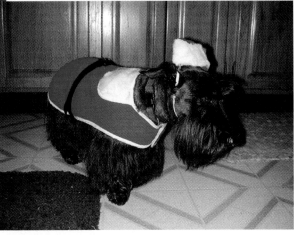

CHAPTER 11
107 **Adjust Hue, Saturation, and Lightness Manually**

*The **Hue/Saturation/Lightness** command allowed me to darken our faces just a bit, increase the saturation lost by the close flash, and bring out the red in the coat and the blue in the sweater.*

CHAPTER 11

108 Restore an Old Photograph

Repair an old photo like this one by improving contrast, restoring faded color and tone, and restoring color/tonal balance.

CHAPTER 11

109 Restore Color to a Washed-Out Photograph

*Boost color saturation on a faded photograph using a duplicate layer and the **Multiply** blend mode.*

CHAPTER 11
110 Change the Color or HSL to Match a Target Value

By controlling the placement of color in this mostly grayscale image, your eyes are immediately drawn towards its subject.

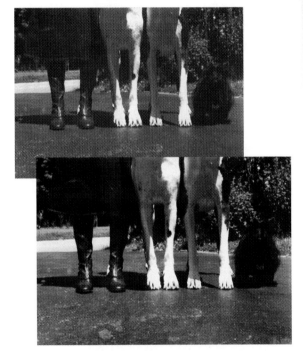

CHAPTER 11
111 Remove a Color Cast

The reddish color cast in this faded photo was instantly corrected with the **Black and White Points** command.

CHAPTER 12
118 Add Motion to an Image

Add motion to an otherwise still photo using the **Motion Blur** filter.

CHAPTER 13

120 **About Layers and the Layer Palette**

With layers, you can build up an image from elements.

CHAPTER 13

123 **Group and Organize Layers**

Grouping the girl and the text layers together allowed me to make the same hue adjustment to both.

CHAPTER 13

124 **Merge or Flatten Layers into One**

If an image contains many layers like this one does, you can merge together the layers you don't need to adjust any more to make the file smaller and easier to manage.

125 About Masks

A frame mask lets you try out the same frame on different pieces of art.

CHAPTER 14

127 Create a Mask from a Selection

I stylized this photo of Lincoln and, using a mask, replaced the background with a majestic sky.

129 Edit a Mask

A too-white sky in the background is easily substituted for two others: a more dramatic one and a more imaginary one.

CHAPTER 15

135 **Frame a Photograph**

This ornate frame and double picture mat complement this "painted" version of a nativity scene.

CHAPTER 15

136 **Add a Decorative Edge**

Rather than framing an image, add a decorative edge to give it a unique look.

CHAPTER 15

138 **Move, Alter, or Distort a Layer**

*With the **Deform** tool, you can distort an image and shape it to fit against a wall, a box, or in this case, a pillow.*

CHAPTER 15
139 "Melt" an Image

Mesh Warp and the *Warp Brush* allow you to add a sense of humor to your images by warping selected portions.

CHAPTER 15
141 Create a Panorama

Stitch together several images to create your own panorama.

CHAPTER 16
142 Age a Photograph

Apply a custom sepia effect to create images with an old-time look.

CHAPTER 16
143 Change a Color Photograph to Black and White

By selectively combining image channels, you can create your own high-quality grayscale image.

Original Color Image   **Photo Created with Grayscale Command**   **Photo Created with Channels**

CHAPTER 16
144 Colorize a Photograph

Colorizing various regions of a black-and-white image turns it into a full-color image with a hand-painted look.

CHAPTER 16
145 Make a Photograph Look Like an Oil Painting

*With some easy prep work and the **Brush Strokes** filter, you can make a photo look similar to a real oil painting like this one on the left.*

Real Oil Painting　　　　　　　　　　**Brush Strokes Filter**

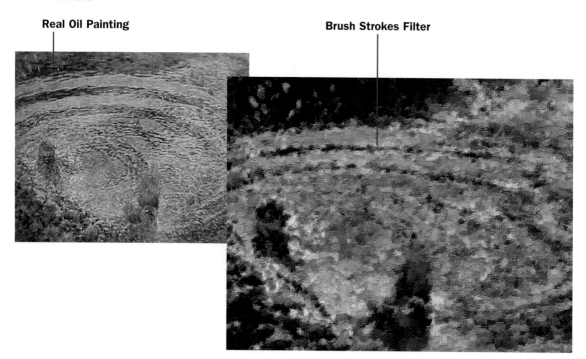

CHAPTER 16
146 Turn a Photograph into a Watercolor

With your choice of an Asian or an ink border technique, you can turn a peaceful scene into a realistic watercolor.

Asian Technique

Ink Border Technique

CHAPTER 16
147 Make a Photograph Look Like It Was Drawn

*Apply several techniques and the **Pencil** filter to create a pencil drawing from a photograph.*

148 **Make a Photograph Look Like Ansel Adams Shot It**

Turn an ordinary color image into a dramatic black-and-white image similar to those created by Ansel Adams.

① Make an Initial Selection

② Select Specks, Holes, or Both

Speck

Hole

③ Adjust Size of Areas to Fix and Click OK

④ View the Result

④ View the Result

Originally, the peace rose area was selected with multiple applications of the **Magic Wand** tool over the pinker regions of the rose. But what makes this rose beautiful is its little splashes of yellow; and those little splashes were being omitted as a result of violating the **Match mode** conditions. In addition, some specks were created by mistake when editing the selection with a gray paint brush. By setting the **Remove Specks and Holes** test square to a large enough value, PSP eliminated the specks and holes in the selection so that it now includes the yellow areas.

PSP does not fill gaps along the edges of the selection. That's because PSP treats a hole separately from a "pit" or "dent" in the outside perimeter of a selection. After applying **Remove Specks and Holes**, any such pits along the edge of a selection remain untouched. You can fix those pits and dents by smoothing the edges of the selection.

69 Remove Jaggies from a Selection

NOTE

PSP offers two ways to modify a selection using anti-aliasing: shape-based anti-aliasing (featured in this task) and recover anti-aliasing (featured in task **82** Clean Up a Selection Edge Before Pasting.

There's a subtle difference between smoothing and anti-aliasing which, once you understand it, may become useful to you: *Smoothing* is a purely geometric process. It finds the best series of simplified curves that fit the jagged line transcribed by the selection boundary. The results significantly change that boundary. Generally, *anti-aliasing* is a process of masking the side-effects caused by curved and diagonal lines, by fuzzifying those lines. The anti-alias process deals not with geometry but with opacity; it adds semi-selected pixels along the borders of a selection. So the question you should ask yourself when preparing to clarify a selection is, do you want to alter the selection lines to iron them out (including or excluding various fully selected pixels), or do you want to even out the appearance of the contents inside those lines at the edges without (significantly) altering those lines?

The shape-based anti-aliasing explained in this task makes use of both geometry and variable opacity. As does smoothing, shape-based anti-aliasing determines the simple lines and curves formed by the selection border. But then, unlike smoothing, it applies anti-aliasing to all diagonal edges and curves it finds, rather than actually changing the border itself. Depending on how you apply this kind of anti-aliasing, it can add semi-selected pixels along the outside or the inside of the selection. Either way,

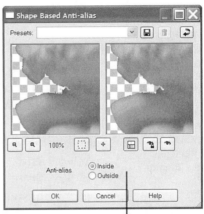

1 Make an Initial Selection

2 Select Where to Anti-alias and Click OK

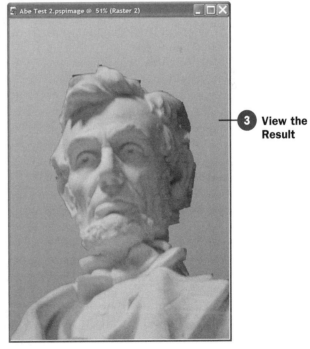

3 View the Result

TIP

If you paste an anti-aliased selection to its own layer, semi-transparent pixels appear along its borders, making it look jagged. Clean up the edge by selecting **Layers, Matting** and then choosing a command based on the color of the background the selection was copied from: **Remove Black Matte, Remove White Matte,** or **Defringe** (if the selection was copied from a colored background).

the anti-aliased edge will include variably selected pixels, or pixels which, if copied and pasted to another location, have less than 100% of their color values copied, and less than 100% applied to the pasted region.

❶ Make an Initial Selection

After making the selection you want to anti-alias, choose **Selections, Modify, Shape Based Anti-alias** from the menu. The **Shape Based Anti-alias** dialog box opens.

❷ Select Where to Anti-alias and Click OK

Select **Inside** (stair-stepped pixels along the inside perimeter of the selection are made partly transparent) or **Outside** (semi-transparent pixels are added to the exterior of the selection) to tell PSP where to smooth the selection with anti-aliasing. Click **OK**.

❸ View the Result

Here, I used an **Outside** anti-alias in moving Mr. Lincoln to a new, gradient-filled background. Notice the result isn't entirely perfect just yet. There are some dark artifacts along the edge of the "Lincoln layer," particularly in his hair, that can still be removed. However, especially along the shoulder area, there's a soft transition between the layer's edge and the foreign, tan-colored background.

Select Everything But the Current Selection

Before You Begin

✔ ❺❽ About Making Selections

See Also

➜ ❻❺ Add Areas to or Subtract Areas from a Selection

When you want to select a particular region of a digital photo, one option is to select the parts you *don't* want to work with, and then invert the selection. Inverting flips the selection so that everything that wasn't selected before is now selected (and everything that was selected, no longer is).

Selection inversion is your best choice when the item you want to select is hard to define, but *everything else* is easy. Suppose that you want to select a woman who happens to be posing against a monotone background. Normally, selecting all the hair, skin, and clothing in light, shade, and shadow would be a lengthy process.

1 Select All Unwanted Regions

2 Choose Selections, Invert

3 View the Result

However, using the **Magic Wand** tool, you can select the almost monochromatic background with just one or two clicks. Invert the selection, and you've selected the woman—as easy as that.

1 **Select All Unwanted Regions**

Using any of the selection tools, select the areas of the image you *do not* want to include in the final selection.

2 Select Selections, Invert

Choose **Selections, Invert** from the menu. Immediately, the marquee changes to indicate all areas of the image you did not select in step 1.

3 View the Result

Here, I originally selected the background. After I inverted the selection, it was easy to quickly transport these two lovely ladies from an everyday high school reunion to a tropical island where, given the choice, I'm sure they'd rather be.

71 Select a Portion of an Image with Channels

Before You Begin

✔ **58** About Making Selections

See Also

→ **72** Select a Portion of an Image with Threshold

→ **148** Make a Photograph Look Like Ansel Adams Shot It

KEY TERM

Channel—One of a handful of components that jointly characterizes the structure of a digital image, such as RGB, HSL, or CMYK. A channel can be addressed independently of the others; it's possible to edit just the green channel of an image.

As you've already seen earlier in this chapter, the **Magic Wand** tool lets you select an entire area whose pixels have similar or equal characteristics with one click in the middle of that area. With most photographs, however, it might be difficult to use the **Magic Wand** (or any other selection tool) to quickly select an object. This is where you can take advantage of PSP's capability to split a color image into three or four *channels*. A channel interpretation of an image represents one component of that image—its redness, blueness, or greenness; or its relative degree of saturation or lightness—as separate black-and-white images, where blackness represents a low amount and whiteness a high amount of that component. So a landscape that includes a bright blue sky would be interpreted with light grey in the blue channel image, and dark grey in the separate red channel image.

By splitting an image into black and white versions of its red, green, or blue components, for example, you might be able to more quickly select the object of your desire. Imagine an image with a person wearing a bright multi-colored sweater, standing against a rather dim background. By splitting the image into separate hue, saturation, and luminance channels, you can use the **Magic Wand** on the saturation channel image to more easily select the brightly lit person and exclude the darker background.

2 Make a Selection

1 Split Image Into Channels

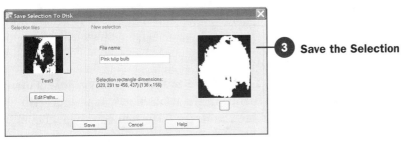

3 Save the Selection

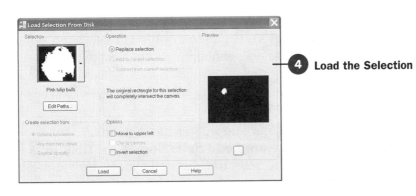

4 Load the Selection

5 View the Result

You can split an image into channels, edit those channels, and reassemble the image, repairing certain types of damage easily. See **103** **Fix a Flash That's Too Close** and **105** **Restore Balance to a Backlit Photograph** for tasks that use that technique.

❶ Split Image Into Channels

To split an image into its red, green, and blue components, select **Image**, **Split Channel**, **Split to RGB**. To split an image into its hue, saturation, and luminance components, select **Image**, **Split Channel**, **Split to HSL**. To split an image into its cyan, magenta, yellow, and black components, select **Image**, **Split Channel**, **Split to CMYK**.

❷ Make a Selection

Look over each of the three or four newly created channel images carefully. What you're looking for is enough contrast between the darker and lighter regions to make it easier for you to select the object you want. Change to the channel image you want to use and select the object using your choice of selection tool(s).

❸ Save the Selection

Select **Selections**, **Load/Save Selection**, **Save Selection To Disk** from the menu. In the dialog box, type a descriptive name for the selection in the **File name** box and click **Save**.

What you are saving to disk is not the data in the selected region itself, but the pattern formed by that selection. The goal is to apply this same pattern, at the same location, to the original color image, enabling you to select that same object there.

❹ Load the Selection

Change to the original image. Select **Selections**, **Load/Save Selection**, **Load Selection From Disk** from the menu. Open the **Selection** list and choose the channel selection you saved in step 3.

If you want to select everything on the color image *except* the region in the saved selection, enable the **Invert selection** check box. Click **Load**. In a moment, PSP will apply the saved selection pattern to the color image, as if you had made that selection directly on that image.

⑤ View the Result

In this example, I used RGB channeling to help isolate a very pink tulip from its very green surroundings. In the red channel image, the pinkness of the tulip caused the region it occupied to glow brightly, as if to say, "Pick me!"

72 Select a Portion of an Image with Threshold

The whole point of threshold adjustment in Paint Shop Pro is to make an image "bipolar" in a very real sense. Threshold converts an image to black and white (no grays), with those portions that are relatively dark converted to pure black, and the remainder to pure white. You control what defines a "relatively dark" pixel (the "threshold"), and PSP does the rest, turning those pixels black and the rest white.

Producing a truly black-and-white image gives you another way in which you can easily select areas of an image with relatively little fuss and bother. You might use this method to enhance the colors in, say, just the darker regions of the image, while leaving the lighter regions alone. As with channel splitting, this task involves saving the selection pattern to disk and reloading the original image.

You can perform this same task and safeguard your image against accidental changes by duplicating the image on another layer, thresholding the copy, making your selection, and then deleting the duplicate layer.

① Display Threshold Dialog Box

Select **Adjust, Brightness and Contrast, Threshold** from the menu.

Before You Begin

✔ **58** About Making Selections

See Also

→ **71** Select a Portion of an Image with Channels

→ **100** Lighten a Subject on a Snowy Background

→ **104** Fix a Flash That's Too Far Away

💡 TIP

Be careful after you apply the threshold technique so that you do not save the thresholded image on top of your original image file.

SNAPSHOT

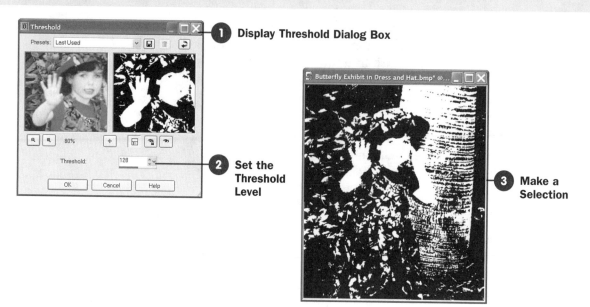

1 Display Threshold Dialog Box

2 Set the Threshold Level

3 Make a Selection

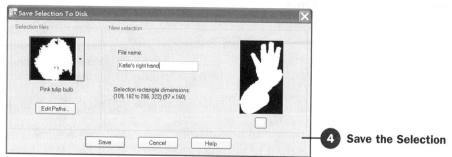

4 Save the Selection

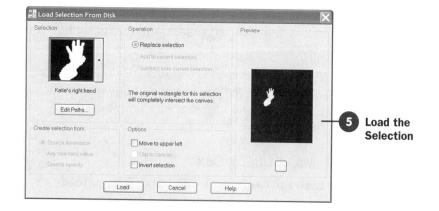

5 Load the Selection

② Set the Threshold Level

Adjust the **Threshold** value to define the threshold—a low threshold allows more pixels to remain white, whereas a high threshold turns more of them black. Click **OK**.

③ Make a Selection

Select the area(s) you want, using your choice of selection tool. Typically, you'll be able to select the region you want with a single click using the **Magic Wand** tool.

④ Save the Selection

To save the selection choose **Selections**, **Load/Save Selection**, **Save Selection To Disk**. In the dialog box, type a name for the selection in the **File name** box and click **Save**.

⑤ Load the Selection

First, restore the image to normal by selecting **File**, **Revert** from the menu. When prompted, click **Yes**.

Choose **Selections**, **Load/Save Selection**, **Load Selection From Disk** from the menu. In the dialog box, open the **Selection** list and choose the selection you saved in step 4. To have PSP select everything *except* the region in the saved selection, enable the **Invert Selection** check box. Click **Load**. In a moment, PSP will apply the saved selection pattern to the color image.

NOTE

There's no right or wrong with this technique; set a **Threshold** value that turns the region you want to select either all white or all black so that you can select it easily.

NOTE

Saving the selection saves just its pattern, not its contents (which would be totally black or totally white).

TIP

Don't click **Undo** to remove the Threshold effect, or you'll undo your **Load/Save Selection** command.

---

73 Edit a Selection

Paint Shop Pro offers another unique, and certainly more obscure, method for you to change the pattern of your selection to whatever you want. You can indicate the selection on the image with the selection overlay (also known as the ruby lithe), and then edit the selection by painting it with any of PSP's painting tools. Because the image is displayed underneath the semi-transparent overlay, it's easy to use the image itself as a guide to the adjustments you make.

Before You Begin

✔ **58** About Making Selections

See Also

→ **127** Create a Mask from a Selection

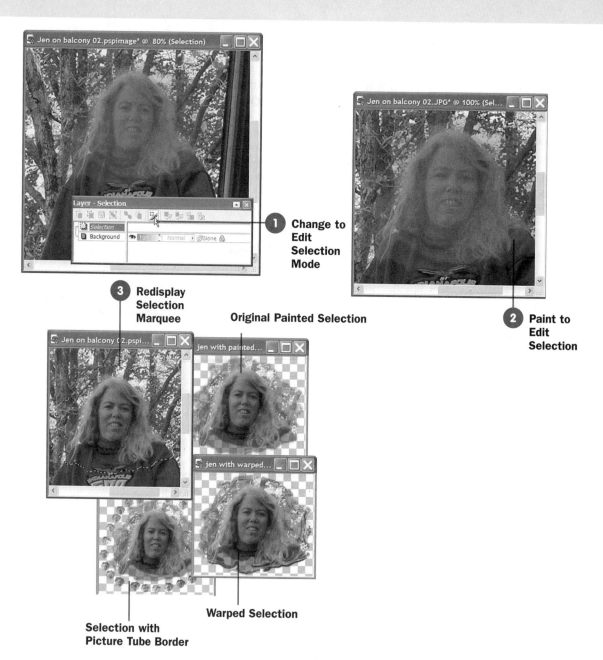

1 Change to Edit Selection Mode

3 Redisplay Selection Marquee

Original Painted Selection

2 Paint to Edit Selection

Selection with Picture Tube Border

Warped Selection

As described in **58** **About Making Selections**, the ruby lithe represents the varying intensities of a selection with proportionally varying opaqueness of red. Fully selected areas are depicted with a deeper red, while lesser selected regions appear with a more transparent red. As long as the **Selection** layer is active, you'll notice that the **Color** palette has temporarily become grayscale. To vary the intensity of a selected area, paint over it with various shades of gray; white adds pixels to a selection while black removes them.

① **Change to Edit Selection Mode**

Select **Selections**, **Edit Selection** from the menu, or click the **Edit Selection** button on the **Layer** palette. A transparent overlay representing the current selection (if any) appears over the image.

② **Paint to Edit Selection**

Select any of the available painting tools and paint with white in the image window to add areas to the selection; paint with black to remove them. Paint with gray to vary the selection's intensity. In addition, you can use any tool or command that works on grayscale images to modify the selection. Note that you can use any painting tool to modify the ruby lithe: the **Paint Brush**, **Airbrush**, or **Warp Brush** tool; the **Clone** tool; the **Dodge**, **Burn**, **Smudge**, **Push**, **Soften**, **Sharpen**, or **Emboss** tool; the **Lighten/Darken** tool; the **Eraser** tool; the **Picture Tube** tool; or the **Flood Fill** tool.

③ **Redisplay Selection Marquee**

To return PSP to normal editing mode, choose **Selections**, **Edit Selection** from the menu or click the **Edit Selection** button on the **Layer** palette. The overlay disappears and is replaced by the familiar selection marquee surrounding every pixel included in the selection, regardless of its intensity. The italicized *Selection* entry is removed from the top tier of the **Layer** palette.

Shown is an image with the original selection, created with the **Paint Brush** tool. Also shown is the selection further

NOTE

If your image is mostly red to begin with, the ruby lithe might be almost (if not entirely) invisible. To solve: In the **Layer** palette, double-click the **Selection** layer. In the **Layer Properties** dialog box change the **Overlay color** and/or adjust the **Opacity** until the ruby lithe is more visible.

TIP

You can manipulate the selection layer's shape, size, and opacity using the same tools you would use to manipulate a content layer. For example, you can use the **Deform** tool to adjust the size and position of the selection, clone the selection with the **Clone Brush**, warp the selection using the **Mesh Warp** tool, or apply any filter that works on grayscale images such as **Gaussian Blur**.

NOTES

On the **Layer** palette, notice that **Selection** has temporarily been given the status of a layer, at the top of the order; this listing disappears when you exit **Edit Selection** mode.

Because the ruby lithe appears on its own layer, whatever you do to it affects the selection marquee only—*not your image*.

8

Copying and Reusing Selections

IN THIS CHAPTER:

In Chapter 7, you learned how to create selections using the various selection tools Paint Shop Pro provides. One of the most wonderful things about selections, however, is that they are reusable. For example, after using a selection to lighten an area, you might decide much later in the process to adjust the area's saturation as well. If you've saved the selection, you won't have to re-create it later if you find you still need it. In this chapter, you'll learn how to save and reuse selections and how to copy the selection to various areas of an image.

74 About the Alpha Channel

Before You Begin

✔ **58** About Making Selections

✔ **73** Edit a Selection

See Also

→ **75** Save a Selection for Reuse

→ **130** Save and Reuse Masks

⒦EY TERM

Alpha channel—A storage area within an image file in which you can save an image's selections and masks. Data stored in an alpha channel can be reused in that image, or in another image if both are open at the same time.

◣NOTE

Selections are saved *temporarily* to the image's alpha channel and deleted when the image is closed, *unless the image uses the PSPImage format.*

One of the key purposes of the *alpha channel* is to serve as a sort of internal "pocket" within an image file for selections—not the data within the selection, but the selection marquee itself. Other data is saved with the selection pattern as well, such as feathering, anti-aliasing, and variable intensity (as described in **73** **Edit a Selection**). By saving a selection to the alpha channel, you can use it in that same image to reselect the region, to select a different region in the image by moving the selection or changing to a different layer, or to select a similar region in another image (provided that both images are open at the time).

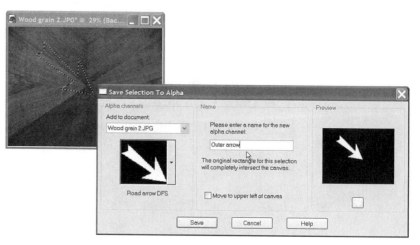

Saving a selection to an alpha channel.

As you know, Paint Shop Pro selects only one region at a time; when one region is selected, the existing selection pattern is discarded. By saving that selection to the alpha channel, however, you can recall that pattern later when needed. The alpha channel can hold as many selection patterns as you like. Suppose that you want to create a series of wooden arrow-shaped buttons for use on a Web site. You've taken a photograph of a parquet floor—and you intend to cut out equivalently shaped chunks from various sections of the floor, saving each selection as a separate image file. After you create the arrow pattern, you can save it to the alpha channel and use it multiple times in that same image. You can also open an image of a different wood pattern and use the arrow selection there as well, provided that the alpha channel image remains open. With the help of the alpha channel, you can construct the pattern once, save it, and reload it any number of times.

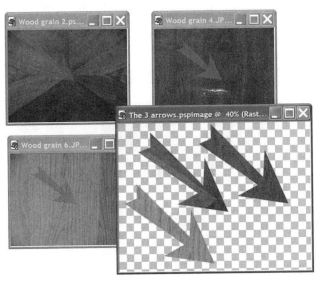

Using an alpha channel selection in one image to cut the same shape from multiple open images.

TIP

You can save a selection permanently for use in any image, regardless of whether the original image is open—see **75** Save a Selection for Reuse.

There are only two things you have to remember about the limits of using the alpha channel: Selections stored in an alpha channel are available within that image only, or within other open images. The alpha channel is considered temporary—its data is therefore cleared when the image is closed *unless you save the image in PSP format, in which case the alpha channel data is retained.* You'll typically use the alpha channel for selections you want to reuse in the same image, during this work session only (unless you're working on an image that uses PSP format). For example, after building a selection that creates a perfect outline around your son, you can save the selection to the alpha channel so that you can recall it whenever you have to make specific changes to your son only and not to the entire image.

NOTE

The other purpose of the alpha channel is to save masks. See **124** About Masks for more information.

Another neat thing you can do with the alpha channel is to build complex selections by using an alpha channel selection to add to or subtract from the current selection in an image. In this example, I started by loading the arrow selection from the alpha channel. Then I loaded a text selection from the alpha channel that I'd created earlier, but instead of replacing the arrow selection in the image, I asked PSP to remove the text area from the arrow selection. When I copied and pasted the resulting selection to a new image, I had a wooden arrow with the words "Look here" cut out of it. If I wanted, I could save this new, combined selection to the alpha channel as well.

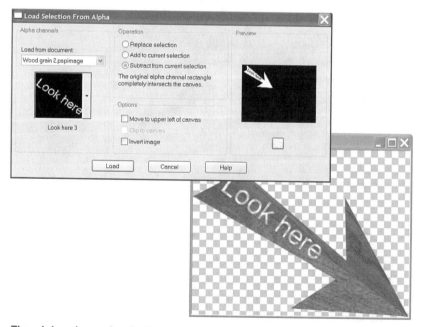

The alpha channel selection can add to or subtract from the current selection.

PART II: Making Selected Changes to an Image

75 Save a Selection for Reuse

If you have a selection you think you might want to reuse, either in this same image or another image, you have two choices: You can save the selection to the image's alpha channel, or you can save it to disk. Saving a selection to the alpha channel makes it available within the current image and to any other image open at the time. Typically, the alpha channel is deleted when an image is closed, so you can use it for selections you want to save temporarily—for this work session. To save selections permanently for use in any image (regardless of the format the image is saved in), save that selection to disk.

1 Finalize Your Selection

Make all adjustments necessary for your selection pattern to appear precisely the way you want it to appear when you reload it later.

2 Save the Selection

To save your selection to the alpha channel of the active image, choose **Selections, Load/Save Selection, Save Selection To Alpha Channel**.

To save your selection to disk, choose **Selections, Load/Save Selection, Save Selection To Disk**.

3 Select Options

When saving to the alpha channel, you can choose various options as desired. To save the selection to the alpha channel of some image other than the current one, open the **Add to document** list and select that image from the list that appears.

To have PSP save the selection pattern without its location—thus enabling the pattern to appear in the upper-left corner of the destination image—enable **Move to upper left of canvas** check box.

Before You Begin

✔ **74** About the Alpha Channel

See Also

→ **76** Reload a Previously Saved Selection

 NOTE

The selections in the alpha channel *are not cleared* when the image is closed if the image is saved in PSPImage format.

NOTE

Once saved, a selection cannot be edited. But you can reload the selection, make changes, and save it again. If you use the same name, you can overwrite the original selection pattern.

TIP

To preview the selection in varying degrees of black against a checkered transparent background, click the **Toggle Transparency Checkerboard** button under the sample image.

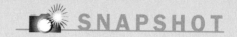

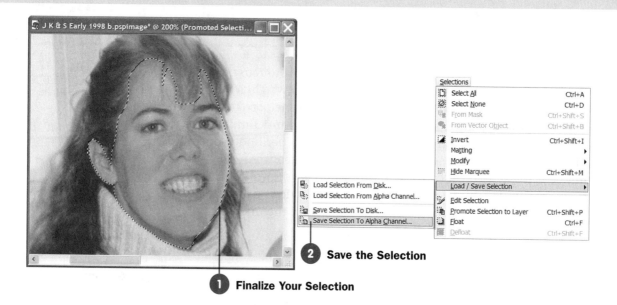

2 Save the Selection

1 Finalize Your Selection

Toggle Transparency
Checkerboard Button

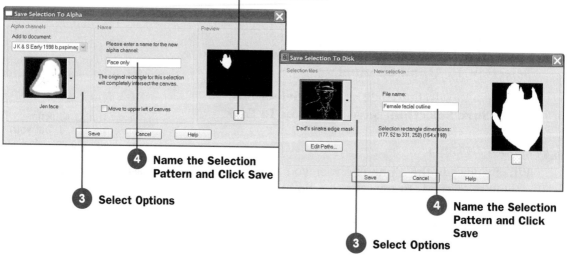

4 Name the Selection
Pattern and Click Save

3 Select Options

4 Name the Selection
Pattern and Click
Save

3 Select Options

4 Name the Selection Pattern and Click Save

Type a name for the selection pattern in the **Name** box and
click **Save**.

76 Reload a Previously Saved Selection

After saving a selection to the alpha channel of an image or to disk, you can recall it for reuse whenever you like. When the selection is reloaded, you can have it appear in the same general location as when it was saved, or in the upper-left corner of the image. The latter option is especially convenient when you're loading the selection into an image that's a different size than the original image from which the selection was created. If a selection already exists in an image when you attempt to reload a previously saved selection, you have the option to replace it, add to it, or to subtract from the selection the area occupied by the loaded selection. You can even invert the selection as it's being reloaded—essentially selecting everything but the area originally in the selection.

Before You Begin

✔ **75** Save a Selection for Reuse

See Also

✔ **73** Edit a Selection

1 Select Load Selection

Open the image and select the layer into which you want to load the saved selection. Then choose **Selections, Load/Save Selection, Load Selection From Alpha Channel** or **Selections, Load/Save Selection, Load Selection From Disk**.

2 Choose the Selection Pattern

If you are loading a selection from the alpha channel of a different image, first select that image from the **Load from document** list. Then open the **Selection** list and choose the selection to reload.

3 Choose Options and Click Load

If the current image already contains a selection, choose the **Replace selection** option to replace it, **Add to current selection** to add to it, or **Subtract from current selection** to erase the part of the existing selection that the selection you are loading overlaps.

If you are loading a selection from disk, choose **Source luminance** to load the selection as it was saved (using variable opacity). To load the selection with each pixel at 100% intensity, choose **Any non-zero value**. To select a

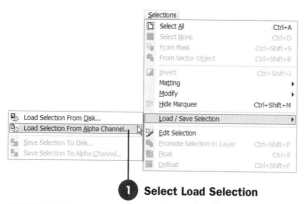

Select Load Selection

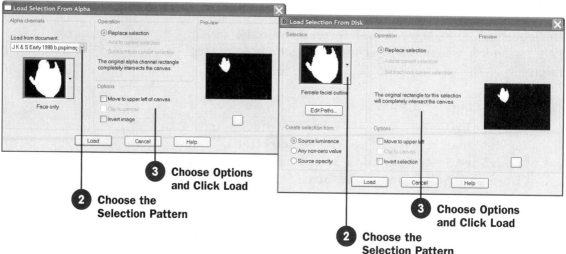

Choose Options and Click Load

Choose the Selection Pattern

Choose Options and Click Load

Choose the Selection Pattern

NOTE

By default, the selection you load appears exactly as far down from the top, and exactly as far to the right, as the original selection before it was saved. To move this selection to a new location, choose **Selections**, **Edit Selection**, and use the **Move** tool to drag the selection overlay to a new location in the image.

rectangular area around the original selection area, choose **Source opacity**.

To move the selection marquee from its original location to the upper-left of the image, enable the **Move to upper left** check box. To cut off a large selection at the edges of the image, enable the **Clip to canvas** check box. To select everything in the image *except* the pattern being loaded, enable the **Invert image** (alpha channel) or **Invert selection** (from disk) check box. When you've made your choices, click **Load**.

77 About Copy and Paste

I assume that you've had some experience with the general concept of cutting, copying, and pasting using the Windows
Clipboard, which enables you to copy material between different
applications. In this discussion, I'll concentrate on what distinguishes cut-and-paste operations with Paint Shop Pro from any
other kind of cut-and-paste operation.

When you make a selection, only the pixels within the selection
marquee are cut or copied to the Clipboard. In the absence of a
marquee, PSP cuts or copies the current layer. As you'd expect,
the **Cut** command removes the item being cut to the Clipboard,
and the **Copy** command simply copies it and does not affect the
original image. In both cases, the item is stored in the area of
memory referred to by Windows as the Clipboard.

PSP makes available another copying command: **Copy Merged**,
which places a copy of pixels on *all visible layers* on the
Clipboard. By contrast, the **Copy** command copies only the pixels within the selection marquee (if any) for just the *current* layer.

Pasting an element from the Clipboard is not a one-click operation. In Paint Shop Pro, it matters not just *where* you paste the
copied element, but also *how* that pasted element should be
treated: Should the copied data become a new image unto itself,
a new layer of the active image, a new selection that belongs
someplace in an existing layer, or a new selection that doesn't
belong anyplace just yet but just floats above the current layer as
a separate entity?

When you paste data using the **Paste As New Image** command, PSP creates a new image window with the previously set
background color or transparency, at the size of the image most
recently created with the **File, New** command, and places the
data in the center of that new image. The **Paste As New Layer**
command creates a new layer in the active image.

The **Paste As New Selection** command creates a new entity
called a *floating selection*, which for the time being does not
belong to any layer at all. After the paste, the copied element

Before You Begin

✔ **58** About Making
Selections

See Also

→ **78** Create a New
Image from a
Selection

→ **79** Copy a Selection
to a New Layer

→ **80** Copy a Selection
and Move It

→ **81** Copy Data into a
Selected Area

→ **120** About Layers and
the Layer Palette

NOTE

Unlike Office, where you
can collect bits and pieces
of material and then paste
them all at once or sepa-
rately, in PSP you can copy
or cut only one thing at a
time.

NOTE

In the absence of a selection, the **Copy Merged**
command copies *the entire
image* to the Clipboard, but
first merges its contents.

floats above the current layer. This gives you an opportunity to position the pasted data, modify it with filters, and use tools to make changes to it. When the copy looks exactly as you want, you *defloat* the selection, which makes it a permanent part of the current layer—in a sense, you "stamp" it onto that layer. However, it's still a selection, so you can continue to make alterations to it, although it's now part of a layer.

The difference between **Paste As New Selection** and **Paste As Transparent Selection** concerns the use of a background color. Suppose that you're copying an element from a graphic with a solid-colored background, such as white. You can quickly select around the element you want using a simple rectangular selection. If you then change the background color on the **Materials** palette to the same white used in the background of your image, and choose **Paste As Transparent Selection**, PSP pastes all the pixels within the selection *except for the ones that match the background color*—in this example, PSP removes the white background pixels from the rectangular selection for you, pasting only the remaining pixels.

The **Paste Into Selection** command allows you to designate the precise area where your pasted element will appear by creating a selection. Before you paste, you use a selection tool to select the region of the destination image where you want the pasted selection to appear. When you do paste, PSP proportionately stretches or shrinks the pasted selection, if necessary, to fit the area you've designated.

Finally, the **Paste As New Vector Selection** command enables you to use the **Object Selection** tool to indicate a vector-based object, such as a star shape or text element, cut or copy it, and paste it elsewhere as a vector-based object. If you use any other command to accomplish this cut-and-paste trick, the vector data you selected is first converted to rasters before it's pasted.

TIP

You can use the **Paste Into Selection** command to fill text you've created as a selection with flowers, fall leaves, or any other graphic you like. You can also use this command to create unique frames around a favorite photo, pasting an image into a heart-shaped selection, for example.

78 Create a New Image from a Selection

There are times when you want to use a portion of an image in a larger composition—a greeting card, place card, invitation, or simply an artistic composition. In such a case, it's simpler to copy the portion you want to use to a new image window, rather than modifying the original image. You might also use this method to save the selection as a separate image where you can make modifications to it, preparing the selection for use in several other images, such as various versions of your company's logo.

1 Copy Selection

Select the area you want to copy and then choose **Edit, Copy** or **Edit, Copy Merged** from the menu. Alternatively, to remove the selection from the active image, choose **Edit, Cut**.

2 Paste As New Image

Choose **Edit, Paste, Paste as New Image** from the menu.

3 View the Result

A new image window, sized to fit the selection, appears. It uses a temporary name and number, such as "**Image1**," until you give the image a permanent name when you save it.

Before You Begin

✔ **58** About Making Selections

✔ **77** About Copy and Paste

See Also

➔ **2** Create a New Image

TIPS

You can also make a selection and click the **Copy** or **Cut** button on the **Standard** toolbar.

To copy or cut all the data on the current layer, you don't have to make any selection at all.

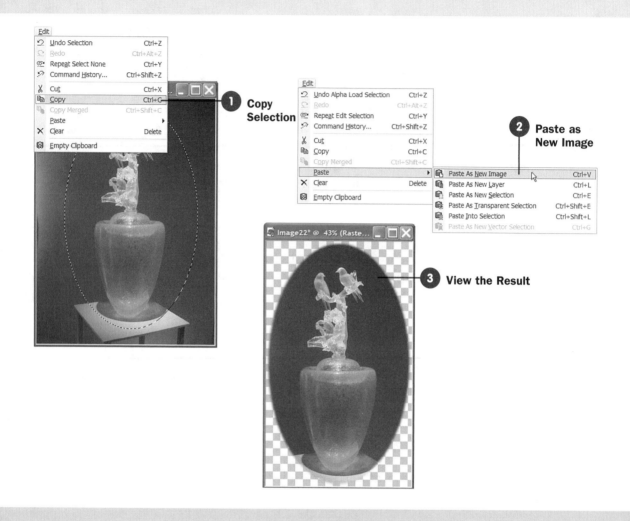

1 Copy Selection

2 Paste as New Image

3 View the Result

---

79 Copy a Selection to a New Layer

Before You Begin

✔ **58** About Making Selections

✔ **77** About Copy and Paste

See Also

→ **120** About Layers and the Layer Palette

One of the fastest growing functions of digital photo editing programs is to add something to a photo that wasn't in the original. In practice, this could get you into trouble, as was the case with one former photographer for the *Los Angeles Times* who was fired during the second Gulf War for using a technique very similar to what you're about to see done here, although without telling his superiors or his readers.

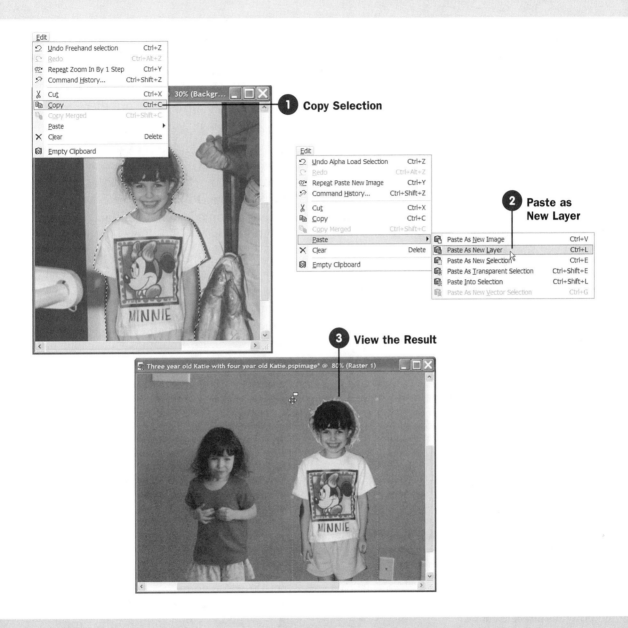

1 **Copy Selection**

2 **Paste as New Layer**

3 **View the Result**

But there are very legitimate purposes for taking the contents of one layer and copying them to a new layer. For example, you might copy a bit of the background in an old photo, paste it to a new layer, and move it over a hole or tear in the layer below. Or

TIP

After copying the selection to a new layer, use the **Move** tool to move the entire layer around as needed. Use the **Deform** tool to move a selection on a layer (without affecting the layer's other contents), or to change the size of a selection.

 TIPS

You can also make a selection and click the **Copy** or **Cut** button on the **Standard** toolbar.

To copy or cut all the data on the current layer, you don't have to make any selection at all.

 TIP

As a shortcut, you can copy a selection to a layer above the current one by simply making the selection and then choosing **Selections, Promote Selection to Layer.**

NOTE

Often, the selected data is not proportionate to the image into which you're pasting it. Use the **Deform** tool to resize and move the selection. See **138** Move, Alter, or Distort a Layer.

you might create a photo montage by copying elements of multiple photos into separate layers of an image. By maintaining each copied element in its own separate layer, you can create dramatic photo effects, such as one layer casting a shadow on another, or one layer iridescently appearing over another.

If you paste a feathered selection to its own layer, semi-transparent pixels appear along its borders, making it look jagged. Clean up the edge by selecting **Layers, Matting** and then choosing a command based on the color of the background the selection was copied from: **Remove Black Matte, Remove White Matte,** or **Defringe** (if the selection was copied from a colored background).

1 Copy Selection

Make your selection, then choose **Edit**, **Copy** or **Edit, Copy Merged** from the menu. Alternatively, to remove the selection from the active image, choose **Edit, Cut**.

2 Paste as New Layer

Open the image into which you want to paste the selection (if different from the current image). Choose the layer *above which* you want the newly created layer to appear. Choose **Edit, Paste, Paste As New Layer** from the menu.

You can paste an entire image onto a new layer in another image by dragging the image from the Browser and dropping it on an open image. See **4 Browse for an Image.**

3 View the Result

The copied selection appears in the center of the new raster layer. Use the **Move** tool to relocate the selection within the layer. In this example, I'm starting to work on a little vignette where four-year-old Katie comes to play with three-year-old Katie. I used the **Deform** tool to bring the newly imported Katie down to size. I've yet to get the junk out of her hair (four-year-old Katie was standing in front of a lighter-colored wall), and I need to create shadows behind her and on her face to make it appear that both Katies are in the same scene. Look for this image in the Color Gallery section of this book.

80 Copy a Selection and Move It

The first problem you'll face after copying a selection is placing it precisely where you want it. When you use the **Paste As New Selection**, **Paste As Transparent Selection**, or **Paste As New Vector Selection** command, you are given the opportunity to move the selection around the current layer until it is exactly where you want it. That's because, for a limited time, the copied selection actually floats above the current layer like a cloud.

After positioning the selection, your next problem might be the way the selection looks compared to the surrounding image data. Fortunately, while the selection is still floating, you can manipulate it however you want—brightening it, blurring it, and so on. After all adjustments are made, your final problem is to get the selection to belong to a layer. This is simple to solve: When you're ready, you simply defloat the selection. Like pasting real wallpaper to a real wall, the defloated selection binds itself to the layer below it, and the selection marquee disappears.

1 Copy Selection

Select the area you want to copy. To select a vector-based object such as a bit of text, use the **Object Selection** tool to click on it. Then choose **Edit**, **Copy** or **Edit**, **Copy Merged** from the menu. Alternatively, to remove the selection from the active image, choose **Edit**, **Cut**.

2 Paste Selection

Open the image into which you want to paste the selection and then choose the layer on which you want the selection to appear. To paste the data as a movable selection, select **Edit**, **Paste**, **Paste As New Selection** from the menu. The copied selection appears in the middle of the current layer without its marquee.

To paste the selection and make its background transparent, set the background color to match the color of the pixels in the background of the selection, and select **Edit**, **Paste**, **Paste As Transparent Selection**. Pixels from the selection

Before You Begin

✔ **58** About Making Selections

✔ **77** About Copy and Paste

See Also

→ **81** Copy Data into a Selected Area

TIPS

At any time, you can *float* any number of selected regions by choosing **Selections**, **Float**. These floating selections are left free to roam, disconnected from layers, until you shuffle their positions and promote them to a regular layer by selecting **Selections**, **Promote Selection to Layer**.

To select multiple vector-based objects, hold down the **Shift** key while clicking with the **Object Selection** tool.

You can also make a selection and click the **Copy** or **Cut** button on the **Standard** toolbar.

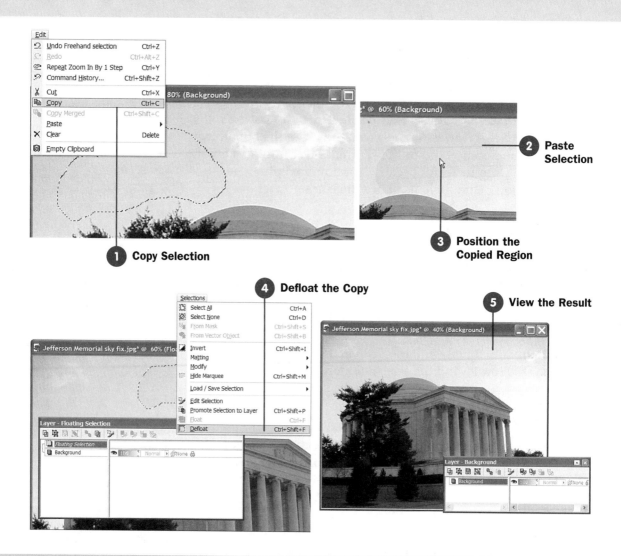

1 Copy Selection

2 Paste Selection

3 Position the Copied Region

4 Defloat the Copy

5 View the Result

If your original selection was vector based, and you select **Paste As New Selection** or **Paste As Transparent Selection**, the copy will be converted to raster data.

that match the background color you set are now omitted from the floating selection.

If your original selection was vector based, and you want to make a vector-based copy, choose **Edit**, **Paste As New Vector Selection**. The object appears as an outline; it's not marked with the familiar handles used to indicate vector-based objects because the copy isn't an object yet.

3 Position the Copied Region

Move the mouse to the location where you want the copied region to appear and click. With a pen tablet, hover the pen over the area where you want the copy to appear and touch that spot.

4 Defloat the Copy

After making changes to the selection as desired (lightening, brightening, resizing, moving, and so on), make the selection part of a permanent layer by defloating the selection. From the menu bar, choose **Selections**, **Defloat**. The floating selection is now part of a layer. If you copied raster data onto a vector layer, click **OK** and a new a raster layer is created.

5 View the Result

The marquee reappears around the selection after defloating. If you want to remove the marquee, choose **Selections**, **Select None**. In this example, I had a fairly good picture of the Jefferson Memorial, but the beautiful cloud above it attracted too much attention. So I cut out a fuzzy portion of the clear blue sky from elsewhere in the photograph and pasted it back to mostly cover up the cloud. The result is less of a distraction, and the eyes remain trained on the structure.

NOTE

With raster data, PSP creates a temporary layer called **Floating Selection** and positions it above the current layer. With vector data, if you've chosen a vector-based layer in the **Layer** palette, PSP adds the copied object to that layer. If you've chosen a raster layer, PSP creates a new *permanent* vector layer directly above the chosen layer. In either case, with vector data, skip step 4.

TIP

Before defloating, you can reposition the **Floating Selection** layer within the layer stack. After defloating, the selection becomes part of the layer below it in the stack.

---

81 Copy Data into a Selected Area

In many types of editing operations, you'll want or need a graphic from another image—perhaps something as simple as a piece of sky—to be applied not only to a certain location but to a specifically defined area of an image. For example, how many photos have you taken where the sky seems washed out? Perhaps you can correct this problem by pasting in a new sky. Or maybe you want to paste flowers into a selection "frame" around a loved one's face. Or perhaps you want to create some patriotic text by pasting a flag into text you've created using a selection.

Before You Begin

✔ **58** About Making Selections

✔ **77** About Copy and Paste

See Also

→ **59** Select a Rectangular, Circular, or Other Standard-Shaped Area

---

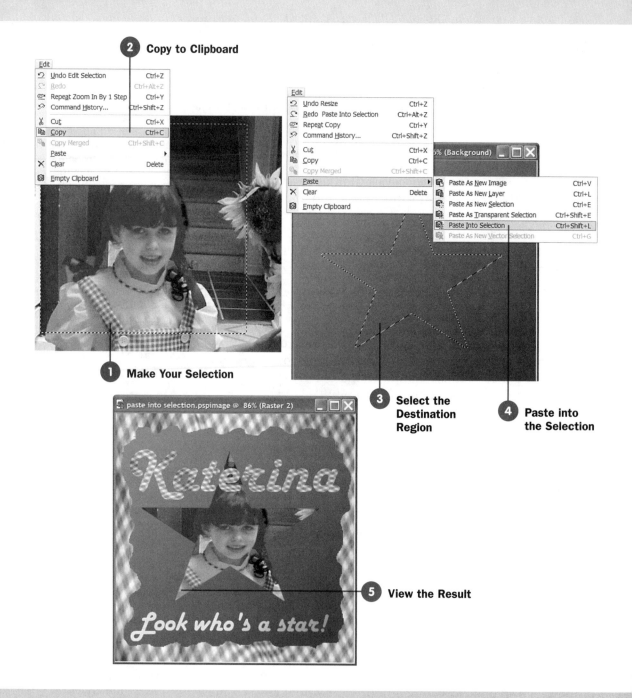

2 Copy to Clipboard

1 Make Your Selection

3 Select the Destination Region

4 Paste into the Selection

5 View the Result

① Make Your Selection

From the **Layer** palette, choose the layer from which the selection is to be made. To select a raster-based region, use the **Selection** tool, the **Freehand Selection** tool, or the **Magic Wand**. To select a vector-based region, use the **Object Selection** tool to click on the object to be copied.

② Copy to Clipboard

From the menu bar, choose **Edit**, **Copy**. Alternatively, to remove the selection from the active image, choose **Edit**, **Cut**.

③ Select the Destination Region

In the destination image, using a selection tool, select the region where you want the copied portion to appear.

④ Paste into Selection

From the menu bar, choose **Edit**, **Paste Into Selection**. The pasted data appears within the selection. PSP stretches or shrinks the pasted data proportionately to fit the width of the selected region—it won't change the shape of the copy if the selected region happens to be nonrectangular. It will simply try to make the best fit possible.

⑤ View the Result

Here, I've done three "paste into selection" tasks: one to paste Katerina into the star shape, a second to paste a portion of Dorothy's dress into text created as a selection, and a third to paste the dress fabric again, this time into a freehand frame. Look for this image in the Color Gallery section of this book.

 TIPS

You can also make a selection and click the **Copy** or **Cut** button on the **Standard** toolbar.

To copy or cut all the data on the current layer, you don't have to make any selection at all.

 NOTE

If you pasted vector-based data—for instance, text—it will be converted into raster data.

82 Clean Up a Selection Edge Before Pasting

Before You Begin

→ **80** Copy a Selection and Move It

See Also

→ **66** Soften the Edge of a Selection

→ **67** Smooth the Edge of a Selection

→ **69** Remove Jaggies from a Selection

 NOTE

Adding anti-aliasing to a selection before pasting it can cause formerly unselected pixels along the edges to become partially or totally selected. In so doing, unwanted contents such as the background of the selected object might appear as part of the pasted data.

 NOTE

When choosing between **Inside** or **Outside** anti-aliasing, look at the previews to see which result you like best. **Inside** changes the pixels nearest the border so that they are almost transparent, gradually fading to opaque as they move inward. **Outside** changes the border pixels to semi-transparent, adding even more transparent pixels as they move outward, smoothing the edge.

One of the minor problems brought about by nonrectangular selections is the introduction of jagged diagonal edges and curves. Paint Shop Pro includes two features that address this problem in different ways. In **69** **Remove Jaggies from a Selection**, I demonstrate how PSP applies anti-aliasing to the shape of a selection to produce at least the illusion of smoother curves and straighter lines.

As an alternative to adding anti-aliasing to a selection before you paste it, you can use the **Recover Anti-alias** command to apply anti-aliasing to a just pasted selection. This way, if you've carefully used the **Magic Wand** or some other selection tool to precisely include the contents you want and exclude the contents you don't want, PSP can smooth out the edges using the colors and contents of just the pixels along those edges. This can introduce some distortions and fuzziness along the edges of a selection; however, the process does not result in PSP altering the selection borders to include any contents from the original image that you did not intend to select.

1 Make Your Selection

Select the object you want to work with.

2 Choose Recover Anti-alias

Choose **Selections, Modify, Recover Anti-alias** from the menu. The **Recover Anti-alias** dialog box opens.

3 Choose Where to Anti-alias

Under **Anti-alias**, choose **Inside** to have PSP apply its fuzzying effects to pixels inside the current selection border. Choose **Outside** to have fuzzying applied beyond the boundaries of the current selection.

4 Set Other Options and Click OK

To include the visible color of pixels from all layers beneath the current one when creating the anti-aliased pixels, enable the **Sample merged** check box.

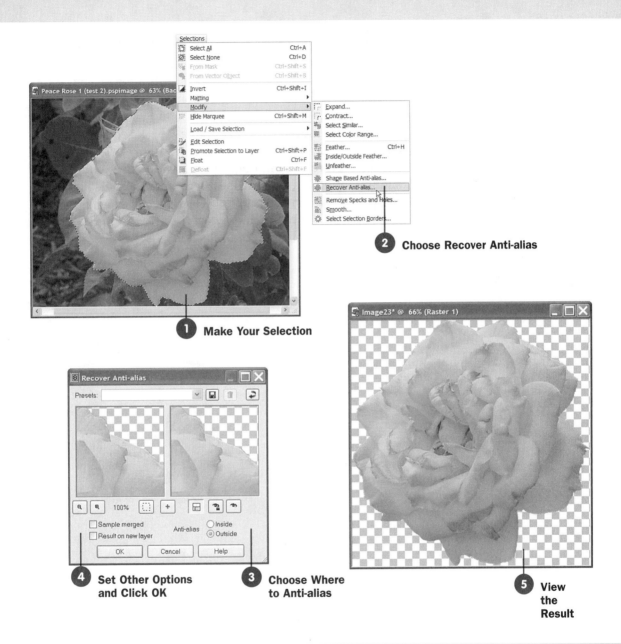

Make Your Selection (1)

Choose Recover Anti-alias (2)

Set Other Options and Click OK (4)

Choose Where to Anti-alias (3)

View the Result (5)

To copy the anti-aliased result to a new layer, enable the **Result on new layer** check box. PSP will copy the selection (without deleting its contents from its original layer) to a new layer above the current one. To finalize your choices, click **OK**.

5 View the Result

In this example, the flower portion of a Peace rose was selected and moved to a new image. The **Recover Anti-alias** command was applied to the **Outside** of the selection border. As a result, although the selection edges ended up slightly fatter, the flower edges were smoother. Also notice that, even though the original selection was extended by a few pixels, it did not include green portions from the leafy surroundings of the original selection.

9

Retouching a Photograph

IN THIS CHAPTER:

A photograph used to be a permanent record of a singular moment in time. With digital imaging, however, a photograph can be improved, enhanced, and even fundamentally changed to hide the "truth" of the original moment it captured. Through retouching, you can repair minor flaws such as scratches and holes and remove distortion caused by the camera lens or high file compression. You can even improve a human subject, removing red eye, erasing freckles and blemishes, and whitening teeth. In this chapter, I'll teach you how to use Paint Shop Pro's tools and filters to retouch your photographs and make them as good as new (or even better!).

83 About Removing Scratches, Specks, and Holes

Before You Begin

✔ **46** About Common Corrections

✔ **58** About Making Selections

✔ **120** About Layers and the Layer Palette

See Also

→ **84** Remove Scratches Automatically

→ **85** Repair Scratches Manually

→ **86** Remove Specks and Spots

→ **87** Repair Holes and Tears

TIP

Like most changes you can make to an image, you can limit your retouching to either a layer or a selection.

It's not uncommon for photographs to acquire small scratches, spots, holes, and tears, even if the photos are not very old. If a photograph is not stored flat with its surface protected from damage, the photo might easily develop surface defects. PSP offers many tools you can use to repair these scratches and other small anomalies:

- **Automatic Small Scratch Removal.** If scratches are small, use this command to get rid of them quickly. See **84** Remove Scratches Automatically.

- **Scratch Remover Tool.** This tool gives you precise control over how scratches, cracks, and small specks are removed. See **85** Repair Scratches Manually.

- **Clone Brush Tool.** This tool allows you to remove defects by cloning or copying parts of an image over top of holes, tears, scratches, or specks. It's perfect for making large repairs that the other tools and filters cannot handle easily. See **132** Remove Unwanted Objects from an Image. You can also repair large holes, tears, and scratches using a technique that borrows data from the undamaged parts of an image. See **87** Repair Holes and Tears.

- **Despeckle.** Does your photograph have a lot of tiny single-pixel dots on it? Use this filter to remove them—no matter their color. See **86** **Remove Specks and Spots**.

- **Salt and Pepper.** Large black or white specks that the **Despeckle** command misses can easily be removed with this filter. See **86** **Remove Specks and Spots**.

- **Noise Filters.** To remove a general scattering of dots or *noise* from a photograph, use any one of these filters: **Edge Preserving Smooth**, **Median**, or **Texture Preserving Smooth**. See **86** **Remove Specks and Spots** and **119** **Smooth an Image Without Losing Crisp Edges or Texture**.

KEY TERM

Noise—A random pattern of pixels that gives an image a grainy texture. Digital still cameras have the same picture-taking electronics as digital video cameras, so the noise that generally cancels itself out when viewed at 30 frames per second can't be ignored on a frozen frame.

NOTE

Many of the tools you might use to remove scratches, specks, and holes require that your image be either grayscale or have a full color depth of 16 million colors. See **31** **Change Color Depth**.

---

84 Remove Scratches Automatically

Printed photographs are fragile by nature and are easily scratched, especially if they are not stored in protective sleeves. The scanning process can actually enhance scratches by introducing halos around them, making them even more noticeable—especially in lower-resolution scans—than they were on the print. By using the **Automatic Small Scratch Removal** command, you can easily remove small, line-shaped scratches across the surface of an image. By its nature, this command is not terribly aggressive at removing scratches, so it's fairly safe to use on just about any image without worrying about introducing fuzziness and unwanted patterns.

Before You Begin

✔ **46** About Common Corrections

See Also

→ **85** Repair Scratches Manually

→ **87** Repair Holes and Tears

→ **132** Remove Unwanted Objects from an Image

TIP

To prevent details from being lost in areas that do not contain scratches, select the scratched area before choosing this command.

1 Choose Automatic Small Scratch Removal

Choose **Adjust, Add/Remove Noise, Automatic Small Scratch Removal** from the menu. The **Automatic Small Scratch Removal** dialog box opens.

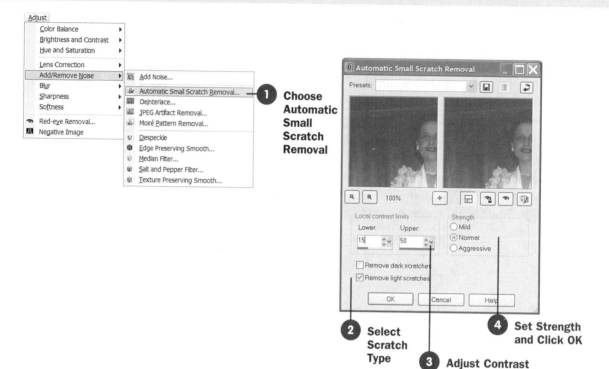

1 Choose Automatic Small Scratch Removal

2 Select Scratch Type

3 Adjust Contrast

4 Set Strength and Click OK

NOTE

For scratches the **Automatic Small Scratch Remover** won't get rid of, try removing them manually with the **Scratch Remover** or **Clone Brush** tools. See **85** Repair Scratches Manually and **132** Remove Unwanted Objects from an Image.

NOTE

If scratches remain while the contrast limits are set to 0 and 50, PSP cannot identify and remove them with this tool; you should try something else.

2 Select Scratch Type

Select the type of scratches you want to remove—dark scratches from a light background, light ones from a dark background, or both.

3 Adjust Contrast

By default, PSP sets the **Lower** contrast level to 0% and the **Upper** level to 50%. (PSP assumes that neighboring pixels with a contrast difference greater than 50% are intentional and not accidental.) PSP then seeks out line-shaped areas that contrast with surrounding pixels by that amount and removes them. To narrow this range, adjust the **Lower** and **Upper** limits.

---

④ Set Strength and Click OK

Adjust the **Strength** as needed. For example, you might change the setting from **Normal** to **Aggressive** to have PSP be less discriminating in identifying scratches, or to **Mild** to have PSP be more careful. Click **OK** to apply the changes.

TIP

Before clicking **OK**, check the image to make sure that no details have been accidentally erased.

85 Repair Scratches Manually

When a photograph contains large scratches or tears, you can remove them quickly using the **Scratch Remover** tool. You use this tool to trace all or part of a scratch or tear—if the tear isn't straight, you might have to apply the tool several times in small sections. As you drag with the tool on the image, you'll see a small rectangle bordered by two "gutters"; the pixels inside the two gutters are used to calculate the color of the pixels that will replace those inside the rectangle, covering up the tear. Proper placement of the rectangle and its two gutters is critical to achieving success. It'll be easier if you zoom in so that you can see the edges of the defect completely, and then drag as narrow a rectangle as possible around the tear so that fewer good pixels are "caught" within its boundaries and replaced.

The **Scratch Remover** tool offers a choice of two tool tips: a rectangle with 90-degree corners, and a flattened hexagon. Use the pointy-ended hexagon when removing scratches close to the edge of some other object; doing so enables you to get in close without actually capturing any of that neighboring object's pixels.

① Select Scratch Remover Tool

Select the **Scratch Remover** tool on the **Tools** toolbar.

② Choose a Brush Tip

On the **Tool Options** palette, click the brush tip you want to use. When working near the boundary of another object, select the pointy-ended tip; otherwise, choose the tip with square corners.

Before You Begin

✔ **83** About Removing Scratches, Specks, and Holes

See Also

→ **84** Remove Scratches Automatically

→ **87** Repair Holes and Tears

→ **132** Remove Unwanted Objects from an Image

TIP

The **Scratch Remover** tool works by copying colors from surrounding pixels and applying them to the defect area in a random pattern. As a result, this tool works best on areas that are smooth, with no background pattern or texture. If the background of your image is not smooth, use the **Clone Brush** tool to remove the scratches instead.

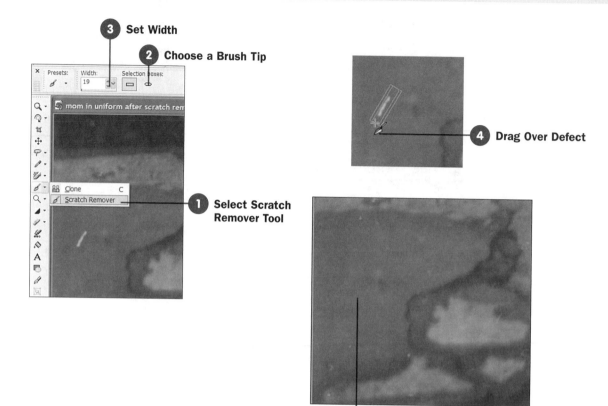

3 Set Width

2 Choose a Brush Tip

4 Drag Over Defect

1 Select Scratch Remover Tool

5 View the Result

NOTE

The **Scratch Remover** tool works only on single-layer images. If you've just scanned in or imported a digital photo, it should have only one layer, so the tool will work just fine. If the image contains more than one layer, however, you must flatten it first or use the **Clone Brush** tool.

3 Set Width

Set the **Width** to a value just greater than the width of the scratch or tear you're trying to remove.

The idea is to capture a few good pixels on either side of the tear to create a good sample; but not so many that the sample becomes distorted. If you're not sure what **Width** to set, select the scratch first with the rectangle **Selection** tool and judge its size using the coordinates shown on the status bar.

4 **Drag Over Defect**

Click just above the beginning of the tear and drag down so that the "gutters" capture pixels on either side of the tear. Don't let the tear itself fall into the gutter (keep it within the rectangle), or the result will make the tear look bigger.

5 **View the Result**

As you can see, the **Scratch Remover** tool easily removes the scratch, leaving a natural-colored patch. By repeating this process in an image, all the scratches and tears can be easily removed.

Sometimes, even when you adjust the **Width** correctly, because of nearby dust specks or a faded background, the **Scratch Remover** continues to create a bad-looking repair. In such a case, try a different tool such as the **Clone Brush**.

TIP

If a tear meanders like a fickle snake throughout your image, you do not have to try to capture the entire tear with one motion. Instead, divide a large tear into smaller repair sections, and sew up the tear one section at a time.

---

86 **Remove Specks and Spots**

Noise can creep into your images in the most innocuous ways— after scanning a newspaper image, capturing an image with a video camera or grabbing it from live video, taking a long exposure with a digital camera (*CCD noise*), over-sharpening an image, or simply letting an image accumulate everyday dust and dirt. You'll notice noise the most in the shadows or the flat, non-textured, nonpatterned areas of an image.

Paint Shop Pro provides many filters you can use to remove noise from an image. **Despeckle** removes nearly black or nearly white single pixel specks, and thus has limited use. The **Salt and Pepper** filter removes specks of the size you specify, whose brightness varies dramatically from that of surrounding pixels. **Salt and Pepper** is great at removing general noise and small specks of dust and dirt from old photographs. The **Median** filter is similar to **Salt and Pepper** except that it changes *all pixels* to match the median brightness of their neighbors, and not just the specks. This task shows you how to use the **Salt and Pepper** and **Median** filters. The **Median** filter works faster than the

Before You Begin

✔ **83** About Removing Scratches, Specks, and Holes

See Also

→ **87** Repair Holes and Tears

→ **117** Remove Distracting Detail

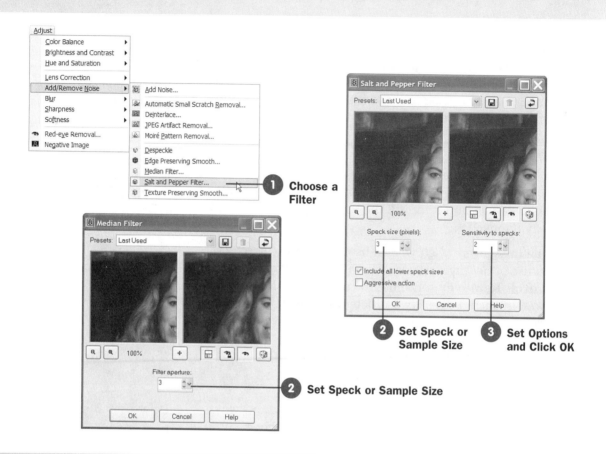

1 Choose a Filter

2 Set Speck or Sample Size

3 Set Options and Click OK

2 Set Speck or Sample Size

KEY TERM

CCD noise—Random distortions introduced into a photo by a digital camera's CCD chip—its principal light detector. CCD noise happens most often during long exposures or at high ISO settings (film speed), and is magnified when "electronic zoom" is used to simulate a close-up of a subject taken at a distance. This type of noise mostly affects the shadow areas of an image, within the red and blue channels.

Salt and Pepper filter because it's less discriminating but it often causes detail to be lost. You might want to try both the **Salt and Pepper** and the **Median** filters on an image and compare the results.

1 Choose a Filter

Choose **Adjust, Add/Remove Noise** from the menu bar, and then choose either **Salt and Pepper Filter** or **Median Filter**. Here, I'll try both filters on an old photo that's acquired some small specks.

2 **Set Speck or Sample Size**

In the **Salt and Pepper Filter** dialog box, adjust the size of the specks you want to remove by changing the **Speck size** value. To remove specks this size and smaller, enable the **Include all lower speck sizes** check box.

In the **Median Filter** dialog box, adjust the area to sample for brightness differences by changing the **Filter aperture** value. Each pixel in the selection or layer is compared to the brightness of its many neighbors and is adjusted accordingly.

3 **Set Options and Click OK**

The **Median** filter has no other options, but in the **Salt and Pepper Filter** dialog box, you can also set the **Sensitivity to specks**. This value tells PSP how different an area must be from surrounding pixels to be considered a speck; higher values tell PSP that an area doesn't have to be that different from its neighbors to be a speck. Enable the **Aggressive action** check box to have PSP change the brightness of specks more drastically than it would normally. Click **OK** to apply the filter.

After using the **Median** filter, you will probably have to sharpen the image. See **114** **Sharpen an Image.**

NOTE

To use the **Despeckle** filter, choose **Adjust, Add/Remove Noise, Despeckle.** The filter works automatically, removing single, very dark or very light specks.

TIP

To prevent loss of detail, first select the areas of your image that contain noise, and then choose the filter. Only the area you selected will be affected by the filter.

NOTE

If you compare the images, you'll see that both filters did a pretty good job at eliminating the small white specks in the shadows of the fireplace. The **Median** filter, however, has blurred the image too much.

87 **Repair Holes and Tears**

Because of their fragile nature, photographs are easily bent, torn, and scratched—especially when they are not stored properly. In earlier tasks, you learned how to repair small tears and to remove specks of dust and such, but what do you do if there are lots of tears, holes, and maybe even old foldlines, and the image is simply in sad shape?

As explained in **132** **Remove Unwanted Objects from an Image,** one way in which you can cover up flaws is to use the **Clone Brush** to copy pixels from an undamaged area. The problem with this method, however, is that unless it's done carefully, the

Before You Begin

✔ **83** About Removing Scratches, Specks, and Holes

✔ **120** About Layers and the Layer Palette

See Also

→ **86** Remove Specks and Spots

→ **132** Remove Unwanted Objects from an Image

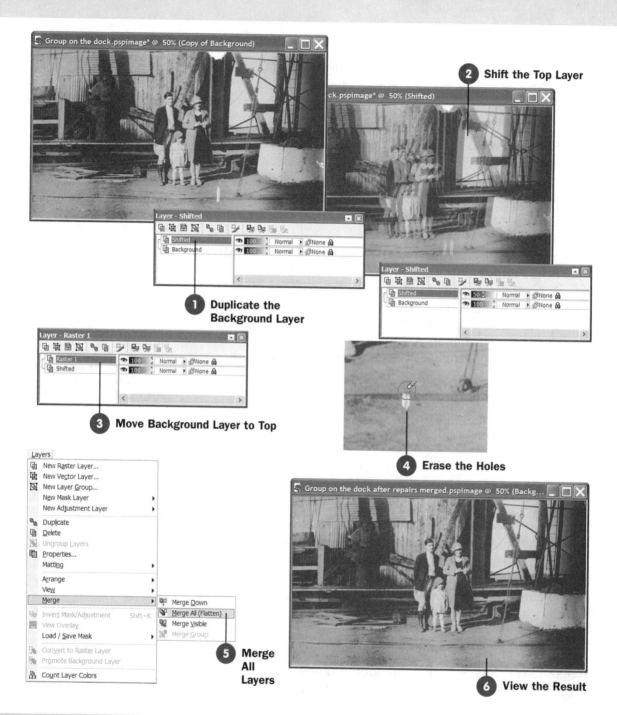

2 Shift the Top Layer

1 Duplicate the Background Layer

3 Move Background Layer to Top

4 Erase the Holes

5 Merge All Layers

6 View the Result

Clone Brush often leaves an unnatural, easily detectable pattern. In this task, you'll learn an alternative method that's both fast and foolproof.

1 Duplicate the Background Layer

Open the image you want to repair and then click the **Duplicate Layer** button on the **Layer** palette. Name the duplicate layer **Shifted**.

2 Shift the Top Layer

In the **Layer** palette, change the **Opacity** of the **Shifted** layer to 50%. This lets you see the **Background** layer content while you're moving the **Shifted** layer. You're going to use pieces of the **Shifted** layer to cover the holes on the **Background** layer. Click the **Move** tool on the **Tools** toolbar and slowly drag the **Shifted** layer up, down, right, or left, until the torn area on the **Background** layer is covered by content from the **Shifted** layer.

 NOTE

In this example, I want to repair the tear just below and to the right of the family, and the hole along the right edge, so I've moved the **Shifted** layer to the right.

3 Move Background Layer to Top

In the **Layer** palette, reset the **Opacity** of the **Shifted** layer to 100%. To be able to move the **Background** layer to the top, you must first promote it to a full raster layer. Select **Layers, Promote Background Layer** from the menu. This changes the name of the **Background** layer to **Raster 1**. Now drag the bottom **Raster 1** layer to the top of the layer stack.

NOTE

After dragging the **Raster 1** layer to the top of the layer stack in step 3, the photo will look as it did originally—tears, holes, and everything.

4 Erase the Holes

Click the **Eraser** tool on the **Tools** toolbar. On the **Tool Options** palette, adjust the **Size** value so that the eraser is slightly bigger than the defect. Soften the edge a bit by setting **Hardness** to 50 and **Density** to 80. Then drag over the defect with the eraser, revealing the **Shifted** layer beneath.

TIP

If your image has large tears you don't want to fix this way, use the **Clone Brush**. See **132** Remove Unwanted Objects from an Image.

5 Merge All Layers

After erasing all the holes and tears, merge the layers into one by choosing **Layers, Merge, Merge All (Flatten)**.

6 View the Result

After erasing the holes and tears using the **Eraser** tool, I followed up with the **Clone Brush** to fill the ghastly tear at the top of the image. Then I merged all layers.

88 Correct Red Eye

See Also

→ **91** Awaken Tired Eyes

KEY TERM

Red eye—An effect caused when a camera flash is reflected by the retina at the back of the eye. It isn't an optical illusion; you're actually photographing a fully illuminated retina in its natural color—bright red.

TIP

When you're shooting your photograph, you can avoid giving your subjects red eye by separating the flash unit from the camera (if possible), or telling your subjects to not look directly at the camera. Some cameras have a red-eye reduction feature, which causes the flash to go off several times. The first series of flashes at lower intensity cause the pupil to contract, thus blocking the reflection, while the final flash at full intensity illuminates the subject for the picture.

When used properly, a camera flash can help lighten shadows and illuminate an otherwise dark image. Unfortunately, using a flash might sometimes have unintended effects, such as *red eye*. In nonhuman subjects such as dogs or cats, the result might be "glassy eye" rather than red eye. No matter; you remove it in the same way: with PSP's **Red-eye Removal** command.

This task explains how to remove red eye in Paint Shop Pro, however you can also remove red eye using Photo Album, if you have that program: Open the image in the **Image View** window, zoom in on the eye you want to fix, click the arrow on the **Red Eye** button, and choose **One Click Removal**. The pointer changes to a circle cross-hair—center this cursor on the red area of the eye and click. If you would rather paint the red out manually, click the arrow on the **Red Eye** button and choose **Red Eye Brush**. Adjust the width of the brush by selecting **Brush Width** from the **Red Eye** menu. Then drag over the red to paint the pupil black. If you have to repaint part of the iris, change the brush color by choosing the **Brush Color** command from the **Red Eye** menu. To paint the glint back in, choose **Highlight Brush** from the **Red Eye** menu and click the pupil.

1 Choose Adjust, Red-eye Removal

Choose **Adjust, Red-eye Removal** from the menu bar. The **Red-eye Removal** dialog box appears.

As you make adjustments, the corrections appear in the right preview pane of the **Red-eye Removal** dialog box.

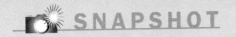
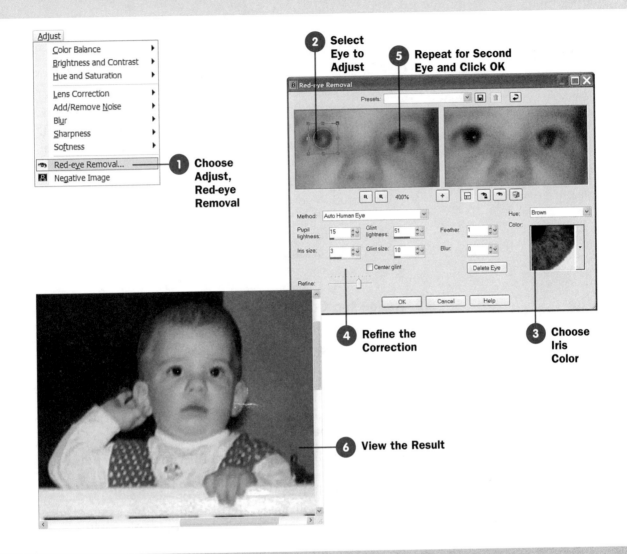

Adjust
- Color Balance ▸
- Brightness and Contrast ▸
- Hue and Saturation ▸
- Lens Correction ▸
- Add/Remove Noise ▸
- Blur ▸
- Sharpness ▸
- Softness ▸
- Red-eye Removal... ━━
- Negative Image

2 Select Eye to Adjust

5 Repeat for Second Eye and Click OK

1 Choose Adjust, Red-eye Removal

4 Refine the Correction

3 Choose Iris Color

6 View the Result

2 Select the Eye to Adjust

Zoom in on the eye you want to adjust using the **Zoom In** and **Select Area** buttons. Change the portion of the image shown in the right preview by dragging if needed.

Open the **Method** list and choose **Auto Human Eye** if you're adjusting a human eye, or **Auto Animal Eye** if you're adjusting a cat, dog, or other animal eye. In the left preview window, click in the absolute center of the *pupil*. A circle-guide appears; drag this guide until it touches the outer rim of the *iris*. For an animal, select only the pupil.

If the pupil shape is not perfectly round, you might have better luck selecting it manually. Choose **Freehand Pupil Outline** from the **Method** list and draw around the pupil, or choose **Point-to-Point** and click along the pupil's edge.

KEY TERMS

Pupil—The black center of the eye which adjusts in size based on the amount of ambient light.

Iris—The colored part of the eye; typically brown, blue, or green.

3 Choose Iris Color

For a human eye, open the **Hue** list and choose the person's actual iris color. Then open the **Color** list and choose the variation of that eye color that matches the person's natural color. For an animal, choose a variation from the **Color** list only.

4 Refine the Correction

To adjust how much of the guide circle is painted with the iris color, drag the **Refine** slider. If you drag the **Refine** slider all the way to the right, PSP paints a whole, round iris, even if it overlaps part of the eyelid. By dragging toward the left, you can prevent part of the eyelid from being painted. You might move the **Refine** slider to the left in a half-opened eye.

KEY TERM

Glint—A tiny reflection of light that appears on the pupil.

Adjust **Pupil lightness**, **Glint lightness**, **Glint size**, and **Iris size** as needed. Position the *glint* in the center of the pupil by enabling the **Center glint** check box. Add a **Feather** to the outside of the pupil or **Blur** the outer edge of the iris if desired by specifying values in these fields.

5 Repeat for Second Eye and Click OK

Repeat steps 2 through 4 to select and correct the pupil of the second eye and then click **OK** to apply the correction.

6 View the Result

The red eye is gone, and with a bit of sharpening, we're left with a cute baby just waking up from his nap.

89 Remove Freckles and Minor Blemishes

Almost everyone has certain...cosmetic distinctions that help identify and even glamorize a person. However, if they're the temporary kind, you might not want a permanent record of them. Sometimes a perfectly good photograph is marred by minor distractions such as a few blemishes, a mole, a cold sore, or a few wrinkles just beginning to show. Is it vain to want to fix nature? Perhaps, but don't let that stop you—especially when it's so easy.

As explained in **132** **Remove Unwanted Objects from an Image,** you can use the **Clone Brush** to paint away minor defects in a photograph by copying good pixels from some other area. But the process is tedious and often easily detectable. In this task, you'll use a quicker method.

1 Duplicate Background Layer

Open the image you want to repair and then click the **Duplicate Layer** button on the **Layer** palette. Name the new layer **Unblurred**.

2 Blur Background Layer

Change to the **Background** layer and select **Adjust, Blur, Blur More** from the menu.

3 Erase Blemishes

On the **Layer** palette, change to the **Unblurred** layer; click the **Eraser** tool. Adjust the **Size** value so that the eraser is slightly bigger than the blemish you want to remove. Soften the edge a bit by setting **Hardness** to 50 and **Density** to 80. Then click the blemish with the eraser, revealing the blurred layer beneath.

4 Merge All Layers

After erasing all the minor imperfections, merge the layers into one by choosing **Layers, Merge, Merge All (Flatten)**.

Before You Begin

✔ **120** About Layers and the Layer Palette

See Also

→ **90** Whiten Teeth

→ **91** Awaken Tired Eyes

→ **132** Remove Unwanted Objects from an Image

TIPS

To see the blurred **Background** layer, hide the top layer temporarily by clicking its eye button on the **Layer** palette.

For very large images such as those at 1048 × 1478 resolution, the **Blur More** filter might not do enough to blur the layer. In such cases, try the **Gaussian Blur** filter (**Adjust, Blur, Gaussian Blur**).

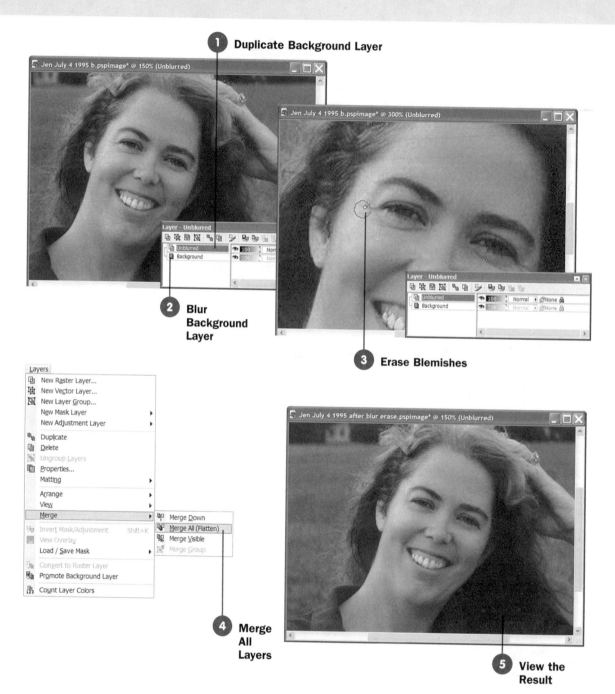

1 Duplicate Background Layer

2 Blur Background Layer

3 Erase Blemishes

4 Merge All Layers

5 View the Result

5 **View the Result**

There, that's better. We didn't erase the detail and character of the face, just improved it a bit. Look for this photo in the Color Gallery section in this book.

---

90 **Whiten Teeth**

There are many products on the market that you can use to whiten your teeth: gels, toothpastes, whitening strips, and bleaches, but none work as fast and as effectively as digital editing. It's not vanity to want to improve mother nature; in our culture today, a great importance is placed on having clean, white teeth, and if a photo will be used in a resume or to advertise a product, you'll want to give the best impression you can by making sure that your subject looks his or her best.

Whitening teeth is tricky, however; you don't want the effect to look obvious and artificial. You'll want to avoid the temptation to use *pure white* to paint over all your teeth, which results in a picket-fence effect that can look genuinely scary. The technique explained here uses the **Dodge** tool, which selectively lightens the brightness of the pixels over which it passes. You must be cautious, however, so that you don't burn out the color and create a fake whiteness.

Before You Begin

✔ **10** About Tools and Tool Options

See Also

→ **89** Remove Freckles and Minor Blemishes

→ **91** Awaken Tired Eyes

 TIP

I always get good results with the **Dodge** tool, but if you don't like its effects, try selecting the teeth, choosing **Adjust, Color Balance, Red/Green/Blue,** and increasing the **Blue** value.

1 **Select the Dodge Tool**

Zoom in on the teeth so that you can see them clearly, and then select the **Dodge** tool on the **Tools** toolbar.

2 **Set Options**

Adjust the **Size** of the **Dodge** tool in the **Tool Options** palette so that the brush tip is just larger than the teeth. Set **Opacity** to 10 or so, **Density** to 100, and **Hardness** to 50.

If you want to prevent over-lightening the teeth and burning them out, select the **Continuous** option. This option prevents the brush from lightening pixels more, even if you pass over them more than once.

 TIP

To isolate the effects of the **Dodge** tool, select the teeth before beginning. You might want to select the gums as well.

SNAPSHOT

② **Set Options**

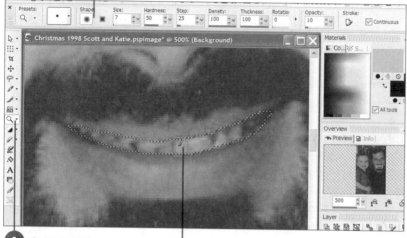

① **Select the Dodge Tool**

③ **Whiten the Teeth**

④ **View the Result**

③ Whiten the Teeth

If the **Continuous** option is not turned on, position the brush tip over the first tooth and click once. The tooth

---

should get just a bit lighter. Click again to lighten a bit more, or move to the next tooth. Repeat until all the teeth are whiter. If the **Continuous** option is set, drag over the teeth to lighten—they will only be lightened up to the **Opacity** amount you select, even if you brush over them several times.

4 **View the Result**

Compare the original (on the left) to the whitened version; you can see that the teeth on the right look better, and yet still natural.

TIP

Remove any remaining imperfections (such as uneven color or spots on the teeth) with the **Clone Brush**. See **132** Remove Unwanted Objects from an Image.

91 Awaken Tired Eyes

They say that the eyes are the window to the soul. It must be true, because if a woman has dark circles under her eyes, we think she looks tired (even if the dark circles are a natural skin condition). By slightly lightening the skin under the eyes, you can take years off a face and brighten a person's outlook. And it's simple to do, using the **Change to Target** tool.

Redness in the eyes caused by chlorine in swimming pools can also make them look tired. To whiten the eyes, select the white parts and choose **Adjust, Hue and Saturation, Hue/Saturation/Lightness**. Then change the color to white by setting **Hue** to –180 and **Saturation** to –100. Then adjust the **Lightness** value to achieve a lighter, yet still natural, white (try 18 to 25).

1 **Select Change to Target Tool**

Select the **Change to Target** tool on the **Tools** toolbar.

2 **Set Options**

On the **Tool Options** palette, open the **Mode** list and select **Lightness.** Set the **Size** to the width of the area you want to lighten. Set **Hardness** to 50 and **Opacity** to 10.

Before You Begin

✔ **10** About Tools and Tool Options

See Also

→ **88** Correct Red Eye

→ **89** Remove Freckles and Minor Blemishes

→ **90** Whiten Teeth

TIP

If your subject is looking into the sun, her pupils might be quite small, making her look tired and sleepy. To widen the pupils, use the **Red-eye Removal** command as described in **88** Correct Red Eye. Move **Refine** to the far right to prevent changes to the iris, and then set **Iris Size** to 1 or 0 to make the pupil as big as you like.

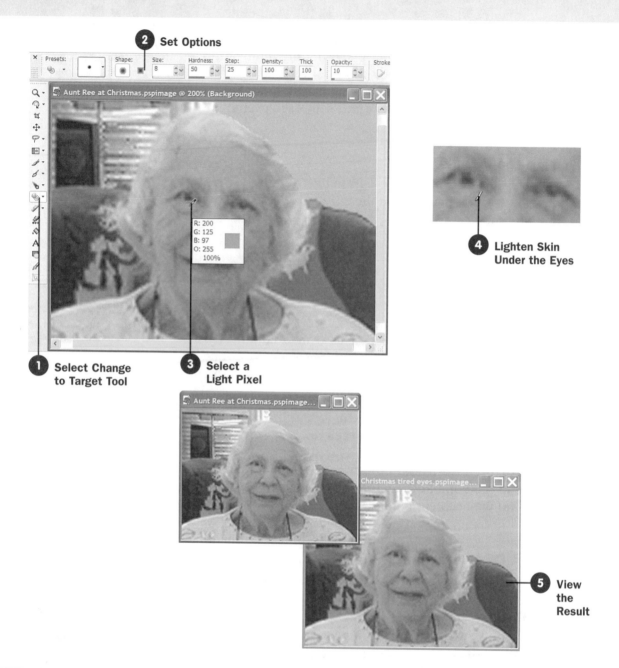

2 Set Options

1 Select Change to Target Tool

3 Select a Light Pixel

4 Lighten Skin Under the Eyes

5 View the Result

R: 200
G: 125
B: 97
O: 255
100%

③ Select a Light Pixel

Press the **Ctrl** key and use the eyedropper to click a skin pixel close to the eye that's fairly light. The **Change to Target** tool uses this pixel's lightness value to lighten the skin you paint over.

④ Lighten Skin Under the Eyes

Drag the **Change to Target** tool over the dark patches under the eye, changing the pixels there to the same lightness value as the pixel you clicked with the eyedropper in step 3.

⑤ View the Result

The final result (on the right) is very natural looking. With lighter patches under her eyes, Aunt Ree looks less tired, and it's easier to see how truly loving, humorous, and wonderful she is.

TIP

If you're lightening a large area of skin, change the source pixel from time to time for a more natural look.

TIP

If you have trouble using **Change to Target**, try creating a copy of the image on a duplicate layer and making your changes to the copy. You can then use the **Opacity** setting to control the amount of the changes you see.

---

92 Remove Barrel, Pincushion, and Fisheye Distortion

Although using a special lens can enable you to capture an image your camera might not have been able to record otherwise, it often leads to distortion of the image, especially at the edges. Paint Shop Pro can easily remove these common distortions:

- **Barrel Distortion.** Associated with the use of a wide-angle lens, or the minimum zoom setting of a zoom lens. Areas at the extreme edges of the image are curved outward, like the sides of a barrel.

- **Pincushion Distortion.** The opposite of barrel distortion. Associated with maximum zoom setting of a zoom lens. Here, the edges of the image look pulled in toward the center, like the top of a pincushion. Both barrel and pincushion distortion are most noticeable when a subject with a straight edge (such as a tall building) is located at the far edge of an image.

- **Fisheye Distortion.** Caused by a fisheye lens, which you might use to capture a full 180-degree view of a large scene.

See Also

→ **137** Change Perspective

→ **138** Move, Alter, or Distort an Image

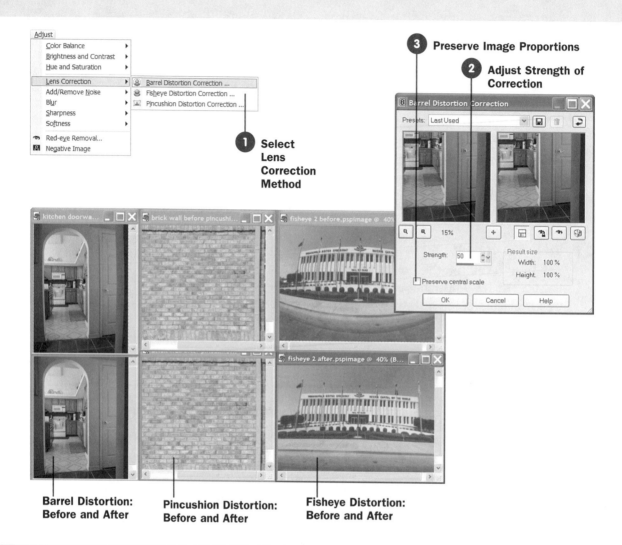

3 Preserve Image Proportions

2 Adjust Strength of Correction

1 Select Lens Correction Method

Barrel Distortion: Before and After

Pincushion Distortion: Before and After

Fisheye Distortion: Before and After

With this type of distortion, the image looks as though it's been pasted to the outside of a ball.

1 Select Lens Correction Method

Choose **Adjust, Lens Correction** and then select the type of correction you need from the submenu: **Barrel Distortion Correction**, **Fisheye Distortion Correction**, or **Pincushion Distortion Correction**. A dialog box specific to the selected correction opens.

2 Adjust Strength of Correction

Adjust the **Strength** value to change the amount of correction applied. Use the right pane in the dialog box to preview the correction effect.

3 Preserve Image Proportions and Click OK

To enlarge the image automatically to accommodate the stretching required by the correction, enable the **Preserve central scale** check box. (If you don't enable the **Preserve central scale** option, the original size of the image is preserved, but data along the edges might be thrown out to place the stretched image back into its original size.) Click **OK**.

4 View the Result

Here are several photos with various lens distortions, before and after correcting them with Paint Shop Pro.

NOTES

If vertical lines are splayed out in opposite directions like a "V", your image suffers from perspective distortion. See **137** Change Perspective.

If you like the look, you can *create* a fisheye distortion on an image using Photo Album. Open the image in the Image View window, choose **Effects, Special Effects,** and click the **Fisheye** tab. Adjust the **Width of Fisheye** and the **Height of Fisheye** using the sliders and then click **Apply.**

93 Remove Imperfections Caused by File Compression

Smaller graphic files offer many benefits: Because of their size, they are easier to store, easier to send as email attachments, and easier to download from a Web page. Unfortunately, one of the side effects of file compression is the introduction of *artifacts* into an image. Artifacts occur when a file has been over-compressed, but they can also happen to a slightly compressed file if it has been saved and resaved a lot of times. These artifacts appear most often in solid or almost solid color areas of an image, and they can be quite distracting.

To repair an image that has artifacts caused by compression, you use the **JPEG Artifact Removal** filter. Basically, the filter blurs the image just a bit to blend the artifacts with neighboring pixels. You control the amount of blurring while simultaneously adjusting the crispness of the image detail.

See Also

→ **42** Compress an Image Using JPEG Format

→ **94** Clean Up Scans of Printed Material

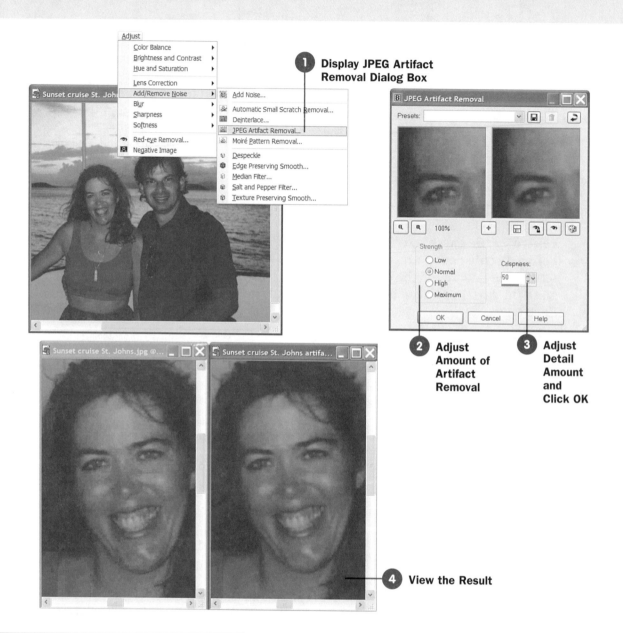

1 Display JPEG Artifact Removal Dialog Box

2 Adjust Amount of Artifact Removal

3 Adjust Detail Amount and Click OK

4 View the Result

① **Display JPEG Artifact Removal Dialog Box**

Choose **Adjust, Add/Remove Noise, JPEG Artifact Removal** from the menu bar. The **JPEG Artifact Removal** dialog box opens.

② **Adjust Amount of Artifact Removal**

Control the amount of blur that's applied to the image by selecting an appropriate **Strength** value. You want to use just enough blur to blend the artifacts away without losing too much detail.

③ **Adjust Detail Amount and Click OK**

Adjust the amount of detail that's retained by changing the **Crispness** value. When you're satisfied, click **OK** to apply the filter.

④ **View the Result**

Even after removing the artifacts from the image (shown on the right), the details still remain.

KEY TERM

Artifacts—Unwanted elements of a digital photo introduced by technology: by the setup of the digital camera, by the format used to compress an image file when saving it, or sometimes by the simple act of resaving an image. In a JPEG image, artifacts typically appear as rectangular blocks of slightly differing colors.

TIP

If your image was taken from a video source, it might contain a different kind of imperfection—visible scan lines. To remove them, use the **Adjust, Add/Remove Noise, Deinterlace** command.

94 Clean Up Scans of Printed Material

Scanning an image for use on a computer is always a tricky business, as you learned in **5** **Scan an Image**. Your scanner might not be able to interpret the colors accurately, and in fact, might introduce problems that never existed in the image at all, such as *moiré patterns*. These patterns typically appear on images scanned from newspapers or magazines, although you might also find them when you scan images printed on textured paper or paper with a silk finish.

Before you follow this task to remove the moiré pattern, do everything you can to scan the best newspaper or magazine image. First, turn on the **Descreen** option on your scanner (if it has one). Then select a resolution equal to *twice your intended output*. For example, if you intend to print the image at 300 dpi, scan it at 600 dpi. Then scan the image and follow these steps to remove any moiré patterns that appear.

Before You Begin

✔ **5** Scan an Image

See Also

→ **93** Remove Imperfections Caused by File Compression

SNAPSHOT

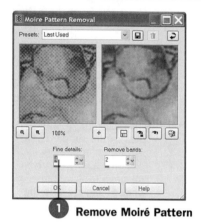

1 Remove Moiré Pattern

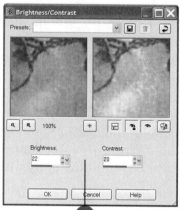

2 Adjust Brightness and Contrast

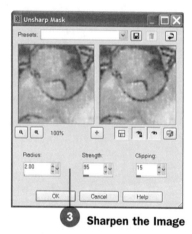

3 Sharpen the Image

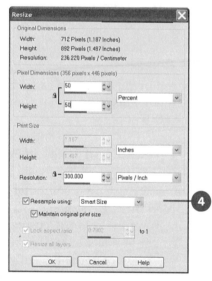

4 Resample the Image

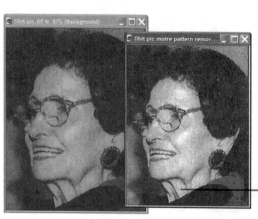

5 View the Result

1 **Remove Moiré Pattern**

Choose **Adjust, Add/Remove Noise, Moire Pattern Removal** from the menu bar. The **Moire Pattern Removal** dialog box opens. You want to blur the image just enough to remove the moiré pattern, but not so much that you lose the detail. Start with a low **Fine details** value, and gradually increase it until the pattern disappears.

Gradually increase the **Remove bands** value until any stripes or large blotches of distracting color disappear. Click **OK** to apply the filter.

2 **Adjust Brightness and Contrast**

Choose **Adjust, Brightness and Contrast, Brightness/Contrast** from the menu. In the dialog box, adjust the **Brightness** and **Contrast** values as needed to restore the brightness lost during scanning. Click **OK.**

3 **Sharpen the Image**

Choose **Adjust, Sharpness, Unsharp Mask** from the menu. In the **Unsharp Mask** dialog box that opens, start with a small **Radius** and gradually increase this value. Adjust the **Strength** value to lessen the effect. To control the level of contrast between neighboring pixels that results in sharpening, adjust the **Clipping** value. Click **OK.**

4 **Resample the Image**

Because you scanned the image at double the actual resolution you'll need, you can resize and resample the image downwards. This causes PSP to crowd the pixels closer together, resulting in a better, denser image. Choose **Image, Resize** from the menu. In the **Resize** dialog box, enable the **Resample using Smart Size** and **Maintain original print size** check boxes. Enter a **Resolution** value that is half the scan rate and click **OK.**

KEY TERM

Moiré pattern—The optical illusion that occurs when one regular geometric pattern—such as a grid made up of dots—overlays another similar pattern slightly askew. For example, two window screens placed on top of each other at an angle form a moiré effect. (From the French, meaning "to make ripples.")

TIPS

To reduce the moiré pattern on a scanned newspaper or magazine image, try scanning the image at a 30-degree angle.

Instead of using the **Moire Pattern Removal** filter, try these other filters to blur the image and remove the moiré pattern: **Median, Gaussian Blur, Salt and Pepper.**

5 View the Result

The original scan contained an obvious dot pattern and was much too dark. The improved version on the right is lighter and dot-free.

As a final step for a black-and-white image, convert it to grayscale—doing so might improve the range of values throughout the image.

10

Correcting the Brightness and Contrast in a Photograph

IN THIS CHAPTER:

If you happen to recall the era when television sets had knobs on them, you'll remember the time spent fiddling with the Contrast, Brightness, and Tone controls. As a kid, I was never allowed to touch these knobs, so when I first started using Paint Shop Pro, I got a sense of freedom by making these adjustments in the **Brightness/Contrast** dialog box. The only problem was, the results looked very much like the pictures on that old TV set.

That was a long time ago, and my knowledge of PSP has grown. I can show you a better way to improve your images, using tools favored by professional photographers and videographers. Unfortunately, these tools are far less intuitive and more scientific than the brightness and contrast controls you've seen in earlier tasks. To make these tools work for you, you have to understand something about the principles of optics—light and color. After you understand optics, you'll be weaned forever from all-purpose brightness and contrast controls that hail from a simpler time, when we tolerated even a low degree of static noise.

95 About Making Histogram Adjustments to Brightness and Contrast

See Also

→ **1** Ensure That What You See Is What You Get

→ **96** Improve Brightness and Contrast

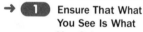

KEY TERM

Histogram—A chart that depicts the relative distribution of pixels in an image that share the same characteristics, such as lightness, saturation, hue, or presence in a particular color channel (red, green, or blue). Use it to determine whether particular colors or brightness values disproportionately predominate, diminishing picture quality.

Granted, the *histogram* is intimidating, and perhaps even confusing at first. But when you come to understand how the information it's telling you can help you manipulate the characteristics of any image more precisely and with better results, you will choose it every time you make adjustments to your photos.

As explained earlier in this book, a pixel can be defined either by the amount of red, green, and blue it contains, or by its hue, saturation, and luminance values. All six of these key characteristics are represented on the histogram.

In the **Histogram** palette shown here, I've displayed the distribution of pixels in each of the color channels by enabling those three check boxes. The dark red, green, and blue pixels are plotted on the left, while the light red, green, and blue pixels are plotted to the right. Medium values appear in the middle. If there are a lot of pixels with a particular value, the line rises; if there are few pixels of that value, it falls. By looking at this particular histogram, I can tell that there are a lot of dark red, blue, and green pixels in the image. And there are relatively few medium-to-light pixels in all the channels, as you can tell by how each line fades away to nothing rather quickly. The histogram also reveals the separation between the green and red channels, which would normally combine optically to make yellow. This lets me know that the yellows have faded from this image in several spots. The loss of yellow is significant, more so than the loss of magenta (as indicated by the separation of the red and blue channels on the chart) because yellow is present in skin tones, whereas magenta is not.

NOTE

I'm not terribly surprised by the faded yellows in this image because yellow ink tends to fade first in old Polaroid prints like this one. (Cyan goes next, and magenta always seems to outlast the other two.)

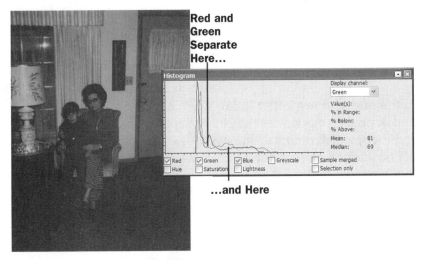

An old Polaroid print whose yellows have faded.

A histogram of the same photo's brightness channel (displayed by disabling all but the **Lightness** check box in the **Histogram** palette) reveals deep chasms along both the left and right sides, indicating an image with neither light brights nor deep darks. Their absence is what causes the lack of contrast in the photo. With the help of the **Histogram Adjustment** dialog box, you can shift the distribution of the green pixels to match the red pixels and restore color balance, and also shift the lightness value of all pixels to fill in the side gaps. Doing so should restore most, if not all, of the original print's luster and brilliance.

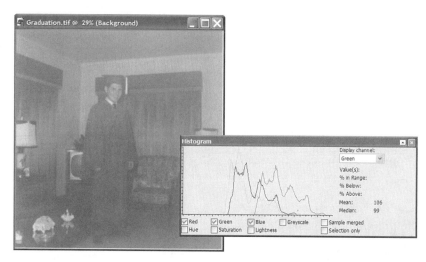

This histogram shows a classic separation between the color channels.

NOTE

Although yellows tend to fade first in old Polaroid prints, the cyan inks are the first to go in old Kodak prints, leaving the reds, pinks, and yellows.

In the image of my father-in-law's graduation (this time, an old Kodak print), you can see the classic separation of the color channels, which occurs as images fade. Notice that the red channel has drifted to the right, taking over the middle-to-light values in the image, making it seem very pinkish. Meanwhile, the blues and greens have faded to almost nothing, present mostly in the darkest pixels. Look for this image in the Color Gallery section in this book.

NOTE

Astonishingly, a histogram of a person's face reveals its own "signature": From left to right, you see first a blue peak, followed by a green one, and then a red one. This is true for faces with any skin tone, dark or light. Correct facial discoloration by adjusting the graphs of the red, green, and blue channels so that the peaks fall in that order.

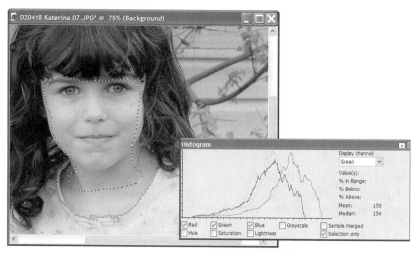

The magic signature of skin tones: blue peak, green peak, red peak.

Understand Image Gamma

Your eyes, like everything else in nature, seek balance. If a scene is too bright, your pupils constrict and the actual brightness of the light is muted. The same thing happens when a scene is too dark; your pupils automatically widen, letting in more light, and you perceive a greater difference between the shadows, *midtones*, and lights than really exists if measured with a light meter. Likewise, if a scene is filled with cool colors (such as a field of blue and purple flowers), your eyes balance the scene by increasing your perception of warm tones such as yellow and red. Again, the colors in the scene do not appear to you as they would if measured by a spectrophotometer.

Unlike your eyes, which constrict bright light from entering, and thus darken all the other light in a scene proportionally (as if grading the light "on a curve"), a digital camera records a brightly lit scene using a *linear system*, measuring the actual light without bias. To create an image that your eyes will see as "natural," a similar grading curve is applied to the light coming onto a digital camera. This curve is based on something called the *image gamma*; by adjusting this one point, the midtones in an image can be made lighter or darker as needed, with correlated adjustments to the light and dark pixels.

Most digital cameras set the gamma at about 1.7, which produces roughly the same grading curve used by the human eye to adjust incoming light under sunny conditions. Photographic film and film processing take this curve into account as well, producing images that look right to the human eye when printed (assuming the proper settings were used to take the photo).

A gamma value of 1.0 implies no bias (adjustment) whatsoever. A gamma greater than 1.0 implies a bias towards brighter midtones; PSP accepts a maximum gamma of 5.0. A gamma value of less than 1.0 implies a bias towards darker, shadowy tones; PSP accepts a minimum gamma of 0.2.

The gamma point I'm talking about here is the *image gamma* and not the *monitor gamma* referred to in **1** **Ensure That What You See Is What You Get**. In that previous discussion, I explained how to adjust the gamma point of your monitor so that its input (the screen image) would match the desired output

KEY TERM

Midtones—Pixels with a luminance value near the middle of those allowed—a value of about 124. The midtones in an image are an object's true color, without shadows or highlights (reflected light).

KEY TERM

Image gamma—On a line that graphs the image's input values against its output (its appearance onscreen against how it looks when printed), the *gamma* is the point at which the pixels in an image are 50% gray.

NOTE

Adjustments to the gamma affect the midtone pixels in an image the most, with smaller adjustments made as you progress to either end of the input/output curve.

NOTE

When you select certain settings on your camera, such as Snow or Night, you're actually choosing a gamma adjustment, which in turn changes the midtones of your image, lightening or darkening them automatically.

(the way the image looks when printed). Here, I'm talking about adjusting the *gamma* of the image itself—the point at which pixels become exactly 50% gray. Like monitor gamma, image gamma is also plotted on a curve, with the vertical axis representing output, and the horizontal axis representing input. When you change the image gamma, you are essentially saying, "Let's make the middle tones in the image (input) appear lighter or darker onscreen (output)." When you click OK to save your adjustment, the lightness values of the image pixels are changed, creating new *input* values if you were to look at the gamma again.

Image with Gamma Lowered to .70

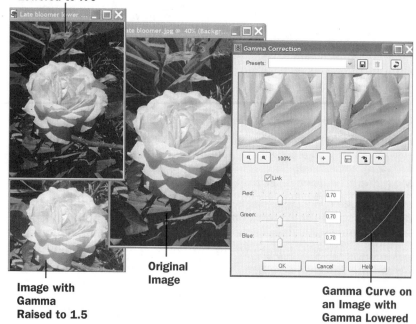

Image with Gamma Raised to 1.5

Original Image

Gamma Curve on an Image with Gamma Lowered

An image of a rose with different gamma adjustments.

Let me reiterate that the adjustments you make to image gamma affect the middle tones the most, with lesser and lesser adjustments as pixels move away in brightness value from the gamma point. As you can see in the image of a rose shown here, lowering the gamma darkened the middle tones, making the peach colors in the rose more apparent. Lightening the gamma lightened the middle tones at the edges of the rose, making them blend more easily into the already light inner petals. (Check out this image in the Color Gallery section of this book.)

Understand Histogram Adjustments

Using the **Histogram** palette as your guide to what's wrong with an image, you can make subtle, controlled changes to its contrast and color balance. To view the **Histogram** palette, select **View**, **Palette**, **Histogram** from the menu or press **F7**. Although you can't change or edit anything in the **Histogram** palette, you can turn on or off the different chart lines it displays. Display the palette as you make changes to an image to help you make the right adjustments. The most important command that affects the values plotted on the histogram is the **Histogram Adjustment** command.

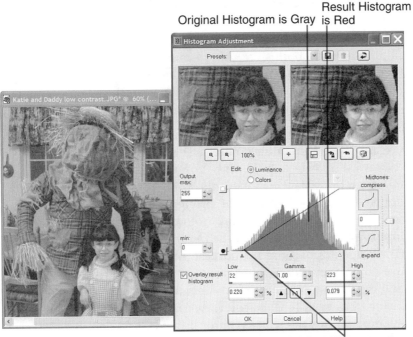

Original Histogram is Gray

Result Histogram is Red

Gaps in the Original Histogram Are Filled by the Adjustments I Made

The gaps on either side of this image's histogram indicate an absence of truly dark and light pixels, causing a lack of contrast and definition in the image.

NOTE

The original values in the image are plotted with a gray histogram; adjusted values (assuming the selections you're making will be applied) appear in a red histogram. You can turn off the red overlay by turning off the **Overlay result histogram** check box.

KEY TERM

Input levels—The minimum and maximum luminance values for an image. Pixels outside this range are changed to the minimum or maximum value allowed.

TIP

When moving the black and white pointers inwards, try not to clip off pixels, which will turn them into pure white or pure black. Doing so creates a loss of contrast that might have existed between light and almost-light or dark and almost-dark pixels.

The histogram displayed in the **Histogram Adjustment** dialog box graphs the distribution of light and dark pixels throughout an image (or a selected region or layer). With this dialog box, you can also display (and adjust) the pixels in a single color channel, such as the red channel. As is true with the **Histogram** palette, the dark pixels of the **Luminance** channel are plotted on the left with light pixels on the right. Midtone pixels are found, well, in the middle. A good image has a fairly even distribution of pixels in all three areas of the **Luminance** channel: darks, midtones, and lights—the graph has very few sharp peaks and valleys. In addition, the plotted area on a good image fills the complete range of values (the chart touches both sides of the white graph window), unlike the low-contrast image shown here, which has gaps along both sides of the original dark gray histogram. (In the sample image, the gaps are hard to see because the gaps in the original plotted values—the dark gray histogram—are filled when the results are plotted—the red histogram shown in light gray in this grayscale figure.) You can improve contrast in such an image by stretching the plotted area to fill, or nearly fill, the gaps on both sides. After I made a few minor adjustments, the red result histogram fills the chart, providing a better distribution of pixels. The difference between the original and the adjusted image as shown in the preview panes is dramatic.

Along the bottom edge of the **Histogram Adjustment** dialog box are three triangular pointers. The black pointer represents the lowest allowable luminance value (the darks); the white pointer represents the highest allowable luminance value (the lights). The range between the two represents the entire allowable spectrum of luminance values, from dark to light, also called the *input levels*. If gaps exist in the original gray histogram along either side, it's because the darkest pixels in the image are not truly black, and the lightest ones are not white. To fill these gaps and increase contrast, move the black and white pointers inwards, as I did for the Scarecrow and Dorothy image. For example, move the white pointer inwards, to touch the edge of the gray graph on its right side. By *narrowing* the range of allowable lightness values (by sliding the white pointer in toward the left), you instruct PSP to lighten the lightest pixels.

These pointers take on a different significance when you're viewing one of the color channels, such as the **Green** channel (enable the **Colors** radio button above the graph). When you move the black pointer inwards, for example, you are not darkening the dark-green pixels; you are making the pixels with a lot of green in them less green. In a similar manner, if you drag the white pointer inwards, you are adding green to those pixels that don't contain a lot of green to begin with.

Superimposed over the histogram is a black line extending from the lower-left to the upper-right of the chart. When this line is perfectly straight, it tells you that no adjustment to the gamma (the image's midtones) has been made. As you adjust the gamma of an image (making the midtones lighter or darker as a result), the line bends at some point to become a curve. A convex bend favors the lights; a concave slope favors darks. The gamma point on the chart is represented by the gray triangle underneath the histogram. Drag this triangle left or right to adjust the image's gamma. If you change the gamma on a color channel, you change the balance of saturation in that channel, tipping the scale towards more saturation (if you move the gamma marker to the right) or less (if you move the marker to the left).

You can make further adjustments to the midtones beyond a gamma adjustment. To maintain subtleties between midtones while concentrating contrast changes to the lightest and darkest colors, you can *compress* the midtones represented in the histogram. This has the effect of bringing out the detail in the lightest and darkest areas of your image. You might want to do this if you notice peaks at both ends of the histogram, with a dip in the middle. On the other hand, if you notice dips on both sides of the histogram with a peak in the middle, you might want to expand the midtones. Doing so will draw out details in the midtones while preserving the natural contrast in lights and shadows. The slider marked **Midtones** at the right edge of the **Histogram Adjustment** dialog box enables you to make these adjustments. The result is a kind of twisting of the black curve at the gamma point.

Along the left edge of the **Histogram Adjustment** dialog box are markers that represent the highest and lowest allowed *output levels* for the chosen channel (**Luminance**, **Red**, **Green**, or **Blue**). Normally, these values are set to 0 (darkest) and 255 (brightest), and you'd never change them for an ordinary

KEY TERM

Output levels—The minimum and maximum luminance values for an image's output (appearance onscreen or in print). Pixels within the image are replotted to fit these new limits—no image data is lost. Narrowing the output level range *reduces* contrast between pixels.

photograph. But to make the darkest pixels lighter, drag the black circle marker up; to make the lightest pixels darker, drag the white circle marker down. You might do this for artistic effect—to achieve a pastel pop-art portrait, for example.

96 Improve Brightness and Contrast

Before You Begin

✔ **95** About Making Histogram Adjustments to Brightness and Contrast

See Also

→ **100** Lighten a Subject on a Snowy Background

→ **108** Restore an Old Photograph

NOTE

You can also change the brightness and contrast in an image with the **Adjust, Brightness and Contrast, Brightness/Contrast** command. Its dialog box is simple, and so is the algorithm it uses to adjust pixel luminance. The resulting image is often quite jarring, lacking the subtlety of shading found in nature.

TIP

Values from previous Histogram Adjustment sessions appear when you open the dialog box. Click the **Reset to Default** button if you want to make your adjustments from scratch.

One of the best ways to improve an image's contrast is by making a histogram adjustment. It allows you to improve the distribution of light and dark pixels in an image, creating darks that are truly dark and lights that are truly light. You can also improve the middle tones, making them slightly lighter or darker as needed.

Paint Shop Pro doesn't apply histogram adjustments equally to all pixels, but instead uses a distribution curve to determine which pixels should be adjusted more than others. This approach allows the **Histogram Adjustment** command to retain as much of the original tonal quality of the image as possible.

1 Display Histogram Adjustment Dialog Box

Choose the layer or area to adjust, and then select **Adjust, Brightness and Contrast**, **Histogram Adjustment** from the menu.

2 Choose a Channel

To adjust the overall contrast in an image, click the **Luminance** radio button. To make an adjustment to the saturation of pixels in a single color channel, click the **Colors** radio button and then select **Red**, **Green**, or **Blue** from the list.

3 Adjust Input Levels if Necessary

If gaps exist on either side of the original gray histogram chart, drag the black or white pointer to the edge of the histogram on that side. Alternatively, you can enter the lowest and highest allowable luminance values in the **Low** and **High** boxes.

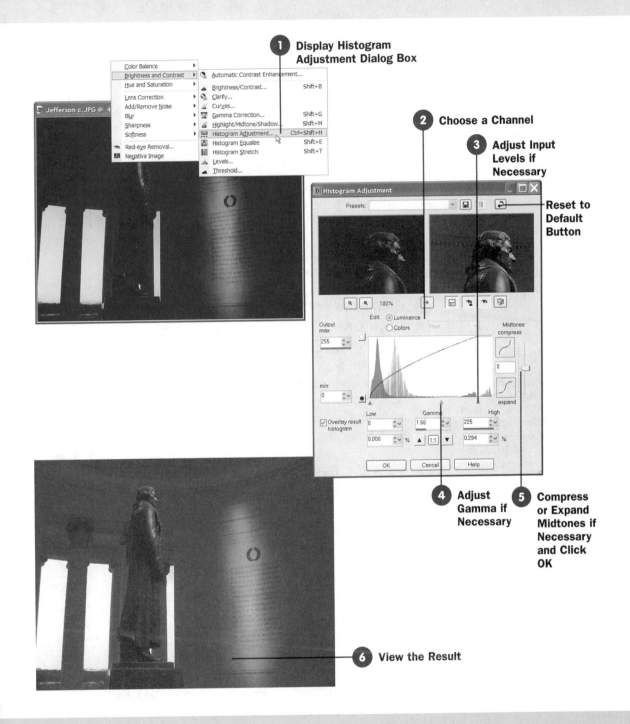

1 Display Histogram Adjustment Dialog Box

2 Choose a Channel

3 Adjust Input Levels if Necessary

Reset to Default Button

4 Adjust Gamma if Necessary

5 Compress or Expand Midtones if Necessary and Click OK

6 View the Result

TIP

As you drag the pointers, watch the percentage amounts displayed below the **Low** and **High** boxes. To restrain from clipping too many almost-dark or almost-light pixels, keep these percentages at or below .1%.

 TIP

The more jagged and striped the result histogram becomes, the fewer gentle transitions between adjacent colors your picture has. As a result, edges in your image could appear noisy rather than clear. The solution—after the histogram adjustment is complete—is to select **Adjust**, **Brightness and Contrast**, **Clarify**. This process knocks off the spikes and fills up the pits throughout the histogram, reintroducing the missing transitions and smoothing out your image.

4 Adjust Gamma if Necessary

To adjust the gamma to make the midtones lighter, drag the gray pointer under the histogram toward the white pointer; to make the midtones darker, drag the gray pointer toward the black pointer.

You can also enter a value (from .20 to 5) in the **Gamma** box—values less than 1 darken midtones, and values greater than 1 lighten them.

The most sensitive adjustments you can make to the **Gamma** value are mere fractional values added to or subtracted from 1.0. You can make a cloudy day appear sunny simply by changing the gamma for the green channel from 1.0 to 1.07, thus enabling more yellows.

5 Compress or Expand Midtones if Necessary and Click OK

Slide the **Midtones** bar up toward **compress** to expand details in highlights and shadows while reducing overall contrast; slide it down toward **expand** to increase detail in the midtones while increasing overall contrast. To apply manual changes, enter a value in the **Midtones** box between –50 (compression) and 50 (expansion).

6 View the Result

In this example, I took a snapshot of a hero of mine, Thomas Jefferson. I shot this picture at dusk, just after the sun set, and used only natural lighting. By shooting without a flash, I retained Jefferson's colors, but the natural interior light simply wasn't enough to illuminate the entire passage on the wall.

My goal in histogram adjustment was to bring back some of the interior detail, such as the entire wall passage, without disturbing Jefferson's dark coppers and red ochres. Sticking with just the **Luminance** channel, I began by sliding the white upper input level cap from 255 to 184, clipping off a small peak in the brights area. Immediately, the walls emerged in their natural color and I could just make out the passage; however, this adjustment also made the sky brighter and washed out Jefferson's colors. To bring back a hint of the darks, I moved the black lower input level cap from 0 up to a mere 3, again clipping off some pixels. This minute adjustment restored the shadow to Jefferson's back and under his cloak.

Next, I adjusted the gamma to 1.54 to lighten the midtones, completely restoring the contrast between the statue and the wall. But I needed more definition in the midtones, so I dragged the Midtones bar up to a compression level of 23. I regained the gentle variety of colors in Jefferson's statue, while restoring some of his more familiar facial features. (Oh, yeah, that's the guy on the nickel!) The result is a photograph that captures the quiet solitude of the low-light conditions inside the memorial, while providing enough detail to retain interest. Look for this image in the Color Gallery section of this book.

97 Improve a Dull, Flat Photo

Today, every individual has it within his or her grasp to duplicate photographs and documents with astounding resolution and brilliance. But scanning photographs is by no means a perfect science. In the act of copying a color photograph, so many translations of color tables and formulas take place that the initial product often ends up washed out, as if it had been left out in the sun for several weeks.

In this task, you'll learn to restore some of a faded, scanned photograph's natural brilliance and contrast by narrowing the range of its input levels. You can also use the steps in this task to improve a badly faded photo, as I have done. When adjusting input levels, it's important to remember that you are telling PSP what constitutes pure white and pure black in an image. If you change the high *input value* from 255 to 240, for example, all the pixels in the image with a lightness value currently above 240 are changed to the lightest allowable *output value*, which is usually left at its default of 255. Thus, by changing the high input value, you make the almost-light pixels in an image much lighter. Pixels currently below 240 are adjusted downward

Before You Begin

✔ **5** Scan an Image

✔ **95** About Making Histogram Adjustments to Brightness and Contrast

See Also

→ **96** Improve Brightness and Contrast

→ **109** Restore Color to a Washed-Out Photograph

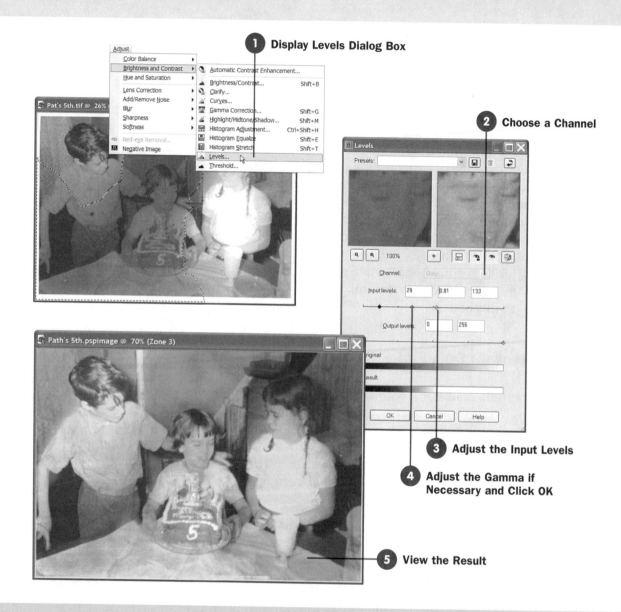

1 Display Levels Dialog Box

2 Choose a Channel

3 Adjust the Input Levels

4 Adjust the Gamma if Necessary and Click OK

5 View the Result

proportionately, based on the image gamma. Lightening light pixels and darkening dark pixels creates more contrast, which is often what's needed in a dull, flat photo. Adjustments similar to the ones discussed here can be accomplished using the

Histogram Adjustment dialog box, as explained in **96** **Improve Brightness and Contrast**. Here the focus is on something simpler to use and understand: the **Levels** dialog box.

1 Display Levels Dialog Box

After selecting the region or layer you want to adjust, select **Adjust**, **Brightness and Contrast**, **Levels** from the menu.

2 Choose a Channel

In the **Levels** dialog box, select the channel you want to adjust from the **Channel** list. The **RGB** channel is essentially the **Luminance** channel (the combined brightness of all three color channels).

3 Adjust the Input Levels

To lighten the lightest pixels in an image, drag the white (clear) diamond marker to the left. If a single channel is selected, this action saturates the least saturated pixels. To darken the darkest pixels in an image (or desaturate heavily saturated pixels in a color channel), drag the black diamond marker to the right. You can also enter numerical values in the appropriate text boxes.

4 Adjust the Gamma if Necessary and Click OK

To change the image gamma, drag the gray diamond pointer in the middle of the **Input levels** scale to the left to lighten midtones (the pixels in an image with a brightness value around 124); drag the marker to the right to darken them. Click **OK** to accept all adjustments.

5 View the Result

In this example, a black-and-white print of my sister Pat's fifth birthday had faded in three different ways, in three different places. A single **Levels** adjustment on the entire photo would have been inappropriate, so I selected each region and feathered and copied each selection to its own layer, so that I could control how each adjustment blended into the final result.

 TIP

Some scanner drivers use their own automatic levels correction when scanning photos. These drivers tend to overestimate the corrections and perform too much contrast adjustment rather than too little. If possible, try turning *off* the automatic correction feature in your scanning software *before* you proceed with the scan, then make any corrections yourself in PSP.

 TIP

Before making adjustments, display the **Histogram** palette so that you can see how your changes affect the image.

NOTES

To lighten the lightest pixels or darken the darkest pixels in an image (reducing contrast), change the high and low **Output levels** values accordingly. Doing so often creates strange results in a photograph, so it's recommended that you leave the **Output levels** values set at 0 and 255.

Many people say that gamma is "a measure of an image's luminance"—this simply isn't so, even though increasing gamma does brighten the brighter pixels. Notice that when you adjust gamma, the darkest pixels remain as dark as they were before, and the brightest pixels stay as bright. Gamma affects only those pixels in between—the midtones.

Pat's center region was really dark, so I lightened it by lowering the high **Input level** from 255 all the way down to 133. I restored contrast by setting the low **Input level** from 0 to 29. I then lowered the gamma from 1.0 to 0.84 to lighten the too-dark midtones. This almost restored Pat's face, but didn't bring back her shock of dark hair. Because she's the subject of the photo, I wanted to add as much detail there as possible, so I selected just her face, used a narrower **Input level** range of 54 and 128 for even greater contrast, and set the gamma to 1.28 to favor darks.

I made separate adjustments to my brother Joe's region on the left, which needed some narrowing of the input levels but not so much. For my sister Beth on the right, I selected the flaky area of print damage on her dress, where peeling film caused a whitening effect, and simply lowered its **Output level** cap from 255 to 238. This grayed the area down to match the facial tones, and any small abnormalities that remained in the dress I ironed out with spot tools. To hide the very slight seams between zones, I used the **Dodge** brush to lighten the darker areas in convenient places, such as the folds in fabric.

98 About Making Curves Adjustments to Brightness and Contrast

Before You Begin

✔ **About Making Histogram Adjustments to Brightness and Contrast**

See Also

→ **Restore Color and Improve Detail**

In **95** **About Making Histogram Adjustments to Brightness and Contrast**, I discuss how the progression from darks to lights in an image can be represented on a curve. When you want to make your midtones lighter or darker, you bend this curve up or down by adjusting the *image gamma*. There's another method for altering this curve that provides you with more flexibility. In the **Curves** dialog box, you can "redraw" this curve, essentially adjusting the lightness value of any pixel in an image, not just the midtones. In this image of my nephew Ryan on a sunset cruise in Hawaii, I created more drama by darkening some of the midtones and lightening some of the lights.

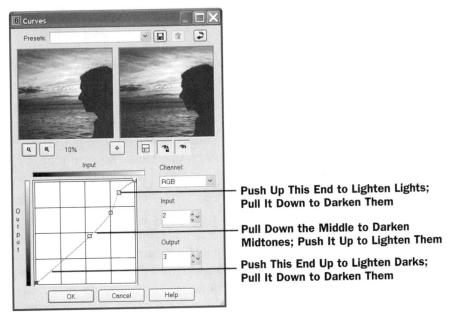

Push Up This End to Lighten Lights; Pull It Down to Darken Them

Pull Down the Middle to Darken Midtones; Push It Up to Lighten Them

Push This End Up to Lighten Darks; Pull It Down to Darken Them

The **Curves** *dialog box lets you adjust the darks-to-lights progression manually.*

The graph in the **Curves** dialog box represents the extent to which the lightness values in an image have been remapped (made lighter or darker). When the graph is a flat, diagonal line, darks are darks, lights are lights, and midtones are left alone. The line doesn't represent how *many* lights and darks there are; that's for the histogram to tell you. What the **Curves** graph tells you instead is which lights, darks, and midtones in the image are being remapped to other lightness values. By redrawing the curve, for example, you could tell PSP to change all pixels with a lightness value of 143 (the pixels' current or input value) to 167 (the pixels' result or output value).

The horizontal axis represents the *input values*—the brightness values currently in the image. The vertical axis represents the *output values*—the values the pixels will have after you click **OK**. To make the light midtones even lighter, for example, you could click above the halfway point on the curve and drag the newly created node up or to the left. To make those pixels darker, drag the node down or to the right instead. With this approach, strange and severe photographic distortions such as the kind observed in damaged Polaroid prints (where middle greens mutate toward gray) can be localized and compensated for without disturbing the rest of the image.

You can move either end of the curve as well; if you drag the left end up, you'll lighten the darks so that they are not completely black. Drag the right end down to darken the lightest pixels. For most photos, this adjustment is not a good idea, but sometimes it's useful to lighten darks—for example, to prevent them from dominating an image and creating black "holes."

There's no apparent limit to the number of nodes you can create within the **Curves** dialog box. To remove a node entirely, drag it off the graph. You can make one last adjustment to the curve if you want: You can drag the nodes at either end of the line to new positions on the graph. To change the low input value (essentially what you do when you drag the black marker on a histogram inwards), drag the node at the left end of the curve to the *right*. To change the high input value, drag the node at the right end of the curve to the *left*. You can set the output values with these nodes as well, although it's typically best to leave them alone. However, if you want to lighten the darkest pixels in your image, click the node at the lower-left end of the curve and drag it up. To darken the lightest pixels, drag the node at the top-right end of the curve down.

You can also use the **Curves** dialog box to make precise color corrections, sometimes without first selecting the region you want to affect. Suppose that you have a picture of some lovely daffodils. Some have white petals with a yellow cup, while others are yellow with pale yellow wisps here and there. You would like to remove the pale yellow wisps, making those daffodils almost solid yellow so that they will contrast more with the white and yellow daffodils. But the idea of selecting all those tiny pale yellow wisps has you pulling your hair out. Luckily for your hair, you suddenly remember that the way your computer's RGB *colorspace* works, the most vivid yellow your computer can produce is represented as {RGB: 255, 255, 0} (full red and green, no blue). To create pale yellow pixels, the computer adds blue. If you work in the **Blue** channel and make a curves adjustment that removes

TIP

The hardest part of using **Curves** is finding the right part of the curve to adjust. Before opening the dialog box, use the **Dropper** tool to sample a pixel you want to adjust and learn its exact lightness value. Then type that value in the **Input** box and either drag or type to create a new **Output** value.

KEY TERM

Colorspace—An internal map used by computers and printing devices that depicts all the possible colors for that device. This allows each device to translate colors from one colorspace to another, resulting in the best color interpretation between the two devices.

the blues in those pale yellow wisps, they'll become more yellow. The exact adjustment I used, and the result, are shown in the figure. Look for this image in the Color Gallery section of this book.

Curves adjustment restores natural vividness to bright colors without using gamma adjustment.

99 Restore Color and Improve Detail

Scientists studying the brain have confirmed what artists have known since the Renaissance: The mind seeks out the darks and lights of a scene first. But after light and shadow have given a subject the illusion of shape and depth, the mind concentrates on that subject's midtones—its natural colors. Scanned, printed photographs lose their lustrous midtones long before their highlights and shadows start to fade, especially when those prints are exposed to direct sunlight. But just because midtones have faded doesn't mean they're gone. With this technique, you can retrieve the natural color from the existing, faded color.

This task uses two PSP features in succession: highlight/midtone/shadow adjustment and curves adjustment. The purpose of

Before You Begin

✔ **95** About Making Histogram Adjustments to Brightness and Contrast

See Also

→ **96** Improve Brightness and Contrast

→ **108** Restore an Old Photograph

→ **109** Restore Color to a Washed-Out Photograph

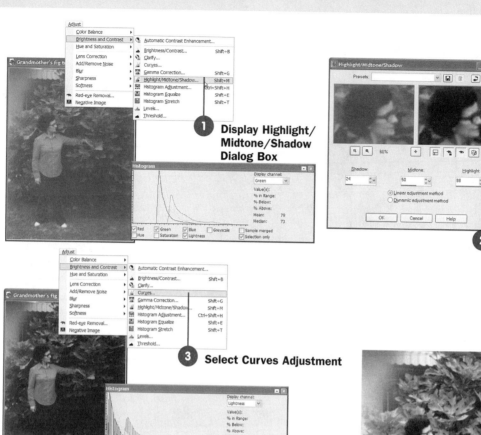

1 Display Highlight/Midtone/Shadow Dialog Box

2 Identify Dark and Light Points and Click OK

3 Select Curves Adjustment

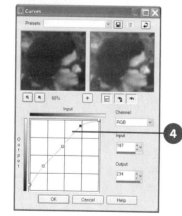

4 Define Curves and Click OK

5 View the Result

the highlight/midtone/shadow adjustment is to identify the darkest and lightest levels in the image and relocate them if necessary to increase contrast and restore color balance. The **Curves** adjustment is used to fine-tune the darks and lights, lighten or darken midtones if needed, and increase or decrease red, green, or blue in the highlights, midtones, or shadows to balance the color.

① Display Highlight/Midtone/Shadow Dialog Box

After choosing an image or selecting a layer or region to adjust, select **Adjust**, **Brightness and Contrast**, **Highlight/Midtone/Shadow** from the menu.

② Identify Dark and Light Points and Click OK

There are two methods you can use to identify the dark and light points in the image: With the **Linear adjustment method** radio button selected, the settings represent *relative strength*. To make the shadows darker, increase the **Shadow** value. To lighten the highlights, decrease the **Highlight** value.

With the **Dynamic adjustment method** option selected, settings represent *actual strength*. To darken the shadows, decrease the **Shadow** value; lighten shadows by increasing the value. Lighten highlights by increasing the **Highlight** value; darken them by decreasing the value.

③ Select Curves Adjustment

At this point, your darks are as dark as they can be, and your lights as light as they can be. Now you can use curves to adjust lightness values and saturation levels throughout an image as needed. Select **Adjust**, **Brightness and Contrast**, **Curves** from the menu.

④ Define Curves and Click OK

In the **Curves** dialog box, open the **Channel** drop-down list box and choose whether to adjust the RGB channel (the combined brightness of all three color channels) or the saturation level of the Red, Green, and Blue channels independently. Then click and drag the curve to adjust the values of pixels at that point. You can change curves for all four

NOTE

If the **Histogram** palette is not showing, select **View**, **Palettes**, **Histogram** to display it. Make sure that the graphs for the **Red**, **Green**, **Blue**, and **Lightness** channels are checked and showing.

TIPS

As you make changes, keep an eye on the **Histogram** palette. For best results, adjust the **Shadow** and **Highlight** values so that both sides of the **Lightness** curve (the yellow line on the **Histogram** palette) just touch the left and right ends of the horizontal scale.

Do not adjust the **Midtone** setting; it too often creates strange results. To adjust the midtones in an image, change the gamma. See **96** Improve Brightness and Contrast. After making adjustments, click **OK**.

channels in one session, before you click **OK** and apply those changes to your image.

For example, you might want to increase the reds in the light pixels to add pink to a face. To do that, drag the right end of the curve for the red channel up or to the left. To simply darken the midtones, select the RGB channel and drag the curve down in the middle.

NOTE

The midtones in your image are represented by the center of the **Curves** graph. If your image is too grainy, especially in the skin tone regions, try flattening the curve in the middle.

TIP

If your curves adjustment results in "spikes and pits" in the histogram, smooth them out by selecting **Adjust, Brightness and Contrast, Clarify**, and setting **Strength of effect** from 1 to 5.

TIP

Similar curves adjustments can be made to the Red, Green, and Blue channels with the **Gamma Correction** dialog box and also with the **Histogram Adjustment** dialog box. However, such adjustments aren't nearly as precise as they are with the **Curves** dialog box.

⑤ View the Result

The first step to restoring this photo of my husband's grandmother and her beloved fig tree was to expand its spectrum so that the darks are really dark, and the lights are light. Using the **Highlight/Midtone/Shadow** command, I adjusted the **Shadow** and **Highlight** values until the histogram touched the left and right sides of the chart. By expanding the amount of darks and lights, I give myself more room to make adjustments within the shadow and highlight areas. For example, I'll be able to lighten some of the shadows underneath the fig tree to keep it from becoming a black hole.

Without employing any gamma correction at all, I used the **Curves** dialog box to restore color balance. I started by adjusting the color channels individually, bringing up the Blue channel in the shadows (dragging the left end of the graph up or to the left) to restore Grandmother's blue slacks, and bringing up the Green channel in the shadows to restore detail in the deep folds of the fig leaves. There isn't a yellow channel in optics, so you often have to restore greens to recover yellows (red and green make yellow). Grandmother loved wearing red, but that shouldn't make the Red channel dominate the image; I created a concave curve to remove the red tint from areas where it didn't belong. (I dragged the middle of the red curve down to lower the presence of reds in the midtones.) These adjustments restored the natural balance between the Red, Green, and Blue channels in Grandmother's face, bringing back her natural skin tone.

After achieving color balance by fiddling with the curves of the Red, Green, and Blue channels, I adjusted the midtones using the RGB channel. I started by creating a convex curve, making the middle values brighter while leaving the extremes (lights and darks) where they were. Although that improved the image immensely, it created an unwanted effect in Grandmother's blouse, accenting the windy wrinkles to make it appear as if pink paint had rained down on it. I put a dent in the middle of the curve (pulled it down just a tiny bit) because the blouse constituted the majority of the image's middle values; the result equalized the blouse colors, bringing back their natural variation. Finally, I boosted the minimum darkness node (I moved the node at the left end of the curve up) so that the darks weren't quite so black. This lightened the base of the fig tree so that it didn't look like a gateway into another dimension and so that Grandmother's hair didn't look so much like a black boulder. The results are colors that look more natural. Some work remains: clarifying some of the blurry spots and extracting Granddad's finger from the upper-left corner. Look for this image in the Color Gallery section of this book.

100 Lighten a Subject on a Snowy Background

Typically, the brightness of snow changes the way your camera handles light from darker objects—and on a snowy day, almost everything is darker than snow. Digital cameras are especially sensitive to bright light reflecting off snow, bleaching out the rest of the scene and causing subjects in the foreground, including people, to appear muted and dark. Furthermore, because many digital cameras tend to "normalize" their light input on the fly, even though the snow is the brightest thing in the image, it might be recorded as gray, while your foreground subjects are made even darker to compensate.

In remedying an image that suffers from this problem, you could start by invoking the **Histogram Adjustment** command, but the lightest lights (the snow) are probably as light as you want them to be anyway. This task shows you how to easily separate your foreground subject from the background snow so that you can select just the subject and restore its detail.

Before You Begin

✔ **95** About Making Histogram Adjustments to Brightness and Contrast

See Also

→ **68** Remove Specks and Holes from a Selection

→ **72** Select a Portion of an Image with Threshold

→ **96** Improve Brightness and Contrast

→ **99** Restore Color and Improve Detail

→ **120** About Layers and the Layer Palette

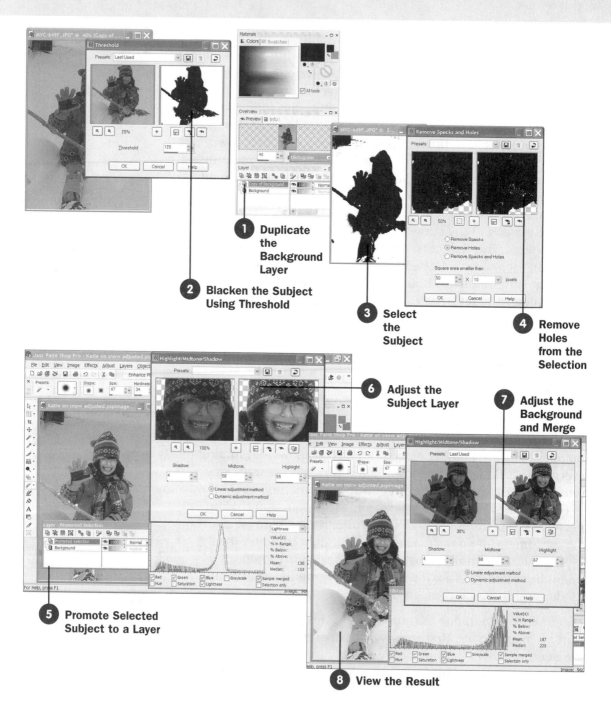

1 Duplicate the Background Layer

2 Blacken the Subject Using Threshold

3 Select the Subject

4 Remove Holes from the Selection

6 Adjust the Subject Layer

7 Adjust the Background and Merge

5 Promote Selected Subject to a Layer

8 View the Result

1 **Duplicate the Background Layer**

In the **Layer** palette, choose the **Background** layer of the image. Then click the **Duplicate Layer** button.

2 **Blacken the Subject Using Threshold**

In the **Layer** palette, choose the **Copy of Background** layer. Then select **Adjust**, **Brightness and Contrast**, **Threshold** from the main menu. Adjust the **Threshold** level until the black area just covers your subject. You'll probably also blacken *some* of the shadows your subject might be casting on the snow; don't worry, that's okay. Click **OK**.

3 **Select the Subject**

Your subject should now be black and the background white, but that's only temporary. Use the **Magic Wand** tool to select the subject.

4 **Remove Holes from the Selection**

At this moment, your selection probably includes some specks of snow on your subject—especially if she's recently been in a snowball fight. These beads of snow will produce holes in your selection. To eliminate that problem, choose **Selections**, **Modify**, **Remove Specks and Holes**. Enable the **Remove Holes** option and then adjust the **pixels** value to a value just big enough to remove the snow specks from the selection, such as 10. Click **OK**.

5 **Promote Selected Subject to a Layer**

In the **Layer** palette, change to the **Background** layer, then select **Selections**, **Promote Selection to Layer** from the main menu. Your subject is now isolated on its own layer, where you can make adjustments that bring out its details without disturbing the snow background.

You no longer need the **Copy of Background** layer, so change to it and then click the **Delete Layer** button in the **Layer** palette. Click **Yes** to confirm the deletion.

 TIP

If your camera has a special setting for snow, by all means use it, but you might still find that adjustments are needed after importing the image into PSP.

NOTE

Why close the holes in your selection and include the specks of snow on your subject? If you don't, chances are your selection will include some bits of snow while excluding other bits. The included snow will appear very white in the final image, whereas the non-included specks will appear very light gray.

 TIP

You might find that certain patches of shadow cast by the subject on the snow have been included in your selection. Because you don't want to bring out their details, remove them from the **Promoted Selection** layer using the **Eraser** tool. (This will be easier to do if you first hide the **Background** layer.)

TIP

Histogram adjustment often creates pits and spikes in the image's histogram. To compensate, select **Adjust, Brightness and Contrast, Clarify.** In the **Clarify** dialog box, under **Strength of effect,** choose a number that restores some natural contrasts to the subject's skin tones without brightening other tones, such as clothes colors. Click **OK**.

 NOTE

Because snow is so white, it has a narrow range of brightness and contrast, making it difficult to set proper **Shadow** and **Highlight** values for the snow alone. You'll get better results by including the darker subject material in the calculation. Don't worry; you won't see any of these adjustments made to the subject in the final image.

6 Adjust the Subject Layer

Display the **Histogram** palette so that you can see your adjustments. Change to the **Promoted Selection** layer and select **Adjust, Brightness and Contrast, Highlight/Midtone/Shadow** from the menu. Use the method explained in **99** **Restore Color and Improve Detail** to expand the brightness range of the foreground area by adjusting the **Shadow** and **Highlight** values.

Your subject might need further adjustment to bring out the natural color of skin tones and bright clothes. If so, select **Adjust, Brightness and Contrast, Histogram Adjustment**. Use the method explained in **96** **Improve Brightness and Contrast** to restore brilliance and clarity to the foreground contents.

7 Adjust the Background and Merge

Choose **Selections, Select None** to deselect the subject. On the **Layer** palette, choose the **Background** layer. Select **Adjust, Brightness and Contrast, Highlight/Midtone/Shadow**. Repeat the method explained in **99** **Restore Color and Improve Detail**, this time to restore the snowy background to a natural level of brightness that's more balanced with respect to the subject. When the image looks good, merge all layers by selecting **Layers, Merge, Merge All (Flatten)**.

8 View the Result

My original photo suffered from a phenomenon common to digital cameras: The brightness of the snow overwhelmed the light detectors, even when the camera was set for bright outdoors. As a result, Katerina's colors were muted and dull. I made histogram adjustments to brighten her clothes, but had my image been one undivided layer, the same changes I made to her clothes and skin tones would have made the snow pink. By separating the snow from the foreground, I was able to shield the snow from the changes I made to the color channels, while applying color-safe changes to the snow.

101 Lighten or Darken a Portion of an Image

In the process of developing a photograph from a negative, photographers use two darkroom techniques to alter the appearance of the developing print, often for artistic effect: To *dodge* is to underexpose a specific portion of a print to light from the negative, causing that portion to become lighter. To *burn* is to increase the light on a portion of a print, causing it to overexpose and become darker.

Paint Shop Pro includes two spot tools you can use to lighten or darken an area of an image: **Dodge** and **Burn**. When you understand the heritage of their names, you know almost everything you need to know about what they do. In effect, these tools work like brushes that lighten or darken whatever they touch. To use them intelligently, you should use several tool options: First, turn on the **Continuous** option, which allows you to stroke over an area as much as you want without building up the effect (continuing to lighten or darken overlapped pixels, which results in noticeable streaks). Adjust the **Opacity** setting to the lightness/darkness value you want, and with the **Continuous** option set, this will control the effect, lightening/darkening pixels by only the **Opacity** amount. Adjust the **Size** of the brush to fit the area you want to change, and adjust the **Hardness** to soften the effect at the edges of the brush stroke.

1 Select Dodge or Burn Tool

Select the layer or region you want to edit. From the **Tools** toolbar, select the **Dodge** tool to lighten or the **Burn** tool to darken.

2 Set Tool Options

On the **Tool Options** palette, set the characteristics you want to use—especially the tool's **Size, Opacity,** and **Limit** (if desired).

3 Lighten/Darken Pixels

Drag the brush over that spot you want to adjust.

Before You Begin

✔ **10** About Tools and Tool Options

See Also

→ **90** Whiten Teeth

 TIP

If you want to build up the lightening or darkening effect in an area, turn off the **Continuous** option, or simply click the **New Stroke** button to start a new stroke.

NOTE

You can also lighten or darken pixels using the **Lighten/Darken** retouch tool. With this tool, you can choose to adjust the RGB or the HSL component to make the pixels lighter/darker.

NOTE

By default, the **Limit** option is set to **None**, meaning that the **Dodge** or **Burn** effect is applied evenly to all pixels you brush over, regardless of their brightness values. To limit dodging or burning to a specific range of brightness values, choose **Shadow, Midtones,** or **Highlights** from this list.

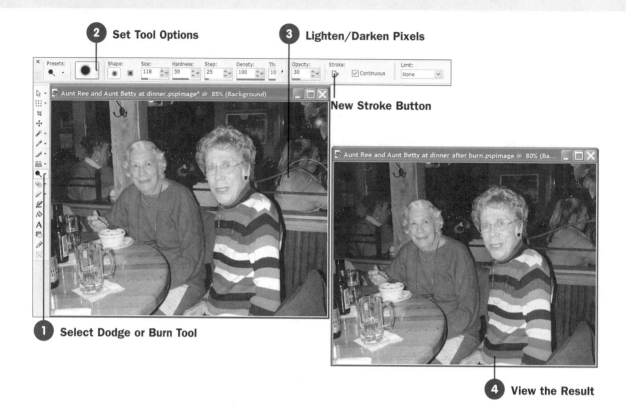

2 Set Tool Options

3 Lighten/Darken Pixels

New Stroke Button

1 Select Dodge or Burn Tool

4 View the Result

4 View the Result

Here, I decided to darken the background a bit to draw more attention to the subjects, Aunt Ree and Aunt Betty. With the **Burn** tool, I darkened some highlights as well, such as the white stripes on Aunt Betty's sweater, Aunt Ree's napkin, and the reflection of the flash in the upper-right corner, all of which seemed to be drawing too much attention.

102 Improve a Nighttime Photo

The perennial problem with photographing a night scene such as a campfire gathering or a winter's evening snowfall is that there's never enough natural light to produce a proper exposure. Increasing the exposure time can introduce blurriness, especially if your subject doesn't hold perfectly still, and using a flash bleaches out the colors of nearby subjects while blackening out anything that's further away than a few feet.

In most nighttime photographs, however, the detail that's almost too dark to see is there—hidden, dormant—and can be rediscovered not so much by increasing contrast but by compounding the saturation levels. The technique you're about to see here borrows a trick from Paint Shop Pro's **Overlay** blend mode, using *white* as the indicator that tells PSP where to turn up the color volume.

① Create a Duplicate Overlay Layer

On the **Layer** palette, click the **Duplicate Layer** button. Set the **Blend Mode** of the new layer (probably called **Copy of Background** or **Copy of Raster 1**) to **Overlay**.

② Choose a White Gradient

To bring out detail at the bottom of the image while leaving the top detail alone, set the **Foreground Material** to a gradient that progresses from transparency to white {RGB: 255, 255, 255}, at an angle of zero degrees (straight down). To do that, first set the **Foreground Color** to white, select the **Fading foreground** gradient, and adjust its angle.

③ Apply a Gradient Flood Fill

From the **Tools** palette, select the **Flood Fill** tool. On the **Tool Options** palette, set **Opacity** to 100, **Blend Mode** to **Normal**, and **Match Mode** to **None**.

Make sure that the **Copy of Background** layer is chosen in the **Layer** palette. In the image window, point to any location and click. Pixels of low brightness toward the bottom of the image are made brighter and more vibrant. Because you applied a gradient fill using transparency,

Before You Begin

✔ **13** Select a Color to Work With

✔ **14** Select a Gradient to Work With

✔ **120** About Layers and the Layer Palette

ⓘ TIP

To capture a nighttime photo, use a flash, but slow the camera's shutter speed as well, so that some ambient light is captured, along with detail the flash might ordinarily black out. On most digital cameras, a slow shutter speed is labeled Night, Slow Sync, or Manual.

 NOTE

For this process to work properly, you should have only one layer in your image; if necessary, select **Layers**, **Merge**, **Merge All (Flatten)** to merge all layers. This command produces the single layer that serves as the **Background** layer for this task.

ⓘ TIP

The detail in your image will be brought out wherever white appears in the duplicate layer. Instead of applying a gradient, you could fill the duplicate layer with white or use a paintbrush to be selective. Dim details that are too bright by painting them with dark gray or black. Where transparency exists, the image's original values will be left alone.

1 Create a Duplicate Overlay Layer

2 Choose a White Gradient

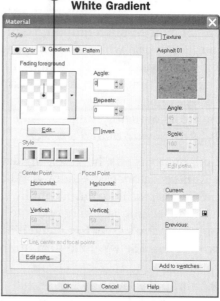

3 Apply a Gradient Flood Fill

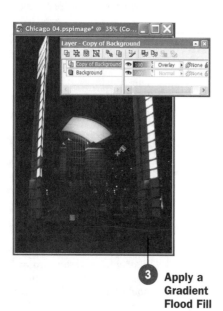

4 View the Result

pixels toward the top of the image are not affected, so a nighttime sky will retain its color.

④ View the Result

This was a quick snapshot taken after sundown, outside the McCormick Place Convention Center in Chicago. With the original image, it was difficult to discern what you were looking at (the outside of a building? a snapshot of a passing spaceship?). After applying the second overlay layer, the building's entrance and unloading area are now easy to identify.

103 Fix a Flash That's Too Close

When you photograph a subject at a very close distance with the flash turned on, inevitably the colors become bleached out and the shadows all fill with midtones. Faced with an overly bright image, you might feel compelled to use the **Histogram Adjustment** command to broaden the contrast between the image's narrow range of colors. Although this command might work, there is a quicker, simpler, and startlingly more effective way to fix a flash that's too close.

The secret is this: The contrast (detail) in an image is stored in its Black channel. If you separate a bleached-out image into its CMYK channels—the fourth one being Black—the Black channel reveals little, if any, information. If you replace the Black channel with a copy of any one of the other color channels (being bathed in light after all, at least one of the other three channels must contain some information) and then combine the four channels back into one image, the detail lost by the close flash will be restored. Whether or not the result is absolutely realistic, it has to be better than what you had before...and in a lot of cases, the results are glowing.

Before You Begin

✔ **71** Select a Portion of an Image with Channels

See Also

→ **102** Improve a Nighttime Photo

→ **104** Fix a Flash That's Too Far Away

🔋 TIP

This is also a good way to get rid of excess noise—simply separate an image into its CYMK channels, run a noise reduction filter on the Black channel, and recombine. Alternatively, blur any or all of the color channels and recombine them. (Because they don't contain the detail, no crispness is lost.)

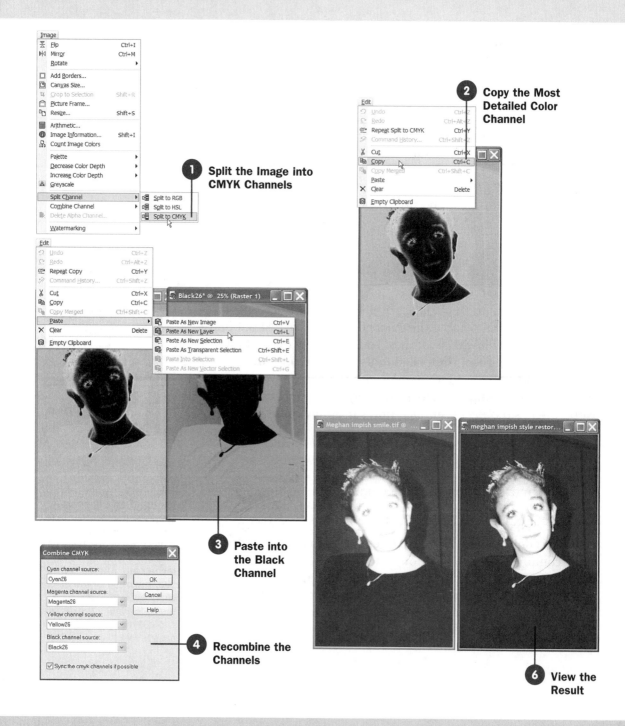

1 Split the Image into CMYK Channels

2 Copy the Most Detailed Color Channel

3 Paste into the Black Channel

4 Recombine the Channels

6 View the Result

❶ Split the Image into CMYK Channels

Select **Image**, **Split Channel**, **Split to CMYK** from the menu. Four new image windows appear, representing the **Cyan**, **Magenta**, **Yellow**, and **Black** channels of the original image.

❷ Copy the Most Detailed Color Channel

Observe the image windows for the **Cyan**, **Magenta**, and **Yellow** channels. Choose the one you believe contains the greatest amount of contrast between its various levels of gray. Activate its window and select **Edit**, **Copy**.

❸ Paste into the Black Channel

Activate the window for the **Black** channel and select **Edit**, **Paste**, **Paste As New Layer**. The entire **Black** channel will be covered over by the data from the color channel you chose in step 2.

❹ Recombine the Channels

Select **Image**, **Combine Channel**, **Combine from CMYK**. The **Combine CMYK** dialog box should list the names from the title bars of the four open channels. Click **OK**. PSP creates a new image window containing the combined data, which you can save as a separate file.

❺ View the Result

At my wedding reception, my husband and I provided several flash cameras so that our guests could capture the action. Little did we know that most of the pictures would contain items the children found most interesting—close-ups of drink cups, people's faces, other children running away, and adults from the waist down. So when I stumbled on a not-quite-usable image of my niece Meghan with an impish, almost-a-woman-but-still-a-child expression, it was worth the effort to save it. The results, though not perfect, are amazing.

NOTE

Photo Album allows you to make simple corrections to flash photographs. In the ImageView window, click either the **QuickFix** button or **Adjust** button.

TIP

If the combined image isn't what you'd hoped it would be, try erasing part of the channel detail you copied in and letting some of the **Black** channel remain. Because the channels are contained on separate layers, this shouldn't be too hard to do.

104 Fix a Flash That's Too Far Away

Before You Begin

✔ **79** Copy a Selection to a New Layer

✔ **96** Improve Brightness and Contrast

✔ **99** Restore Color and Improve Detail

✔ **120** About Layers and the Layer Palette

See Also

→ **103** Fix a Flash That's Too Close

NOTE

Photo Album allows you to make simple corrections to flash photographs. In the ImageView window, click either the **QuickFix** button or **Adjust** button.

 TIP

To help grab the foreground, try using the **Threshold** or **Split Channel** command. See **71** Select a Portion of an Image with Channels or **72** Select a Portion of an Image with Threshold.

NOTE

To minimize the "halo" effect that can occur when you edit two parts of an image separately (as we do in this task), feather the selection somewhat.

One of the main problems with flash photography is that distant objects get little light, certainly not enough to bring out the detail needed for a nice photograph. And if they do get much light at all, it's because they reflect unnatural glare instead of soft, warm light. In some flash images, it doesn't matter whether background objects are lit because they are unimportant. But if the distant object is your sister dancing her first dance with her new husband, the lack of light and detail is a problem.

You might try the **Histogram Adjustment** command to lighten the darkness levels of distant objects and increase the gamma, but you don't want to apply these same changes to other subject matter in the near foreground. You'll want to separate the foreground and background matter and apply the gamma changes to the background only.

1 Promote the Foreground to Layer

Use a selection tool to select the foreground subject—such as a person near to the camera. Place the selection on its own layer by choosing **Selections**, **Promote Selection to Layer** from the menu. Rename the new layer **Foreground**.

2 Promote the Background to Layer

Change to the **Background** layer and choose **Selections**, **Invert**. This command selects the background (everything you didn't select in step 1). Choose **Selections**, **Modify**, **Inside/Outside Feather**. Select **Both**, set **Feather amount** to at least 6, and click **OK** to feather the selection. Finally, choose **Selections**, **Promote Selection to Layer** and rename this new layer **Surroundings**.

3 Adjust the Foreground Layer

Choose **Selections**, **Select None** to deselect the background. Change to the **Foreground** layer. Adjust the foreground as needed, improving detail and color balance. In this example, I used the **Histogram Adjustment** and **Curves** commands to lighten the midtones and restore the white to my brother Mike's sweater.

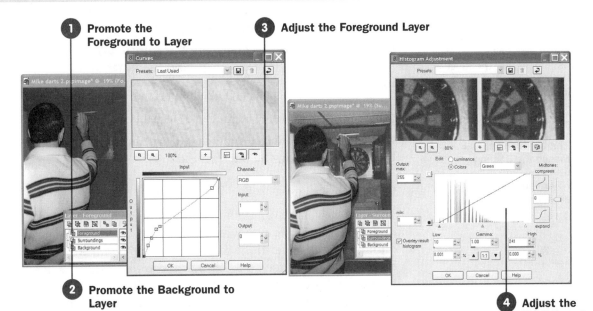

1 Promote the Foreground to Layer

3 Adjust the Foreground Layer

2 Promote the Background to Layer

4 Adjust the Background Layer

5 Correct Any Halo Effect

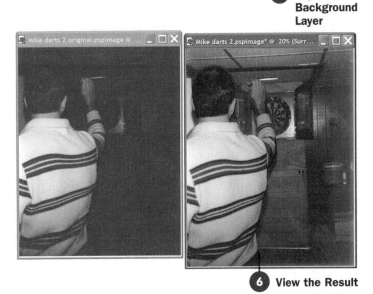

6 View the Result

TIP

To bring out detail where the flash didn't hit, lighten the midtones. For the most control, use the **Histogram Adjustment** command. For this image, I set the **Low** value normally but clipped .3% of the brights when setting the **High** value. I increased the **Gamma** value to 2.3, and moved the **Midtones** slider down to expand the midtones.

4 Adjust the Background Layer

On the **Layer** palette, choose the **Surroundings** layer. Make adjustments to the background to lighten it and improve detail.

5 Remove Any Halo Effect

Use the **Eraser** tool to remove any over-brightened pixels that might exist on the background layer.

6 View the Result

This project is far from done. There are numerous scratches and specks yet to be removed, and permanent fingerprint damage to the lower-right corner. Cropping could easily eliminate the strange band of fuzziness along the right side. Manual color correction could still be applied to the center of the dartboard, and the glare effect to the lower-right of the dartboard could be reduced. Still, the difference between this and the original is dramatic, and certainly tells the story I meant to capture: my brother, Mike, beating someone at darts (name withheld to protect the innocent).

105 Restore Balance to a Backlit Photograph

Before You Begin

✔ 75 Save a Selection for Reuse

✔ 96 Improve Brightness and Contrast

✔ 99 Restore Color and Improve Detail

See Also

→ 64 Select Areas of Similar Color, Brightness, or Opacity

→ 101 Lighten or Darken a Portion of an Image

How many times has this happened to you? You and your spouse are someplace special—someplace you want to remember forever—and another couple asks if you could take their picture in return for them taking your picture. You frame your unknown subjects perfectly; they, on the other hand, place the two of you square in front of the sunset. As a result of the sun being placed behind you, you are now the proud owner of a perfect silhouette.

You're about to see how to regain at least some, if not all, of the information from a drastically backlit photograph that you might otherwise discard as unsalvageable—a photograph in which the facial features of the subject are indistinguishable. Even in the most distressed of backlit situations, some information still exists—some small slice of something that distinguishes shadows from midtones from highlights. This task shows you how to exploit that information to produce, if not a perfect photograph, at least something you won't want to throw away. To restore a partly or more moderately backlit photograph—where at least you can make out some facial detail—you won't need to follow every step in this process, so I'll show you which steps you can skip. If you have Photo Album, you can use it to make corrections to backlit photographs, assuming they are not that bad. In the ImageView window, select **Adjust** from the **Adjust** button menu.

1 Copy the Foreground to a Separate Layer

Select the foreground objects hidden in shadow by the back-lighting and save the selection pattern (for use in a later steps) to the Alpha channel by choosing **Selections, Load/Save Selection, Save Selection to Alpha Channel**. Then copy the selection to its own layer by choosing **Selections, Promote Selection to Layer**.

2 Separate Shadows from Highlights if Necessary

If you can make out *some* facial features—not just the eyes and nose, but cheekbones and foreheads—skip this step. Otherwise, select the new layer and choose **Adjust, Brightness and Contrast, Highlight/Midtone/Shadow**. Increase the **Shadow** setting and decrease the **Highlight** setting until you can distinguish lights from darks, and the facial features are distinguishable. Now you have something to work with. Click **OK**.

3 Split Image into CMYK Channels

Select **Image, Split Channel, Split to CMYK** from the menu. Four new windows open, one for each color channel and Black.

4 Correct Contrast of Black Channel

Invert the Black channel image (which is, in effect, a negative of the image) by selecting **Adjust, Negative Image**. A positive image will enable you to better judge the contrast adjustments you make. Next, select **Selections,**

→ **107** Adjust Hue, Saturation, and Lightness Manually

→ **114** Sharpen an Image

→ **116** Blur a Background to Create Depth of Field

 TIP

For best results, scan your backlit photo using the highest possible resolution—generally 600 dpi. If the print has a satin finish, don't worry; by applying some selective blurring and then reducing the final image's size, that texture will vanish. Make certain that your print is perfectly clean before you scan; wipe it clear of fingerprints.

TIP

For a badly backlit image, it is almost comically easy to select the damaged region. Use the **Magic Wand** tool, set **Match Mode** to **RGB Value**, and set **Tolerance** to a value inversely proportional to the degree of damage—low numbers for high damage, high numbers for low damage.

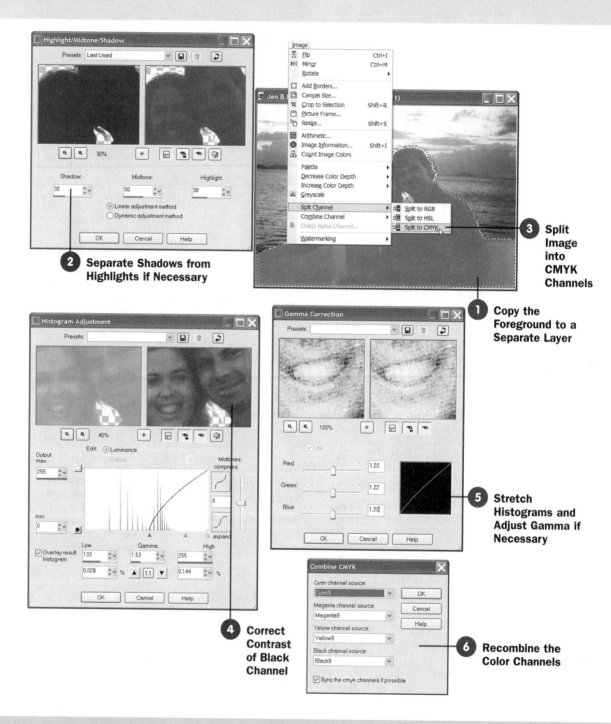

2 Separate Shadows from Highlights if Necessary

3 Split Image into CMYK Channels

1 Copy the Foreground to a Separate Layer

5 Stretch Histograms and Adjust Gamma if Necessary

4 Correct Contrast of Black Channel

6 Recombine the Color Channels

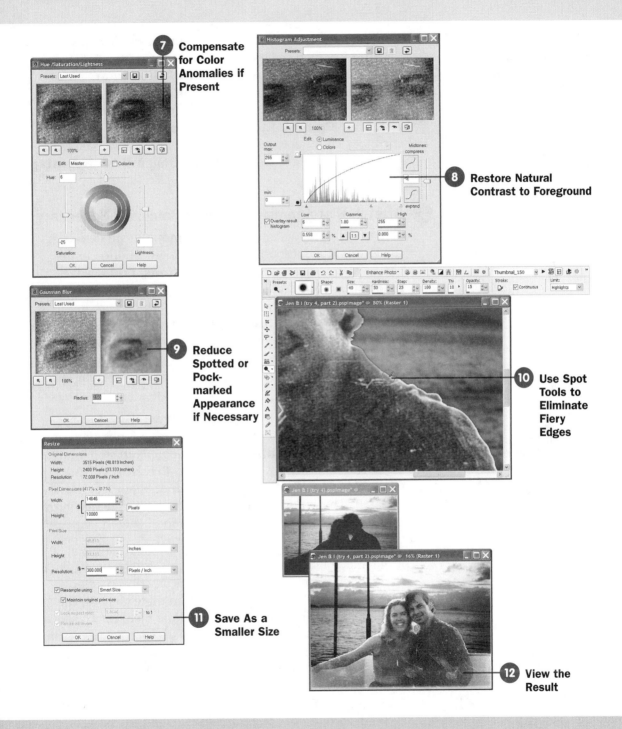

7 Compensate for Color Anomalies if Present

8 Restore Natural Contrast to Foreground

9 Reduce Spotted or Pock-marked Appearance if Necessary

10 Use Spot Tools to Eliminate Fiery Edges

11 Save As a Smaller Size

12 View the Result

TIP

For moderately damaged images, increase the **Gamma** setting to about 1.4. For badly damaged images, increase **Gamma** to a value between 1.8 and 2.2. *Remember the Gamma number you use*; whatever value you specify here, you will be using it three more times.

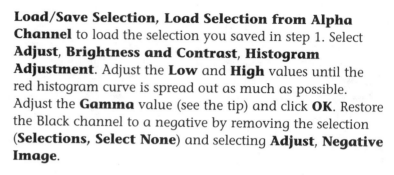

Load/Save Selection, Load Selection from Alpha Channel to load the selection you saved in step 1. Select **Adjust**, **Brightness and Contrast**, **Histogram Adjustment**. Adjust the **Low** and **High** values until the red histogram curve is spread out as much as possible. Adjust the **Gamma** value (see the tip) and click **OK**. Restore the Black channel to a negative by removing the selection (**Selections, Select None**) and selecting **Adjust, Negative Image**.

5 **Stretch Histograms and Adjust Gamma if Necessary**

Skip this step if you can discern the major facial details in the Cyan, Magenta, and Yellow channels. Change to the Cyan color channel and select **Selections, Load/Save Selection, Load Selection from Alpha Channel** to load the previously saved selection from the Alpha channel. Select **Adjust, Brightness and Contrast, Histogram Equalize** to expand the histogram curve for the selection to cover the entire range from darks to lights, maximizing the contrast for the selection as much as possible without losing information.

Select **Adjust, Brightness and Contrast, Gamma Adjustment** and enter the same gamma number you used in the **Histogram Adjustment** dialog box in step 4 for the Black channel. Finally, select **Adjust, Brightness and Contrast, Clarify**. Enter a **Strength** of about 3 or 4 and click **OK**. This will remove some of the pits in the histogram that the **Histogram Equalize** command caused. Repeat this step for the other two color channels.

If the image has borderline details, try this technique: Skip step 5 and recombine the channels as described in step 6. Save the result. Then go back, perform these steps on the still open color channels, and recombine them into a second new image. Load the Alpha channel selection to this second image (**Selections, Load/Save Selection, Load Selection from Alpha Channel**), copy the foreground, and paste it into the first recombined image as a new layer. Set the layer's **Blend Mode** to **Overlay** and its **Opacity** between 25 and 50. The results should be splendid.

 TIP

You might want to blur the selection in each of the color channels (except Black) to reduce the noise in the final recombined image. Select **Adjust, Blur, Blur More**.

6 Recombine the Color Channels

Select **Image**, **Combine Channel**, **Combine from CMYK**. Click **OK**. PSP creates a new image window containing the product of the recombined color channels. If you like what you see, you can close the Black, Cyan, Yellow, and Magenta images; otherwise, return to them, make additional adjustments, and recombine them into a second new image. You can also close the original image from step 2.

NOTE

If you skipped step 5, and you don't like the results so far, simply close the new image window without saving. Then try again, this time performing step 5.

7 Compensate for Color Anomalies if Present

In the new image, reload the foreground selection from the Alpha channel again by choosing **Selections, Load/Save Selection, Load Selection from Alpha Channel**. This prevents any additional changes from disturbing the background of the image. If you used the **Histogram Equalize** method earlier, most likely your foreground is *over-saturated*. To correct this problem, select **Adjust, Hue and Saturation, Hue/Saturation/Lightness**. Slide the **Saturation** bar down—between –20 and –30. If the skin tones are too red, slide the **Hue** bar to 6.

8 Restore Natural Contrast to Foreground

With the foreground still selected, select **Adjust, Brightness and Contrast, Histogram Adjustment**. Any adjustment to the **High** and **Low** points may be slight; however, gamma correction will probably be necessary (again). Try a **Gamma** value between 1.6 and 2.0. If the contrast is extreme, try compressing the midtones; in severe cases of backlighting, try expanding the midtones instead.

TIP

In cases of extreme restoration, following this final histogram adjustment, *do not use the Clarify command*. For whatever reason, in such an extreme case, PSP injects blacks and grays in areas where color should be.

9 Reduce Spotted or Pock-marked Appearance if Necessary

Skip this step in less-than-extreme cases. To remove graininess introduced by a satin finish on the original print and extreme backlighting, make sure that the foreground is still selected and select **Adjust, Blur, Gaussian Blur**. Set **Radius** to 2.5 and click **OK**.

See more on Gaussian blur in **116** Blur a Background to Create Depth of Field. See more on the Unsharp Mask filter in **114** Sharpen an Image.

Resharpen the selection by selecting **Adjust**, **Sharpness**, **Unsharp Mask**. Set **Clipping** to 0, set **Radius** to 1.5, and set **Strength** to 250. Click **OK**. You have removed much, if not all, of the graininess, and you have created some mid-tones you didn't have before.

⑩ Use Spot Tools to Eliminate Fiery Edges

At this point, there is probably a white halo around the entire foreground area. To eliminate it, select the **Burn** tool. In the **Tool Options** bar, enable the **Continuous** check box, set **Opacity** relatively low—about 15—and brush out the halo. To avoid burning anything but the halo, set the **Limit** to **Highlights**. Use a lower **Opacity** setting if you want to keep some of the natural highlights caused by the sun at your back.

⑪ Save As a Smaller Size

By all means, save your result in its current size first. Then, to reduce any remaining graininess, select **Image**, **Resize**. Select **Maintain original print size**, change **Resolution** to a value between 200 and 300 for printing or to 100 for onscreen use, and click **OK**.

⑫ View the Result

There's an actual photograph here. But there's much work to be done before it's completely fixed. Most notably, the foreground remains grainier than the background. For less serious cases of backlighting, the graininess won't be nearly so bad as it is here. Another problem is the damage to the photo: Fingerprints not noticeable on the print suddenly look like white gashes or tears. Still, it's almost unbelievable that I was able to get anything from such a dismal start.

Correcting Color and Saturation

IN THIS CHAPTER:

TIP

If the color in an image looks right onscreen, but wrong when printed out, you have a problem with the color balance of your monitor and printer. See **1** Ensure That What You See Is What You Get for ways to solve this dilemma.

There are many reasons why the color balance in an image might be wrong. Perhaps the photo is faded with age or sun exposure, perhaps it was shot in low-light conditions, or perhaps the adjustments you've made to correct a brightness or contrast problem have caused a problem with the color. Whatever the cause, you'll find many tools in Paint Shop Pro to help you fix the problem.

106 Correct Color Manually

See Also

→ **54** Achieve Color Balance Automatically

→ **109** Restore Color to a Washed-Out Photograph

→ **110** Change Color or HSL to Match a Target Value

→ **111** Remove a Color Cast

 TIP

You can fix color problems in some photos with **Automatic Color Balance**, which balances the colors in a photo based on the type of light (warm incandescent or cold florescent) that was used when the picture was taken. See **54** Achieve Color Balance Automatically.

Although the eye is more sensitive to differences in lightness and contrast than it is to color, when the color spectrum in a photograph is out of balance, it stands out like a sore thumb. Paint Shop Pro offers many ways to balance the color in an image; in this task, you'll learn how to use PSP's **Manual Color Correction** tool. It works by balancing all the colors in a layer or selection against the target color of a single source object in the photo, such as hair, skin tone, grass, sky, wood, and so on. You select a *source color* to change (for example, you select a section of grass), then choose the *target color* the object should be (a lush green or a dry tan). PSP then uses this information to balance all the colors in the layer or selected region accordingly.

Even though the **Manual Color Correction** tool is targeted for use in balancing colors in an image, there's nothing in the rules that says you have to use the tool that way. Instead of adjusting all the colors in an image, select someone's hair and use this tool to make them blond, brunette, or redhead—or select the siding on your house and try out various paint colors. Just remember that *all* the colors within the current selection or layer will be adjusted based on the target color you choose, and not just objects that happen to be the same hue as the source color. If you want to change a red ball to green, select only the red ball. If no selection is made, the red ball becomes green, but other color changes are made as well, turning the sky purple perhaps, and the grass blue.

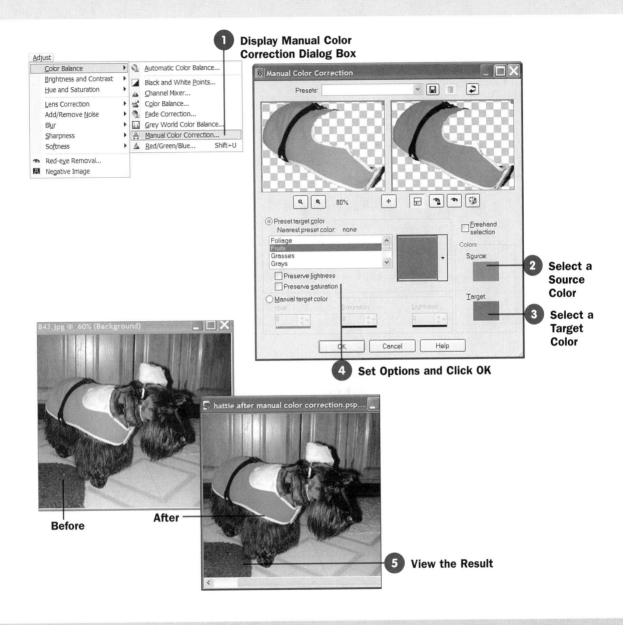

1 Display Manual Color Correction Dialog Box

2 Select a Source Color

3 Select a Target Color

4 Set Options and Click OK

Before

After

5 View the Result

1 Display Manual Color Correction Dialog Box

From the **Layer** palette, select the layer to affect. If you want to change only the colors within a portion of a layer,

TIP

Typically, if the color of one object is obviously "off," the colors of the other objects in the photo are equally wrong, even if you can't see those discrepancies as well. However, if you want to correct the color of only one item, first select that object and then follow these steps.

NOTE

The **Gray World** option that appeared in this dialog box in earlier versions of PSP now has its own dialog box (choose **Adjust, Color Balance, Gray World Color Balance**). **Gray World** assumes that the average of all colors in an image is middle gray, and makes adjustments in a fashion similar to **Automatic Color Balance**.

select that region. Then choose **Adjust, Color Balance, Manual Color Correction** from the menu bar to open the dialog box.

② Select a Source Color

In the left preview pane of the **Manual Color Correction** dialog box, click on a single pixel of the color you're trying to fix or drag to select a rectangular region whose colors will then be averaged into a single source color.

To select an irregularly shaped region of pixels to use as the source, enable the **Freehand selection** check box and draw around the pixels you want to select.

③ Select a Target Color

To choose a target color from the "gallery" of recognized colors, enable the **Preset target color** radio button and then choose a category, such as **Fruits**. Then open the color list and select a color from that category of colors.

If you have a specific target color in mind, enable the **Manual target color** radio button and enter the **Hue, Saturation,** and **Lightness** values you want.

④ Set Options and Click OK

Enable the **Preserve lightness** check box to prevent adjustments to the brightness of the source pixels, and thus, the rest of the layer or selection. Enabling this option allows you to retain the nuances of light and shade while adjusting the color. Enable **Preserve saturation** to prevent similar adjustments to the saturation of the source pixels. Click **OK**. PSP changes the source pixels you choose in step 2 to match the target color you select in step 3. PSP then adjusts all the other colors within the selection or layer accordingly.

⑤ View the Result

I started with a pretty good picture of Hattie, Aunt Betty's prized Scottish Terrier. After using the **One Step Photo Fix** command to adjust the contrast, color, and saturation, the photo was still "off." Although her fur, the floor, and the rug were all the right color, her Santa outfit was orange-ish, faded from the flash and old age. So I selected just the outfit, chose a natural red fruit color from the **Manual Color Correction** dialog box, and the result is very merry indeed! Be sure to see this in the Color Gallery.

107 Adjust Hue, Saturation, and Lightness Manually

A pixel's color value can be defined by three components: hue, saturation, and lightness. A pixel's *hue* represents its location on the color wheel, such as red, green, or yellow. *Saturation* defines the relative amount of that hue within a pixel—quantifying, for instance, the range between a clear red (full saturation) to a colorless gray (no saturation). *Lightness* defines the amount of white in a pixel, from black (no light) to white (all light) to somewhere in between (light pink). To make adjustments to these individual components of the pixels within an image, use the **Hue/Saturation/Lightness** command.

Many images taken with digital cameras seem to lack saturation. A boost of saturation by just even a few degrees can revive an otherwise dull image, infusing it with excitement and drama. By reducing the saturation in a color image, you can create a black-and-white photo, often with better results than simply converting the image to grayscale.

By adjusting the hue of a selected object, you can change its color from red to green, for example. By reducing the lightness of an image's background, you can make it fade into the distance—placing more importance on the subject of your image. With the **Hue/Saturation/Lightness** command, you can also address the hue, saturation, and lightness of an image's *channels*, making the reds more saturated, for example, or the greens less so.

① Display Hue/Saturation/Lightness Dialog Box

Choose **Adjust, Hue and Saturation, Hue/Saturation/Lightness** from the menu bar.

See Also

→ **108** Restore an Old Photograph

→ **109** Restore Color to a Washed-Out Photograph

→ **110** Change Color or HSL to Match a Target Value

→ **111** Remove a Color Cast

KEY TERM

Channel—One of a handful of components that jointly characterize the structure of a digital image, such as RGB, HSL, or CMYK. One channel can be addressed independently of other channels; thus, it's possible to edit just the green channel of an image.

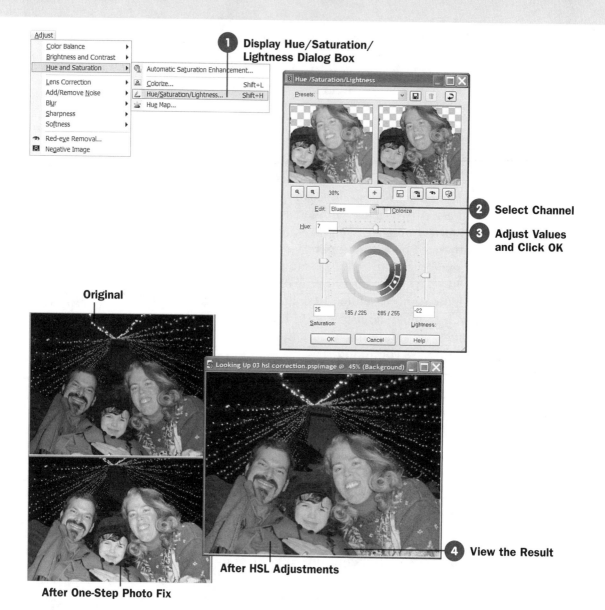

Original

After One-Step Photo Fix

After HSL Adjustments

1 Display Hue/Saturation/ Lightness Dialog Box

2 Select Channel

3 Adjust Values and Click OK

4 View the Result

2 Select Channel

Select the channel you want to work on from the **Edit** list. To affect all channels equally, select **Master** from this list.

3 Adjust Values and Click OK

Adjust the **Hue, Saturation,** and **Lightness** values as needed by dragging the appropriate slider. Positive values increase the saturation/lightness, while negative values decrease them. View the results of your adjustments in the right preview pane.

4 View the Result

Here's the original image and two corrections. The first is the result of using the **One-Step Photo Fix** feature, which includes the **Automatic Color Balance** command. With the control that the **Hue/Saturation/Lightness** command gave me, I selected just the people, lowered the lightness a bit and increased the saturation. I played with the red and the blue channel to make Katie's coat a nice red and my sweater a deeper blue (because both of them were washed out by the flash). The result is more pleasing and less "reindeer in the headlights." Compare these images yourself in the Color Gallery section of this book.

TIP

Enable the **Colorize** check box to remove all color from an image and essentially turn it into a black-and-white photo. If you then adjust the **Hue** value, you can create a sepia image. See **142** Age a Photograph, **143** Change a Color Photograph to Black and White and **144** Colorize a Photograph.

108 Restore an Old Photograph

Unless they are stored under perfect conditions, most photographs do not age gracefully. Their colors fade and shift, tears and cracks appear, and they lose the contrast and depth typical of new photos. Fortunately, there are several things you can do to restore an old photo to its former glory. If you need to repair tears and holes, you can use the **Clone Brush** or the technique discussed in **87** **Repair Holes and Tears**. Then you can follow the steps in this procedure to restore contrast and depth with a histogram adjustment, restore the color and make any additional adjustments to the contrast by applying a fade correction, and remove any remaining color cast by balancing the color.

1 Perform a Histogram Adjustment

Choose **Adjust, Brightness and Contrast, Histogram Adjustment**. In the **Histogram Adjustment** dialog box, move the **Low**, **Gamma**, and **High** sliders until you have

Before You Begin

✔ **55** Adjust Brightness and Contrast Automatically

✔ **96** Improve Brightness and Contrast

See Also

→ **54** Achieve Color Balance Automatically

→ **87** Repair Holes and Tears

→ **109** Restore Color to a Washed-Out Photograph

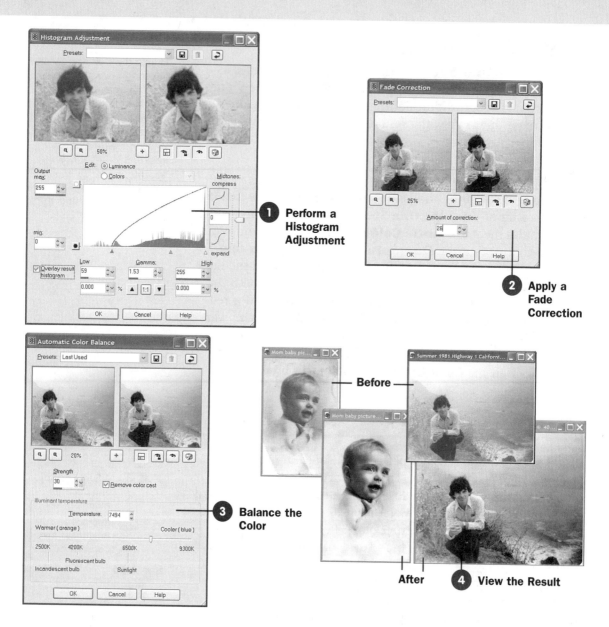

1 Perform a Histogram Adjustment

2 Apply a Fade Correction

3 Balance the Color

Before

After

4 View the Result

a pleasing distribution of darks, mediums, and light tones in the image and then click **OK**. See **96** **Improve Brightness and Contrast** for help.

2 **Apply a Fade Correction**

Choose **Adjust, Color Balance, Fade Correction**. The only value you need to adjust in the **Fade Correction** dialog box is the **Amount of correction**. Your eyes will tell you the amount that looks best. When you like the results, click **OK**.

If you don't like the results of using the **Fade Correction** command, undo them; after you perform step 3, use **Automatic Saturation Enhancement**.

3 **Balance the Color**

To balance the color and remove any remaining color cast, choose **Adjust, Color Balance, Automatic Color Balance**. In the **Automatic Color Balance** dialog box, enable the **Remove color cast** check box and then move the slider to adjust the illuminant temperature to achieve the color balance you're looking for. Click **OK**. See **54** **Achieve Color Balance Automatically**.

4 **View the Result**

Here I show two examples: one a badly faded color photograph from a California trip my husband took years ago, and an equally faded, torn, and smudged baby photo of my mother. Both are doing much better, thank you. Look for these images in the Color Gallery section of this book.

TIP

The **Fade Correction** command is not available for grayscale images. For a black-and-white photo stored in 16 million color format, you might want to do only a minor fade correction, if any.

TIP

If you're not satisfied with the results of the color balance, try the **Gray World Color Balance** or **Manual Color Correction** commands on the **Adjust, Color Balance** menu.

---

109 **Restore Color to a Washed-Out Photograph**

Over time, any photo might lose its color through a gradual fading process. Typically, an old photo will also lose contrast as well, becoming flat and lifeless. The fade correction technique discussed in **108** **Restore an Old Photograph** will work on such images, but what if a photo simply needs a little color burst? And what if the problem affects only certain areas? It would be nice to have more control over where the color is enhanced.

In this task, you'll learn a technique to boost colors in an image by using a duplicate layer and the **Multiply** blend mode. This

Before You Begin

✔ **10** About Tools and Tool Options

✔ **120** About Layers and the Layer Palette

See Also

→ **103** Fix a Flash That's Too Close

→ **108** Restore an Old Photograph

→ **125** About Masks

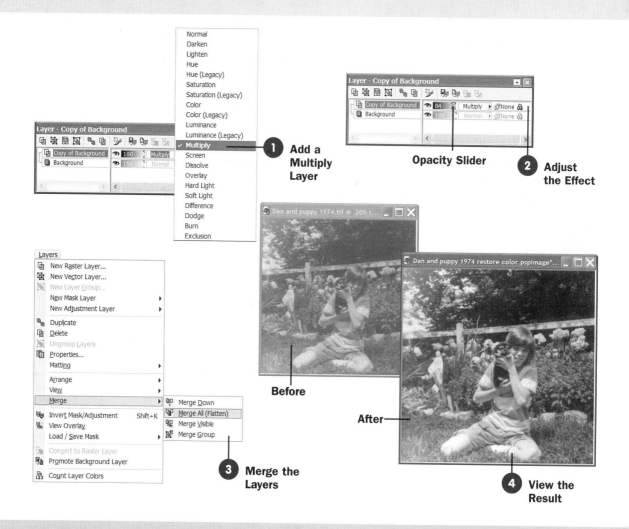

Before

After

1 Add a Multiply Layer

Opacity Slider

2 Adjust the Effect

3 Merge the Layers

4 View the Result

TIP

If your image has gotten darker with time and lost color, you can use this same technique with the **Screen** blend mode instead.

blend mode is similar to laying two transparencies over top of each other—in effect, doubling (and darkening) the color. Because you're using layers, you can control the effect with the **Opacity** slider and/or masks.

1 Add a Multiply Layer

After cropping and repairing any defects in the image such as tears or holes, add a new layer by clicking the **Duplicate Layer** button on the **Layer** palette. Open the **Blend Mode** list and select **Multiply**. The colors in the original image immediately become more saturated, but darker. If the **Multiply** mode produces too much color or the effect is too harsh, try using the **Overlay** or **Soft Light** blend mode.

2 **Adjust the Effect**

If desired, adjust the amount of extra saturation by changing the **Multiply** layer's **Opacity** value on the **Layer** palette.

3 **Merge the Layers**

Merge the layers by choosing **Layers, Merge, Merge All (Flatten)**.

4 **View the Result**

Before you finish, you'll probably want to lighten the image a bit with a histogram, levels, or curves adjustment—see **96** Improve Brightness and Contrast, **97** Improve a Dull, Flat Photo, and **99** Restore Color and Improve Detail. The image might also need sharpening with an **Unsharp Mask** (see **114** Sharpen an Image). As you can see, my younger brother's photo has regained its youth. See the dramatic difference in the Color Gallery section in this book.

NOTE

If the colors have really faded, you might want to repeat step 1 several times, adding several **Multiply** layers to build up the color.

TIP

You can also focus the effect by inserting a mask layer below the **Multiply** layer to mask out areas you do not want to oversaturate.

---

110 **Change Color or HSL to Match a Target Value**

Paint Shop Pro contains several retouch tools that can help you perform amazingly precise changes to your images. Suppose that you want to lighten a few small areas of a person's face that are in shadow. You could select just these areas and use the **Hue/Saturation/Lightness** command to adjust the lightness; but if you're trying to lighten the selected portion to the same lightness as some other part of the face or body, it would be difficult for you to guess the setting to use. Instead, using the **Change to Target** retouch tool, you can select a pixel whose lightness, hue, or saturation you like, and then brush over just those pixels whose luminance you want to change to that same value. You can also change the color of a pixel (a combination of

Before You Begin

✔ **10** About Tools and Tool Options

See Also

→ **91** Awaken Tired Eyes

→ **106** Correct Color Manually

→ **107** Adjust Hue, Saturation, and Lightness Manually

4 Adjust Tool Options

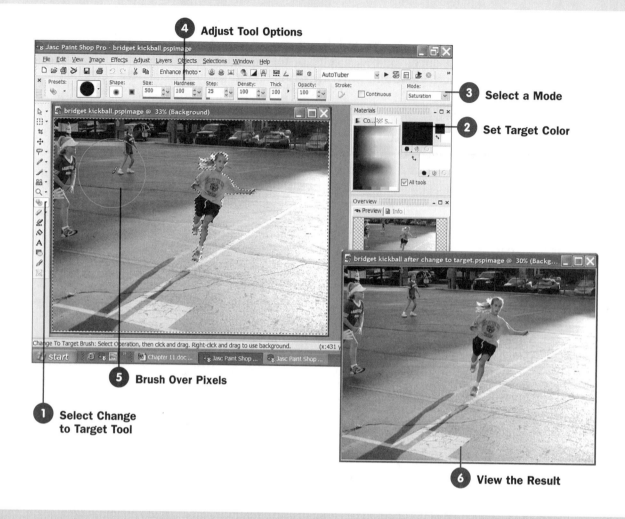

3 Select a Mode

2 Set Target Color

5 Brush Over Pixels

1 Select Change to Target Tool

6 View the Result

 TIP

Try using the **Change to Target** tool (with the **Lightness** option) to lighten dark skin under your eyes so that it matches surrounding skin. Change the color of a shirt from green to blue with the **Hue** option. Try repairing faded spots in an old photo with the **Saturation** option.

hue and saturation) to match those of some other pixel—something you can't do easily with the **Hue/Saturation/Lightness** command. As you've gathered, the retouch tools use a brush tip, so you have all the options of a normal painting tool available to you (such as **Opacity**, **Density**, **Hardness**, and so on). The brush tip gives you even more control over the changes you make.

Retouch tools other than **Change to Target** allow you to gradually alter the hue, saturation, or lightness of an area upward or downward as you continue to brush over it. However, because none of these tools uses a target color, it's easy for you to overdo an alteration. When you use a retouch tool other than **Change to Target**, make your changes on a duplicate image layer and use that layer's **Opacity** setting to control how much of the change you see.

① Select Change to Target Tool

Click the **Change to Target** tool on the **Tools** toolbar to select it.

② Set Target Color

Press **Ctrl** and click a pixel that has a characteristic you like, such as a saturation level or lightness you want to apply. The **Foreground** color is changed to match the pixel you click.

③ Select a Mode

In the **Tool Options** palette, open the **Mode** list and select the characteristic you want to change: **Color, Hue, Lightness**, or **Saturation**.

④ Adjust Tool Options

Adjust the **Size** of the brush to fit the item you want to change. To make gradual soft changes, lower the **Hardness**, **Density**, and **Opacity** values as desired.

⑤ Brush Over Pixels

Brush over the pixels you want to change; they are immediately adjusted to match the selected characteristic of the target color.

⑥ View the Result

Using a target color of pure black {HSL: 255, 0, 0} and the **Saturation** mode, I've desaturated the background around my godchild Bridget, to draw your attention to her. Using the **Change to Target** tool this way creates a better-looking grayscale background than using the **Grayscale**

TIP

To prevent the **Change to Target** tool from affecting pixels you don't want to change, first create a selection that includes the pixels you want to change. Those pixels outside the selected region are not affected.

command, and it was convenient because I also wanted to use the tool to color the base. Next, I picked up the yellow from her shirt and used the **Color** mode to change the color of second base to that same yellow. The resulting photo is more dramatic and places the focus squarely on the runner, Bridget. Look for this in the Color Gallery section in this book.

111 Remove a Color Cast

As a photograph ages, it often assumes a color cast—a shift of all its colors towards a single color such as yellow or red. The fact is, the colors aren't *changing*; certain inks are merely fading faster than others. Depending on the print process used in developing your aged photo, it could emerge from its long and historic journey through time covered in either a dull red or a muted bluish-gray overtone.

You can use many commands to remove the color cast from an image and restore its true colors: **Auto Color Balance**, **Manual Color Balance**, **Gamma Correction**, **Red/Green/Blue**, **Channel Mixer**, and **Hue/Saturation/Lightness**. The method you choose depends on the amount and kind of color cast in the image and your own personal comfort with a particular command. In this task, you'll learn how to use the **Black and White Points** command to remove a color cast.

❶ Find White and Black Points

To discern which points should be pure white and pure black in an image, temporarily change the image to grayscale by selecting **Image, Grayscale**. Then select **Adjust, Brightness and Contrast, Levels**. The **Levels** dialog box appears.

To find the white point: On the **Input levels** scale, slide the black pointer to the right until the fewest possible white spots remain in the preview window—ideally just one. This is your white point. Remember its relative position because you have to select it in step 2.

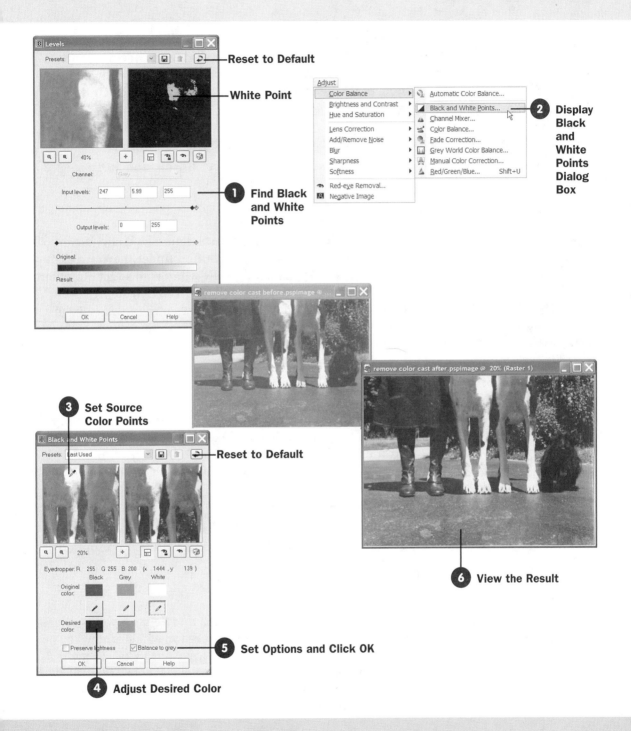

Reset to Default

White Point

2 Display Black and White Points Dialog Box

1 Find Black and White Points

3 Set Source Color Points

Reset to Default

6 View the Result

5 Set Options and Click OK

4 Adjust Desired Color

TIP

Essentially, the **Black and White Points** command shifts the colors in an image left or right on the color wheel to compensate for shifts that occur as a photo ages. You can also use the **Color Balance** and **Channel Mixer** commands on the **Adjust, Color Balance** menu.

NOTE

You'll get the best results if you can also set the **Grey** point, but it's often difficult to identify a pixel in your image that should be middle gray. If you select the wrong pixel, your image will look cartoonish; for that reason, you may find it best to *not* select a **Grey** point.

NOTE

To limit the palette of target colors to a grayscale palette, enable the **Balance to grey** check box. If this option is not selected, you can set the target color to any color you want, not just black, gray, or white.

To find the black point: Click the **Reset to Default** button at the top of the dialog box and then slide the white pointer to the left until only one black spot remains. Make a note of the black point then click **Cancel**. Click **Undo** to return the image to full color.

2 Display Black and White Points Dialog Box

Choose **Adjust, Color Balance, Black and White Points** from the menu bar.

3 Set Source Color Points

In the **Black and White Points** dialog box, click **Reset to Default**. Click the dropper button under the **White** column and click in the left preview window to select a pixel in the area of the white point you discovered in step 1. Then click the dropper under the **Black** column and click in the left preview window to select a pixel in the area of the black point.

4 Adjust Desired Color

For any of the three columns, you can adjust the target color to which the source pixels will be shifted. For example, perhaps the selected **White** pixel should be shifted to a very unsaturated blue. Click the column's **Desired** color box, and choose the color that you want to use as the target.

5 Set Options and Click OK

To preserve the lightness of the original pixels, enable the **Preserve lightness** check box. After setting your options, click **OK**.

6 View the Result

After setting the black, white, and middle gray points, the reddish color cast was completely removed, returning my Aunt Ree's two Great Danes and my Aunt Betty's Scottish Terrier, Heather, to their normal colors. (Those are Aunt Ree's feet on the left.) Look for this image in the Color Gallery section of this book.

12

Controlling Sharpness and Clarity

IN THIS CHAPTER:

A great photograph is the result of the photographer (or graphic editor) exercising control over three elements: light and dark, color, and sharpness. In previous chapters, you've learned how to master brightness and contrast and how to master color; in this chapter, you'll learn how to control the third element of a memorable photograph: sharpness.

112 About Sharpness

Before You Begin

✔ **71** Select a Portion of an Image with Channels

✔ **120** About Layers and the Layer Palette

✔ **125** About Masks

See Also

→ **113** Create an Edge Mask

→ **114** Sharpen an Image

 TIP

One of the quickest ways to "sharpen" an image is to add more contrast. A fast way to do that is to duplicate the image onto another layer, and change that layer's blend mode to either **Soft Light** or **Hard Light**.

 TIP

Because the **Sharpen/ Sharpen More** commands don't offer any control over the process, some edges might be sharpened too much (the contrast is increased beyond what looks good). If you get bad results, undo them and try the **Unsharp Mask** or the **Sharpen** retouch tool on the **Tools** toolbar (both allow you to adjust the effect).

In capturing or converting an image to digital format, the image often loses clarity and sharpness. For example, you might have a perfectly sharp photograph, but after scanning, it appears slightly fuzzy at the edges of a face or a tree leaf. Or perhaps in choosing a lower resolution on your digital camera, the images you've taken aren't as sharp as you'd like them to be when viewed at the size you want to use. Luckily, with a bit of patience and skill, a lack of sharpness in most images is easy to fix.

Paint Shop Pro offers several tools you can use to sharpen an image:

- **Sharpen.** Sharpens an image by increasing the contrast at the edges of objects in a photograph. Here, an *edge* is defined as two or more adjacent pixels with some degree of contrast. Where edges are found, the brightness difference between the adjacent pixels is increased.

- **Sharpen More.** Works like the **Sharpen** command, only more strongly. The contrast between pixels along an edge is increased even more. Both **Sharpen** and **Sharpen More** work automatically, on the entire image or selection, without further input from you.

- **Unsharp Mask.** Although it seems this command was named wrong, it's actually one of the strongest sharpening tools available to you. It works so well because it works *backwards*. Literally, the **Unsharp Mask** command generates a *blurred* version of the region it's supposed to sharpen and keeps that version in memory. That part is the mask. It then subtracts the luminance data of the pixels in the "mask" from that of the corresponding pixels in the original version, the result being, strikingly enough, a sharper image with more well-distributed regions of sharp contrast. **Unsharp Mask** increases the level of contrast along high to mid-level contrast edges. In its dialog box, you choose the level of contrast that defines the edges you want adjusted. You also control the amount of contrast change you want to apply, and the size of the area around the edge to which you want the change applied.

- **Clarify.** This is a good sharpening tool to use when the image is kind of hazy or slightly out of focus because it provides an overall adjustment of the brightness and contrast. Use this command after adjusting an image's histogram with either the **Histogram Adjustment** or **Curves** command, to smooth out the histogram and remove pits and jagged peaks. Smoothing a histogram adds transitions between the various tones in an image, which in turn provides depth and apparent sharpness. In Chapter 10, "Correcting the Brightness and Contrast in a Photograph," you'll find several examples that use the **Clarify** command. It has only one option: **Strength of effect**, which you typically set to 2 or 3.

113 Create an Edge Mask

Sharpness, of course, is a perception, and what looks sharp to you might not look sharp to someone else. Although in conversation, we tend to define sharpness in terms of "crisp edges," PSP uses the term to mean "high contrast." Normal sharpening can produce crisp edges in most circumstances, but it can also lead to noise and variance inside objects where your eyes expect *low* contrast. There is a tried and true method of applying the sharpening tools, however, which produces crisp edges while leaving non-edge pixels alone:

1. First, sharpen only the edges (and not the overall image) by creating an *edge mask*. This mask has the added advantage of allowing changes to gradually blend into the unsharpened areas of an image. I'll show you how to create an edge mask in a moment. By the way, when you're trying to judge

Before You Begin

✔ **97** Improve a Dull, Flat Photo

✔ **112** About Sharpness

✔ **115** Blur an Image to Remove Noise

✔ **119** Smooth an Image Without Losing Crisp Edges or Texture

See Also

→ **114** Sharpen an Image

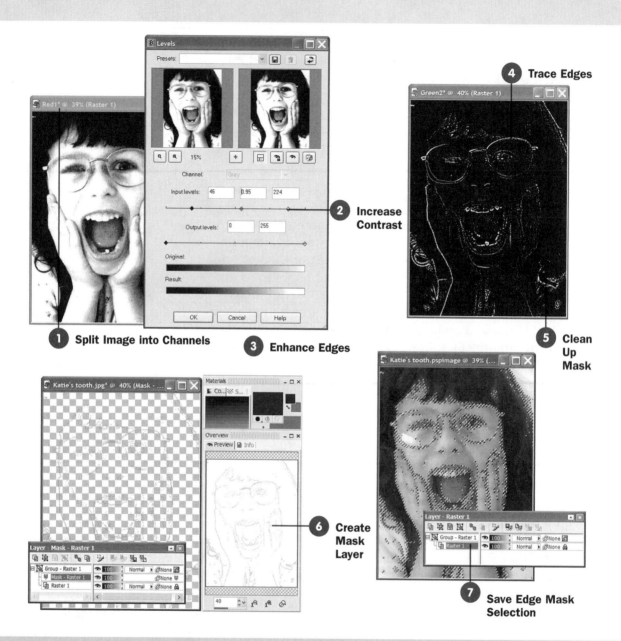

4 Trace Edges

2 Increase Contrast

1 Split Image into Channels

3 Enhance Edges

5 Clean Up Mask

6 Create Mask Layer

7 Save Edge Mask Selection

whether an image is sharp or not, be sure to look at the image at 100% zoom.

2. After applying the initial sharpening through the edge mask, make whatever other changes you need to correct the image. For example, you might balance the colors or improve the brightness.

3. As a final step, adjust the image's resolution to suit your purposes (for example, 300 dpi for printing), and then perform an overall sharpening or clarification to the entire image. This second pass is necessary because the additional changes you make to an image to correct its color and its brightness often end up fuzzying its edges.

1 Split Image into Channels

Split the image into channels using the **Image, Split Channel, Split to RGB** or **Split to HSL** or **Split to CMYK** command. Look for the channel that contains the most contrast at the edges you want to sharpen. Typically, in images that include faces and skin tones, the **Red** or **Green** channel works best.

2 Increase Contrast

Choose **Adjust, Brightness and Contrast, Levels**. On the **Input levels** scale, drag the black and white pointers inward until you achieve a high level of contrast along the edges you want to sharpen. Click **OK**.

3 Enhance Edges

Remove any noise that might later be perceived as edges by selecting **Adjust, Add/Remove Noise, Edge Preserving Smooth**. Specify a large **Amount of smoothing**, such as 20. Click **OK**.

Resharpen the edges again by choosing **Adjust, Sharpness, Sharpen More**. Finally, enhance the edges a bit by improving their contrast. Choose **Effects, Edge Effects, Enhance**.

4 Trace Edges

Trace the edges in your image by applying either the **Find All** or the **Trace Contours** filter. Choose **Effects, Edge Effects, Find All** or **Trace Contours**.

KEY TERM

Edge mask—A selection that encompasses only the edge pixels in an image, thus preventing unwanted changes to everything else.

TIP

When performing the final sharpening pass, simply sharpen the image until it looks good onscreen. If you intend to print the image on an ink jet printer or a half-tone press, however, you'll need to over-sharpen the image slightly to compensate for the fuzziness introduced by the printer itself.

TIP

If none of the channels produces a grayscale image with high-contrast edges, try creating one with a copy of the original image. Select **Adjust, Color Balance, Channel Mixer**, and check the **Monochrome** option. Adjust the **Source channels** and the **Constant** (a brightness coefficient) values until the edges you want to sharpen contrast as much as possible with their surroundings.

NOTE

The **Trace Contours** filter is usually better at *not tracing* background noise, but it might not find all the edges in some photos. In most cases, the **Find All** filter does a better job for you.

A mask works by blocking alterations in the area where the mask is black, and allowing them where it is white. So *if you used the **Trace Contours** filter,* you'll have to invert the image by choosing **Adjust, Negative Image**. The edges of your channel image should now be white and the background black.

With some images, you might not see the edges very clearly after applying the **Find All** or **Trace Contours** filters. To make the edges more white and the background more black, select **Adjust, Brightness and Contrast, Threshold**, and set **Threshold** to a value that eliminates random white pixels that are not part of edges. Click **OK**.

⑤ Clean Up Mask

Clean up the mask as needed. For example, you might want to apply a slight blur to feather the white edges so that the sharpening you apply later on won't seem so abrupt. The blur will also remove any additional noise still left in the mask—grainy areas that show as white, but yet are not edges. Select **Adjust, Blur, Blur More**.

TIP

To remove any final areas from the mask that you don't want to sharpen, paint them over with a black paint brush before proceeding to step 6.

⑥ Create Mask Layer

Create a mask layer in the original image using the black-and-white pattern you just formed in the channel image. First, switch to the original image. Then select **Layers, New Mask Layer, From Image**. If you see a confirmation dialog box, click **OK**. In the **Add Mask from Image** dialog box, choose the name of the channel image from the **Source window** list. Select the **Source luminance** option. Turn off the **Invert mask data** option. Click **OK**. The mask image should look like a faint pencil sketch.

TIP

Before saving the selection, you might want to apply a slight feather to it to provide a wider edge for sharpening and to soften the effect so that it's not so abrupt. Select **Selections, Modify, Feather**. Set a low **Number of pixels** such as 4, and click **OK**.

⑦ Save Edge Mask Selection

To create a selection that includes only the edges you want to sharpen, choose **Selections, From Mask**. Save the selection by choosing **Selections, Load/Save Selection, Save Selection to Alpha Channel**. Type some obvious name in the **Name** box, such as **Edge mask**. Click **Save**.

Close the channel image (you won't need it any more). Change back to the original image and delete the mask layer (you won't need it, either). In the **Layer** palette, click the mask layer, and click the **Delete Layer** button. In the dialog box that appears, click **No** because you do not want the mask merged with your image.

Now you're ready to sharpen just the edges of your image with the **Unsharp Mask**. See **114** Sharpen an Image.

114 Sharpen an Image

It is the illusion of focus that places a viewer's mind within a photographic scene. Unless you're daydreaming at the moment, your eyes are focused on something. The illusions of depth and dimension are established in your mind literally by the appearance of what you're *not* focused on. A good photograph's job is to lead your eyes toward something worth being focused on.

Focus is the single most difficult illusion to restore if your photograph doesn't have it to begin with. From a digital perspective, *blur* is the equal distribution of color and other characteristic values from individual pixels throughout their neighbors. Because blur scatters in all directions, there's no absolute way even for a computer to detect which values in a set of pixels are the result of scatter and which ones are native. But the **Unsharp Mask** filter goes about as far as applied mathematics can go to just that end. It makes an almost preposterous-sounding logical assumption: The product of the data from a duplicate image that's *even blurrier than the original* (unsharp), subtracted from the original data, must yield something cleaner, clearer, and sharper. And believe it or not, it actually does.

1 Display the Unsharp Mask Dialog box

To sharpen only the edges in the image, load your edge mask first, as described in **113** Create an Edge Mask. Hide the selection marquee so that you can see the image as you sharpen by choosing **Selections, Hide Marquee** or by pressing **Ctrl+Shift+M**. Then choose **Adjust, Sharpness, Unsharp Mask**.

Before You Begin

✔ **112** About Sharpness
✔ **113** Create an Edge Mask

 TIP

To sharpen a specific area, try the **Sharpen** tool on the **Tools** toolbar. You can control the effect by changing the **Opacity** and **Density** settings.

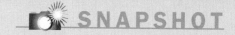
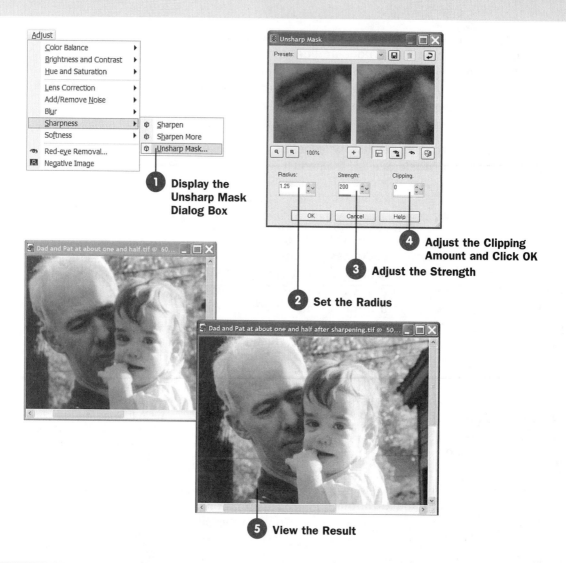

1 Display the Unsharp Mask Dialog Box

4 Adjust the Clipping Amount and Click OK

3 Adjust the Strength

2 Set the Radius

5 View the Result

2 Set the Radius

The **Radius** controls the area of change—the number of pixels around an edge pixel that should have their contrast adjusted. Adjust the **Radius** value as desired.

③ Adjust the Strength

Adjust the **Strength** of the effect as desired. At higher **Strength** values, the **Unsharp Mask** tends to even out similar colors over a broad area, creating wider patches of solid colors and more outstanding contrasts between those patches.

Typically, if you chose a small **Radius**, you'll need a higher **Strength** setting to produce a good result. With a small **Radius** value, start the **Strength** setting at 200% and increase it gradually; with a large **Radius** value, start the **Strength** setting at 100% and decrease it until you get a good result.

④ Adjust the Clipping Amount and Click OK

The **Clipping** value is basically the filter's tolerance factor—the difference in brightness that defines the edge to be sharpened. The higher the **Clipping** value, the less contrast between pixels is needed to define an edge. Adjust this value, and when you like the effect, click **OK**.

⑤ View the Result

Here's a sweet photo of my sister Pat, at about one and a half, with my dad. The dappled shade from a nearby maple makes the photo interesting. After adjusting the brightness and contrast and repairing the scratches, I finished with an overall sharpening for a very satisfying result.

TIP

If the subject is close and has a lot of fine detail (as in a close-up of your son's face), use a large **Radius** setting, such as 2.5 to 3.5. If the subject is far away with little detail (as in a landscape), use a much lower setting, such as .5 to .75. For medium shots, such as a family photo (head to toe), use a radius of about 1.0 to 2.0.

TIP

Start with a **Clipping** value of 0 and increase it gradually to reduce the sharpening applied to non-edge areas.

---

115 Blur an Image to Remove Noise

I've run into this many times, and perhaps you have too—after scanning in an old color photo with a satin (nonglossy) finish, an obvious graininess appears. Satin finishes were popular years ago because they were less shiny and more natural in appearance, and they didn't pick up fingerprints as readily. Unfortunately, they make lousy scans. To remove the noise caused by the satin finish, you can try the techniques discussed in **86** Remove Specks and Spots, but I've found that the simplest fix is to blur the image slightly and then edge-sharpen it as discussed in **114** Sharpen an Image.

Before You Begin

✔ **112** About Sharpness

See Also

→ **86** Remove Specks and Spots

→ **114** Sharpen an Image

→ **119** Smooth an Image Without Losing Crisp Edges or Texture

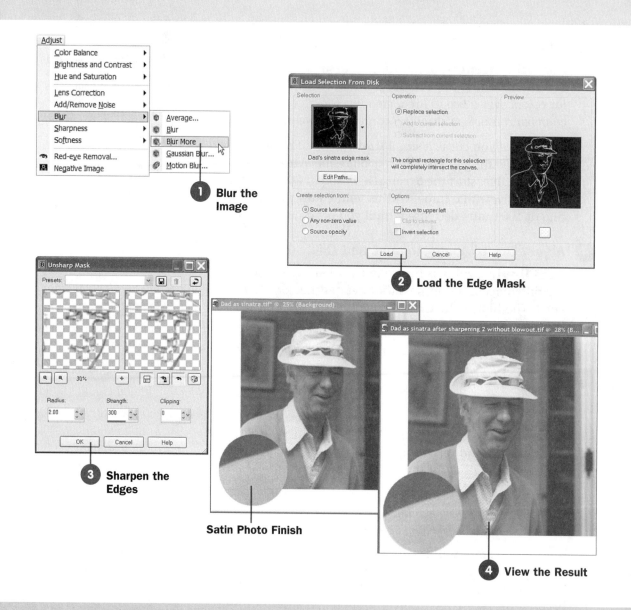

Adjust
- Color Balance
- Brightness and Contrast
- Hue and Saturation
- Lens Correction
- Add/Remove Noise
- Blur — Average...
- Sharpness — Blur
- Softness — Blur More
- Red-eye Removal... — Gaussian Blur...
- Negative Image — Motion Blur...

1 Blur the Image

Load Selection From Disk

2 Load the Edge Mask

Unsharp Mask

3 Sharpen the Edges

Satin Photo Finish

4 View the Result

Paint Shop Pro has several filters that blur an image: **Soften** uses a simple formula to blend the colors of nearby pixels while also decreasing their contrast. **Soften More**, **Blur**, and **Blur More** do the same thing, only more strongly. **Average** blends pixels as well, while adjusting the brightness of each pixel to match the average of the pixels within a radius you specify. **Gaussian** blends pixel colors using a more sophisticated formula, within a radius you choose, with less blurring occurring at the edge of the radius. **Motion** blurs by blending pixels in the direction and at the strength you select. **Soft Focus** attempts to create the same blur as a soft focus filter on a camera as explained in **134** **Create a Soft Focus Effect**. For the purpose of blurring to remove noise, the **Blur** and **Blur More** filters work best.

① Blur the Image

To remove the texture pattern caused by the satin finish on the photo, choose **Adjust, Blur, Blur More**. If you can still see the satin texture, blur the image just a bit more by choosing **Adjust, Blur, Blur** or **Blur More**, depending on what you think it needs.

② Load the Edge Mask

Choose **Selections, Load/Save Selections, Load Selection from Disk** to load the edge mask you created earlier. Choose the mask from the **Selection** list and click **Load**.

③ Sharpen the Edges

Choose **Selections, Hide Marquee** so that you can see the edges in the image and judge when they are sharp. Zoom in on the image so that you can see the edges up close. Choose **Adjust, Sharpness, Unsharp Mask**. Select the **Radius**, **Strength**, and **Clipping** needed to create a nice sharp edge and click **OK**.

④ View the Result

Here, Dad's picture is just a bit sharper than before, yet the graininess from the satin finish has been completely removed.

NOTE

Before blurring the image, make an edge mask for use in sharpening it later on. See **113** **Create an Edge Mask** for instructions.

116 Blur a Background to Create Depth of Field

Before You Begin

✔ **120** About Layers and the Layer Palette

✔ **131** Erase Part of an Image

See Also

→ **115** Blur an Image to Remove Noise

→ **117** Remove Distracting Detail

→ **118** Add Motion to an Image

→ **119** Smooth an Image Without Losing Crisp Edges or Texture

✎ NOTE

Blurring the background of any photo creates a false *depth of field*—a false distance—between the area in focus and the area that's not. That's because objects far away are naturally blurry and less sharp.

One of the easiest ways to make a photograph more interesting is to blur the background, drawing focus to your subject. For example, you might have caught the perfect expression on your son's face during a recent Easter egg hut, only to have the photo ruined by a background that's cluttered with other kids, their parents, or cars in the parking lot. Blur the background a bit, and those distractions fade into the distance.

To accomplish this magic, you could select your subject, invert the selection, and then apply a blur. This assumes that your subject is easy to select, which it is often not. Instead, this task explains how to duplicate the image on a new layer, apply a Gaussian blur, and then erase the areas on the original layer you want to blur. Although you could use any blur command with this technique, the **Gaussian Blur** filter provides total control over the blur amount, which is based on the radius size you select.

1 Add Duplicate Layer

On the **Layer** palette, click the **Duplicate Layer** button, or select **Layers, Duplicate** from the menu.

2 Blur the Background Layer

On the **Layer** palette, change to the **Background** layer. Select **Adjust, Blur, Gaussian Blur** from the menu. Select a large **Radius**, such as 7 or 8. Click **OK**. The image will still look like it's in focus because the unblurred duplicate layer is blocking the blurred **Background** layer from view.

3 Select the Eraser Tool

To erase portions of the unblurred duplicate layer (so that the blurred background layer shows through in those areas), click the **Eraser** tool. Set the **Opacity** and **Density** to 100. Adjust the **Size** to fit the area you want to blur.

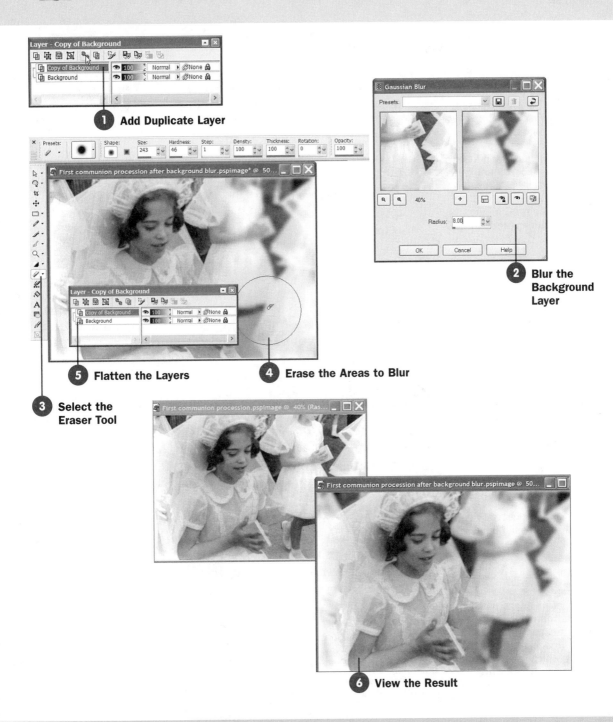

1 Add Duplicate Layer

2 Blur the Background Layer

3 Select the Eraser Tool

5 Flatten the Layers

4 Erase the Areas to Blur

6 View the Result

TIP

You can use this opportunity to blur parts of your subject as well, clearing up skin blemishes, for example, by blurring them. However, if you blur part of a person's face, do not blur the important features that give the face definition, such as the eyes, mouth, nose, eyebrows, and jaw line.

4 **Erase the Areas to Blur**

On the **Layer** palette, change to the **Copy of Background** layer. Use the **Eraser** tool to erase the background so that the blurred layer appears. If you make a mistake and erase something you wanted to keep, drag with the right mouse button to "unerase."

5 **Flatten the Layers**

After you have blurred the background, flatten the layers together by choosing **Layers, Merge, Merge All (Flatten)**.

6 **View the Result**

By blurring the background of this photo of my first communion, your eyes jump to my face, and then down to the small prayer book I'm holding, without zigzagging around, looking at the other girls in the procession.

---

117 **Remove Distracting Detail**

Before You Begin

✔ **60** Select by Drawing Freehand

See Also

→ **116** Blur a Background to Create Depth of Field

 TIP

You can soften selected areas of an image using the **Soften** tool on the **Tools** toolbar. The tool provides total control over the effect, which is similar to the **Soften** filter.

In **116** **Blur a Background to Create Depth of Field**, you learned how to remove distractions from behind your subject by blurring them. This blur also places some distance between the subject and the background by increasing the apparent depth of field. In some images, you might find distractions in the foreground as well, such as too many footprints in the sand, an uncut lawn, piles of fallen leaves, or a busy pattern on a blanket. Whatever the distraction, you can apply a mild blur to make the foreground less noticeable, and your subject more prominent. The trick here is to apply a subtle blur that lessens the distracting texture without removing it completely.

1 **Select the Foreground Area to Blur**

Click the **Freehand Selection Tool** and select the general area you want to blur. You don't have to be terribly precise in your selection; the idea is to remove the distraction, but not blur the foreground completely.

1 Select the Foreground
Area to Blur

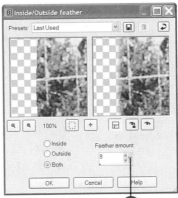

2 Feather the
Selection

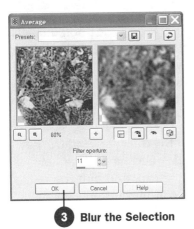

3 Blur the Selection

4 View the Result

2 Feather the Selection

Choose **Selections, Modify, Inside/Outside Feather**. In
the dialog box, click **Both** to apply the feathering to both
sides of the selection marquee. Enter a large value, such as
8 or 9, in the **Feather amount** box and click **OK**.

3 **Blur the Selection**

Select **Adjust, Blur, Average**. Enter a **Filter aperture** value that's large enough to blur the distraction, but not enough to be terribly noticeable. Click **OK**.

 TIP

If you want, increase the apparent depth of field by inverting your selection and sharpening the subject just a bit more.

4 **View the Result**

In this photo of the "Terrible Trio"—Bob, Dennis, and me—the background was a plain brick wall that created no particular distraction. However, the dark, rough texture of the grass and the garden seemed to catch my eye too much. So I softened it with a slight blur.

---

118 **Add Motion to an Image**

Before You Begin

✔ **120** About Layers and the Layer Palette

✔ **124** Merge or Flatten Layers into One

✔ **131** Erase Part of an Image

TIP

The **Motion Blur** filter is also useful in creating glowing text (by adding a motion blur above and below the text). Paint Shop Pro provides several additional filters that can create a sense of movement in an image, such as **Ripple, Twirl, Warp, Wave,** and **Wind**. You'll find these filters on the **Effects, Distortion** menu. See **139** "Melt" an Image.

A fun way to increase drama in an otherwise static photograph is to add the illusion of motion with the **Motion Blur** filter. For example, you could take a picture of your car, blur the background behind it using **Motion Blur**, and make the car look as if it is going very fast even though it's really parked on your driveway.

The **Motion Blur** filter blurs pixels in the direction and by the amount you specify. To create a realistic effect, you'll want to leave the leading edges of your subject sharp, and blur the rest. You can select the area to blur, or you can blur a duplicate image layer and erase selected areas of the nonblurred layer, as explained in this task.

1 **Create Duplicate Layer**

Click the **Duplicate Layer** button on the **Layer** palette, or select **Layers, Duplicate** to copy the entire image to a separate layer. Name this new layer **Unblurred**.

2 **Blur the Background Layer**

On the **Layer** palette, change to the **Background** layer. Then select **Adjust, Blur, Motion Blur**. In the dialog box, adjust the **Angle** of the blur to suit the image—blurring occurs in the direction you select. Then set the **Strength** of the blur and click **OK**.

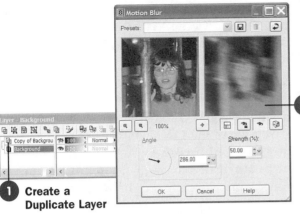

2 Blur the Background Layer

1 Create a Duplicate Layer

3 Erase the Areas to Blur

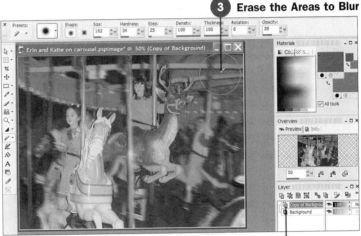

4 Merge the Layers

5 View the Result

If you want to view the **Motion Blur** effect on the image as you make adjustments, click the **Visibility Toggle** button (the eye) on the **Layer** palette for the **Unblurred** layer to hide it before opening the **Motion Blur** dialog box.

③ Erase the Areas to Blur

Make sure that all layers are visible (the eye icon should be showing for each layer in the **Layer** palette). On the **Layer** palette, change to the **Unblurred** layer. Select the **Eraser** tool and lower the **Hardness** to create a soft brush. Adjust the **Size** as needed, and erase the part of the image you want to blur. For a realistic effect, keep the forward edges of your subjects sharp and blur only the middle and trailing portions. To blend the motion blur along the edges of your subject, lower the **Opacity** of the **Eraser** tool.

④ Merge the Layers

Choose **Layers, Merge, Merge All (Flatten)** to combine all the layers back into a single layer.

⑤ View the Result

By panning my camera in the direction of the carousel when I took this photo, I managed to keep my daughter Katerina and her cousin Erin, in perfect focus. To restore a natural sense of movement and to make the photograph more dramatic, I added a strong motion blur. Look for this image in the Color Gallery section of this book.

TIP

If you erase an area you want to keep sharp, drag the **Eraser** with the right mouse button, and it will "unerase." With a pen tablet, there's a trick: Turn the pen upside down, but place the "right button" or rocker switch under your *thumb*. Hold the thumb button down, and then *hover* the pen (don't touch down) over the area you want to unerase.

---

119 Smooth an Image Without Losing Crisp Edges or Texture

See Also

→ **115** Blur an Image to Remove Noise

One problem with using most of the blur filters is that they blur *everything*—edges included. If your objective is to smooth an image to remove noise, preserving your edges is important because they provide detail. In **115** Blur an Image to Remove Noise, you learned how to apply a blur to smooth out an image and to resharpen its edges. In this task, you'll learn how to blur an image while retaining edges, using the **Edge Preserving Smooth** filter. The advantage in using this method is that it's

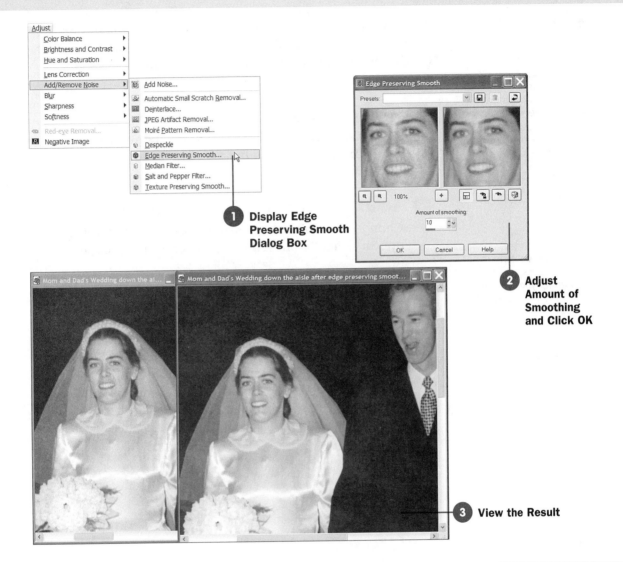

1 Display Edge Preserving Smooth Dialog Box

2 Adjust Amount of Smoothing and Click OK

3 View the Result

simple and fast; the disadvantage is that you don't have as much control over what areas should be blurred, and what areas should be treated as edges and left alone.

Use **Edge Preserving Smooth** to remove noise or reduce graininess in a low-light photograph. It's also handy in smoothing the skin, which anyone over age 25 will appreciate. The **Edge**

TIP

If you want to create a hand-painted look for an image, try applying the **Edge Preserving Smooth** filter first, to flatten the details while retaining object shapes. See **144** Colorize a Photograph, **145** Make a Photograph Look Like an Oil Painting, and **156** Turn a Photograph into a Watercolor.

 TIP

The higher the **Amount of smoothing** value, the more smoothing you get, but the less fussy PSP is about what constitutes an edge. For best results, use as low a smoothing value as you possibly can.

Preserving Smooth filter has a cousin that you might find useful in certain situations: the **Texture Preserving Smooth** filter, which smoothes an image while retaining some of the sharp changes in contrast that define a texture.

1 Display Edge Preserving Smooth Dialog Box

Choose **Adjust, Add/Remove Noise, Edge Preserving Smooth** from the menu bar to open the **Edge Preserving Smooth** dialog box.

2 Adjust Amount of Smoothing and Click OK

Change the **Amount of smoothing** value until the image appears smooth, but still retains clear edges. Click **OK**.

3 View the Result

Here's a picture of Mom and Dad, leaving the church just after getting married. The photo was printed on photo paper with a textured finish, so there was quite a lot of noise in the original scan. I reduced the resolution from 600 to 300 dpi using the **Resize** command, which helped some. The **Edge Preserving Smooth** filter easily took care of the rest, as you can see by looking at Mom's veil, her satin dress, and the dark background in these side-by-side comparisons.

PART III

Advanced Skills

IN THIS PART

13

Managing Multiple-Layer Images

IN THIS CHAPTER:

The power of layers is the power of control. On a layer, you can isolate a single part of your image—its background, subject, text, and so on—and perform a unique adjustment on that part alone. This separation of elements allows you to make corrections and create special effects that would otherwise be incredibly time consuming or just impossible without layers.

120 About Layers and the Layer Palette

Before You Begin

✔ **10** About Tools and Tool Options

See Also

→ **79** Copy a Selection to a New Layer

→ **121** Create a Layer

→ **122** Create an Adjustment Layer

→ **126** Create a New Mask

NOTE

The **Background** layer cannot be renamed. Nor can you add transparent pixels to the **Background** layer, adjust its opacity, or change its blend mode. To enable such changes, convert the **Background** layer to a regular layer by selecting **Layers, Promote Background Layer.** PSP renames the layer "Raster," followed by a number—generally 1.

New images begin with a single layer. If you import a photograph or scan one in, the image file contains a single layer called **Background** or **Raster 1**. To create complex images, you can add layers. A layer typically begins its life as a transparency; it does not block any part of the layers below it. As you paint, draw objects, or copy data to this new layer, that new data obscures whatever occupies that exact same spot on the layers below it (that is, when your blend mode is set to **Normal**, which is the default). Like old-style animation film cels, the layers in an image build on each other, forming a complete picture. For instance, you could place a small bunny on a layer above your daughter's Easter picture, creating the illusion of a bunny in front of her feet.

Want the bunny peeking out behind your daughter in the Easter photo? No problem—just switch the order of the layers, placing the bunny layer below the layer your daughter occupies on the **Layer** palette so that your daughter (on the layer above) partially obscures the bunny. If the "daughter" layer blocks the bunny completely, just erase part of the daughter layer and let the bunny show through. To make erasing easier, temporarily lower the **Opacity** value of the daughter layer so that you can see where the bunny is located on the layer behind it.

Building an image in layers gives you complete control over the image's final appearance. You can adjust the brightness, contrast, sharpness, and saturation of each layer separately. You can control how much one layer overlays the other by simply adjusting its **Opacity** setting. You can mix the pixels of an overlaying layer with those below it by choosing a unique blend mode.

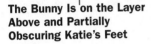

The Bunny Is on the Layer Above and Partially Obscuring Katie's Feet

Partial Opacity Helps in Erasing Part of Katie's Image to Reveal the Bunny Layer Below

Two versions of the Easter bunny photo: one with the bunny in front, one behind.

NOTE

Need a refresher course on what opacity is and what the various blend modes do? Jump back to **10** About Tools and Tool Options.

Another way to blend one layer with the layers beneath it is to add a *mask layer*, which provides you with total control over the blending process. With a mask, you can prevent parts of the layers lower in the layer stack from appearing in the image. The degree to which a mask blocks lower layers depends on the shade of gray you use in the mask. For example, with a black-to-white gradient, you could gradually fade from total blockage of the layers below to total visibility. See **125** About Masks.

With layers, you can perform many feats of image editing wizardry such as these (look for a few examples of layered images in the Color Gallery in this book):

- **Paste two photos together to create a panorama.** Simply place a copy of each photo on its own layer in a new image that's wide enough to accommodate the entire panorama you want to create. Then reduce the **Opacity** of the top layer and use the **Move** tool to position the bottom layer into place so that the edges match. Blend the two edges by softly erasing the top layer, and merge the final result. See **141** Create a Panorama.

KEY TERM

Mask layer—A grayscale layer that acts as a filter, covering up parts of other layers that lie beneath it in the layer stack (or in the same layer group). Where a mask is black, the layers beneath are covered, often revealing other content that the layer is not masking; where it is white, the masked layers are visible. Where a mask is gray, partial blocking of the masked layers occurs.

- **Create a scrapbook page.** Gather several related photos and copy each onto a new layer of a larger image file. Position each photo as you like and blend each layer carefully into a composite photo, as shown in the figure. You can add special effects such as **Soft Focus**, **Brush Strokes**, or **Charcoal** to each layer, giving the separate images their own special look.

Three carefully blended photos that create a photographic timeline.

- **Patch holes and tears.** As described in **87** **Repair Holes and Tears**, you can position a copy of the undamaged portion of an image on a layer below the original and "erase" the holes and tears to reveal unblemished parts underneath.

- **Repair old or faded photographs.** As explained in **109** **Restore Color to a Washed-Out Photograph**, you can restore faded color by duplicating an image on another layer and changing its blend mode to **Multiply**. This mode blends pixels from different layers and compounds their brightness.

- **Control changes.** As explained in many tasks throughout this book, it's often best to make changes to a duplicate of an image on another layer. That way, if the effect of an attempted alteration is in the right direction but too strong, you can tone it down by adjusting the duplicate layer's opacity, revealing some of the original layer beneath. If your edits take you down the wrong path, you can simply remove the layer and start over. The original image is undisturbed.

Another way to try out changes, such as curves and level adjustments, is to add an *adjustment layer*. See **122** **Create an Adjustment Layer.**

- **Add text or other drawn objects.** When you add text or create drawn objects such as rectangles and ellipses, PSP automatically places them on their own layers. This gives you total control over their placement, size, and other characteristics.

You might be asking, how *many* layers should a PSP image have? Your image should have only as many layers as there are elements of your original photograph that are worthy of independent treatment and editing, plus however many layers are necessary to provide the image with the visual effects you want for it. Spending a few minutes separating elements into their own layers could save you several hours of hassle down the road.

You can create empty layers and add things to them, although you don't have to do so. You can just as easily duplicate the data on one layer to create another—for example, you might duplicate the **Background** layer (the only layer in most photographs) to make changes to its copy. You can also create a layer from another image, or from a selected part of an image (see **79** **Copy a Selection to a New Layer**). After you've added a layer to an image, its name appears in the **Layer** palette. To make changes to any layer, click its name in the list on the left side of the palette. This action activates the layer, highlighting your choice. The layer's name also appears in parentheses in the image window's title bar.

🔍 **KEY TERM**

Adjustment layer—A special layer that allows you to make a specific color or contrast adjustment to the layers that show through it, without directly altering those layers' pixels.

💡 **TIP**

Suppose that your photo features three people seated on a park bench on a sunny day. Do you need three separate layers, one for each person? Only if there are changes you want to make to one or two of those people that you don't want reflected in the others. Do you need to separate the people from the trees and other items in the background? Probably—because in most cases, it's the people you want to improve (with better contrast, saturation, and sharpness) and not the background.

💡 **TIP**

To move, resize, rotate, or distort the data on a layer, use the **Deform** tool. See **138** Move, Alter, or Distort a Layer.

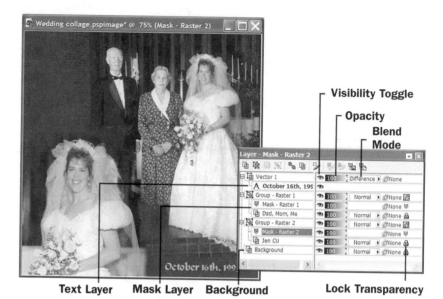

*The **Layer** palette.*

You manage how a layer interacts with other layers by using the following controls on the **Layer** palette:

<img> **NOTE**

A reduction in the opacity of a layer affects the entire layer, not just the edges. To fade one layer into another along its edges (as in the wedding image shown), add a mask to gradually block the content along a layer's edge.

- **Visibility Toggle.** Click the eye button to temporarily hide a layer. Hiding a layer allows you to see the content of lower layers more clearly.

- **Opacity.** Normally, a layer is set to 100% opacity, meaning that the data on the layer completely covers the data on layers below. You can fade one layer onto another by lowering the opacity of the top layer.

- **Blend mode.** Control how pixels from a top layer mix with pixels in layers below by selecting a blend mode. Typically, the blend mode is set to **Normal**, which means that no blending occurs at all—the top pixel simply overlays the bottom one. For more on blend modes, see **10** **About Tools and Tool Options.**

- **Lock Transparency.** With this button turned on, transparent pixels on a layer are unaffected by any changes you might make, such as color fills, brightness/contrast adjustments, and so on. This option is turned off by default, which means that for editing purposes, transparent pixels are treated just like any other pixel on the layer.

If you look back at the wedding figure, notice on the **Layer** palette that some layers have been grouped together (layers in the same group are indented underneath the group layer). Grouping allows you to make changes that affect several layers at one time. For example, you could make the same contrast and brightness adjustment to several layers, while leaving the layers not in the group alone.

 TIP

Grouping is also extremely helpful when using masks, when you want to distinguish between layers that are masked and layers that are not. You'll learn more about grouping layers in **123** Group and Organize Layers.

New Raster Layer
New Vector Layer
Duplicate Layer
Delete Layer

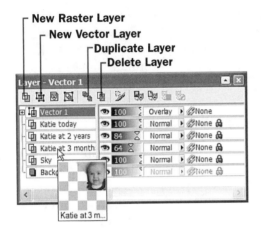

Katie at 3 m...

*Manage layers with these buttons in the **Layer** palette.*

The **Layer** palette helps you quickly perform several basic layer management tasks:

- **Create an empty layer.** If you want to create a transparent layer and then add data to it using the painting or drawing tools, click either the **New Raster Layer** or **New Vector Layer** button on the **Layer** palette, or select **Layers, New Raster Layer** or **Layers, New Vector Layer** from the menu. See **121** Create a Layer.

- **Rename a layer.** When an image contains several layers, it's hard to keep track of the data that's on each layer. If you rename each layer with a more descriptive name, it'll be easier for you to work with all of them. To rename a layer, right-click its name in the **Layer** palette, select **Rename** from the pop-up menu, type a new name, and press **Enter**.

- **View the contents of a layer.** To view the contents of just a single layer, move the mouse pointer over the layer's name and hold it there for a moment. A small thumbnail of the layer's contents appears.

- **Copy a layer.** Make a copy of the currently selected layer by clicking the **Duplicate Layer** button, or by selecting **Layers, Duplicate** from the menu.

- **Remove a layer.** To remove the currently selected layer, click the **Delete Layer** button, or select **Layers, Delete** from the menu. If you select a group layer and then click **Delete Layer**, all the layers in that group are deleted.

121 Create a Layer

Before You Begin

✔ **120** About Layers and the Layer Palette

See Also

→ **79** Copy a Selection to a New Layer

→ **122** Create an Adjustment Layer

→ **126** Create a New Mask

🔍 KEY TERMS

Vector layer—A layer whose data is comprised of objects defined mathematically by a series of points.

Raster layer—A layer whose data is comprised of individual pixels.

There are two types of layers you can create for new image data: *vector* and *raster*. Initially, new vector and raster layers are full of transparent pixels; however, the type of layer you create determines the type of data you can put on it. A vector layer can contain drawn objects such as text, circles, rectangles, and lines whose shapes are recorded geometrically. A raster layer can contain data comprised of rows upon rows of single pixels, each with its own hue, saturation, and lightness value (or its own red, green, blue value if you prefer that color model). A raster layer might contain a photograph or objects drawn with the paint tools, or it might be filled with paint or other bitmapped data.

① Select Layer Position

On the **Layer** palette, click in the layer stack *below* where you want the new layer to appear. The new layer will appear above this layer.

② Create New Layer

To create a new raster layer, click the **New Raster Layer** button on the **Layer** palette, or select **Layers, New Raster Layer** from the menu.

To create a new vector layer, click the **New Vector Layer** button on the **Layer** palette, or select **Layers, New Vector Layer** from the menu.

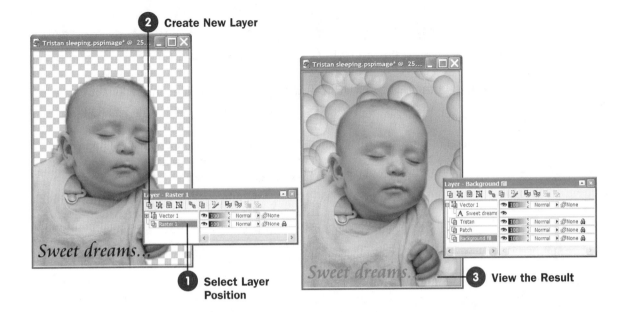

② **Create New Layer**

① **Select Layer Position**

③ **View the Result**

Initially, your new layer will be empty (completely transparent). Add raster or vector data as desired. If you have to move, resize, or distort the data on a layer at any time, use the **Deform** tool. See **138** **Move, Alter, or Distort a Layer**.

③ **View the Result**

I started with a great photograph of my grandnephew Tristan slumbering peacefully. I selected the dark background, filled it with transparency, and added some text on a vector layer. Then I added a new raster layer, which I filled with a blue gradient. After applying the filter **Balls and Bubbles** (**Effects, Artistic, Balls and Bubbles**) to the raster layer, I moved it down in the stack below the layer with Tristan on it so that it would act as the background. I then added another layer in which I created a patch to fill the space where his arm seemed to be missing (this space was created when I removed the person holding him). The result, I think, is rather sweet.

NOTE

Although you can create layers in any image, you'll only be able to save the layers as separate (non-merged) layers if the image uses PSP format.

TIP

You can copy data and paste it onto its own layer in any image by selecting **Edit, Paste, As New Layer**. You can also copy the data in a selection to a new layer in the same image by choosing **Selections, Promote Selection to Layer**. See **79** **Copy a Selection to a New Layer**.

122 Create an Adjustment Layer

NOTE

An adjustment layer normally affects only the layers below it in the stack. However, if the adjustment layer is placed in a group, it affects only the layers below it *in that group*.

TIP

If you make a selection and then create an adjustment layer, PSP automatically adds a mask to the adjustment layer that prevents it from affecting the nonselected area of the image.

An adjustment layer is like a filter for a color or contrast adjustment—it gives the appearance of changes made to the layers below without actually altering the content of those layers at all. There are several types of adjustment layers you can insert into an image. Each performs a specific type of adjustment to the color or contrast of a layer: **Brightness/Contrast**, **Channel Mixer**, **Color Balance**, **Curves**, **Hue/Saturation/Lightness**, **Invert**, **Levels**, **Posterize**, and **Threshold**. All these adjustments are discussed in the tasks listed in the **See Also** section, except for a few: **Channel Mixer** and **Color Balance** allow you to shift the colors in an image, removing a color cast (see **111** Remove a Color Cast for a similar procedure); **Invert** reverses the colors in an image, in a manner similar to the **Difference** blend mode (see **10** About Tools and Tool Options); **Posterize** divides an image into several levels of brightness, based on the number you select—you might use this command to make an image look as if it were created by CorelDraw or a similar drawing program. See **147** Make a Photograph Look Like It Was Drawn.

You might use adjustment layers to isolate changes to specific parts of an image, or to simply try out a series of changes you're unsure of. If you get a result you don't like, delete the adjustment layer or change its settings.

1 **Select Position for Adjustment**

On the **Layer** palette, click in the layer stack *above* where you want the adjustment layer to appear. Layers *below* this position in the stack will be affected by the adjustment. For example, if you want the adjustment layer to affect *all layers below and including* the **Bird** layer, click the **Bird** layer in the **Layer** palette. If the **Bird** layer is in a layer group, the adjustment layer will affect only the **Bird** layer and other layers below it *in that group*.

2 **Create Adjustment Layer**

Select **Layers, New Adjustment Layer**; from the menu that appears, select the type of adjustment you want to apply, such as **Levels** or **Curves**. The **Adjustment** layer is added to the stack above the layer you selected in step 1.

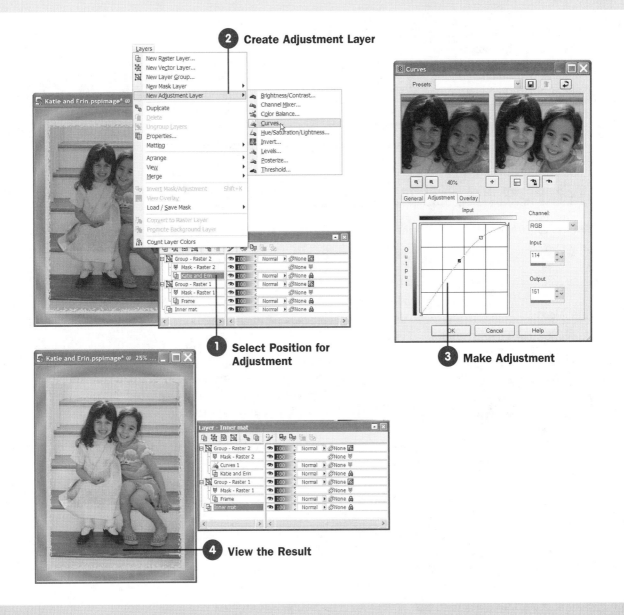

2 Create Adjustment Layer

1 Select Position for Adjustment

3 Make Adjustment

4 View the Result

3 **Make Adjustment**

The appropriate dialog box appears (for example, if you add a **Curves** adjustment layer, the **Curves** dialog box appears). On the **Adjustment** tab, make the correction in the normal manner and click **OK**.

TIP

If you later want to adjust the settings you make in the dialog box, simply double-click the name of the adjustment layer on the **Layer** palette, make your changes, and click **OK**.

④ View the Result

Here, I added a frame and mat around a photograph of my daughter Katerina and her cousin Erin. The only problem was that the photo was shot with available light and was therefore a bit dark. I added an adjustment layer above the image of the girls so that my **Curves** adjustment would affect them and not the frame and mat.

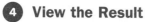 Group and Organize Layers

Before You Begin

✔ **10** About Tools and Tool Options

✔ **120** About Layers and the Layer Palette

See Also

→ **79** Copy a Selection to a New Layer

→ **121** Create a Layer

→ **122** Create an Adjustment Layer

→ **126** Create a New Mask

NOTE

Just because layers are in a group doesn't mean you have to treat them as a conglomerate; you are still free to apply an adjustment or change the opacity of a single layer, even if it's located within a group. You can change the position of a layer within the group, even moving it out of the group if necessary.

When layers are grouped together, they act as one unit. You can easily move a group up or down in the layer stack, change the group's opacity and blend mode, or move the layers in a group together, anywhere on the image canvas. When you place an adjustment or mask layer in a group with other layers, its effect is limited to the layers in that group.

Some layer groups are created automatically. When you add text or draw a vector object such as a triangle, it's placed in its own vector group—a group with just one layer, until you add more vector objects to it. If you insert a mask, it's placed in a group with the current layer. You can add other layers to these automatic groups, and you can create your own layer groups manually. Of course, some rules apply to rearranging layers: You cannot move the **Background** layer or move any layer below it. (If you want to move the **Background** layer, change it into a regular layer by selecting **Layers, Promote Background Layer**.) You cannot place vector and raster layers in the same group. And finally, you cannot move an adjustment layer or mask layer to the bottom of its group because both layer types must have a layer below them that they can affect.

① Select First Layer to Group

Click the **New Layer Group** button on the **Layer** palette or select **Layers, New Layer Group**. This action creates a group with the current layer as the only layer in that group.

2 Move Other Layers into Group

In the **Layer** palette, click the name of a layer you want to add to the group. Then drag the layer up or down the layer stack and drop it within the group. As you drag, a black line marks where the layer will be placed when you release the mouse button.

3 Make an Adjustment That Affects the Group

Click the group's name in the **Layer** palette and then select how to affect all layers in that group:

- To view the layer names in a group on the **Layer** palette, click the plus sign in front of the group's name. To temporarily hide the names of the layers in a group, click the minus sign.

- Adjust the **Opacity** slider for the group or select a new blend mode.

- Drag the group up or down in the layer stack to change its position in the stack.

- Click the **Group Link Toggle** button for the group to lock the layers in that group together as a unit for the purpose of repositioning them. Then click the **Move** tool on the **Tools** palette, click any layer in the group, and move the layers in the group as one unit within the image canvas. If you turn off the **Group Link Toggle** button and use the **Move** tool to move a layer, you'll move just that layer (even if the layer is part of a group).

- Insert an adjustment layer above the top layer in the group to affect just the layers in that group.

4 Remove Layers As Needed

To remove a layer from a group, select its name in the **Layer** palette. Then drag and drop the layer anywhere in the stack, or select **Layers, Arrange, Move Out of Group**.

 TIP

If you select a layer and choose **Layers, Arrange, Move Into Group**, the layer is moved into the group directly below it in the layer stack.

 TIP

Layers can appear on top of something in the image only if they are above that layer in the stack. You can nest a group within another layer group if you like.

 TIP

You can link selected layers to each other (regardless of the group they are in, if any) so that you can move the linked layers together on the layer canvas using the **Move** tool. To link layers, click the **Layer Link** button (located to the right of the **Blend Mode** list on the **Layer** palette) for each layer you want to link and set it to the same number, such as 2.

 TIP

To ungroup all the layers in a group, click the group name in the **Layer** palette and select **Layers, Ungroup Layers**.

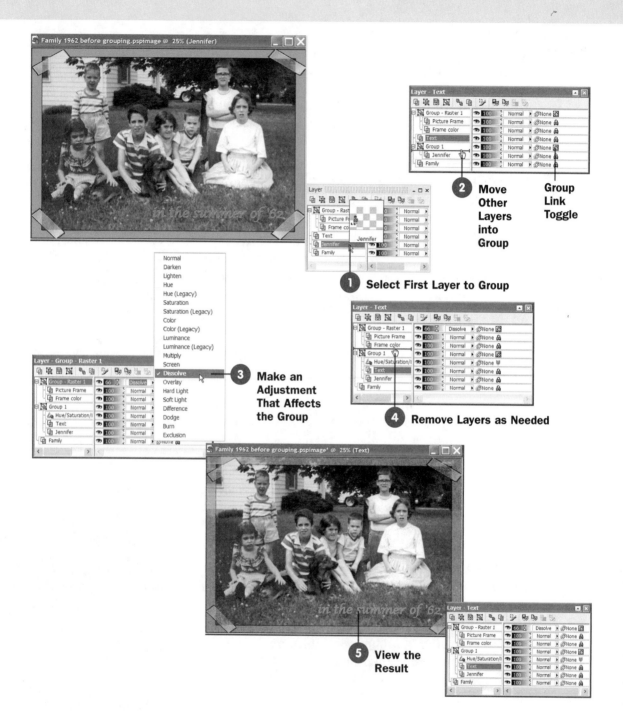

2 Move Other Layers into Group

Group Link Toggle

1 Select First Layer to Group

3 Make an Adjustment That Affects the Group

4 Remove Layers as Needed

5 View the Result

5 **View the Result**

By grouping the bitmapped text and the little girl together, I was able to use a **Hue/Saturation/Lightness** adjustment to change both to the same color. This layer group enabled me to play around with colors for both elements until I found one I liked best. The group with the picture frame and frame color work the same way—by grouping them together, I can change the color of the frame easily. Look for this image in the Color Gallery.

124 Merge or Flatten Layers into One

Because PSP format is the only format that supports layers, you must merge the layers of your image together (flatten them) into a single layer if you want to save the image in any other format. When layers are merged together, the pixels are blended based on the opacity and blend mode used by each layer. Vector data such as text and drawn objects are converted to raster data so that they can be blended with the pixels on other layers.

You can merge all the layers in a group (which you might do if you want to apply some special effect to the group, such as **Colored Pencil**), merge two neighboring layers, merge only the visible layers, or merge all the layers in an image. Because merging reduces an image's system requirements, you might merge a few layers that you know you won't have to change again, even as you're still editing an image. Another reason for merging layers is simply to make the image more manageable.

1 **Prepare Layers for Merging**

To merge one layer with the layer below it, click that layer in the **Layer** palette. To merge all the layers in a group, click the group name or any layer in that group. To merge visible layers only, click the **Visibility Toggle** button on the **Layer** palette to hide any layers *you do not want to merge*. (The eye icons for the layers you do not want to merge should not be showing.)

Before You Begin

✔ **120** About Layers and the Layer Palette

See Also

→ **121** Create a Layer

NOTE

If you save your image in Photoshop format (.PSD), you can also save the layers without merging. Photoshop is a graphics editor like Paint Shop Pro.

TIP

Before merging layers, make a copy of the image and save it in PSP format. This enables you to return to the copy at a later time, make additional changes, and flatten the image again.

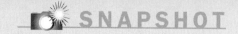

Visibility Toggle

1   Prepare Layers for Merging

2   Merge Layers as Desired

2   Merge Layers as Desired

Select **Layers, Merge** and then select the command that merges the layers you want. To merge the current layer with the layer below it, select **Merge Down**; to merge the layers in the current group, select **Merge Group**; to merge only the visible layers, select **Merge Visible**; to merge all layers, select **Merge All (Flatten)**.

14

Creating and Using Masks

IN THIS CHAPTER:

The mask in Paint Shop Pro is unusual among the program's many tools in that you actually build it yourself. It's a straightforward tool that does exactly what its name suggests it does: You place a mask like a cardboard cut-out on top of (above) other layers to partially block them from view or to protect certain portions from being affected by changes you make. If you've ever painted a sign using letters from a stencil, you know already what a mask is supposed to do. This chapter focuses specifically on building masks and implementing them in your projects.

125 About Masks

Before You Begin

✔ **120** About Layers and the Layer Palette

See Also

→ **122** Create an Adjustment Layer

→ **126** Create a New Mask

→ **127** Create a Mask From a Selection

→ **128** Create a Mask From an Image

KEY TERM

Mask—A layer comprised only of grayscale pixels, whose color determines the amount of filtering to be applied to corresponding pixels in lower layers. Black pixels in a mask block lower layers entirely. Gray pixels partially block lower layers, whereas white pixels allow changes and the content of lower layers to pass through completely.

When creating a photographic composition made up of several elements, masking lets you easily hide the portions of each element you don't want displayed. Suppose that you want your subject matter to appear behind a frame. A *mask* can prevent the center of the frame layer from displaying, allowing a photograph placed lower in the layer stack to appear within the gap. Suppose that you want to highlight your daughter's latest culinary adventure (a Christmas cookie) by placing it on a fir tree background. You could use a mask to prevent the countertop surrounding the cookie from showing through. Want to add some text to an image and fill that text with data from a different image? By placing one image on top of the other on different layers, and inserting a mask with a hole in the shape of the text in-between, you can easily create the effect you're looking for.

The basic purpose of a mask is to selectively reveal some content from a layer or layers behind it, and obscure the rest. In some ways, a mask can be considered the *opposite* of a selection. A selection includes material; a mask *excludes* material. But using a mask might provide you with more options than simply copying selected data to a layer. For example, if you simply copied a portion of one image and pasted it into a layer above a different image, you could certainly position the copied data wherever you liked, and even make it larger or smaller. However, you would lose the ability to revise the border around the inset portion. You could crop it down, but you couldn't widen it or extend it on just one side to reveal anything you hadn't copied to begin with.

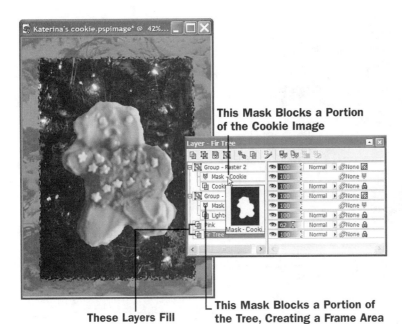

This Mask Blocks a Portion of the Cookie Image

These Layers Fill the Frame Area

This Mask Blocks a Portion of the Tree, Creating a Frame Area

Masking lets you reveal the portions of an image you want to see.

Masks do more than simply block portions of a layer from view; when used with adjustment layers, masks also allow you to protect areas of an image from changes you make. See **122** Create an Adjustment Layer.

NOTE

Using a mask to cover the portion of the copied layer you don't want to use provides versatility. Because a mask is just a grayscale layer, you can paint on it with black to block lower layers, paint with white to reveal them, or paint with gray to partially obscure them. You can change the mask with any painting tool or any other PSP tool that works on grayscale images, such as the blur, soften, and effects filters. To reveal more of the inset image, you paint along the edges of the mask "window" with white to make it bigger. When you group the mask together with the inset image, PSP treats only the revealed portion as its own layer—your viewer never sees the mask, only its product. Another benefit of using a mask is that it allows you to switch out the inset image until you find one that creates the exact image you're looking for. Look for a few examples of masking in the Color Gallery.

NOTE

You can vary the amount of filtering created by a mask by varying the shade of gray you use to paint the mask. Darker gray pixels block more completely than lighter gray ones; almost-white pixels hardly block the pixels on lower layers at all.

A pure black mask in the center of this frame enables one DeLaJuen original to be replaced with another.

TIP

You can create a mask in several different ways: by simply painting on a mask layer with black, white, or any shade of gray; by making a selection and filling that selection with black to create a mask with that shape; or by copying a grayscale version of the data within an image and letting the image itself create a mask.

Suppose that you want to take a photo of you and your spouse sitting on your front lawn, and replace your front lawn with a more exotic location. Make a copy of the image and use various contrast adjustments (such as **Threshold**, **Channel Map**, **Curves**, or **Levels**) to blacken the background, leaving a white silhouette. Then use this black and white image to create the mask you need. Place the mask on the layer above the two of you, and the lawn instantly disappears. Insert a copy of a tropical island image on the bottom layer, and you and your spouse are sipping Mai Tais instead of swatting mosquitoes.

As you already know, a mask blocks data *only* on the layers beneath it in the layer stack. So how did our tropical island trick work? If you place the mask *above* the image of you and your spouse *and* the image of the tropical island, wouldn't the background of both layers be blocked? Well, the answer is yes and no. Yes, the mask would block both layers, unless it was placed in a group with one or more other layers. In that case, the mask would block data *only on the layers in that same group*. In the case of our island foolery, if you place the mask in a group with the lawn layer, only the background from the lawn layer is blocked, allowing the lower, tropical island layer to be seen.

This Mask Blocks Only the Layer It Is Grouped With

Take a vacation with Paint Shop Pro.

TIP

The pattern of a mask might be something you need to use for more than just one image or project; for that reason, you can save a mask pattern separately to disk or to an image's alpha channel. Say you're creating a photo documentary of a home redecoration project. You're building a series of before-and-after shots, where the "before" part is inset in the same frame in every image. By saving the frame's mask to disk, you can easily recall it and apply it to the same corner of each "after" shot.

126 Create a New Mask

A new mask does one of two things: It reveals everything or conceals everything. That's because, when you create a new mask using the most common method, the mask is either all white (revealing) or all black (concealing). You must first choose the layer you intend to mask and then create the new mask to apply specifically to that layer. From there, you can apply black to conceal those portions of the masked layer you want hidden, apply white to reveal those portions you want shown, or apply in-between shades of gray to apply grades of transparency in accordance with their darkness—darker gray conceals more, lighter gray reveals more. But first, you have to bring the new mask into existence.

Before You Begin

✔ **125** About Masks

See Also

→ **120** About Layers and the Layer Palette

→ **123** Group and Organize Layers

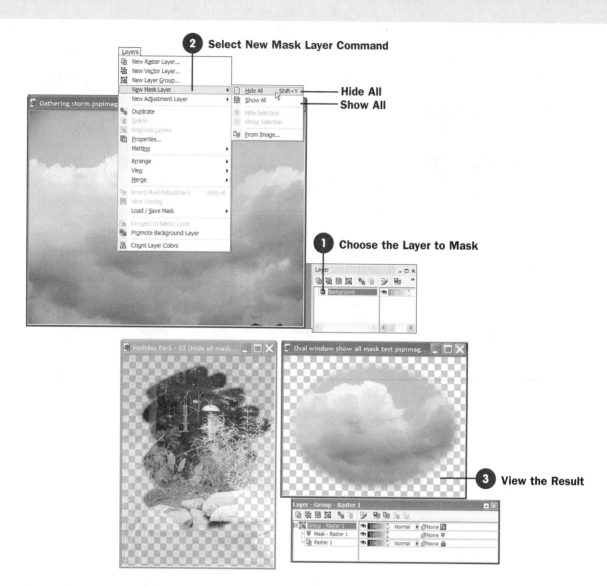

2 Select New Mask Layer Command

Layers
- New Raster Layer...
- New Vector Layer...
- New Layer Group...
- New Mask Layer ▶
  - Hide All   Shift+Y —— **Hide All**
  - Show All   —— **Show All**
  - Hide Selection
  - Show Selection
  - From Image...
- New Adjustment Layer ▶
- Duplicate
- Delete
- Ungroup Layers
- Properties...
- Matting ▶
- Arrange ▶
- View ▶
- Merge ▶
- Invert Mask/Adjustment   Shift+K
- View Overlay
- Load / Save Mask ▶
- Convert to Raster Layer
- Promote Background Layer
- Count Layer Colors

Choose the Layer to Mask ①

Layer
Background

3 View the Result

Layer - Group - Raster 1
- Group - Raster 1   100   Normal   None
- Mask - Raster 1   100   None
- Raster 1   100   Normal   None

Creating a new mask results in the introduction of a *layer group* into your image. The layers and other parts of a layer group collectively produce a single image component, which Paint Shop

Pro treats as a single layer. The product of a layer and the mask on top of it is merely the filtered portion, which you manage as though it were one layer unto itself. In the **Layer** palette, you can rearrange this layer group, apply variable opacity to it, and even apply a separate blend mode to it. In a sense, after the mask has done its work, PSP doesn't care about the mask anymore, and is concerned solely with what the mask lets through.

❶ Choose the Layer to Mask

In the **Layer** palette, choose the layer you want to mask.

❷ Select New Mask Layer Command

Select **Layers**, **New Mask Layer**, and then select **Hide All** to create a new mask that obscures everything, or **Show All** to create a new mask that reveals everything. If a confirmation dialog box appears, click **Yes**. Paint on the mask with white to change what it reveals, or black to change what it obscures. Use gray to partially obscure.

❸ View the Result

Here are two examples of masks, one of which began as a **Hide All** mask, the other as a **Show All**. With the **Hide All**, I applied a total mask over a garden image, then used a wide-nosed airbrush to paint a white wash over the area I wanted to show. For the **Show All** mask, I selected a heavily feathered ellipse centered in the middle of the cloud image, then inverted the selection to indicate the perimeter of the image. I then flood-filled the selected region with pure black, hiding the rectangular portion of the border and part of the feathered region.

 TIP

You can save the masks you create and reuse them so that you don't have to start from scratch each time. In addition, PSP comes with several masks ready for you to use, such as various types of picture frames. See **130** Save and Reuse Masks.

NOTE

When you create a mask, a new layer group is automatically created; it includes the new mask on top of the chosen layer. The mask is grayscale, so when you select it from the **Layer** palette, the **Materials** palette will display a color palette of white, black, and various shades of gray.

TIP

You delete a mask layer by selecting it in the **Layer** palette, and then clicking the **Delete Layer** button or by selecting **Layers**, **Delete**. You'll be asked whether you want to merge the mask with the layer below it before it's removed. Merging replaces the layer below with the product of the layer after being masked, so you can keep the results without keeping the mask.

127 Create a Mask from a Selection

 TIP

You can also create a text
selection using the **Text**
tool, and use that selection
to create a mask. Such a
mask is typically used to
fill the text with part of an
image. Just create a selection, copy the image, and
choose **Edit, Paste, Paste
into Selection**.

 TIP

You can create the selec-
tion in an image other than
the one in which you want
to use it, if you like.

In **126** **Create a New Mask**, you learned how to build a mask by
starting with a blank slate, so that you can paint the areas of
that mask that you want to reveal or block out. That method
works best when the shape of the revealed or obscured area is
not defined by something in the image itself—in other words, if
it's rectangular or a gradient fill area or some freestyle pattern. If
your intention is instead to build a mask that reveals a specific
object—for instance, a person in your foreground—and obscures
everything else, it would be easier for you to use Paint Shop Pro's
selection tools to identify and select the revealed area, then tell
the mask to obscure everything else.

When you create a mask from a selection, you use selection tools
to build a pattern. For instance, you can use the **Magic Wand**
tool or the **Edge Seeker** to indicate specific areas of the image
based on their content. You then use the selection as a pattern on
which you base a new mask. The mask can either use the pattern to indicate what the mask should obscure, or what it should
reveal. As you're about to see, the selection doesn't have to be
perfect, because after creating the mask, you can paint on it to
clear up any parts you missed or selected accidentally.

1 **Build a Selection Pattern**

Create a selection in the shape of the region you want to
mask or reveal.

2 **Create a Mask from the Selection**

Select the layer you want to mask and then choose **Layers,
New Mask Layer, Show Selection** to create a mask that
blocks everything but the selected area; select **Layers, New
Mask Layer, Hide Selection** to create a mask that blocks
only the selected area. If you see a confirmation dialog box,
click **Yes**; PSP places the current layer and the new mask in
the same group.

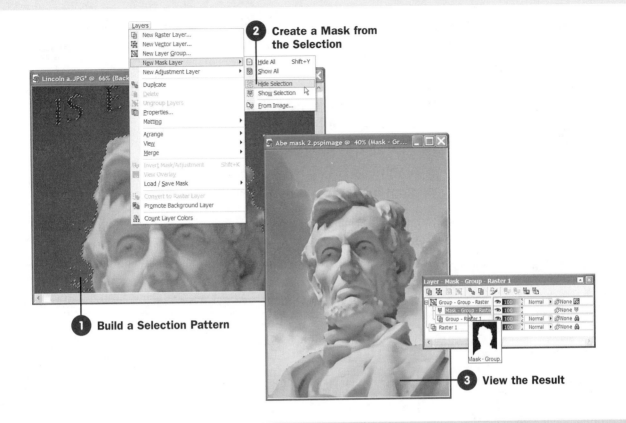

1 Build a Selection Pattern

2 Create a Mask from the Selection

3 View the Result

3 View the Result

In this example, I stylized a photo of the Lincoln Memorial, smoothing out his chiseled features. Then I used the **Magic Wand** tool to select the wall behind him. I used this selection to produce a new **Hide Selection** mask layer that blacks out the wall. The selection wasn't perfect (some of the letters in the wall were omitted from the original mask), so I touched up the mask with some quick strokes with a black paintbrush. This was much easier than perfecting the selection before I created the mask. Then I replaced the original background with an awe-inspiring sky. Look for this image in the Color Gallery.

> **NOTE**
>
> When you create a mask layer, PSP builds a group containing the mask and the layer behind it that is being masked. When you point to that lower layer on the **Layer** palette, the thumbnail shows you the entire, unaltered layer. However, if you select the masked layer and paste it to another layer or another image, *what is pasted is the mask-reversed portion of that layer*. In other words, what you paste is the part of the original layer that is *not* masked by the mask.

128 Create a Mask from an Image

Before You Begin

✔ **125** About Masks

✔ **129** Edit a Mask

See Also

→ **127** Create a Mask from a Selection

When you create a mask from an image, Paint Shop Pro generates a grayscale copy of that image and uses that copy as the mask. You might create the mask from a different image to leave an impression of that other image on the current one. For example, you could imprint the wave pattern of a pond on the serene image of a small child. However, in most cases, what you typically want to do is make a mask from the current image to block portions of that image from view or from changes you want to make. You might even modify the image mask after creation. For example, you could use the information the mask contains (the location of objects and their edges) to paint a mask that includes or excludes certain objects.

1 Duplicate the Background Layer

Make a copy of the image on another layer: On the **Layer** palette, select the **Background** (or **Raster 1**) layer. Then click the **Duplicate Layer** button or select **Layers, Duplicate** from the menu.

2 Generate a Mask from the Image

In the **Layer** palette, choose the **Copy of Background** layer. Then select **Layers, New Mask Layer, From Image**.

From the **Source window** list in the **Add Mask from Image** dialog box, select the active image. Under **Create mask from**, choose how PSP is to interpret the data from the original image: To create a grayscale mask whose luminance data is directly copied from the original image, choose **Source luminance**. To paint transparent pixels black in the mask, choose **Any non-zero value**. Choose **Source opacity** if your original image includes both pure and partial transparencies that you want to make black in the mask. To block light data and reveal dark areas, click the **Invert mask data** check box and then click **OK**.

✎ NOTE

You could skip step 1 and create the mask directly from the **Background** layer, but doing so links the layers and makes it much more difficult to insert the image you want to substitute (in my example, a more dramatic sky) for the part of the original image you're masking. As an alternative, you can copy the image itself, create the mask in the second file, and import the mask from that second image after adding your substitute sky layer.

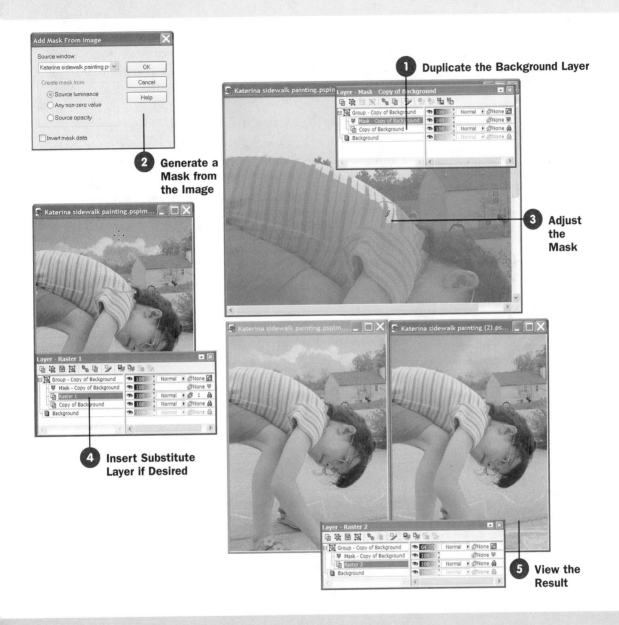

1 Duplicate the Background Layer

2 Generate a Mask from the Image

3 Adjust the Mask

4 Insert Substitute Layer if Desired

5 View the Result

3 **Adjust the Mask**

At first, not much has changed. You can't see the mask
(unless you hold the mouse pointer over its name in the

TIP

To make your mask visible so that you can edit it more easily, select the **Mask** layer and choose **Layers**, **View Overlay**. PSP represents the mask with a "ruby lithe." The redder regions represent the darker areas of the mask; the more transparent areas represent lighter areas. *You do not have to display the ruby lithe to paint on the mask layer.*

NOTE

When you paste the substitute layer into the middle of the layer group, the new layer appears in the center of the image and by default is *linked* with the other two layers. As a result, you can't move the new layer without also moving the mask and the **Copy of Background** layer. On the **Layer** palette, click the **Layer Link Toggle** button once to unlink the layers; remember to relink the layers after you move the substitute layer into position.

Layer palette), but you can see its effects. As a grayscale copy of the image, the mask blocks or almost blocks dark areas, while leaving light areas visible or partially visible. See **129** **Edit a Mask**, for ways to alter the mask.

④ Insert Substitute Layer if Desired

If the purpose of the mask is to protect parts of your image from some kind of adjustment, you can skip this step. If you want to insert an image so that it appears in the areas not blocked by the mask, open that other image and select **Edit**, **Copy**. Change back to the image you're modifying and select the **Copy of Background** layer. Select **Edit**, **Paste**, **Paste as New Layer**, and the substitute image (in this example, the sky) appears on a layer just below the mask. Use the **Deform** tool to reposition and resize the substitute image so that it fits the hole you want it to fill.

Because you no longer need it, on the **Layer** palette, choose the **Copy of Background** layer and then click the **Delete Layer** button. Click **Yes** to confirm.

⑤ View the Result

In this example, I shot a photo of my daughter that included a relatively uninteresting, gray sky. In fact, that particular early evening, some beautiful thunderstorm clouds were just brewing, but just out of frame. I did shoot those clouds; and by creating a mask from the image of Katerina, I was able to substitute a more interesting sky for the duller one. To create the mask, I duplicated the image layer, used **Threshold** to blacken almost everything but the sky, and added a bit of black paint to touch up the mask where it was needed. To see where I needed to use the black paint, I turned on the ruby lithe, as you can see in the step-3 figure. Even though it appears that I'm painting with red, my brush is filled with black paint. The mask appears red when the ruby lithe is displayed, but if you view it by holding your mouse pointer over the mask layer's name in the **Layer** palette, you'll see only black, white, and gray.

You might be wondering, "Why did I paint the mask black everywhere except the sky? Isn't the sky what I want to substitute?" Well, here it's just a matter of how you want to arrange your layers. I used the mask to block my substitute sky layer, so that the only clouds that showed through were the ones at the top of the image, in the sky area. That way, the portion of the image with Katie in it was not blocked by the substitute sky layer, even though that layer was higher in the stack. With the mask in place, I can make any number of substitutions for the sky. (Look for these images in the Color Gallery in this book.)

TIP

The amount of content revealed by the mask can be adjusted *after the fact* by changing the **Opacity** setting for the substitute layer. You can also change the **Opacity** setting for the group, which adjusts the mask as well, causing a blending of the substitute sky and the original.

129 Edit a Mask

After your mask layer has been created, you will probably have to alter it in some way to make it do what you want it to do. As you know, you apply black to those areas you want the mask to obscure, white to areas you want to reveal, and varying shades of gray to apply partial blocking. You can edit the mask using any tool, feature, or command you would use to edit any other grayscale image or layer. In this task, you'll see the effects of the most commonly used mask-editing tools and how you can use them for your own purposes.

1 Change to Mask Layer

On the **Layer** palette, choose the mask layer you want to edit.

2 Make the Mask Visible

On the **Layer** palette, click the **Mask Overlay Toggle** button; alternatively, select **Layers, View Overlay**. The color red (the ruby lithe) marks the areas of the mask that are blocking the layer(s) beneath it, or in the same group as the mask; dark red blocks more completely than light red.

The ruby lithe representing the mask is displayed at 50% opacity so that you can see the underlying layers. To make the mask more visible, right-click the mask layer and select **Properties**. Increase the **Opacity** setting for the mask as

Before You Begin

✔ **126** Create a New Mask

✔ **127** Create a Mask from a Selection

✔ **128** Create a Mask from an Image

See Also

→ **10** About Tools and Tool Options

→ **72** Select a Portion of an Image with Threshold

TIP

You don't actually have to display the mask to edit it; you can make changes as long as the **Mask** layer is selected. But if you're going to paint the mask (and not use a command such as **Threshold** to edit it), I recommend turning on the ruby lithe as explained in step 2.

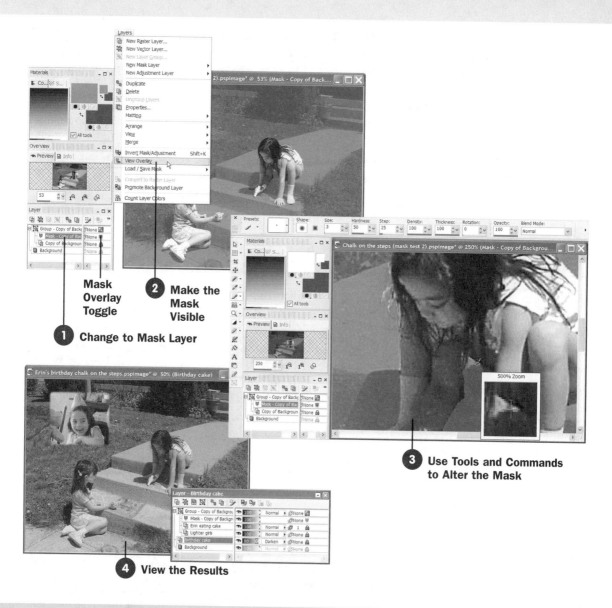

Mask Overlay Toggle

1 Change to Mask Layer

2 Make the Mask Visible

3 Use Tools and Commands to Alter the Mask

4 View the Results

desired. Change the overlay color by clicking the **Overlay color** color picker, choosing another color (such as black, if it makes more sense to you to paint with black and have it show up as black on the lithe, rather than red), and clicking **OK**. Click **OK** again to change the overlay.

3 Use Tools and Commands to Alter the Mask

While your mask layer is chosen, the **Materials** palette shows only grayscale color choices. You can draw directly onto the mask using the **Paint Brush** or **Airbrush** tools. You can select areas and fill them using the **Flood Fill** tool. You can apply special effects such as a blur or a texture. You can use any contrast adjustment tool to change the black/white areas, (The **Threshold** command is especially useful for this purpose.) If you're going to spot paint with black to clean up the edge of the mask against your subject, as I am doing here, invoke the **Magnifier** by pressing **Ctrl+Alt+M**.

 TIP

If you've created a **Hide All** mask, all the lower layers are masked, and it might be hard to make edits that reveal selected areas of the image. Easy solution: On the **Layer** palette, turn down the **Opacity** of the **Mask** layer to around 50% and let the contents of the layers below peek through to guide your painting tool.

4 View the Results

Here, I started with a mask created from a selection of Katerina and her cousin Erin, which I drew using the **Edge Seeker** tool. This mask allowed me to make the girls lighter with a histogram and curves adjustment while leaving the grass and sidewalk as it was.

Because this photo was taken at Erin's birthday party, I used the **Selection** tool to create a "window" of white in the mask so that I could inset an image of the birthday girl on a layer below. I added a soft feather to a square selection and filled the area with white. I copied the selection through the alpha channel to an image of Erin enjoying her birthday cake. This enabled me to copy an area that fit the window, leaving the rest of that layer transparent so that the girls (on a lower layer) would still show.

 TIP

As a final touch of whimsy, I cut out her cake from another image and pasted it on its own layer below the masked group. Using the **Deform** tool and the **Darken** blend mode for that layer, I was able to make it look as if Katerina was drawing a birthday cake in chalk. Because this layer was not part of the masked group, it was easy to place the cake under her arm.

---

130 Save and Reuse Masks

Paint Shop Pro comes with its own stash of reusable masks, mostly for adding framed or decorated edges to the perimeter of an image or an inset frame. The most reusable form of mask you can create is something that establishes a nice border. What might surprise you is that PSP's border masks, although numerous in shape, actually have a limited number of styles.

Before You Begin

✔ **74** About the Alpha Channel

✔ **125** About Masks

See Also

→ **75** Save a Selection for Reuse

Because a selected region can contain various degrees of selection, and a mask can contain various degrees of masking, when either one is stored to an image's alpha channel, PSP treats them *essentially the same*. Thus, you can save a selection and recall it later as a mask, or vice versa. Variable intensities recorded in a selection are recalled as varying shades of gray in the mask, and gray areas of a mask are recalled as variable degrees of selection. However, this is only true for alpha channels; masks stored to disk cannot be recalled as selections, nor vice versa.

A mask automatically stretches or shrinks to fill the size of the image into which it's loaded, so you don't have to worry about size when creating a frame mask.

In this task, I'll create my own frame mask that features wood grains for a realistic look and then save it for reuse. Because it's a mask and not a clip of an image, I can insert a raster layer below the frame layer to give the wood grain any color I need for the current image. Because the mask is based on real wood, whatever effect I choose will be somewhat realistic. This reusable mask is probably more convenient when saved separately to disk, although it can also be saved within the alpha channel of an image.

1 Create the Original Mask Content

Create a mask whose design is practical for use in multiple projects. For a frame, you'll want the mask to be completely whitened in its center, so that your image can appear there.

For my wood frame, I started with a photo of a wood table. I then adjusted the contrast and clarified the image a lot to draw out the grain pattern. After converting the image to grayscale, I created a rectangular center selection and filled it with white. To create the bevel, I saved the selection, created a larger selection, then recalled the inner selection and *subtracted* that from the larger rectangle. This left me with a narrow band that I then filled with white, but this time at only 50% opacity.

2 Create a Mask from the Image

For your mask image to be stored, PSP must recognize it as a mask layer. Select **Layers**, **New Mask Layer**, **From Image**. In the **Add Mask from Image** dialog box, select the **Source opacity** option and click **OK**.

3 Save the Mask

To save the mask so that you can use it with any image, select **Layers**, **Load/Save Mask**, **Save Mask to Disk**. Type a name for the mask and click **Save**.

To save the mask to the alpha channel of the image file in which the mask was created, select **Layers**, **Load/Save Mask**, **Save Mask to Alpha Channel**. To use the alpha-channel mask in any other image, however, you'll have to open the file that contains the alpha-channel mask first.

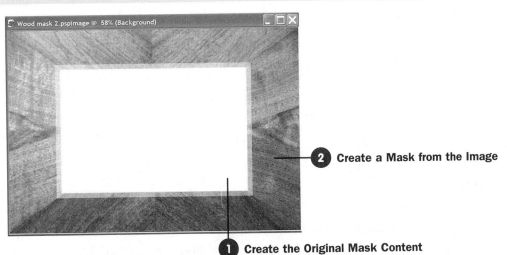

2 Create a Mask from the Image

1 Create the Original Mask Content

3 Save the Mask

4 Load the Mask

5 Select Mask Size

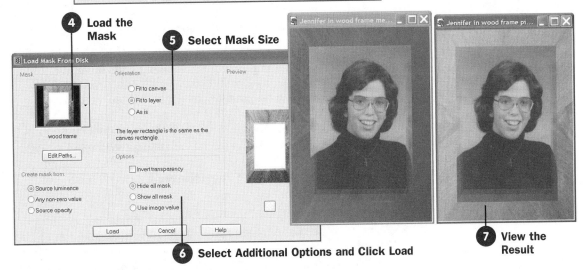

7 View the Result

6 Select Additional Options and Click Load

4 Load the Mask

Open the image in which you want to use the new mask. Select **Layers, Load/Save Mask, Load Mask From Disk** or **Load Mask From Alpha Channel**. If you're asked to promote the **Background** layer to a full layer, click **OK**.

If you're loading a mask from disk, select how you want the mask adjusted: To use the mask as is, select **Source luminance**. To have PSP change any gray values to white, select **Any non-zero value**. The **Source opacity** option turns the mask entirely white—which is the same as adding a **Show All** mask.

TIP

If you're loading a frame mask, you might want to resize the image to allow room for the frame. See **30** Change the Working Area Without Affecting Image Size.

5 Select Mask Size

To have PSP stretch the mask to fill the size of the image (the canvas), choose **Fit to canvas**. If the active layer is larger than the rest of the image, and you want the mask to fit just that layer, choose **Fit to layer**. To load the mask in its original size, choose **As is**.

A layer can be larger than the image canvas if you reduce the size of the image canvas after filling layers with data. Any non-**Background** layers with data already on them are left at their original, larger size—no data is lost, it's just hidden by the reduced size of the canvas.

TIP

After making your choices, click **Load**.

6 Select Additional Options and Click Load

If you selected the **As is** option for the mask size, you must select what happens to the area *outside* of the mask (if the mask is smaller than the canvas). To fill that area with black, select **Hide all mask**. To fill that area with white, select **Show all mask**. To fill the area with white or black depending on how the original mask was created (with **Hide All** or **Show All**), select **Use image value**. To invert the mask so that dark values are loaded as lights and vice-versa, enable the **Invert transparency** check box.

7 View the Result

When I placed the frame mask around this image, the parts that the mask hid appeared white (the color of the canvas). So I added a new raster layer and moved it under the masked layer group. I then filled the new layer with the color I wanted the wood frame to be: reddish brown for a cherry finish, soft yellow for pine, or dark brown for black walnut.

15

Creating Visual Effects

IN THIS CHAPTER:

TIP

The easiest way to experiment with special effects is to use the **Effect Browser**: choose **Effects, Effect Browser**. Most effects allow you to select from various presets, or to make your own adjustments to their settings. You can combine effects by applying them one after the other.

Up until now, the tasks in this book have focused on how to improve contrast, color balance, and sharpness for images, and how to repair damage caused by old age or improper storage. Now that you have improved your images to the point at which they look good, it's time to have some fun. Paint Shop Pro comes with a number of **Effects** filters, such as **Brush Stroke**, **Aged Newspaper**, **Colored Foil**, **Neon Glow**, **Hot Wax Coating**, **Balls and Bubbles**, **Kaleidoscope**, **Sandstone**, and **Rough Leather**. Most of these filters I'll leave for you to explore. Instead, in this chapter, you'll learn how to create your own effects, such as removing distractions (and fingers) from a photo, placing the subject on a new background, applying a romantic soft focus effect to an image, adding a picture frame, applying a decorative edge, distorting an image, combining images to create unique greeting cards or scrapbook pages, and pasting several images together to create a wide panorama.

131 Erase Part of a Layer

Before You Begin

✔ **10** About Tools and Tool Options

✔ **120** About Layers and the Layer Palette

See Also

→ **132** Remove Unwanted Objects from an Image

→ **133** Replace a Background with Something Else

NOTE

Even if a layer contains no transparent pixels, lower layers might show through if the top layer uses a lower **Opacity** setting or a **Blend** mode that favors the lower layer's pixels.

As you learned in **120** **About Layers and the Layer Palette**, you can create an image by building it up, one layer at time. When a layer is placed on top of another layer, it obscures the layer underneath, except in the places where the top layer is transparent. In those areas, the bottom layer peeks through. To create the top layer, you can start with a layer that's already transparent, and then copy or draw whatever you want on that transparent layer. The data you add to the layer blocks the data in that same spot on any layers below it in the layer stack. If you create a layer using a selection, the area around the selection will be transparent, again allowing the lower layers to peep through.

You can also create a new layer by copying an image or layer from someplace else; in such a case, the new layer might not have any transparent pixels. That's where this task comes in— here you'll learn how to use the **Eraser** tool to erase parts of a layer, creating transparent pixels wherever you brush.

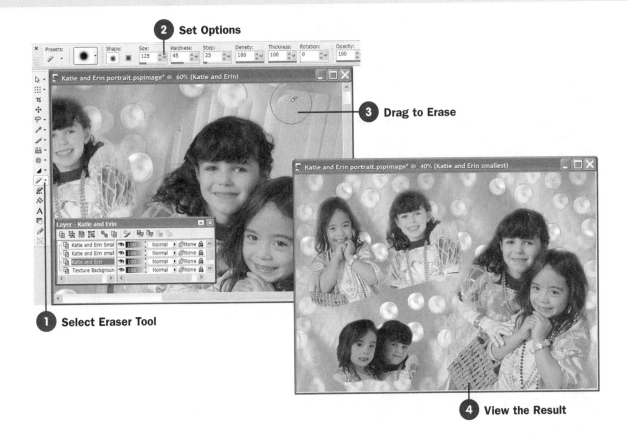

2 Set Options

3 Drag to Erase

1 Select Eraser Tool

4 View the Result

---

1 ### Select Eraser Tool

On the **Tools** toolbar, click the **Eraser** tool. (If it's not displayed, click the arrow on the **Background Eraser** tool and select **Eraser**.)

2 ### Set Options

On the **Tool Options** palette, select the brush tip, **Size**, **Hardness**, and other options you want. If you lower the **Opacity**, you'll only partially erase pixels as you drag over them (in other words, they'll become partially transparent).

NOTE

Because the **Background** layer does not allow transparent pixels, if you use the **Eraser** tool on it, you'll actually paint with the foreground color.

TIP

To erase pixels in a perfectly straight line, click at the beginning of the line you want to erase, press **Shift**, and click at the end of the line. A path of pixels the width of your **Eraser** between these two points is erased.

TIP

You can also erase pixels on a layer by selecting an area and pressing **Delete**.

③ Drag to Erase

In the **Layer** palette, change to the layer you want to erase—if you want to erase pixels from the **Background** layer (and not paint with the foreground color), you must promote it first by selecting **Layers, Promote Background Layer**. Click and drag with the **Eraser** tool. To prevent yourself from accidentally erasing something you don't want to, you can make a selection first—the **Eraser** works only within the selection. To "unerase" an area (restore pixels you erased earlier), drag with the right mouse button.

④ View the Result

By selectively erasing portions of three pictures, I was able to create a unique image of two little girls playing dress-up. I created the background, by the way, by copying a piece of the satin from one of the dresses, and adding pearls by applying the **Balls and Bubbles** filter (twice) and the **Pearls** preset.

132 Remove Unwanted Objects from an Image

Before You Begin

✔ **10** About Tools and Tool Options

See Also

→ **87** Repair Holes and Tears

→ **131** Erase Part of a Layer

→ **133** Replace a Background with Something Else

Using the **Clone Brush**, you can easily remove unwanted objects from an image, such as telephone poles, wires, trash cans, a thumb that wandered in front of the lens, or a few stray hairs blown in the wind, by simply copying over these distractions with pixels located somewhere else. To use the **Clone Brush**, you right-click on the image to indicate the source area, then you click or drag to paint with pixels copied from the source. Be sure to "cover your tracks," and avoid creating a noticeable pattern as you copy. The best way to do that is to lower the **Opacity**, **Density**, and **Hardness** settings so that the pixels you clone blend with existing pixels, paint with single clicks or very short strokes, use a large brush to avoid copying multiple times to the same area (but still small enough that you don't copy things you don't want), and vary the source area you're copying from by right-clicking to establish a new source point every so often.

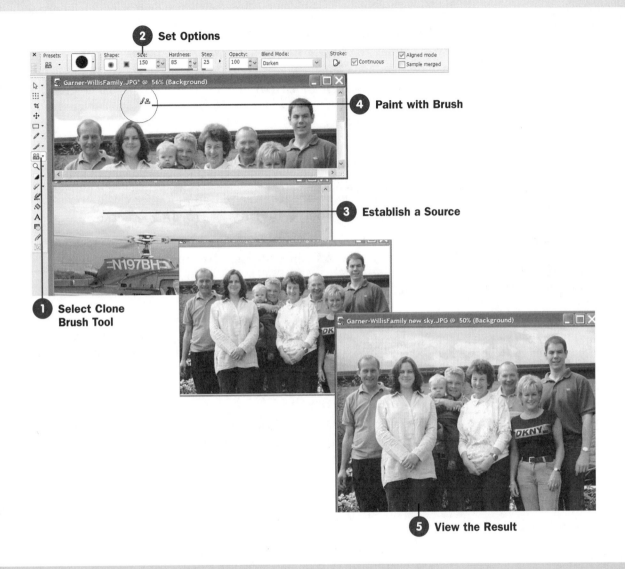

2 Set Options

4 Paint with Brush

3 Establish a Source

1 Select Clone Brush Tool

5 View the Result

The source you select for the **Clone Brush** can be located within a different image, a different layer, or the same layer. For example, you might clone the sky from one image into another to brighten up a washed-out white sky. Or you might clone a squirrel from one photo onto the head of your brother in another photo to create a comic image.

You might also be able to remove objects from an image in the same way you repair tears and holes. See **87 Repair Holes and Tears.**

① Select Clone Brush Tool

Click the **Clone Brush** tool on the **Tools** toolbar. (If it's not displayed, click the arrow on the **Scratch Remover** tool and select **Clone Brush**.)

② Set Options

In the **Tool Options** palette, select a brush tip, then enable the **Aligned mode** check box. Set other options as desired. For example, to copy visible pixels from a multilayered image, select **Sample merged**; to hide the "clone tracks," lower the **Opacity**, **Density**, or **Hardness** setting.

You can build up an area slowly by lowering the **Opacity** setting and disabling the **Continuous** check box. This allows you to paint the cloned pixels a little at a time with each brush stroke.

③ Establish a Source

Right-click on the same layer, a different layer, or in another image to establish the location of the source pixels.

④ Paint with Brush

Left-click on the image or drag with short strokes to copy pixels from the source. Repeat until the repair has been made or until the undesirable object has been removed.

⑤ View the Result

This photo of my friend Kate Garner and her family was snapped on a bright but overcast day. It's pretty good—the color is right, the image is sharp, and hey, everybody's smiling! But the all-white sky behind them looks like a large piece of cardboard. So I opened a photo taken in Hawaii—where the sky is never boring—and simply cloned it into the family portrait. I could have selected the sky area first so that I wouldn't accidentally clone over somebody's head, but instead I used the **Darken** blend mode, which tells the brush to paint over only those pixels that are lighter than the source. So the all-white sky gets painted over, but the

NOTE

With the **Aligned mode** option enabled, the source point changes from the original source in the direction you move the mouse. If the option is turned off, the source point never changes, and you copy the same pixels with each stroke.

TIP

To change the source as you brush, right-click a different area or press **Shift** and left-click.

darker hair and skin on the heads that happen to pop into the sky area do not.

133 Replace a Background with Something Else

One of the simplest special-effects tricks you can pull off is to remove the background from around a subject and replace it with something else. For example, are you the only one who didn't make it to a recent family reunion? There's no reason you have to remember that fact forever—just use the **Background Eraser** to remove the background from a recent photo of yourself and then replace the background with the reunion photo. After a few minutes' work, you'll be partying with your cousins. Of course, there are legitimate reasons for replacing an image background as well—if you have a photo of someone in a black suit against a dark background, you won't be able to do much using PSP's contrast controls to separate them visually. Better to select the subject and place him or her on a lighter background that provides more contrast.

Erasing the background from around a subject has typically been a time-consuming task, but Paint Shop Pro's new **Background Eraser** has some special options to help you do the job quickly. To control which pixels get erased, adjust the **Tolerance** and **Sampling** options: Typically **Auto Tolerance** (which adjusts the tolerance level on the fly, based on the color of the pixels you brush over) is your best bet; however you can set a **Tolerance** value manually if you like. Of the **Sampling** options, **Continuous** (which causes the brush to sample pixels located at the center of the brush tip at each step and erase matching pixels) is typically your best bet, although you might use **Once** (which samples pixels only when you first click), **ForeSwatch**, or **BackSwatch** (which erases pixels that match the current foreground or background color) occasionally.

1 Select Background Eraser Tool

On the **Tools** toolbar, click the **Background Eraser** tool. (If it's not displayed, click the arrow on the **Eraser** tool and select **Background Eraser**.)

Before You Begin

✔ **10** About Tools and Tool Options

See Also

→ **131** Erase Part of a Layer

→ **132** Remove Unwanted Objects from an Image

NOTE

Normally, the **Limits** value is set to **Contiguous**, which erases matching pixels under the brush tip *only if they touch the center pixel.* This might make it difficult to erase the background if it peeks through your subject (as the sky does through tree branches). Use **Discontiguous** in such a case. Use **Find Edges** to stop the erasure of matching pixels at any "edges."

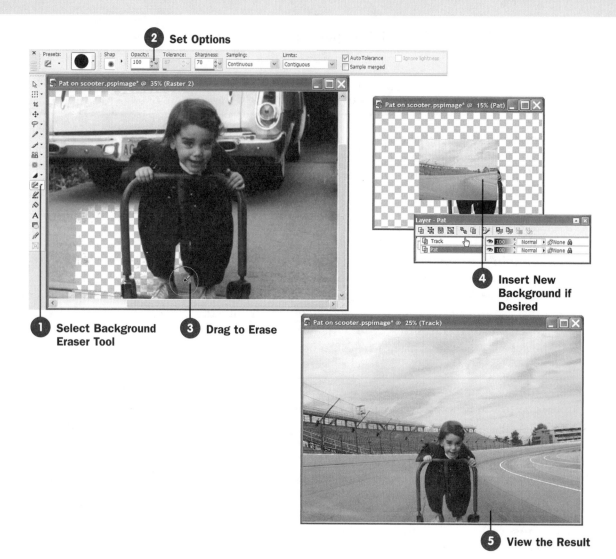

② Set Options

① Select Background Eraser Tool

③ Drag to Erase

④ Insert New Background if Desired

⑤ View the Result

 TIP

To include pixels from lower layers in the sample, enable the **Sample merged** check box. Enable the **Ignore lightness** check box to ignore differences in brightness and instead erase pixels of similar saturation.

② Set Options

On the **Tool Options** palette, select the brush tip, **Size**, **Hardness**, **Tolerance**, **Limits**, **Sampling**, and other options you want. If you lower the **Opacity**, you'll only partially erase pixels as you drag over them (in other words, they'll become partially transparent).

③ Drag to Erase

In the **Layer** palette, change to the layer you want to erase—if you want to erase pixels from the **Background** layer, you must promote it first by selecting **Layers, Promote Background Layer**. Click and drag with the **Background Eraser** tool. To "unerase" an area (restore pixels you erased earlier), drag with the right mouse button.

TIP

To prevent yourself from accidentally erasing something you don't want to, make a selection first—the **Background Eraser** erases only the pixels within the selection.

④ Insert New Background if Desired

After erasing the background from around a subject, you can replace it with something else if you like, or leave the transparent pixels so that you can place the image against a Web page background or on your Windows desktop. To replace the background, simply open the image you want to use as the background, click **Copy**, and then paste the new background to a new layer in the original image by selecting **Edit, Paste, Paste As New Layer**. In the **Layer** palette, drag this layer *below* the layer whose background you've erased. Resize and reposition the new layer if needed using the **Deform** tool.

⑤ View the Result

This image was a case of "had to do." My sister Pat let me borrow a wonderful image of her pushing a walker around our driveway, and when I looked at it, I couldn't help but imagine her racing someplace "sportier." What better background could I use than a photograph of the track out at the Indianapolis Motor Speedway? When I pasted the track background image onto a new layer in the scooter image, it automatically turned grayscale, so I didn't have to fuss with converting it first. (This is actually a picture of turn 1 at IMS, which veers to the left as you're coming into it, but because I wanted to show the turn behind Pat, I used the **Mirror** command to flip it vertically so that it looks like she is coming out of the turn and driving in the same direction the Indy cars do.)

134 **Create a Soft Focus Effect**

Before You Begin

✔ **120** About Layers and
the Layer Palette

✔ **131** Erase Part of a
Layer

See Also

→ **116** Blur a
Background to
Create Depth of
Field

 TIP

To soften the bright areas
in the background so that
they don't dominate the
image, be sure to enable
the **Include scattered light**
option.

NOTE

Although you can apply the
Soft Focus filter to a selection, you will probably not
like the result because it
won't blend well with the
rest of the layer, even if you
feather the selection.

 TIP

For a soft, blurry look, try
the **Dream, New morning,
Very soft,** or
Youthen/Youthen 2 preset.
For a more focused effect,
try **Soft portrait** or
Painting. For a big blur, try
Fog, Watercolor, or **Blurred
big halo.**

To apply a soft, romantic look to an image, you can use the **Soft
Focus** filter. This filter applies a soft blur to the entire layer or
selection and adds a glow around any bright areas it finds. The
filter comes with many presets to help you get started; you can,
of course, modify these settings as you like. The **Softness** and
Edge importance settings control the amount of overall blur
and the degree to which edges are blurred. A higher **Softness**
value causes more blur, while a higher **Edge importance** value
protects the edges from being blurred too much.

You can control the glow or halo that follows the contours of
objects in the image by adjusting the **Amount, Halo size,** and
Halo visibility settings. The **Amount** value controls the
strength of the glow; lower values cause the halo to appear only
around very bright areas. The **Halo size** setting controls the
width of the glow effect. To create a subtle glow, use a low **Halo
visibility** setting; higher settings create a more obvious glow
around bright areas. Because there are so many settings to
adjust, and because the **Soft Focus** filter blurs the entire layer or
selection, I like to control the effect somewhat by using it on a
duplicate layer, and then softly sharpening important features
such as a person's eyes, nostrils, and mouth. In this task, you'll
learn how to perform this same trick.

1 Duplicate Image

If the image has more than one layer, select the layer you
want to soften from the **Layer** palette. Then click the
Duplicate Layer button on the **Layer** palette, or select
Layers, Duplicate.

2 Select Soft Focus Filter

Select **Adjust, Softness, Soft Focus** from the main menu.
The **Soft Focus** dialog box appears.

3 Adjust Settings and Click OK

The easiest way to apply a soft focus is to open the **Presets**
list, select a preset, and then adjust the settings as desired.
Click **OK** to apply those settings.

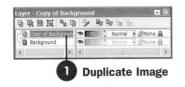

1 Duplicate Image

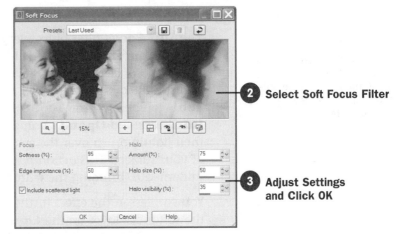

2 Select Soft Focus Filter

3 Adjust Settings and Click OK

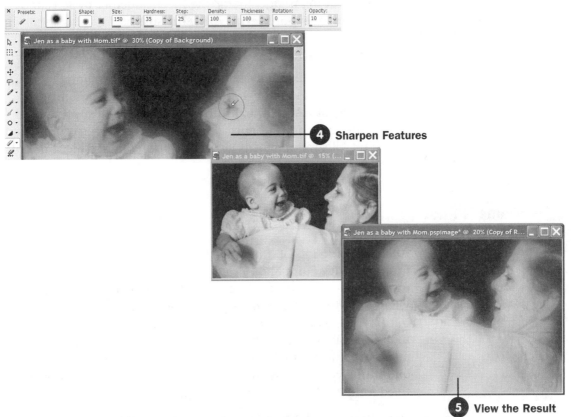

4 Sharpen Features

5 View the Result

TIP

If you sharpen too large an area, brush back over it using the right mouse button, which "unerases" the soft focus layer.

4 Sharpen Features

The **Soft Focus** filter blurs everything, including the features of your subject's face. This causes the image to lose impact because the viewer's eye depends on sharp features to distinguish a person. Select the **Eraser** tool from the **Tools** toolbar. On the **Tool Options** palette, lower the **Hardness** and **Opacity** values to create a soft brush, and then lightly brush over the eyes, nostrils, and mouth areas of your subject. This action reveals the original, sharp layer underneath, bringing the features back into focus.

You can lessen the effect further by lowering the **Opacity** of the soft focus layer on the **Layer** palette. After you're satisfied with the image, merge the layers together by selecting **Layers, Merge, Merge All (Flatten)**.

5 View the Result

I've always liked this picture of my mother smiling down on me as a young baby, but I thought a soft focus might improve it just a little. I started with the **Dream** preset and made some adjustments. Then I sharpened our features just a bit, placing the focus clearly on our looks of delight and love.

135 Frame a Photograph

See Also

→ **130** Save and Reuse Masks

→ **136** Add a Decorative Edge

After spending lots of time creating the perfect image, why not frame it? With Paint Shop Pro, it's easy to add a frame around any image—from large gilt to thin jet black, Paint Shop Pro provides you with many frame styles to choose from. Before adding a frame, you can even insert a single, double, or triple mat for that professional look. Obviously, you won't take the trouble to add a graphic "frame" around an image that you intend to print and frame yourself, but you might add a frame to an image destined for a card, scrapbook, or Web page.

You can also add a mat or picture frame to an image using Photo Album. Many of the offerings are similar to those you'll find in Paint Shop Pro, but some are different and worth a look.

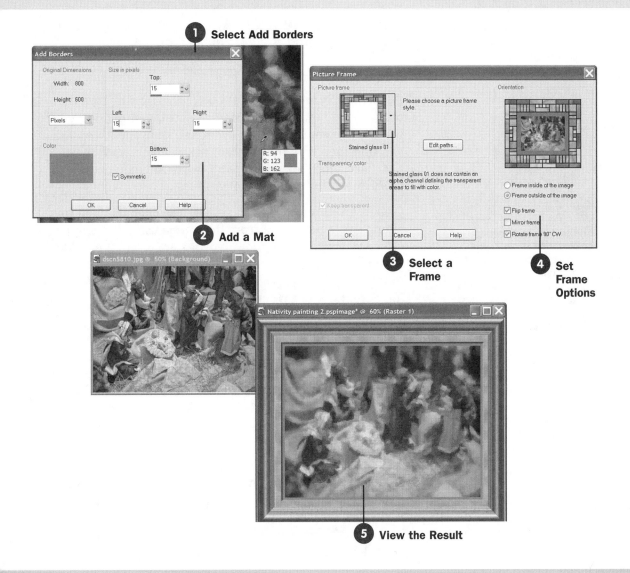

1 Select Add Borders

2 Add a Mat

3 Select a Frame

4 Set Frame Options

5 View the Result

Select **Effects, Add Border** to add a mat, or **Effects, Add Picture Frame** to add a frame in Photo Album.

1 Select Add Borders

If your image contains more than one layer, flatten the image so that you can add a mat by selecting **Layers,**

 TIP

Create your own reusable frame from any image, such as a bunch of lovely flowers or some fall leaves. See 130 **Save and Reuse Masks**.

Merge, Merge All (Flatten). Then select **Image, Add Borders.** The **Add Borders** dialog box appears.

② Add a Mat

Enable the **Symmetric** check box to make sure that the mat is added evenly to all sides. Select the dimension you want to use (such as pixels or inches) from the list on the left, and then type the width of the mat you want in the **Left** box. The **Top**, **Right**, and **Bottom** boxes change to this same value automatically.

Click the **Color** box, select a color, and click **OK**. You might want to pick up a color from the image using the dropper. Click **OK** to create the mat. Repeat steps 1 and 2 to add a second or third slightly larger mat. Add a beveled edge to a mat by selecting its area with the **Magic Wand** and choosing **Effects, 3-D Effects, Inner Bevel**.

③ Select a Frame

Select **Image, Picture Frame**. The **Picture Frame** dialog box appears. Open the **Picture frame** list and choose the frame style you like. The frame appears in the preview window so that you can see how it looks with the image (and the mat you just added).

④ Set Frame Options

To place the frame within the existing borders of the canvas (and possibly cover up part of the image), select **Frame inside of the image**. To automatically expand the canvas so that the frame does not cover any part of the image, select **Frame outside of the image**.

To flip the frame on its horizontal axis, select **Flip frame**. To flip the frame on its vertical axis, select **Mirror frame**. Rotate the frame clockwise by selecting **Rotate frame 90° CW**. Click **OK**.

⑤ View the Result

I started with a picture of my church's new Christmas nativity. I duplicated the background, blurred the outer area, and

TIP

Add texture to a medium-colored mat by selecting the mat area and filling it with a lighter-colored texture chosen from the **Materials** dialog box. You can also select a textured mat from those pictured in the **Picture Frame** dialog box.

NOTE

Some frames contain transparent areas you can fill with your own color. In such a case, turn off the **Keep transparent** option, click the **Transparent color** box, and select the color to use.

enhanced the edges of the nativity on the **Background** layer. I applied the **Brush Stroke** filter to the duplicate layer, adjusted the **Opacity** to blend the two layers, and create an nice-looking oil painting. Such effort deserves a beautiful frame, so I added an inner and outer mat (the outer mat sports a bevel and a texture I painted on), and selected the **Gold 01** frame. Look for this image in the Color Gallery in this book.

136 Add a Decorative Edge

If you don't like the formality of a frame, you can finish off an image with a decorative edge. Paint Shop Pro provides many edge styles to choose from—or you can create your own. To add a decorative edge from Paint Shop Pro's collection, you use the **Picture Frame** command as described in **135** **Frame a Photograph**. Just select one of the edge styles from the **Picture frame** list.

To apply your own edge to an image, you create a mask with the center painted white so that the image shows through. That's the technique you'll learn in this task. As you might recall, a mask works by partially blocking the data on the layers beneath it. Where a mask is white, the lower layers show through; where it is black, the lower layers are blocked from view. Gray allows the lower layers to show through at less than 100% opacity (semi-transparently).

You can create your decorative edge mask in one of two ways: You can start with a *Show All-mask* and then paint the edges black to obscure those parts of the image, or start with a *Hide All mask* and paint the parts of the center white where you want the image to show through. To make changes to the mask, you can use any of the painting or drawing tools such as the **Paint Brush, Airbrush, Warp Brush, Picture Tube Tool, Pen**, or **Preset Shapes**. You can create a selection and fill it with white, black, or gray using the **Flood Fill** tool. You can also use the **Text** tool to form a unique edge by creating white, black, or gray text. Any command that works on grayscale images can be applied to a mask as well, such as **Contours, Balls and Bubbles,** or **Cutout**.

Before You Begin

✔ **126** Create a New Mask

✔ **130** Save and Reuse Masks

See Also

→ **135** Frame a Photograph

TIP

You can add a decorative edge to your images in Photo Album. Simply open the image in **Image View** and select **Effects, Add Photo Edge**.

EY TERMS

Show All mask—An all-white mask through which the entire image appears.

Hide All mask—An all-black mask through which the entire image is prevented from appearing.

1 Add Mask Layer

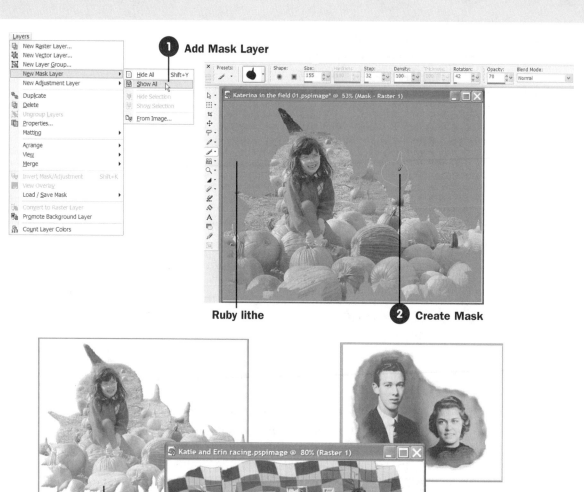

Ruby lithe

2 Create Mask

3 View the Result

1 Add Mask Layer

Select **Layers, New Mask Layer, Hide All** (if you want to paint to *reveal* the part of the image you want to show) or **Layers, New Mask Layer, Show All** (if you want to paint to *hide* the edge of the image). If you see a dialog box asking you to promote the layer, click **OK**.

2 Create Mask

On the **Layer** palette, change to the **Mask** layer if necessary. Then paint or fill an area with white to reveal the image; paint or fill an area with black to hide a portion of the image. Use gray to feather or partially obscure the edge.

 NOTE

If you want to see the mask, turn on the ruby lithe by clicking the **Mask Overlay Toggle** on the **Layer** palette, or selecting **Layers, View Overlay**.

3 View the Result

Here are three possible edge effects you might try. To edge the image of the girl in the pumpkin patch, I started with a **Hide All** mask, and then turned down its **Opacity** to reveal the image underneath. I then brushed white pumpkins and maple leaves in various sizes and **Rotation** angles along the edge of the part I wanted to show and filled the center of this area with white. If you look at the step-2 figure, you can see the special pumpkin brush I created just for this image; in the figure, I'm *stamping* instead of *brushing* with white paint on the **Mask** layer, which of course, reveals the image below the orange layer. After changing the orange layer to white (because I didn't like the color), I merged the layers and used the **Cutout** filter twice to enhance the edge of the masked shape by brushing the top-left edge with cream and the lower-right edge with dark green. By applying the highlight (cream) and shadow (dark green) colors that you select to opposite sides of the masked area, this filter gives the irregular shape a rounded, three-dimensional appearance.

To edge the image of Katerina and her cousin Erin racing pedal cars, I pasted sections of a checkered flag onto a new layer, overlapping them slightly until they filled the layer. (I could have used the flag itself as a mask, but I wanted small squares and more of them.) After pasting the sections onto the flag layer, I created a mask from it. The white

TIP

Create your own brush tips such as a maple leaf by selecting the leaf shape from an image of fall foliage. Save the selection as a new brush tip by clicking the **Create brush tip from selection** button in the **Brush Tip** list of the **Paint Brush** tool.

checks revealed the image below, and the black checks blocked it. I cut out a section in the center and filled it with white so that I would have a portion where the flag didn't appear. Then I changed the color of the black-and-white checks in various places, playing with the opacity of the mask. Finally, I merged the layers and erased around the edges, creating the flag shape.

The last image of my mother and father's graduation pictures was a little less ambitious. I first positioned the two images on different layers and then merged them, using the **Smudge** tool to blend the two photos at the edges. Next, I added a **Hide All** mask, drawing the edge I wanted using the **Freehand Selection** tool, feathering and filling the selection with white. After merging the result, I used the **Airbrush** tool to brush small wisps of black along the edges of the resulting image. Look for this trio of images in the Color Gallery in this book.

137 Change Perspective

See Also

→ **50** Straighten an Image

→ **51** Crop a Portion of an Image

→ **132** Remove Unwanted Objects from an Image

→ **138** Move, Alter, or Distort a Layer

NOTE

If you take a picture looking up instead of straight ahead (for images of tall objects such as buildings or monuments), you'll also get perspective distortion.

There will be times when you cannot face your subject head on and take a picture. Perhaps you tried to photograph a building from across the street, but to get all of the building in the photo, you had to stand off to one side so that you could step back far enough. The trouble is, you'd rather have a shot of the building looking straight at it. Luckily, you have Paint Shop Pro, and its **Perspective Correction** tool can fix just such an image.

The **Perspective Correction** tool works in a manner similar to the **Straighten** tool discussed in **50** Straighten an Image. When you click the tool, a rectangle bounding box appears. Place the four nodes of this box on the corners of the object whose perspective you want to correct, and Paint Shop Pro makes the appropriate adjustments. For example, you could place the nodes on the four corners of the front wall of the building whose image you want to correct, and after you click **Apply**, Paint Shop Pro adjusts the wall (and everything else in the image) by the exact same amount so that the wall ends up facing you straight on. To help you line up the nodes correctly, you can display additional gridlines within the bounding box.

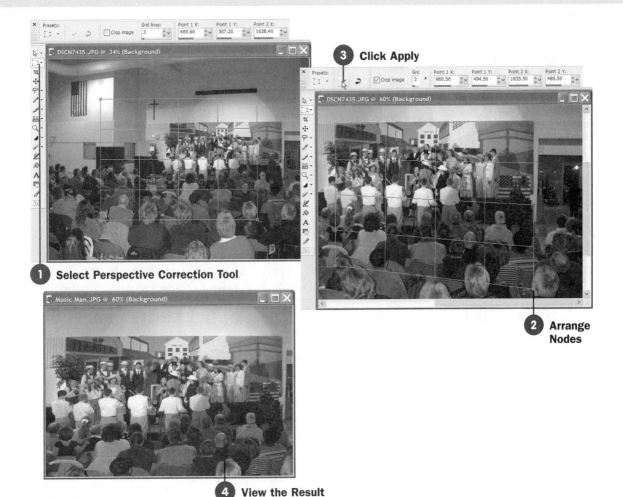

3 Click Apply

1 Select Perspective Correction Tool

2 Arrange Nodes

4 View the Result

1 **Select Perspective Correction Tool**

On the **Layer** palette, change to the layer you want to straighten. On the **Tools** toolbar, click the **Perspective Correction** tool. A bounding box appears on the image. To display additional gridlines, change the **Grid lines** value on the **Tool Options** palette.

NOTE

After the image perspective is changed, empty areas will appear along the sides of the image. You can have PSP crop the image for you by enabling the **Crop image** check box on the **Tool Options** palette. Alternatively, you can use the **Clone Brush** tool as explained in **132** Remove Unwanted Objects from an Image to "paint in" the empty areas with colors and details from other parts of the photograph.

NOTE

You can also change the perspective of an image if you know the exact angle of adjustment you want. Select **Effects, Geometric Effects, Perspective — Horizontal** or **Perspective — Vertical**.

2 **Arrange Nodes**

Drag each of the four nodes on the corners of the bounding box and place them on the four corners of the object you want to adjust.

3 **Click Apply**

Click **Apply**. PSP adjusts the perspective of the image. If you did not select the **Crop image** option to have PSP automatically crop the adjusted image, the areas created by the changes are filled with the current background color.

4 **View the Result**

My niece, Caitlin, recently appeared in her 8th grade's production of *Music Man*. My brother, Mike, brought his camera to record the event, but because he didn't want to disturb anyone in the audience, he stood off to one side. Using the **Perspective Correction** tool, I was able to change the perspective of the stage so that the resulting image looked as if he had stood right in front of the stage.

138 Move, Alter, or Distort a Layer

Before You Begin

 120 About Layers and the Layer Palette

See Also

→ **139** "Melt" an Image

EY TERMS

Skew—To tilt (sheer) a layer right, left, up, or down.

Distort—To stretch a corner of a layer in any one direction.

You can have a lot of fun with the **Deform** tool, although it has its serious side as well. On the serious side, the **Deform** tool can be used to reposition, resize, or rotate the data on a layer. This is especially useful when you copy an image to a layer because you'll typically have to resize and move it into a position that coordinates with the data on other layers. For fun, the **Deform** tool can be used to *skew* and *distort* a layer. When you click the **Deform** tool, a bounding box with four corner nodes appears. Additional nodes appear in the middle of each side of the bounding box. By dragging these nodes, you can resize, skew, or distort a layer. In the center of the bounding box is the rotation handle, which you can use to rotate the data on a layer.

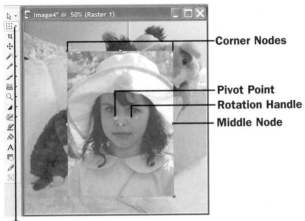

- Corner Nodes
- Pivot Point
- Rotation Handle
- Middle Node

1 Select the Deform Tool

2 Alter the Layer

3 View the Result

1 Select the Deform Tool

In the **Layer** palette, click the layer you want to alter. You cannot alter the **Background** layer, so if necessary, promote it to a regular layer by selecting **Layers, Promote Background Layer**. Select the **Deform** tool on the **Tools** toolbar. A bounding box appears on the layer. If you can't

NOTE

You can deform a selection if you first promote it to its own layer. Choose **Selections, Promote Selection to Layer**. See **79** **Copy a Selection to a New Layer**.

see the nodes on the bounding box, resize the image window to make it bigger than the canvas.

❷ Alter the Layer

To resize the layer, drag by a corner node. To resize a layer and retain its proportions (its aspect ratio), drag a corner node using the right mouse button.

To move the data on the layer around on the image canvas, click anywhere within the bounding box and drag.

To rotate a layer, drag the rotation handle. Normally, the layer rotates around its center, but you can move this pivot point by simply dragging it.

To skew a layer (tilt it), press **Shift** and drag a middle node the direction in which you want to tilt the layer. For example, to skew a layer so that it leans to the right, drag the middle node located on the top or bottom side of the layer to the right.

To distort a layer, press **Ctrl+Shift** and drag any of the nodes in any direction. The layer is stretched in the direction you drag.

❸ View the Result

I started here by taking a picture of a pillow on a sofa, surrounded by my daughter's special "puppets." Then I copied a picture of her to another layer above the pillow layer. I used the **Deform** tool to resize the portrait layer because it was so much larger than the rest of the image. Then I skewed and distorted the layer to match the outline of the pillow. A little erasing to reveal Spice Cat's head and paws and Spirit's feet, and a quick change to the **Multiply** blend mode, and the portrait pillow is complete. Look for this image in the Color Gallery in this book.

TIP

If you don't want to hold the **Shift** key as you skew a layer, change the **Mode** to **Shear** in the **Tool Options** palette. To distort a layer without holding **Ctrl+Shift**, change the **Mode** to **Free**.

"Melt" an Image

If you want to give parts of an image a Salvador Dali look, (the famous artist who loved melting clocks, violins, and other household objects, surreal, almost faceless people, and leafless, lonely trees), Paint Shop Pro has several tools you can try. The most powerful of these is the **Mesh Warp** tool, in which a meshlike grid is placed over the selection or layer. By dragging the nodes located at the grid intersections, you can pull pixels in any direction, warping the image.

If you want to be freer when warping an image, you can paint various warp effects onto an image with the **Warp Brush**. This tool is especially useful in blending the effect of the **Mesh Warp** on a selection with surrounding pixels. The **Warp Brush** is also handy when you want to warp a small area of an image. The **Warp Brush** features several types of warp modes, including **Push** (smears pixels in the direction you drag), **Expand** (pushes pixels out from the brush in all directions), **Contract** (the opposite of **Expand**), **Right Twirl** (rotates pixels clockwise around the center of the brush), **Left Twirl** (the opposite of **Right Twirl**), **Noise** (moves pixels under the brush in a random pattern), **Iron Out** and **Unwarp**. (Both remove the warp effect if it has not yet been applied; **Iron Out** works immediately whereas **Unwarp** works a little at a time, based on how long you hold the brush over a spot.) All the tools, with the exception of **Iron Out**, work very slowly; the longer you hold the brush in one spot, the more the effect warps that area.

1 Select the Mesh Warp Tool

To warp the entire current layer or selection, click the **Mesh Warp** tool on the **Tools** toolbar. If necessary, click the arrow on the **Deform** tool and select **Mesh Warp** from the list. A mesh grid appears over the image.

2 Set Options

In the **Tool Options** palette, make sure that the **Show grid** check box is enabled, then adjust the **Mesh horizontal** and **Mesh vertical** values to display the number of gridlines you want. To position the gridlines evenly both

See Also

→ Move, Alter, or Distort a Layer

TIP

There are many distortion filters you might try, such as **Wave, Ripple,** and **Wind;** you'll find them on the **Effects, Distortion Effects** submenu. The filters work on a selection or a layer. In addition, you can have fun with the **Smudge** and **Push** tools, which act like a finger smearing pixels of paint.

SNAPSHOT

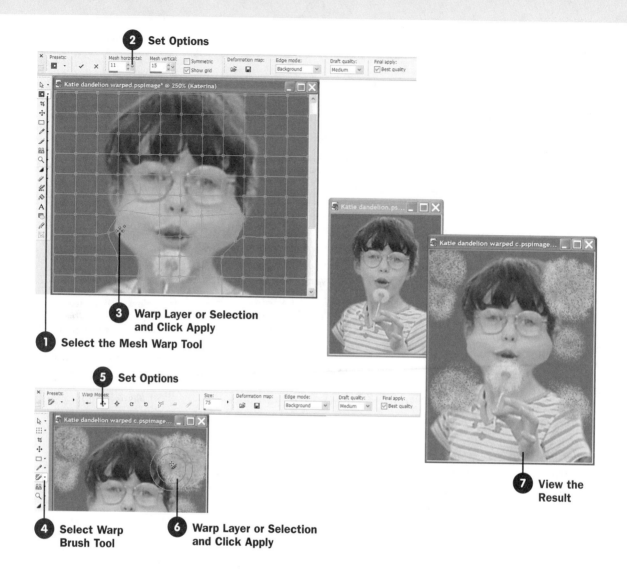

2 Set Options

3 Warp Layer or Selection and Click Apply

1 Select the Mesh Warp Tool

5 Set Options

4 Select Warp Brush Tool

6 Warp Layer or Selection and Click Apply

7 View the Result

vertically and horizontally, enable the **Symmetric** check box.

Adjust the **Draft quality** setting: **High** gives you a better quality onscreen while you work, but it takes more time for each adjustment to process. To work faster, choose **Low** or **Course**.

3 **Warp Layer or Selection and Click Apply**

Drag a mesh node to warp pixels under it. Reposition as many nodes as you like until you achieve the affect you want, then click **Apply** (the check mark in the **Tool Options** palette). To abort your changes, click **Cancel** (the X).

4 **Select Warp Brush Tool**

To warp selected areas of a layer or selection, click the **Warp Brush** tool on the **Tools** toolbar. If necessary, click the arrow on the **Paint Brush** tool and select **Warp Brush** from the menu.

5 **Set Options**

Select a **Warp Mode**. Adjust the **Size, Hardness, Strength**, and **Step** as desired. **Hardness** defines the size of the inner circle, in which the effect is produced at 100% of the **Strength** setting.

Adjust the **Draft quality** setting: In most cases, you should choose **Medium** because it provides good quality and speed. **High** gives you slightly better quality, but it takes more time for each adjustment to process. To work faster but with lower quality on the warp effect, choose **Low** or **Coarse**.

6 **Warp Layer or Selection and Click Apply**

Position the brush over an area and click. The effect gets stronger the longer you hold the brush over the same area. When you've warped the image as you like, or if you want to switch settings, click **Apply** (the check mark in the **Tool Options** palette). To abort your changes, click **Cancel** (the X).

7 **View the Result**

I had some fun here with an image of my daughter playfully blowing a dandelion at the camera. Using **Mesh Warp**, I stretched her cheeks to exaggerate her pose. I then painted dandelion puffs on another layer using the **Airbrush**, and then puffed them out using the **Warp Brush** set to **Expand**. Look for this image in the Color Gallery in this book.

 NOTE

If you save a map of your deformations and reload it on another image, *and the map is smaller than the image canvas*, the **Edge mode** you selected when you created the warp tells PSP how to fill the outer area between the map and the edge of the canvas: **Background** (outer area is filled with the background color if the deformation map is loaded on the **Background** layer, otherwise this area is made transparent), **Fixed** (pixels along the edge of the deformation map are duplicated and used to fill the outer area), or **Wraparound** (the outer area is filled with edge pixels copied from the other side of the deformation map).

 TIP

Press **Shift** when dragging a node to drag the entire row/column. Press **Ctrl** when dragging a node to create a gentle curve.

 TIP

You can also use the **Warp Brush** and **Mesh Warp** tools to warp bitmapped (raster) text.

140 **Blend Two Images into One**

Before You Begin

✔ **10** About Tools and Tool Options

✔ **120** About Layers and the Layer Palette

✔ **138** Move, Alter, or Distort a Layer

If you have two photographs with similar themes, you can blend them into one image using Paint Shop Pro. For example, you could blend a portrait of your recent graduate with a photo of him receiving his diploma. By using Paint Shop Pro's layer and blend mode features, you can create a ghostly image of one photo on top of the other. For example, you could place the faint image of your son's face off to one side, quietly contemplating the significance of his great accomplishment.

1 Copy Secondary Image to a Separate Layer

Open the main image, such as an image of a high school. Open the secondary image, such as a graduation portrait, and select **Edit, Copy**. Change to the main image and select **Edit, Paste, Paste as New Layer**. A copy of the secondary image appears on a layer above the main image layer. Name this new layer **Secondary**. Close the secondary image because it is no longer needed.

2 Resize and Position Secondary Image

Change to the **Secondary** layer. Click the **Deform** tool and drag a corner node with the right mouse button to resize the new layer proportionately, as needed. Click in the middle of the secondary image and reposition it on the **Secondary** layer so that its location complements the main image.

> **NOTE**
>
> If you can't see the corner nodes when trying to resize a layer with the **Deform** tool, you can enter the percentage by which you want to reduce the secondary image in the **Deform** tool's **Scale X (%)** and **Scale Y (%)** boxes on the **Tool Options** palette.

3 Change Layer Blend Mode to Hard Light

On the **Layer** palette, change the **Blend Mode** for the **Secondary** layer to **Hard Light**. The **Secondary** layer appears as a ghost over top of the main image.

4 Clean Up Secondary Layer and Merge

On the **Layer** palette, change to the **Secondary** layer if necessary. Then click the **Background Eraser** tool on the **Tools** toolbar and remove any portions of the layer you don't want to use in the final image. For example, you might erase the background from around a person's portrait.

1 Copy Secondary Image to a Separate Layer

2 Resize and Position Secondary Image

3 Change Layer Blend Mode to Hard Light

4 Clean Up Secondary Layer and Merge

5 View the Result

On the **Layer** palette, adjust the **Opacity** of the **Secondary** layer to make it appear even more ghostly. When you're satisfied with the effect, select **Layers, Merge, Merge All (Flatten)**.

5 **View the Result**

I decided to show you two examples of this technique, one sedate, the other more playful. The first image blends a graduation portrait of my Mom with a picture of her old high school. The second image blends three photos: a close-up of a leaf after a morning rain, my daughter Katerina the ballerina, and a larger Katie seemingly touching the smaller image trapped in a rain drop.

141 Create a Panorama

Before You Begin

✔ **2** Create a New Image

✔ **120** About Layers and the Layer Palette

✔ **138** Move, Alter, or Distort a Layer

⬥NOTE

The 2" × 11" size is adequate for an eight-image horizontal panorama; feel free to adjust these measurements to fit your needs.

Some places, such as the Grand Canyon, the Great Smoky Mountains, or the Vietnam Veterans Memorial in Washington D.C., are just too large to photograph with a single shot. That shouldn't stop you from trying to capture their majesty, however. If you carefully take a series of overlapping photographs, you can use Paint Shop Pro to "stitch" them together into a single, panoramic image.

1 **Create a New Image**

Select **File, New** or click the **New** button on the **Standard** toolbar. Set the **Image Dimensions** to 2" high by 11" wide. Specify a **Resolution** of 300 pixels per inch for print or 100 for onscreen use. Select a white background and click **OK**. Save the image in PSP format with the name **Panorama**.

2 **Copy First Image to Its Own Layer**

Open the image you want to place on the left in your panorama and select **Edit, Copy**. Change to the **Panorama** image, select the top layer from the **Layer** palette, and select **Edit, Paste as New Layer**. Rename the new layer **Pan 1**.

3 **Resize and Position the Pan 1 Layer**

Click the **Deform** tool on the **Tools** toolbar. Change to the **Pan 1** layer and resize it to fit the **Panorama** image by dragging a corner node *with the right mouse button*.

1 Create a New Image

3 Resize and Position the Pan 1 Layer

2 Copy First Image to Its Own Layer

4 Copy, Resize, and Position Additional Images

5 Merge and Crop the Final Image

6 View the Result

TIP

To make the process of resizing and placing the images easier, enlarge the canvas so that it's larger than the **Panorama** image. See **30** Change the Working Area Without Affecting Image Size.

To make the images fit together perfectly, make use of the **Deform** tool's capability to rotate and skew a layer.

You can create a panorama easily using Photo Album. Select the images to use and then click the **Panorama** button. Click the **Settings** button, select the options you want, and then click the **Create** button.

Reposition the **Pan 1** layer along the left side of the image window.

④ Copy, Resize, and Position Additional Images

Repeat steps 2 and 3 to copy each additional image in your panorama to its own layer. Resize and position each image so that the images overlap. To make it easier to position each additional image, temporarily reduce its **Opacity** on the **Layer** palette, and then return it to 100% before placing the next image.

⑤ Merge and Crop the Final Image

Chances are you had to rotate or skew at least one or two images to meld them with their neighbors. If necessary, use the **Eraser** tool to gently remove portions of overlapping layers that do not meet up perfectly. After positioning each layer precisely, merge the result into a single layer by selecting **Layers, Merge, Merge All (Flatten)**. Click the **Crop** tool on the **Tools** toolbar and crop the result, removing any empty regions.

⑥ View the Result

After stitching together eight separate images, I'm left with a panorama of a suburban neighborhood.

16

Creating Artistic Photographs

IN THIS CHAPTER:

The first step to turning a photograph into a work of true art is to capture the perfect composition. This isn't a task that Paint Shop Pro can help you with; only you have the ability and skill to manipulate the light, steer the subject, anticipate the perfect moment, and produce a scene that attracts the adoration of people's eyes. But after you've done that, you can manipulate your composition so that it appears—at least partly—to have been rendered by hand instead of by pixel. In these tasks, you'll learn how to make a photograph look old, hand-painted, or rendered in pastels, oils, pencils, or watercolors.

142 Age a Photograph

Before You Begin

✔ **59** Select a Rectangular, Circular, or Other Standard-Shaped Area

✔ **97** Improve a Dull, Flat Photo

✔ **122** Create an Adjustment Layer

See Also

→ **143** Change a Color Photograph to Black and White

→ **144** Colorize a Photograph

NOTE

PSP has a special **Sepia Toning** filter, which you'll find on the **Effects, Artistic Effects** menu. Try it out if you want, but in this task you'll learn to do a much better job in just a few more steps.

Although ancient photographs are generally identifiable by their rich sepia tones and over-extended contrasts, these effects were not caused by aging. In fact, ironically, well-preserved daguerreotypes of the late 1800s are probably more true to their original appearance than an equally well-preserved Kodak Brownie-box snapshot of the 1930s. If you have a modern photo that you'd like to cast in a 19th century motif, Paint Shop Pro gives you the tools you need not only to simulate the daguerreotype tones of that period, but also to give your photo just the right amount of distress.

In this task, you'll create an old-time oval frame (on a separate layer), and apply a sepia-like finish with dark brown edges to the image, which is typical of old photos of that time. Two additional characteristics typify 19th century photography: blemishing—as a result of imperfectly ground lenses—and over-dramatized contrasts caused by overexposure. For best results, choose a portrait-like photo (a school or portrait studio image works best). Adjust its brightness and contrast in the usual manner before you begin this task—I'll show you how to strengthen the contrast in the steps. For an authentic look, you might want to replace the background of the image with a dark brown sunburst gradient before you start the task.

① Create an Oval Frame

Promote the background layer (so that you can manipulate it) by selecting **Layers**, **Promote Background Layer**.

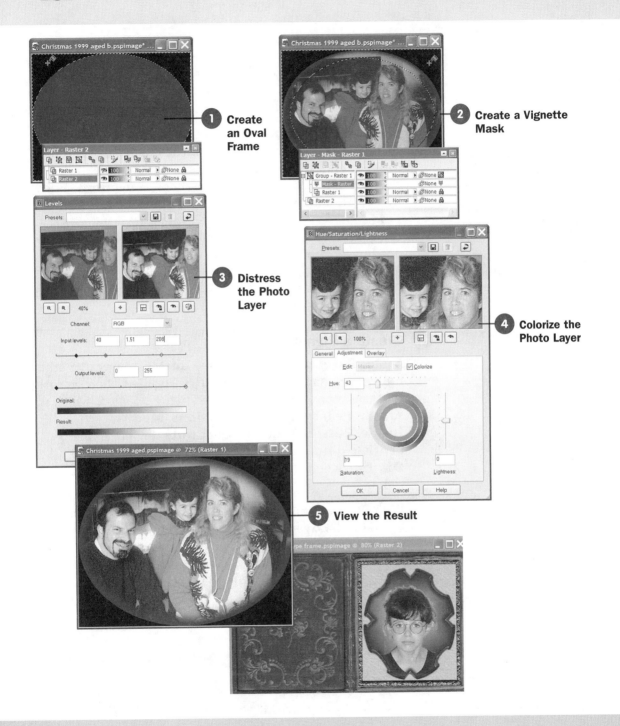

1 Create an Oval Frame

2 Create a Vignette Mask

3 Distress the Photo Layer

4 Colorize the Photo Layer

5 View the Result

Then create the frame layer (**Layers**, **New Raster Layer**). Move the frame layer to the bottom of the stack in the **Layer** palette. So that you can see what you're doing on the frame layer, click the **Visibility Toggle** button on the **Raster 1** layer (the former **Background**) to off.

Choose the **Selection** tool from the **Tools** toolbar, choose **Ellipse** selection type, and set **Feather** to 0. On the frame layer, drag to select a large oval area in the center. (If the selection is not perfectly centered, choose **Selections**, **Edit Selection** and use the **Move** tool to adjust it.) Use the **Flood Fill** tool to fill the selection with a reddish-brown color {RGB: 79, 54, 11}. The reddish-brown area will help to age the edges of the image later on. Save this selection (**Selections**, **Load/Save Selection**, **Save Selection to Alpha Channel**). Invert the selection (**Selections**, **Invert**) and flood the corners with pure black.

NOTE

You can mat your image in shiny gold like the old daguerreotypes by filling the corners of your frame with gold instead of black {RGB: 255, 222, 121}. Feather the selection by 8 and add the **Effects**, **Artistic Effects**, **Hot Wax Coating** filter three times to the selection to make gold.

② Create a Vignette Mask

On the **Layer** palette, choose the **Raster 1** layer (the original image), and click the **Visibility Toggle** button on so that you can see its contents. Modify the selection (which is still inverted) by choosing **Selections**, **Modify**, **Inside/Outside Feather**. Select **Outside** and set the **Feather amount** to a fairly high number, such as 35. Click **OK**. This action selects the corners and a bit of the oval center.

With the **Raster 1** layer selected, create a **Show All** mask by selecting **Layers**, **New Mask Layer**, **Show All**. With the **Flood Fill** tool, fill the selection with black. This masks the photo so that only the center portion of the oval interior shows through, feathered along the edges with the reddish-brown color used in step 1.

NOTE

When you add **Random** noise to an image, the colors of the noise pixels are chosen at random. But the colors of **Uniform** and **Gaussian** noise pixels are determined based on the colors of surrounding pixels. As a result, these two noise options can smooth out an otherwise erratic or jagged histogram.

③ Distress the Photo Layer

On the **Layer** palette, choose **Raster 1** and deselect everything (**Selections**, **Select None**). Select **Adjust**, **Add/Remove Noise**, **Add Noise**. Select the **Gaussian** option, and set the **Noise** value to 10%. Click **OK**.

To overdo the contrast for an old-time look, select **Layers**, **New Adjustment Layer**, **Levels**. Select the **RGB** channel, and drag the gamma marker (the center diamond) *to the left*. For this example, I set gamma to 1.51. Next, narrow the input levels for the white and black points by dragging the markers inwards. Come close to the first hash marks on either side, but don't go over. Click **OK**. Finally, select **Adjust**, **Sharpness**, **Sharpen More**.

④ Colorize the Photo Layer

To control the sepia coloring, create an adjustment layer: With **Raster 1** still selected, choose **Layers**, **New Adjustment Layer**, **Hue/Saturation/Lightness**. Enable the **Colorize** check box. Set **Hue** to 43 and **Saturation** to 19. (These values create the most convincing sepia color, in my opinion, but feel free to make adjustments for your image.) Click **OK**.

⑤ View the Result

Perhaps the smiles in this first image detract from its antiquated appearance—it seems that people hardly ever smiled in photographs back then! But the combination of the **Gaussian** noise and **Sharpen More** filters resulted in some quaint specks and slight, though bearable, defects that lend to the aged look.

I had so much fun creating the first example that I did another so that you could compare the look of a gold mat and daguerreotype frame. Look for these two images in the Color Gallery in this book.

TIP

You can double-click the **Hue/Saturation/Lightness** layer to redisplay the dialog box and make further adjustments. You can also adjust the **Opacity** setting of the adjustment layer to lessen the sepia-tone effect.

---

143 Change a Color Photograph to Black and White

Although it literally takes one step to convert any color image to grayscale (**Image**, **Greyscale**), there's no guarantee that the result will be an attractive image. Professional photographers know that to get the best black-and-white print, you must use special black-and-white film; if you shoot an image in color and then print it in black and white, the image no longer contains the same points of drama and impact.

Before You Begin

✔ **124** Merge or Flatten Layers Into One

See Also

→ **71** Select a Portion of an Image with Channels

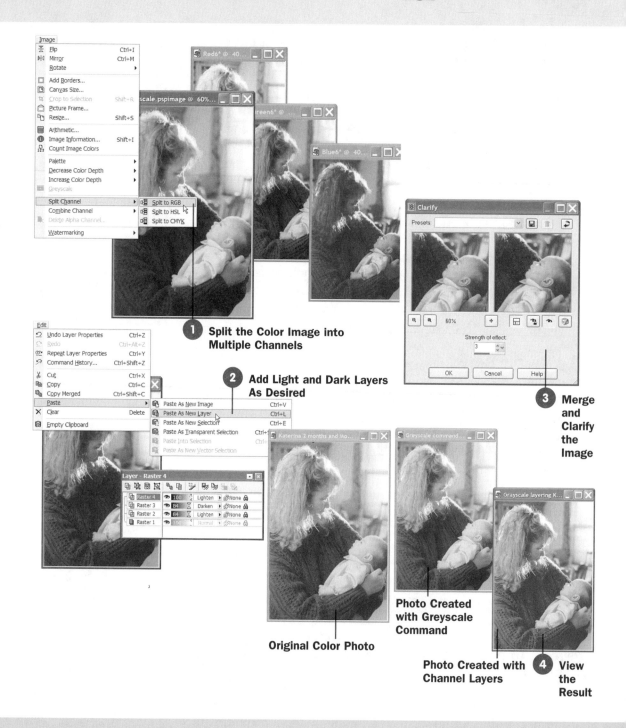

1 Split the Color Image into Multiple Channels

2 Add Light and Dark Layers As Desired

3 Merge and Clarify the Image

Original Color Photo

Photo Created with Greyscale Command

Photo Created with Channel Layers

4 View the Result

By separating a color image into channels, you have an opportunity to isolate each of the most dramatic elements of an image into a monochrome plane of its own. Sunlight bouncing off a subject, for example, shows greater reflectivity on some channels than on others. Low-level light bouncing off a colored object shows up as middle gray on one or two channels, black on the others. Those dark areas can provide both drama and balance in the final image. With the method you're about to see, you can pick and choose the lights and darks you want to create the perfect black-and-white image.

 NOTE

For best results, do the normal brightness, contrast, and color corrections on your color photo before splitting it into channels as directed in the task.

❶ Split the Color Image into Multiple Channels

Open your image and select **Image**, **Split Channel**, **Split to HSL**. Close the **Hue** and **Saturation** windows and save the **Lightness** window with the name **Grayscale**.

Change back to the color image, and select **Image**, **Split Channel**, **Split to RGB**. Analyze these three channels to determine which ones provide the most dramatic lights and darks; the **Lightness** channel (the renamed **Grayscale** image) will provide the middle grays. Close any windows you don't like, and the color image window as well, because you don't need it anymore.

TIP

If none of the Red, Green, or Blue channels offer anything with high black-and-white contrast, try the **Image, Split to CMYK** command. Close the **Black** channel and invert the **Cyan, Magenta, and Yellow** channels by selecting **Adjust, Negative Image.**

❷ Add Light and Dark Layers As Desired

To borrow the dramatic lights from one of the channel images, activate that image and select **Edit, Copy**. Change to the **Grayscale** image. On the **Layer** palette, choose the topmost layer. Select **Edit**, **Paste**, **Paste As New Layer** to paste in the copied data. Change the **Blend Mode** of the new layer to **Lighten** for a nominal effect or to **Screen** for a bolder effect.

To borrow the darks from one of the channel images, follow the preceding instruction to copy and paste it as the top layer in the **Grayscale** image. Then change the **Blend Mode** to **Darken** for a nominal effect or to **Multiply** for a bolder effect.

Adjust the **Opacity** for each new layer to control how *much* of the light or dark effect it contributes to the final image.

TIP

If the final product of your channel layering needs a contrast adjustment, add an adjustment layer to the top of the layers stack by selecting **Layers, New Adjustment Layer, Levels**. See **97** **Improve a Dull, Flat Photo**.

Repeat this step for as many channel layers as you care to add.

③ Merge and Clarify the Image

When you're satisfied with your layered result, select **Layers**, **Merge**, **Merge All (Flatten)**. All the layers are merged into a single **Background** layer.

Finally, select **Adjust**, **Brightness and Contrast**, **Clarify**. Set the **Strength of effect** value to no higher than 3 and click **OK**. This setting brings back some of the intermediate gray values that the preceding adjustments and mergers tend to cancel out.

④ View the Result

When you compare the image created using the **Greyscale** command with the one created through channel layering, you'll immediately notice a greater depth of shadows, midtones, and highlights. What layering in this manner gives you that ordinary grayscaling doesn't is the ability to retain the natural glowing edges and deep shadows that existed in the color version of this photograph.

144 Colorize a Photograph

Before You Begin

✔ **64** Select Areas of Similar Color, Brightness, or Opacity

✔ **75** Save a Selection for Reuse

✔ **107** Adjust Hue, Saturation, and Lightness Manually

✔ **117** Remove Distracting Detail

See Also

→ **135** Frame a Photograph

→ **142** Age a Photograph

There's no perfect way to truly convert a black-and-white photograph—especially an old one—into an image that's both colorfully rich and colorfully accurate. So you have to concede at the outset that what you're working on is an artistic interpretation—an old-time hand-painted color rendition of a black-and-white original. Like those artists of the past, you get to choose what colors you want to wash over each region of your image. What you want to avoid, however, is a paint-by-number look—especially difficult when colorizing the skin because you can choose no single hue that will give you a natural look. Luckily, I have several techniques I can pass on that will give you a finished image to rival efforts you might have to pay hundreds of dollars for.

In a nutshell, you'll first select major regions in the image, such as an article of clothing, a tree trunk, or an exposed part of the

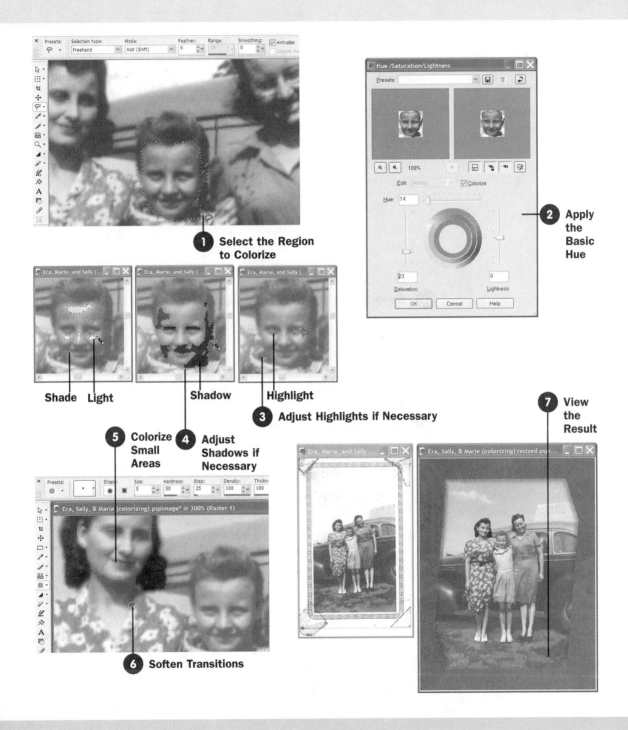

① Select the Region to Colorize

② Apply the Basic Hue

Shade Light Shadow Highlight

③ Adjust Highlights if Necessary

⑦ View the Result

⑤ Colorize Small Areas

④ Adjust Shadows if Necessary

⑥ Soften Transitions

body (such as the head and neck together, an arm, or a leg). Then you'll apply a single hue such as light green. Skin is the hardest to colorize, as you'll see when you apply a single color to the face. The result is quite unrealistic and flat looking. To give a person the illusion of depth and to make the colorizing effect more realistic, you'll then select smaller areas of the skin—the shadows and highlights—and tint them with blue (for the shadows) or yellow (for the highlights) to make them appear to recede or come forward. You can repeat this process for inanimate objects as well, if you feel they do not look very realistic after applying a single hue. After colorizing large areas, you'll select smaller areas, such as jewelry or lips, and colorize them with a single hue. Finally, you'll use the **Soften** tool where needed to soften harsh edges between color regions.

① Select the Region to Colorize

Choose the region to colorize using any selection tool. To make it easier for you to make alterations to this same region later on, save the selection to the image's alpha channel by choosing **Selections, Load/Save Selection, Save Selection to Alpha Channel**.

② Apply the Basic Hue

Select **Adjust**, **Hue and Saturation**, **Hue/Saturation/Lightness**. Enable the **Colorize** check box. Adjust the **Hue** value to the color you want to apply. The middle color ring indicates the hue you are applying *at full strength*. If you're colorizing a skin area, try a value of 10 to 18 for Caucasian skin tones, 16 to 26 for African and Middle Eastern skin tones, or 26 to 32 for Asian skin tones. Next, set the **Saturation** slider to adjust the amount of hue to apply. Darker skin requires heavier **Saturation** values than lighter skin; usually, you need to saturate Caucasian skin by no more than 20, for African skin, you might require a **Saturation** value of as much as 40. A very slight **Lightness** adjustment of no more than +5 might be necessary when applying heavy saturation in a scene with direct sunlight. Click **OK**.

③ Adjust Highlights if Necessary

For skin and some inanimate objects, it's necessary to add more color to the highlight and shadow areas to create a realistic effect. If you're not colorizing a skin area, skip steps 3 and 4. Choose **Selections**, **Select None** to cancel all selected areas. Choose the **Magic Wand** from the **Tools** toolbar. On the **Tool Options** palette, set **Mode** to **Add (Shift)**, **Match Mode** to **Brightness**, and **Tolerance** to a low value above zero—I do well with 4. Then select the brightest/lightest areas of the object so that you can adjust the colors for these areas separately.

Next, select **Adjust**, **Hue and Saturation**, **Hue/Saturation/Lightness**. This time, *disable* the **Colorize** check box. Depending on the strength of the light, set the **Hue** slider to a value from 16 to 21. This setting adds a more yellow tint to the selected region. If necessary, *reduce* the **Lightness** value by setting it to a value no lower than −3 to prevent the yellower patch from standing out too prominently. Click **OK**.

④ Adjust Shadows if Necessary

Choose **Selections**, **Select None** to cancel all previous selections. This time, select the darkest/shadow regions of the object using the **Magic Wand**. For a face, these areas include the underside of the nose, the "rim" of the face, the unlit sides of the cheeks, and the shadows cast by sockets over the eyes and, most notably, the chin over the neck.

Select **Adjust**, **Hue and Saturation**, **Hue/Saturation/Lightness**. With the **Colorize** check box disabled, set the **Hue** slider to a value from 6 to 9. If necessary, reduce the **Saturation** value slightly to prevent a blue color cast over the region. Click **OK**.

⑤ Colorize Small Areas

Repeat steps 1 through 4 to colorize all the large areas of the image. Small features such as blue eyes and red lips should be handled separately. Select the small area you want to colorize and then choose the

NOTE

The highlights you select in step 3 should generally reflect the greatest amount of light—for a face, the sides of cheeks facing the sun, the tip of the nose, the front of the forehead. For a solid object, select the areas that reflect the most direct light or that include glares or streaks.

TIP

You don't have to colorize every object in your image. In my example, I left the shingled rooftop just the way it was.

Hue/Saturation/Lightness command again. Enable the **Colorize** check box. For eyeballs (excluding the pupil) and teeth, reduce **Saturation** to a value *near but above* 0. Natural lips require a **Hue** setting of about 10 for Caucasian and 14 for African and Asian, with a **Saturation** of about 25. Ruby-red lipstick requires a **Hue** setting of about 5 and **Saturation** turned up to 40. Click **OK**.

6 Soften Transitions

One of the unwanted side effects of colorizing elements adjacent to one another—for instance, a person's neck and a blouse's neckline—is the appearance of harsh borders. You can easily eradicate this with a quick application of the **Soften** tool. See **117** Remove Distracting Detail.

7 View the Result

This vintage World War II era photograph clearly needed some repairs to begin with. First of all, probably because Brownie-box cameras were often held at chest level, the entire picture was shot at a 5 degree angle to the ground. I straightened that first, and then replaced the flat white sky with a more interesting one.

NOTE

The final product does not appear like an original color print, and probably wouldn't unless I were to spend a lot more time using spot tools such as the **Paint Brush** and **Airbrush** for detail. For demonstration purposes, I went for an effect that was simply pleasing to the eye.

The skin tones for these three sisters were nearly identical, using a **Hue** setting of 14 with **Saturation** settings between 20 and 24. The dresses for Aunt Sally in the middle and Great Aunt Marie on the right were easily colorized with single hues. For my husband's grandmother on the left, who always wore bright red, I spent more time selecting the darker flowers from the print and coloring them with a deep red (Hue: 3). I left the white flowers as they were, but colorized their centers with a violet shade.

The station wagon was a pre-war, two-tone Buick. Two-tone cars of that time were capped with either silver or copper, so I used artistic license and chose copper. I tinted the reflective spots in the black zones of the car—especially the front fender—slightly toward the yellow, using the same method I used for the skin tones. I could have replaced the ground with one from a recent photo, but I didn't. Instead, I kept the vintage Oklahoma oilfield "turf," consisting of patches of grass surrounded by dusty red clay.

After colorizing the photo, I could have cropped the image to square it up, but I would have lost both fenders, the hubcap, and all the curves of the Buick, which lend character to the photo. So I instead invented this whimsical, yet symmetrical, frame for it. See **135** **Frame a Photograph**. Look for this image in the Color Gallery in this book.

145 Make a Photograph Look Like an Oil Painting

I've learned quite a bit about oil painting since I married a painter who is the son of a professional artist. I've made a few real oil paintings myself; my husband, a few more. His mother, Maria DeLaJuen, a few *thousand* more. What distinguishes oil from acrylic are the variations in its textures and the fact that colors blend with one another on the canvas. By comparison, acrylic brushstrokes are more uniform in texture and more solid in color.

Paint Shop Pro does a fairly good job of simulating the technical characteristics of oil painting, but you can't expect it to emulate the style and creative expression of a professional artist. To see just how good a job it does, I created a unique test: On my office wall is an original 2001 DeLaJuen oil painting called *Bird Dance*. On my computer is the real digital photograph upon which *Bird Dance* was based; for the painting, my mother-in-law Maria printed the photo and taped it to her easel for reference. Could I make PSP simulate even a few of Maria's techniques, and somehow make the original photograph resemble an oil painting? The result was surprisingly good, albeit not as good as a real oil painting.

1 Apply the Edge Preserving Smooth Filter

Blur the original photograph (while preserving object outlines) by selecting **Adjust**, **Add/Remove Noise**, **Edge Preserving Smooth**. Set **Amount of smoothing** to a fairly high value for a still life, such as 30. For a portrait, use a lower number such as 15. Click **OK**.

Before You Begin

✔ **56** Adjust Saturation Automatically

✔ **86** Remove Specks and Spots

✔ **112** About Sharpness

✔ **119** Smooth an Image Without Losing Crisp Edges or Texture

See Also

→ **146** Turn a Photograph into a Watercolor

1 **Apply the Edge Preserving Smooth Filter**

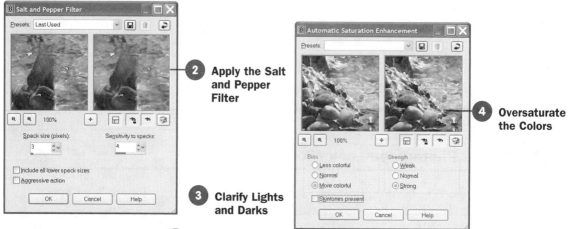

2 **Apply the Salt and Pepper Filter**

3 **Clarify Lights and Darks**

4 **Oversaturate the Colors**

5 **Apply the Brush Strokes Filter**

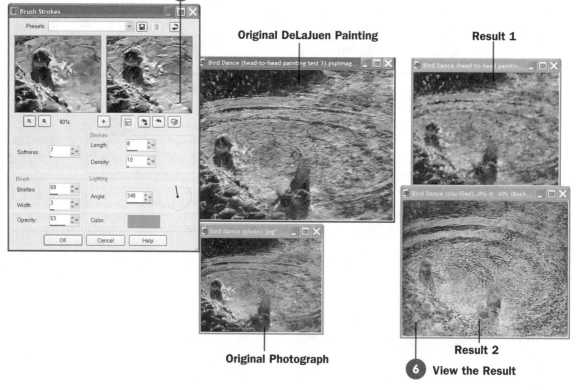

Original DeLaJuen Painting

Result 1

Original Photograph

Result 2

6 **View the Result**

2 Apply the Salt and Pepper Filter

Get rid of speckles in the image so that the painting effect won't emphasize them: Select **Adjust**, **Add/Remove Noise**, **Salt and Pepper Filter**. Set **Speck size (pixels)** to 3 and **Sensitivity to specks** to 4. Click **OK**.

3 Clarify Lights and Darks

To broaden the range of tones in the image, select **Adjust**, **Brightness and Contrast**, **Clarify**. Set **Strength of effect** to 5 (the strongest) and click **OK**.

4 Oversaturate the Colors

Select **Adjust**, **Hue and Saturation**, **Automatic Saturation Enhancement**. Select **More colorful** and **Strong**, and click **OK**. With the colors in the image more saturated, the **Brush Strokes** filter will have more to work with in step 5.

5 Apply the Brush Strokes Filter

Select **Effects**, **Art Media Effects**, **Brush Strokes**. Select a preset from the **Presets** list, and then adjust the settings slightly to fit the image. I typically start with **Small thin oil** and make modifications to fit the image.

The **Softness** setting applies a Gaussian blur that controls how much colors bleed into one another. This blurring creates the illusion of paint being mixed on the canvas (an oil and not acrylic technique), especially when the **Bristles** option is set to a low value.

To simulate brushstrokes, adjust the **Bristles** value as desired. A low value such as 30 is similar to what a painter might expect from a camel-hair brush; a higher value such as 150 resembles a thinner, sable brush. At its highest settings (from 200 to 256), the effect ceases to resemble a brush at all, and takes on the character of a palette knife held flat against the canvas. The **Width** setting adjusts the relative size of this brush tip, and **Opacity** affects the illusion of how much paint is on the brush. Higher **Opacity** settings create bolder texture ridges along each brushstroke's edge.

NOTE

My mother-in-law taught me that the best oil paintings avoid unsaturated pigments like the plague. She has never mixed black with any paint to "gray it down." To create the grayish colors found in the photo, she took two pure, saturated colors from opposite sides of the color wheel, mixed them with white as needed, and dabbed the two colors close to each other throughout the area. Your eye blends these two colors, creating a grayish tone. So in step 4, you'll ensure pure colors in your image by oversaturating them.

TIP

The **Small thin oil** preset assumes a more liquid texture, as if the brush were loaded with copal medium. For some scenes, this preset option looks too much like a photo shot through a shower window. The **Sloppy oil** preset is interesting and well textured, although the direction of the brush strokes is random, and the texture of the strokes resembles more acrylic than oil. The **Oil** and **Oil painting** presets are, quite simply, unconvincing.

If you simply can't get the brush strokes thin or small enough for the effect you desire, click **Cancel**, then resize your image (**Image**, **Resize**). I doubled the size of the photo for this example so that I could make the brush strokes small enough to match those in the actual painting.

For even more spectacular results, try repeating the **Brush Strokes** filter using slightly different settings. Although the results might be less distinguishable, one side effect of applying the filter a second time is that *primary and secondary colored strokes emerge*, mimicking a tried-and-true pointillist technique.

The **Length** setting affects not only the length of each brushstroke, but also their direction. At low values, brushstrokes tend to be uniform and almost cubic; at higher values, they follow the contours of objects. **Density** is a subtle setting that affects the "rigor" in which strokes are made; higher values generate bolder strokes.

As **Width** and **Density** increase, PSP generates larger "collision zones" where the brushstrokes run over one another. These zones create pockmarks that are tinted independently of the rest of the canvas, using the **Lighting** color. Try a lukewarm neutral color such as {RGB: 125, 126, 67} (murky yellow), and an **Angle** that's *almost* directly overhead, such as 348. When you've found settings you like, click **OK**.

6 View the Result

I tried twice to change the photo of two sparrows splashing in a shallow bird bath into one that resembled Maria's *Bird Dance* painting. For the first attempt with the **Brush Strokes** filter, I set **Softness** to 7 and **Opacity** to 54 to keep the motion blur on the sparrows' wings. To simulate a sable brush, I set **Bristles** to 160 and **Width** to 5. To recreate the pointillist technique she used, I set **Length** to 8 and **Density** to 15. The results included some beautiful effects along the rocks, especially where the whites appear to have been dabbled on at the last—I could almost hear Maria reminding me to add my "chalkies" last. There's still some motion blur in the wings, and the spray flying off the male sparrow on the left uses strokes that follow the spray's direction. However, when viewed from a distance or at very small size, the product of these settings looks perhaps too photorealistic.

The second attempt looks more like a painting. Not like Maria's painting, mind you, but like somebody's. To simulate a bigger, camel-hair brush, I reduced **Bristles** to 76, then increased **Width** to 8 and **Opacity** to 73. The bigger brush results in smaller looking strokes by proportion. To retain the dabbled effect, I set **Density** to 10. The brushstrokes did lose their sense of direction, and there's no longer a feeling that any one area of color was painted with any more or less vigor or texture than any other area. But the larger collision zones between brushstrokes do convey a painted look, and reduce if not eliminate any photorealism.

What's missing from both tests—especially in comparison to the real DeLaJuen painting—is any sense of character. The first test retained some of the smaller water rings embedded in the larger ones; Maria's painting dramatized them. You can feel the direction of the wind in Maria's work, especially by how smooth the upper-left corner's water rings are by comparison to the more turbulent lower-right corner. Of course, a computer can't play with its work like an artist can with hers. Seen from a great distance, the real *Bird Dance* painting reveals an embedded prismatic rainbow; PSP would never have "thought" to embed a secret image. Not that I truly expected PSP to exhibit its own artistic character, but I was intrigued—if not just a little shocked—to discover that it could simulate one or two painter's techniques. View these images in the Color Gallery in this book.

TIP

You can select areas of the image before applying the **Brush Strokes** filter. In this way, you can mix painting styles across the image, better simulating an actual artist's technique. Remember to soften the transitions between regions. Remember that using a small brush creates the illusion of closeness, while a larger brush creates distance; you can accidentally disturb the illusion of depth if you make poor choices.

146 Turn a Photograph into a Watercolor

The secret to enabling Paint Shop Pro to generate a simulation of a watercolor from a photograph is to present it with a photograph that looks like a watercolor to begin with. A snapshot of the family hugging Donald Duck in front of Epcot Center simply isn't a candidate, nor particularly are any photos where *people* are the predominant subjects. Instead, you want still, wistful scenes with large areas of a single color and few details.

Different watercolor techniques apply two differing styles of compositions, so for this task, I'll show two examples. The Asian watercolor technique uses very few pigments—generally black, terre verde (green), raw umber (brown), perhaps cobalt blue—with large sections of the white paper showing through as the background. The key here is to make the image look like it was carefully produced by dragging a tapered-tip brush of paint through a patch washed with clear water. Our Asian example involves a wintry setting with two spruce trees in a white wilderness. The second example mimics a more vividly colored

Before You Begin

✔ **60** Select by Drawing Freehand

✔ **75** Save a Selection for Reuse

✔ **97** Improve a Dull, Flat Photo

✔ **99** Restore Color and Improve Detail

✔ **120** About Layers and the Layer Palette

See Also

→ **145** Make a Photograph Look Like an Oil Painting

1 Fill Background with White or Light Color

2 Remove Unwanted Elements

3 Correct the Composition's Color

4 Smooth the Foreground

5 Apply Brush Stroke Effect

6 Apply Textured Paper

Asian Brush Technique

Ink Border Technique

7 View and Tweak the Result

watercolor-and-ink technique. Here, the background is a faint wash of color, with the foreground subject using more vibrant hues, sharply defined by black ink. No, this isn't cheating; ink is often used in watercolor paintings for retaining the edges, especially because fine inks have natural oils that repel water, thus helping to keep the watercolor within its boundaries.

① Fill Background with White or Light Color

On the **Tools** toolbar, choose the **Freehand Selection** tool. On the **Tool Options** palette, set selection type to **Freehand**, set **Smoothing** to a high value such as 20, and set **Feather** to a high value such as 40. In the image window, draw a meandering boundary around your image, excluding objects that don't contribute to the composition (houses, cars, nuclear power plants).

Next, select **Selections**, **Promote Selection to Layer**. On the **Layer** palette, rename this new layer **Composition**. Cancel the selection (**Selections**, **Select None**) and choose the **Background** layer. With the **Flood Fill** tool set at a **Match Mode** of **None**, fill everything with white for the Asian technique; for the ink border technique, fill everything with a light color picked up from the background such as a very light green mixed with the **Backdrop** texture.

② Remove Unwanted Elements

Remove any unwanted material from the **Composition** layer, such as half of a flower or a corner of a barn. On the **Layer** palette, choose the **Composition** layer. From the **Tools** toolbar, select the **Airbrush** tool. On the **Tool Options** palette, set **Size** to 30, **Hardness** to 50, and **Opacity** to 5. Using the foreground color you applied to the **Background** layer, carefully apply the airbrush to the unwanted portions.

For the ink border technique only, isolate the subject on its own layer by changing to the **Composition** layer, selecting the subject. (I selected the butterfly and its flower.) Save this selection to the alpha channel so that you can use it later to apply the ink border by choosing **Selections**,

Load/Resave Selection, Save Selection to Alpha Channel. Promote the selection to a layer by selecting **Selections, Promote Selection to Layer**. Name this new layer **Foreground**.

③ Correct the Composition's Color

For the Asian technique, you want your colors to be muted and desaturated. My example of the winter trees already qualifies, but if your image requires desaturation, change to the **Composition** layer and select **Adjust, Hue and Saturation, Hue/Saturation/Lightness**. set **Saturation** to a low negative setting, such as –67. Click **OK**. Lighten the background colors of the composition to ease the transition between the composition and the white (paper) background. Because my background was snow, I simply lightened it using the **Curves** command (**Adjust, Brightness and Contrast, Curves**). You can also try running the **Lighten/Darken Brush** tool, set to a medium **Opacity**, around the edges of the composition, or use the **Eraser** tool set to a medium **Opacity**.

For the ink-border technique, you want to wash out the background colors. Cancel the selection and switch to the **Composition** layer. From the menu bar, select **Adjust, Brightness and Contrast, Levels**. Adjust the **Input levels**: Drag the white pointer left to about 155. Drag the gamma (the gray pointer) left to about 3.0. If necessary, under **Output levels**, drag the minimum level (the black pointer) to the right a few ticks to 28. Click **OK**.

NOTE

In step 4, for the ink border technique, you separate the colors into lights and darks. This is because light colors in watercolor are generally formed by a low ratio of pigment to water, letting the *paper* do the job of lightening the color; while darker colors are formed with a high ratio of pigment to water.

④ Smooth the Foreground

For both techniques, the texture of the foreground matter must be smoothed. For the Asian technique, choose the **Composition** layer; for the ink border technique, choose the **Foreground** layer. Then select **Adjust, Add/Remove Noise, Edge Preserving Smooth**. Set the **Amount of smoothing** to 30. Click **OK**. Then select **Adjust, Add/Remove Noise, Salt and Pepper Filter**. Set **Speck size (pixels)** to 3 and **Sensitivity to specks** to 4. Click **OK**.

For the ink border technique only, you must reduce the mid-tones in the **Foreground** layer. Switch to the **Foreground** layer. Select **Adjust, Brightness and Contrast, Curves**. Create a curve that eliminates the midtones, leaving mostly lights and darks. Click **OK**.

⑤ Apply Brush Stroke Effect

For the Asian technique, choose the **Composition** layer; for the ink border technique, choose the **Foreground** layer. Then select **Effects, Art Media Effects, Brush Strokes**. Select **Watercolor** from the **Presets** list. For the Asian technique only, make a few adjustments: Set **Softness** to 7, **Length** to 20, and **Density** to 4. Click **OK**.

For the ink border technique only, change to the **Composition** layer and select **Layers, Merge, Merge Down**. The merged layer is now called **Background**. Next, select **Effects, Artistic Effects, Colored Edges**. Set **Color** to a middle gray {RGB: 128, 128, 128}, reduce the **Luminance** value to a value below 0, such as –17, set **Blur** to 25, and **Intensity** to 23. Click **OK**. The background now looks so wet that you'll be afraid to touch your monitor for fear of getting paint on you.

The ink border technique requires one further enhancement: the ink border. Change to the **Background** layer and load the foreground selection from the alpha channel: Choose **Selections, Load/Save Selection, Load Selection from Alpha Channel**. Then choose **Selections, Modify, Select Selection Borders**. Enable the **Outside** and **Anti-alias** options and set **Border width** to 4. Click **OK**. Next, on the **Material** palette, set the foreground color to a very dark gray. Set the texture to **Backdrop**. Select the **Flood Fill** tool, and with **Match Mode** set at **None**, fill each of the ribbon-like selected regions. This gives the appearance of the thin, dark ink border separating the bolder pigments in the foreground from the gentle wash in the background.

⑥ Apply Textured Paper

To complete the watercolor effect, you want the "paper" to have a textured, nubby appearance. Select **Effects,**

TIP

If there's anything you need to "fudge" in the image, do it before step 5. For example, in the Asian example, I used the **Clone Brush** tool to paint a hill in the distance over an outdoor sauna.

Texture Effects, Texture. Choose **Old paper** from the Texture list. Set **Depth** to 2 and click **OK**.

7 View and Tweak the Result

The Asian technique example looks good just like this; a frame might disturb the tranquility. The ink border technique example benefits from the addition of white along the edges, perhaps using one of PSP's built-in picture frames. Look for these images in the Color Gallery in this book.

---

147 Make a Photograph Look Like It Was Drawn

Before You Begin

✔ **71** Select a Portion of an Image with Channels

✔ **97** Improve a Dull, Flat Photo

✔ **107** Adjust Hue, Saturation, and Lightness Manually

✔ **119** Smooth an Edge Without Losing Crisp Edges or Texture

💡 TIP

To make an image look like it was drawn by a drawing program such as CorelDRAW, apply the **Effects, Artistic Effects, Posterize** filter with a value set to between 7 and 10. Apply **Adjust, Add/Remove Noise, Edge Preserving Smooth** set at 30. Then sharpen the image and adjust its contrast as needed.

PSP has a few different pencil stroke filters, the most common being **Pencil**. But left to its own devices, this filter is applicable only to images in which you want to emphasize every detail, because its job is to isolate relatively solid areas of color and draw outlines around them. Faces, with their large patches of color, often end up looking like a slice of onion. The **Colored Pencil** filter is no better. The solution I've discovered to creating a drawn effect from a photograph involves first lightening the image to achieve a pastel look, while saturating the colors so that they are not lost. Next you create a smoothed gray layer that retains the edges while softening the colors. You then create an edge layer, to enhance the edges a bit more. Finally, you apply the **Pencil** filter to this smoothed, lightened, edgy image, where it more accurately simulates a hand-drawn look.

1 Oversaturate and Lighten the Image

Select **Adjust**, **Hue and Saturation**, **Hue/Saturation/Lightness**. Set the **Saturation** slider to a value between 35 and 50. Generally, you'll also have to set the **Lightness** slider to a high value (between 25 and 50). Click **OK**.

2 Create a Smoothed, Grayscale Layer

Select **Image**, **Split Channel**, **Split to HSL**. Close the windows for the **Hue** and **Saturation** channels; you won't need them. Activate the window for the **Lightness** channel,

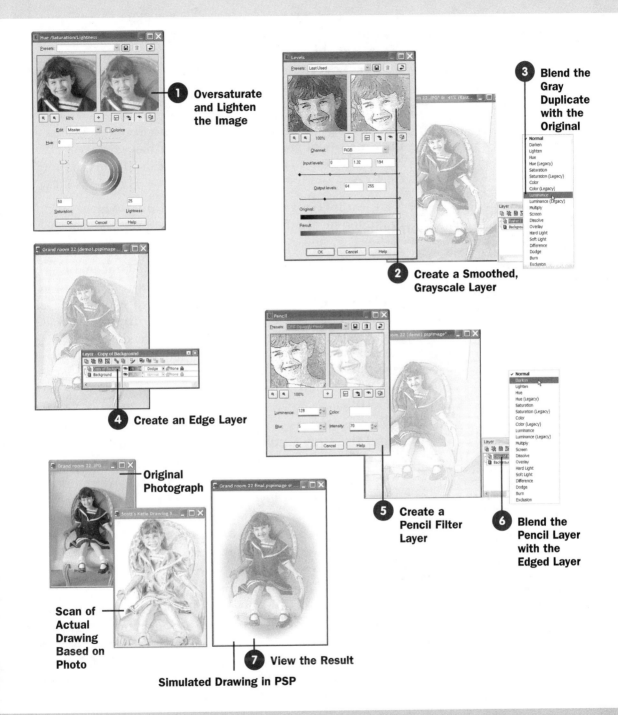

1 Oversaturate and Lighten the Image

2 Create a Smoothed, Grayscale Layer

3 Blend the Gray Duplicate with the Original

4 Create an Edge Layer

5 Create a Pencil Filter Layer

6 Blend the Pencil Layer with the Edged Layer

Original Photograph

Scan of Actual Drawing Based on Photo

7 View the Result

Simulated Drawing in PSP

and from the menu bar, select **Edit, Copy**. Then activate the original image window and select **Edit**, **Paste**, **Paste as New Layer**. Close the **Lightness** window because you won't need it anymore.

With the new, gray layer chosen, select **Adjust**, **Add/Remove Noise**, **Edge Preserving Smooth**. Adjust the **Amount of smoothing** value to achieve the level of detail you want to retain (a value between 10 and 20). Click **OK**.

Next, select **Effects**, **Edge Effects**, **Enhance More**. This command makes the smoothed edges crisper.

The darkest shade on the gray layer should be no darker than a line you can draw with a #2 pencil. To make this change to the image, select **Adjust**, **Brightness and Contrast**, **Levels**. Under **Output levels**, raise the minimum level (the black pointer) to 64. Under **Input levels**, drop the maximum level (the white pointer) down to a value between 180 and 200. Then slide the gray pointer to the *left* to increase the gamma from 1.20 to 1.40. Your eyes will tell you what settings convey a sense of *graphite*. Click **OK**.

③ Blend the Gray Duplicate with the Original

On the **Layer** palette, change the **Blend Mode** for the gray layer to **Luminance**. Color is supplied by the oversaturated layer below the gray layer. To add a bit more color from that lower layer, set the **Opacity** of the gray layer to between 70 and 80. Finally, select **Layers**, **Merge**, **Merge All (Flatten)**.

④ Create an Edge Layer

The next step is to overemphasize the edges. Select **Layers**, **Duplicate** or click the **Duplicate Layer** button on the **Layer** palette. Change to the duplicate layer (probably called **Copy of Background**) and select **Effects**, **Edge Effects**, **Find All**. The image briefly appears reversed, like a negative spray-painted on black velvet.

TIP

If the image has a low level of detail, consider *overdoing* this effect by selecting the **Enhance More** command again. This reduces the sense of photorealism in favor of impressionism.

NOTE

If you were to just apply **Edge Preserving Smooth** to the oversaturated layer, you'd create generalized color regions, but you'd also dislocate some of that color, especially along the edges. As a result, you could lose the content of important features such as faces. By using a separate layer and blending the two, none of that content is lost.

On the **Layer** palette, change the **Blend Mode** for this velvet layer to **Dodge**. The colors from the layer beneath it return, with the overemphasized borders surrounding them. You might have to reduce the **Opacity** of the new border layer to as low as 75 so that the emphasis on borders doesn't appear too pronounced. Then select **Layers, Merge, Merge All (Flatten)**.

⑤ Create a Pencil Filter Layer

Select **Layers, Duplicate**. With the duplicate (**Copy of Background**) layer chosen, select **Effects, Art Media Effects, Pencil**. The **Luminance** value determines the level of contrast needed to identify an edge. Set **Luminance** to 128. Set **Blur** to 5 to simulate a pencil width; a higher value creates a large brush stroke effect. Set **Intensity** to 70—this is the most realistic setting I've found for a pencil stroke that's not too gentle, not too bold.

Finally, click the **Color** sample and select the color of the "paper" background—typically, you'll use white {RGB: 255, 255, 255}. Click **OK**. The result creates the sketchy appearance you need to simulate a pencil drawing, although it doesn't have the bold edges. Recall, though, that you already created those earlier, so all you need to do now is blend the two.

⑥ Blend the Pencil Layer with the Edged Layer

With the new sketchy layer chosen, set the **Blend Mode** for that layer to **Darken**, then reduce **Opacity** to a value between 66 and 80 (depending on the impact of the sketchiness on the results). To embolden the impact even further, set **Blend Mode** to **Multiply**; you might have to reduce **Opacity** even further, to a value between 40 and 50.

Finally, select **Layers, Merge, Merge All (Flatten)** to reveal the final product.

⑦ View the Result

Without using a spot tool such as PSP's own **Paint Brush**, it's difficult, if not impossible, to replicate the appearance of

If you want the image to be a bit darker and bolder, you can accomplish this with gamma correction. Select **Adjust, Brightness and Contrast, Gamma Correction**. In the dialog box, with the **Link** option enabled, slide the gamma down to about 0.8 and click **OK**.

For a bolder look, set **Blur** to 5 and **Color** to white. Then set **Luminance** to between –150 and –245.

a real drawing from a photograph alone. For instance, when you compare the example created in PSP to my husband's drawing based on the same photo, you notice that none of the playfulness and exaggerated contrasts of the sailor suit in the *real* drawing can be re-created in the simulated one. Also missing are the pencil strokes moving in various directions, as they would when drawn by a human hand, although the **Pencil** filter does a fair job of simulating the graininess you would see when applying color with the edge of a pencil. Look for this image in the Color Gallery in this book.

148 Make a Photograph Look Like Ansel Adams Shot It

Before You Begin

✔ **71** Select a Portion of an Image with Channels

✔ **96** Improve Brightness and Contrast

✔ **114** Sharpen an Image

See Also

→ **143** Change a Color Photograph to Black and White

KEY TERM

Zone system—A method of measuring the reflective light from various zones (areas) of an object and applying the appropriate exposure so that the resulting black-and-white print was exactly as the artist desired, full of detail and variances of tone.

Ansel Adams [1902–1984], perhaps more than any photographer of the twentieth century, established photography as an art form. No longer were the operation of a camera and the development of a print from a negative seen purely as mechanical acts for which any individual could be trained. Like any great painter, Adams produced new, personal visions of the latent truth in a scene using a technique he developed himself called the *zone system*.

Although Adams did shoot in color, the images usually singled out as masterpieces are his distinct monochromes—images that don't try to reproduce a scene as much as to isolate, exploit, and reveal some signature portion of it, such as the majesty of a mountain. In this task, you'll learn a method that simulates some of the visual style and developmental approach of the master.

① Isolate the Red Channel

Start with a majestic color image, such as one of the Grand Canyon, a smoky mountaintop, a Hawaiian volcano, or a waterfall. Select **Image**, **Split Channel**, **Split to RGB**. Close the original image and the windows for the **Green** and **Blue** channels; you won't need them. In honor of Ansel and his red filter, we'll be using the **Red** channel.

1 Isolate the Red Channel

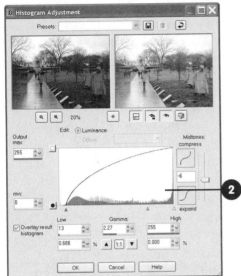

2 Adjust the Channel's Histogram

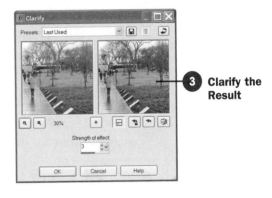

3 Clarify the Result

4 Apply the Unsharp Mask

Original Images

Ansel Adams Versions

5 View the Result

2 Adjust the Channel's Histogram

From the menu bar, select **Adjust**, **Brightness and Contrast**, **Histogram Adjustment**. In the **Histogram Adjustment** dialog box, adjust the black and white pointers so that the resulting histogram extends to the left and right edges (you can clip some pixels at either end if you like). Adjust the gamma so that the "humps" are located in the middle of the graph and at the two ends. To further distinguish lights from darks, drag the **Midtones** slider down no further than –10, to *expand* the distance between lights and darks on the graph. Ansel Adams often captured black-and-whites with three discernable zones of light: whites, blacks, and lots of middle grays. Click **OK**.

3 Clarify the Result

Select **Adjust**, **Brightness and Contrast**, **Clarify**. Set **Strength of effect** to 3 and click **OK**. This setting evens out the histogram, supplying a better range of tone. If the image contains a minimum of detail, repeat this step.

4 Apply the Unsharp Mask

From the menu bar, select **Adjust**, **Sharpness**, **Unsharp Mask**. In the dialog box, set **Radius** to 3, **Strength** to 100, and **Clipping** to 100. These settings sharpen the image and create points of bright highlights. Click **OK**.

5 View the Result

For this example, I used a photo of the Korean War Memorial, taken during a recent visit to Washington, D.C. I also applied these techniques to an image of a leaf wet with dew. By widening the midtones and sharpening the contrasts, I was able to re-create, at least in part, the look of a couple of Ansel Adams' photographs. Look for these images in the Color Gallery in this book.

Index

Symbols

A

C

D

fisheye distortion, removing, 275-277

fixing. *See also* correcting

overflashed photographs, 313-315

underflashed photographs, 316-318

flashing marquee, image selection indicator, 9-11

flat photographs, improving, 295-298

flattening layers, 377-378

Flip command (Image menu), 171-172

flipping images

horizontally, 171-172

vertically, 173

Float command (Selections menu), 247

floating selections, 241-242, 247

folders (images), 51

foreground colors, selecting (Materials palette), 83-84

formats (images)

converting, 148-151

GIFs

image compression, 152-156

uses, 140

Web publishing licensing permissions, 140

JPEG 2000

alpha transparency, 142

browser support, 142

uses, 141-142

JPEGs

artifacts, 141

image compression, 156-159

lossy compression, 141

PNGs

image compression, 159-162

interlacing, 143

uses, 143

TIFF, 143

frame viewfinders in digital cameras, 20

framing photographs, 408-410

freckles, removing, 269-271

freehand drawn areas, selecting, 202-204

freehand mode (Pen tool), Web:17-20

Freehand Selection tool, image selection, 11, 197, 202-204

Full Screen Edit command (View menu), 30

Full Screen View command (View menu), 30

G

gamut (colors), 42-45

GIF Optimizer, image compression process, 152-156

GIFs (graphics interchange format), 140

image compression process, 152-156

uses, 140

Web publishing licensing permissions, 140

glint (eyes), 268

gradients, 81

angles, setting, 87

central point settings, 87

design uses, 85

focal point settings, 87

inversion of, 87

repeat settings, 87

selecting, 85-87

styles, applying, 86

graphics, Pantone color-matching system, 23

Greyscale command (Image menu), 431

Grid command (View menu), 31

grids, object alignment, 31

grouping layers, 369, 374-377

guidelines, adding to images, 31

Guides command (View menu), 31

H

hard light, 342

blend mode (Tool Options palette), 74

hardness value (Tool Options palette), 76

height of images, setting, 47

hiding

palettes, 30, 33

toolbars, 30-32

Tools toolbar, 66

hierarchies (layers), 8

Highlight/Midtone/Shadow dialog box

Dynamic adjustment radio button, 303

Linear adjustment radio button, 303

Histogram Adjustment dialog box, 292

Histogram palette, 33

histograms, adjusting, 284-286, 289-292

holes

image selection areas, removing, 218-220

images, patching (layers), 366

photographs

removing, 256-257

repairing, 263-265

horizontal flipping (images), 171-172

Hot Wax Coating command (Artistic Effects menu), 430

flipping
    horizontally, 171-172
    vertically, 173
floating selections, 241-242
folders, selecting from, 51
formats
    converting, 148-151
    GIF, compression, 140, 152-156
    JPEG, 27-28, 141, 156-159
    PNG, compression, 143, 159-162
    PSP, 27-28
    PSPImage, 143
    TIFF, 27-28, 143
gradients
    angles, 87
    central point settings, 87
    design uses, 85
    focal point settings, 87
    inverting, 87
    repeat settings, 87
    selecting, 85-87
    styles, 86
guidelines, adding, 31
height, setting, 47
HSL, changing to match target values, 335-338
hues, manual adjustments, 329-331
importing from digital cameras, 57-58
information details, displaying, 51, 100-103
jaggies, cleaning up, 252-254
large, scrolling (Pan tool), 106-107
layers
    adjustment layer creation, 367, 372-374
    blending, 7, 365
    copying, 370

distorting (Deform tool), 416-418
empty, 369
erasing portion of, 398-400
flattening, 377-378
grouping, 369, 374-377
hierarchies, 8
hole patching, 366
isolating, 8
mask layers, 365
merging, 377-378
moving (Deform tool), 416-418
number of, 367
opacity values, 364
order of, 364
organizing, 374-377
panorama creation, 365
photographic repair, 366
promoting, 364
purpose of, 7-8
removing, 370
renaming, 369
scrapbook creation, 366
selecting, 8
uses, 364
viewing contents, 370
lightness, manual adjustments, 329-331
locating, 50-51
luminance
    input levels, 290
    output levels, 291
magnifying (Magnifier palette), 108
manual color correction, 326-329
masks
    creating from images, 388-391
    creating from selection, 386-387

creation methods, 382-383
deleting, 385
editing, 391-393
examples, 380-381
filtering levels, 381
patterns, 383
purpose of, 380
reusing, 393-396
saving, 385, 393-396
materials, saving for reuse (Materials palette), 93-94
melting effect (Mesh Warp tool), 419-421
midtones, 287-288
moiré pattern, reducing, 53
motion effects, adding, 356-358
moving, 51
    with pen tablets, 14
multiple changes, undoing, 39
nighttime, improvement methods, 311-313
overflashed, repairing, 313-315
patterns
    angle settings, 88
    repeat settings, 88
    selecting, 88
pen tablets, erasing, 14
people
    blemish removal, 269-271
    freckle removal, 269-271
    teeth whitening, 271-273
    tired eyes, awakening, 273-275
perspective, modifying (Perspective Correction tool), 414-416
portions
    darkening, 309-310
    lightening, 309-310
portrait sheets, printing, 136-140
pre-publishing guidelines, 164-166

images   463

importing images from digital cameras, 57-58

Increase Color Depth command (Image menu), 123

increasing

    image brightness, 292-295

    image contrast, 292-295

input levels for image luminance, 290

inserting new backgrounds in images (Background Eraser), 403-405

Inside/Outside Feather command (Modify menu), 214

installing ICM profiles

    monitors, 45

    printers, 45

interface for workspace, 28-30

interlacing (PNGs), 143

interpolating pixels, 198

Invert command (Selection menu), 224

inverted image selections, 222-224

iris (eyes), 268

isolating layers, 8

J

jaggies

    cleaning up, 252-254

    image selection areas, removing, 220-222

    smoothing, 216-217

    softening, 214

JASC Web site, monitor calibrations chart, 44

Joint Photographic Experts Group. See JPEGs

JPEG 2000 (Joint Photographic Experts Group 2000)

    alpha transparency, 142

    browser support, 142

JPEG Optimizer

    chroma subsampling, 156

    image compression process, 156-159

JPEGs (Joint Photographic Experts Group), 27-28, 141

    artifacts, 141

        removing, 277-279

    image compression process, 156-159

    lossy compression, 141

    uses, 141

L

landscapes, digital photography guidelines, 21

large images, scrolling (Pan tool), 106-107

launching Effects Browser, 398

Layer palette, 33

    controls

        blend mode, 368

        lock transparency, 368

        opacity value, 368

        visibility toggle, 368

    layers, creating, 370-371

    masks

        creating, 385

        deleting, 385

    New Raster Layer button, 369-370

    New Vector Layer button, 369-370

layers

    adjustment, 7

        creating, 372-374

    adjustment layers, 367

    blending, 7, 365

    contents, viewing, 370

    copying, 370

    creating, 370-371

    data

        distorting (Deform tool), 367

        moving (Deform tool), 367

        resizing (Deform tool), 367

    Difference blend mode, 7

    distorting (Deform tool), 416-418

    empty, creating, 369

    flattening, 377-378

    grouping, 369, 374-377

    hierarchies, 8

    holes, patching, 366

    images

        blending effects, 422-424

        selections, copying, 244-246

    isolating, 8

    mask layers, 365

    masks

        creating, 383-385

        creating from images, 388-391

        creating from selection, 386-387

        deleting, 385

        editing, 391-393

        reusing, 393-396

        saving, 385, 393-396

    merging, 377-378

    moving (Deform tool), 416-418

    number of, 367

    opacity, 7-8

    opacity values, 364

    order of, 364

    organizing, 374-377

    panoramas, creating, 365

    photographs, repairing, 366

    portions, erasing, 398-400

    promoting, 364

    purpose of, 7-8

    raster, creating, 370-371

M

pincushion distortion, removing, 275-277

pixels

anti-aliasing effect, 22

brightness

Curves dialog box adjustments, 299-301

histogram adjustments, 284-286, 289-292

edge mask, creating, 343-347

HSL (hue, saturation, and luminance) parameters, 23

image gamma, 287-288

image print guidelines, 130

image resolution, 21, 115

raster data, 21-23

vector data, 21-23

interpolating, 198

neighboring, 68

noise, 257

resampling process, 117-119, 130

bicubic method, 119

bilinear method, 119

weighted average method, 119

resolution, modifying, 120

RGB (red, green, blue light) parameters, 23

PNG Optimizer, 159-162

PNGs (Portable Network Graphics), 143

image compression process, 159-162

interlacing, 143

polarizing filters, use in digital photography, 19

portrait sheets

printing, 136-140

templates, selecting, 138-139

positioning text

along curves, Web:23-25

on images, Web:20-23

ppi (pixels per inch) versus dpi (dots per inch), 130

Preferences menu commands, File Format Associations, 29

Preview in Web Browser command (View menu), 30

previewing scanned images, 54

Print button (Standard toolbar), 133

Print dialog box

Copies option, 133

Landscape orientation, 131

Orientation option, 134

Portrait orientation, 131

Positions option, 134

Print Size option, 134

Properties option, 133

Quality option, 133

Size option, 133

Print Image Managing. *See* PIM

Print Layout command (File menu), 139-140

printers

color

CMYK pigment, 25-26

pigment, 25

subtractive process, 25

ICM profile, installing, 45

photo quality, 16

resolution, 47

printing

contact sheets, 50, 135

images, 131-134

aspect ratio guidelines, 131

copy guidelines, 129

format selection guidelines, 131

home versus professional guidelines, 129

image position, 134

number of copies, 133

paper orientation, 134

paper selection, 133

paper selection guidelines, 128-129

paper size, 133

pixel guidelines, 130

print quality, 133

print size, 134

quality guidelines, 128-129

resolution guidelines, 130

size guidelines, 128

portrait sheets, 136-140

Promote Selection to Layer command (Selections menu), 246

PSP (Paint Shop Pro), 4

interface for workspace, 28-30

new tools, 4

PSPImage format, 143-147

publishing images, pre-publishing guidelines, 164-166

pupils (eyes), 268

Q - R

QuickTime movies (Photo Album), 3

raster data

image backgrounds, 47

pixels, 21-23

raster layers, creating, 370-371

rectangular shaped areas, images, selecting, 200-202

red eye

glint, 268

iris, 268

pupils, 268

removing, 266-268

Red-eye Removal command (Adjust menu), 266

Redo command (Edit menu), 38

reducing

colors

    error diffusion method, 125

    nearest color method, 125-126

    ordered dither method, 125

    moiré pattern effects, 53

regions of images, selecting, 9-11

Remove Specks and Holes command (Modify menu), 218

removing

artifacts, 277-279

barrel distortion, 275-277

blemishes, 269, 271

color cast from photographs, 338-340

distracting textures from photographs, 354-356

fisheye distortion, 275-277

freckles, 269-271

holes

    from photographs, 256-257

    image selections, 218-220

image noise via blurring, 349-351

jaggies from image selections, 220-222

layers, 370

marquees, 196

moiré patterns from scanned images, 279-282

pincushion distortion, 275-277

red eye from photographs, 266-268

scratches from photographs, 256-257

    Automatic Small Scratch Removal, 257-259

    Scratch Remover tool, 259-261

specks from photographs, 218-220, 256-257, 261-263

spots from photographs, 261-263

unwanted objects from images (Clone Brush), 400-402

renaming

images, 51

    from digital cameras, 59-60

layers, 369

repairing

faded photographs, 366

holes in photographs, 263-265

old photographs, 366

overflashed images, 313-315

underflashed images, 316-318

replacing backgrounds in images (Background Eraser), 403-405

resampling

images

    bicubic method, 119

    bilinear method, 119

    pixel insertion, 117-119

    weighted average method, 119

pixels, 130

Resize command (Image menu), 119

Resize dialog box, 119

resizing

data on layers (Deform tool), 367

image canvas, 120-122

resolution

images, 46, 115

    changing, 120

    selecting for scanning purposes, 52

    setting, 47

pixels, 21

    raster data, 21-23

    vector data, 21-23

printer output, 47

restoring

balance in backlit photographs, 318-324

color to washed-out photographs, 333-335

faded colors, 301-305

old photographs, 331-333

palette size, 33

reusing

masks, 393-396

saved materials (Materials palette), 93-94

RGB (red, green and blue) model, 26-27

pixel parameters, 23

Rotate command (Image menu), 170

rotating images, directional options, 170

rotation value (Tool Options palette), 77

rule of thirds (digital photography), 17

rulers, displaying, 31

Rulers command (View menu), 31

S

Salt and Pepper filter, photographic noise removal, 261-263

sample merged value (Tool Options palette), 77

saturation

images, correcting, 187-188

manual adjustments, 329-331

saturation blend mode (Tool Options palette), 71

Save As command (File menu), 145

Save As dialog box, 146

Save command (File menu), 145

Save command (Workspace menu), 31

toolbars

docking, 32

function of, 31

hiding, 30, 32

Photo, 32

Script, 32

Standard, 32

Tools, 32

viewing, 30-32

tools

options

saving for reuse (Tools Options palette), 95-96

setting (Tools Option palette), 66-80

preset options, 79

selecting, 79-80

Tools Options palette, 33

handles, 80

tool options, saving for reuse, 95-96

Tools toolbar, 32

arrow indicator, 66

hiding, 66

tools, selecting from, 79-80

viewing, 66

tracing edges of selected areas

Edge Seeker, 206-208

Smart Edge, 208-210

tripods, use in digital photography, 20

troubleshooting

dull/flat photographs, 295-298

nighttime photograph exposure, 311-313

TWAIN (Technology Without An Interesting Name)-compliant scanners, 53

typesetting text along curves, Web:23-25

U - V

underflashed photographs, fixing, 316-318

Undo command (Edit menu), 37-38

Ungroup Layers command (Layers menu), 375

Unsharp Mask tool, 342

image sharpening, 347-349

unwanted objects, erasing (Clone Brush), 400-402

USB/FireWire cable, connecting to computers, 55

variable intensity, selecting, 198-199

VCDs (Photo Album), 3

vector data

image backgrounds, 47

layers, creating, 370-371

pixels, 21-23

vertical flipping (images), 173

View menu commands

Full Screen Edit, 30

Full Screen View, 30

Grid, 31

Guides, 31

Palettes, 30

Preview in Web Browser, 30

Rulers, 31

Snap to Guides, 31

viewing

layer contents, 370

palettes, 30, 33

thumbnail images, 49

toolbars, 30-32

Tools toolbar, 66

virtual drives, digital camera image storage, 57

visibility toggle control (Layer palette), 368

W

Wacom Graphire pen tablet, 12-14

Warp Brush tool, image melting effects, 419-421

washed-out photographs, restoring, 333-335

watercolor effects

Asian technique, 443-448

black ink technique, 443-448

Watermarking command (Image menu), 109-113

Web Galleries (Photo Album), 3

Web sites

JASC, monitor calibration chart, 44

PhotoScientia, monitor gamma adjustments, 45

Pictorio.com, photographic paper, 129

weighted average resampling, 119

white balance (images), 18, 184

white point of monitors, adjusting, 44

whitening teeth, 271-273

WIA (Windows Image Acquisition)-compliant scanners, 53

width of images, setting, 47

Workspace menu

Default command, 31

Load command, 31

Save command, 31

X - Y - Z

zone system effect (Ansel Adams), 452-454

Zoom tool

percent settings, 104

zooming in/out, 103-105

Key Terms

Don't let unfamiliar terms discourage you from learning all you can about Paint Shop Pro. If you don't completely understand what one of these words means, flip to the indicated page, read the full definition there, and find techniques related to that term.

Adjustment layer
A special layer that allows you to make a specific color or contrast adjustment to the layers that show through it. **367**

Alpha channel
Data saved with an image for reuse when needed. **101**

Alpha transparency
Variable transparency, or the ability to vary the amount of transparency in an image. **142**

Anti-aliasing
The addition of semitransparent pixels along the curved edge of a raster shape or selection. **22**

Artifacts
Unwanted elements of a digital photo introduced by technology. **141**

Black point
Item in a photo that should be pure black. **180**

Canvas
The geometric platform that provides the coordinate system for every image. **120**

CCD noise
Random distortions introduced into a photo by a digital camera's CCD chip. **262**

Channel
One of a handful of components that jointly characterizes the structure of a digital image, such as RGB, HSL, or CMYK. **224**

Chroma
A measure of color values as described by two coordinates in a geometric space. **157**

Color cast
The predominance of a particular color throughout an image. **182**

Color depth
The number of colors in an image. **46**

Colorspace
An internal map used by computers and printing devices that depicts all the possible colors for that device. **300**

Contact sheet
A printout of a group of images, where each image is displayed in a small, thumbnail size. **135**

Cropping
The process of selecting a portion of an image to keep. **177**

Defloat
To reduce a floating selection from an independent element that's unattached to an image, to a portion of a layer in that image. **242**

Depth of field
The distance between the closest in-focus object to your camera and the furthest in-focus object away from your camera. **19**

Distort
To stretch a corner of a layer in any one direction. **416**

Dithering
A technique for simulating a color whose value does not appear in an image's palette. **152**

DPI
Dots per inch. **53**

Edge mask
A selection that encompasses only the edge pixels in an image, thus preventing unwanted changes to everything else. **345**

Error diffusion
Any of several mathematical techniques that attempt to compensate for large error values. **125**

Feather
To produce a fuzzy border around the inside, outside, or both edges of a selection. **197**

Filter
A series of computer instructions that modify the pixels in an image. **11**

Glint
A tiny reflection of light that appears on the pupil in an eye. **268**

Gradient
A gradual transition between two colors. **81**

Hide All mask
An all-black mask through which the entire image is prevented from appearing. **411**

Histogram
A chart that depicts the relative distribution of pixels in an image that share the same characteristics. **284**